Artificial Intelligence Algorithms and Generative AI in Education

Artificial Intelligence Algorithms and Generative AI in Education

Guest Editors

Antonio Sarasa Cabezuelo
María Estefanía Avilés Mariño

MDPI

Basel • Beijing • Wuhan • Barcelona • Belgrade • Novi Sad • Cluj • Manchester

Guest Editors
Antonio Sarasa Cabezuelo
Facultad de Informática
Universidad Complutense
de Madrid
Madrid
Spain

María Estefanía Avilés Mariño
E.T.S. de Ingenieros
Industriales
Universidad Politécnica
de Madrid
Madrid
Spain

Editorial Office
MDPI AG
Grosspeteranlage 5
4052 Basel, Switzerland

This is a reprint of the Special Issue, published open access by the journal *Algorithms* (ISSN 1999-4893), freely accessible at: https://www.mdpi.com/journal/algorithms/special_issues/LD3B4ZHJO0.

For citation purposes, cite each article independently as indicated on the article page online and as indicated below:

Lastname, A.A.; Lastname, B.B. Article Title. *Journal Name* **Year**, *Volume Number*, Page Range.

ISBN 978-3-7258-6115-6 (Hbk)
ISBN 978-3-7258-6116-3 (PDF)
https://doi.org/10.3390/books978-3-7258-6116-3

Contents

About the Editors

Antonio Sarasa Cabezuelo

Antonio Sarasa Cabezuelo is an associated professor at Complutense University of Madrid in the Department of Computer Systems and Computation. He earned his doctorate with research on XML application development and language processor construction. He is active in research on language engineering, software, and applications. His academic focus includes computational linguistics, software engineering, and the development of intelligent educational systems. Antonio's work concerns AI-driven adaptive learning platforms and educational software to transform teaching, learning, and assessment.

María Estefanía Avilés Mariño

Maria Estefanía Avilés Mariño is a researcher and associate professor at Universidad Politécnica de Madrid in the Department of Applied Linguistics to Science and Technology. She holds a degree in English Philology, a Master's in Teacher Training, and a PhD in English Linguistics, awarded with distinction. Her research interests focus on applied linguistics, English for specific purposes, and digital education technologies. She has contributed to international projects and collaborates with research groups at UCM and UAH. María Estefanía integrates her expertise in linguistics with the study of AI applications in education, emphasizing innovative tools for language learning and digital pedagogy.

Preface

This Reprint, "Artificial Intelligence and Generative AI in Education," brings together a collection of research articles that examine the expanding role of intelligent algorithms, machine learning models, and generative systems in shaping the future of education. This compilation reflects the growing recognition that artificial intelligence is not only a technological advancement but also a catalyst for reimagining how knowledge is created, disseminated, and applied in teaching and learning contexts.

The primary aim of this Reprint is to provide a comprehensive overview of current developments at the intersection of artificial intelligence and education, offering both theoretical insights and practical applications. The included works explore topics such as adaptive learning environments, personalized tutoring, AI-assisted assessment, ethical frameworks, and the emerging challenges of integrating generative AI into modern classrooms. Together, they form a multidisciplinary dialogue bridging computer science, pedagogy, cognitive psychology, and educational design.

This Reprint was motivated by the need to capture the rapid evolution of AI technologies and their growing influence on educational practices and research. By addressing both opportunities and concerns, the collected papers contribute to a deeper understanding of how intelligent systems can enhance equity, engagement, and effectiveness in learning across diverse contexts.

This Reprint is intended for researchers, educators, technology developers, and policymakers who seek to understand and responsibly apply artificial intelligence to improve learning outcomes. It invites readers to reflect on the implications of technological transformation while inspiring innovation grounded in ethical and pedagogical principles.

Antonio Sarasa Cabezuelo and María Estefanía Avilés Mariño
Guest Editors

algorithms

MDPI

Article

Analysis of ChatGPT-3.5's Potential in Generating NBME-Standard Pharmacology Questions: What Can Be Improved?

Marwa Saad [1], Wesam Almasri [1], Tanvirul Hye [2], Monzurul Roni [3] and Changiz Mohiyeddini [1,*]

[1] Department of Foundational Medical Studies, Oakland University William Beaumont School of Medicine, 586 Pioneer Drive, Rochester, MI 48309, USA; marwasaad@oakland.edu (M.S.); walmasri@oakland.edu (W.A.)

[2] College of Medicine, Rosman University, Henderson, NV 89014, USA; thye@roseman.edu

[3] College of Medicine Peoria, University of Illinois, Peoria, IL 61605, USA; roni@uic.edu

* Correspondence: mohiyeddini@oakland.edu; Tel.: +1-248-370-3905

Abstract: ChatGPT by OpenAI is an AI model designed to generate human-like responses based on diverse datasets. Our study evaluated ChatGPT-3.5's capability to generate pharmacology multiple-choice questions adhering to the NBME guidelines for USMLE Step exams. The initial findings show ChatGPT's rapid adoption and potential in healthcare education and practice. However, concerns about its accuracy and depth of understanding prompted this evaluation. Using a structured prompt engineering process, ChatGPT was tasked to generate questions across various organ systems, which were then reviewed by pharmacology experts. ChatGPT consistently met the NBME criteria, achieving an average score of 13.7 out of 16 (85.6%) from expert 1 and 14.5 out of 16 (90.6%) from expert 2, with a combined average of 14.1 out of 16 (88.1%) (Kappa coefficient = 0.76). Despite these high scores, challenges in medical accuracy and depth were noted, often producing "pseudo vignettes" instead of in-depth clinical questions. ChatGPT-3.5 shows potential for generating NBME-style questions, but improvements in medical accuracy and understanding are crucial for its reliable use in medical education. This study underscores the need for AI models tailored to the medical domain to enhance educational tools for medical students.

Keywords: ChatGPT; AI; NBME; pharmacology; medical education

1. Introduction

Chat Generative Pre-trained Transformer (ChatGPT-3.5) is an artificial intelligence (AI) software developed by OpenAI [1]. ChatGPT is trained on various datasets and modeled to generate human-like responses [2]. ChatGPT is trained on information from up to September 2021, limiting its knowledge base to events prior to September 2021 [1,3]. ChatGPT is continually being updated and improved by OpenAI [4]. Our study focused on assessing ChatGPT-3.5, the free version of ChatGPT, trained on 175 billion parameters [5]. In the first couple of months since its launch in November 2022, ChatGPT gained approximately 100 million users [6]. Relative to other online platforms such as Netflix, Airbnb, Twitter, Facebook, and Instagram, which took several months to years to reach 1 million users, ChatGPT reached 1 million users in 5 days [7]. As of June 2023, ChatGPT has reached over 1.6 billion visitors and an average of 55 million visitors daily [7].

The National Board of Medical Examiners (NBME) is an organization that owns the United States Medical Licensing Examination (USMLE), which writes Step exams for medical students to take during their medical education. The USMLE Step 1 exam comprises a number of disciplines, such as pathology, physiology, pharmacology, biochemistry and nutrition, microbiology, immunology, gross anatomy and embryology, histology and cell biology, behavioral sciences, and genetics [8]. Pharmacology makes up approximately 15–22 percent of the questions in the USMLE Step 1 [8].

Previous studies have assessed the performance of ChatGPT in USMLE Step exams using the NBME and AMBOSS datasets [9]. It was found that ChatGPT answered the NBME Step 1 exam with 64.4 percent of questions correct, the NBME Step 2 exam with 57.8 percent of questions correct, the AMBOSS Step 1 exam with 44 percent of questions correct, and the AMBOSS Step 2 exam with 42 percent of questions correct [9]. The ability of ChatGPT to perform with a passing grade of over 60 percent in the NBME Step 1 exam prompted our interest in assessing its ability of ChatGPT to generate NBME-style pharmacology multiple-choice questions that meet the NBME Item-Writing Guidelines [10,11].

Previous research has assessed the ability of ChatGPT to take an Ophthalmic Knowledge Assessment Program (OKAP) exam, which is created for ophthalmology residents [12]. The study found that ChatGPT performed at the level of a first-year resident, providing insight into its capabilities and knowledge base.

ChatGPT offers promising benefits in scientific research, healthcare practice, and healthcare education [13]. In scientific research, it has been found to be a useful tool in academic research and writing [14]. In healthcare practice, ChatGPT shows the potential to assist in documentation, disease risk prediction, improving health literacy, and enhancing diagnostics [15,16].

In healthcare education, ChatGPT has been found to be beneficial in its ability to pass exams such as the USMLE Step exams and ophthalmology residency examinations [12,13]. ChatGPT shows promising potential in healthcare and can be a useful tool for medical education [17]. Additionally, ChatGPT has been found to be beneficial in the rapid generation of clinical vignettes, which could help reduce costs for healthcare students [18].

However, there are concerns that ChatGPT can potentially provide inaccurate information and references [19]. With the plethora of resources available to students during Step preparation, the process can be both time-consuming and overwhelming to students. If ChatGPT-generated questions are medically accurate and abide by the NBME guidelines, they can be a valuable resource for medical students [11].

This study aimed to evaluate ChatGPT-3.5's capability to generate NBME-style pharmacology multiple-choice questions, adhering to the NBME Item-Writing Guidelines [11]. Our objective was to generate recommendations for enhancing and fine-tuning ChatGPT-generated NBME questions for medical education. If the questions and answers generated by ChatGPT align with the standards outlined in the NBME Item-Writing Guide, it has the potential to serve as a valuable resource for medical students seeking free NBME practice questions for USMLE Step exams [11].

2. Materials and Methods

Stage 1: Defining a suitable prompt for ChatGPT to generate NBME-style pharmacology multiple-choice questions, adhering to the NBME guidelines.

OpenAI provides "GPT best practices" that assist in the use of ChatGPT. Some of the strategies include writing clear instructions by providing details, specifying tasks, providing examples, and specifying the complexity of the response [20]. Another strategy includes asking ChatGPT to adopt a persona [20].

To develop suitable prompts for ChatGPT to generate the most optimal clinical vignettes, we adopted the following steps:

Step 1. The selection of organ systems and related drugs: We selected 10 medications from the following organ systems and their given corresponding drugs in parentheses: hematology/lymphatics (warfarin), neurology (norepinephrine), cardiovascular (metoprolol), respiratory (albuterol), renal (lisinopril), gastrointestinal (bisacodyl), endocrine (metformin), reproductive (norethindrone), musculoskeletal (cyclobenzaprine), and behavioral medicine (trazodone).

Step 2. Prompt engineering: We conducted prompt engineering to formulate questions that align with NBME standards using 'ChatGPT best practices'. This step involved an iterative process following these stages:

1. A pharmacology expert provided 12 NBME-style questions as examples.
2. IT experts developed the initial prompt based on these examples and generated 12 questions.
3. Refinement for Complexity and Clinical Relevance: The prompts were iteratively refined to enhance complexity and ensure alignment with NBME standards through the following steps:
    (A) Iterative refinement: Initial broad prompts were progressively adjusted, emphasizing clinical scenarios and reducing basic recall. For example, instead of asking "What is the primary side effect of metformin?", the prompt would specify a more detailed clinical vignette, such as: "Create a scenario involving a diabetic patient prescribed metformin, focusing on a less common but clinically significant adverse effect".
    (B) Use of clinical variables: Prompts were further developed to incorporate variables like patient history, comorbidities, and lab results. This helped generate more nuanced questions that required deeper analysis, mimicking the integrated reasoning expected in NBME Step exams.
    (C) Expert feedback integration: Ongoing expert reviews provided feedback on medical accuracy, clinical relevance, and adherence to NBME guidelines, such as avoiding simple distractors and ensuring that the questions tested applied medical knowledge [11].
    (D) Adherence to item-writing guidelines: Prompts were fine-tuned based on the *NBME Item-Writing Guide* recommendations, such as avoiding negatively phrased lead-ins (e.g., "except") and ensuring that questions could be answered without seeing the multiple-choice options [11].
4. Validation and iterative refinement through expert review: After multiple iterations, a standardized prompt template was developed and validated by pharmacology experts, ensuring that it consistently generated questions aligned with NBME standards. In addition, the pharmacology experts continuously reviewed the generated questions to identify specific areas for improvement, such as advising the AI to focus on particular drug-related topics or ensuring greater clinical relevance in the scenarios.
5. The IT expert revised the prompt and generated the subsequent series of questions.

After 12 iterations, the pharmacology experts confirmed the quality of the generated questions, and the refined prompt was adopted as the finalized standard. The standard prompt reads as follows (with brackets indicating the different medications to be assessed): 'Can you provide an expert-level sample NBME question about the (mechanism of action, indication, OR side effect) of (drug) and furnish the correct answer along with a detailed explanation'?

Step 3. Using the above prompt, we asked ChatGPT to generate a question for either the mechanism of action, indications, or side effects for each of these 10 medications. The mechanism of action, indications, and side effects topics were randomly selected to be assessed and evaluated for each medication.

Step 4. The questions and answers generated by ChatGPT were assessed using a grading system that was created following the *NBME Item-Writing Guide* [11]. The *NBME Item-Writing Guide* provides the following specific criteria for writing clinical vignettes that are used to design USMLE Step exam questions [11]. We adapted the following criteria from the *NBME Item-Writing Guide* [11]:

1. Give the correct answer with a medically accurate explanation.
2. Question stem avoids describing the class of the drug in conjunction with the name of the drug in the drug.
3. The question applies foundational medical knowledge, rather than basic recall.
4. The clinical vignette is in complete sentence format.
5. The question can be answered without looking at multiple-choice options, referred to as the "cover-the-option" rule.

6. Avoid long or complex multiple-choice options.
7. Avoid using frequency terms within the clinical vignette, such as "often" or "usually"; instead, use "most likely" or "best indicated".
8. Avoid "none of the above" in the answer choices.
9. Avoid nonparallel, inconsistent answer choices, ensuring all follow the same format and structure.
10. The clinical vignette avoids negatively phrased lead-ins, such as "except".
11. The clinical vignette avoids general grammatical cues that can lead you to the correct answer, such as "an" at the end of the question stem, which would eliminate answer choices that begin with consonants.
12. Avoid grouped or collectively exhaustive answer choices. For instance, the answer choices are "a decrease in X", "an increase in X", and "no change in X".
13. Avoid absolute terms, such as "always" and "never", in the answer choices.
14. Avoid having the correct answer choice stand out. For example, this can happen when one of the answer choices is longer and more in-depth relative to the other answer choices.
15. Avoid repeated words or phrases in the clinical vignette that clue the correct answer choice.
16. Create a balanced distribution of key terms in the answer choices, ensuring none stand out as too similar or too different from the others. (*NBME Item-Writing Guide*).

Stage 2: Assessing the quality of ChatGPT-generated questions.

To evaluate the quality of the questions generated by ChatGPT, we employed the following steps:

Step 1. Expert panel review: All ChatGPT-generated questions and answers underwent evaluation by a panel consisting of two pharmacology education experts with a significant teaching background in medical schools in the USA. These experts were well-versed in the *NBME Item-Writing Guide* and had experience with NBME-style exam questions in pharmacology [11].

Step 2. Calibration process: Two randomly selected questions generated by ChatGPT were presented to the experts for evaluation. The experts independently utilized the aforementioned 16 different criteria to individually score each question and assigned a score of 0 or 1 for each criterion, resulting in a quality score ranging from 0 to 16 for each question. A higher score indicated better adherence to the *NBME Item-Writing Guide* [11]. Subsequently, the experts convened to discuss and reconcile any discrepancies in their evaluations, arriving at a consensus.

Step 3. Independent evaluation: Following the calibration process, the experts individually and independently assessed the remaining ChatGPT-generated questions and provided their respective scores.

Estimated question difficulty: The expert panel was also asked to rate the difficulty of each question on a scale using the question 'On a scale from very easy to very difficult, how would you rate the difficulty of this question for students?'. The responses ranged from 1 (very easy) to 5 (very difficult).

3. Results

3.1. *Inter-Rater Reliability*

Using Cohen's Kappa coefficient, an inter-rater reliability analysis was conducted to assess the internal consistency of the scores assigned by two pharmacology education experts during the evaluation of 10 questions generated by ChatGPT. The resulting Kappa coefficient of 0.76 indicated a good degree of agreement between the two experts beyond what would be expected by chance. Hence, we averaged the experts' ratings.

3.2. *Quality of ChatGPT-Generated Questions*

According to expert 1, the average score for the ChatGPT-3.5 questions was 13.7 out of 16 (85.6%). According to expert 2, the average score for the ChatGPT-3.5 questions was

14.5 out of 16 (90.6%). Thus, the average score between the two experts was 14.1 out of 16 (88.1%).

The most pronounced difference between expert ratings was related to the question on the reproductive system, which was scored 11/16 by expert 1 and 14/16 by expert 2. The individual scores for each of the organ systems are represented in Figure 1.

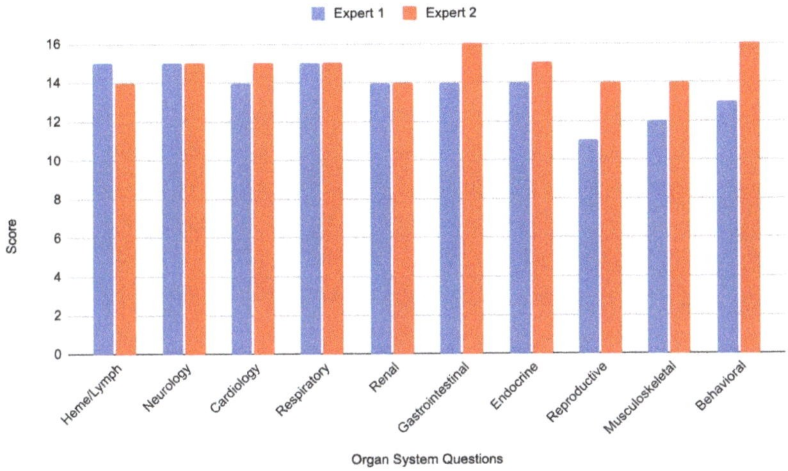

Figure 1. ChatGPT-3.5-generated question scores.

Given the high inter-rater reliability, we then averaged the expert ratings. The average quality score of hematology/lymphology was 13.5/16. The average quality score of neurology and respiratory was 15/16. The average quality score of cardiology and behavioral was 14/16. The average quality score of renal and endocrine was 14.5/16. The average quality score of gastrointestinal was 15/16. The average quality score of reproductive was 12.5/16. The average quality score of musculoskeletal was 13/16.

3.3. *ChatGPT-3.5's Fulfillment of NBME Criteria*

In the next step, we analyzed how often, based on the expert ratings, ChatGPT-3.5 fulfilled the aforementioned 16 characteristics of a valid NBME-style question when generating questions for each of the ten organ systems. Figure 2 shows the results.

According to expert 1, ChatGPT-3.5 fulfilled criteria 2, 6–10, and 13 in all 10 questions (100% degree of fulfillment). Criteria 4, 11, and 14 were satisfied by 9 out of 10 (90% degree of fulfillment). Criteria 1, 12, and 16 were fulfilled by 8 out of 10 (80% degree of fulfillment). Criterion 15 was fulfilled by 7 out of 10 (70% degree of fulfillment), criterion 5 was fulfilled by 6 out of 10 (60% degree of fulfillment), and criterion 3 was fulfilled by 3 out of 10 (30% degree of fulfillment).

According to expert 2, criteria 2, 4, 6–10, and 12–14 were fulfilled by 10 out of 10 (100% degree of fulfillment). Criteria 5 and 15 were fulfilled by 9 out of 10 (90% degree of fulfillment), criteria 1 and 16 were fulfilled by 8 out of 10 (80% degree of fulfillment), criterion 11 was fulfilled by 7 out of 10 (70% degree of fulfillment), and criterion 3 was fulfilled by 5 out of 10 (50% degree of fulfillment).

Additionally, the average rating of the criteria addressed by each expert was analyzed. Criterion 1 was addressed on average 8/10 times. Criteria 2, 6, 7, 8, 9, 10, and 13 were addressed on average 10/10 times. Criterion 3 was addressed on average 4/10 times. Criterion 4 was addressed on average 9.5/10 times. Criterion 5 was addressed on average 7.5/10 times. Criteria 11, 15, and 16 were addressed on average 8/10 times. Lastly, criterion 14 was addressed on average 9.5/10 times.

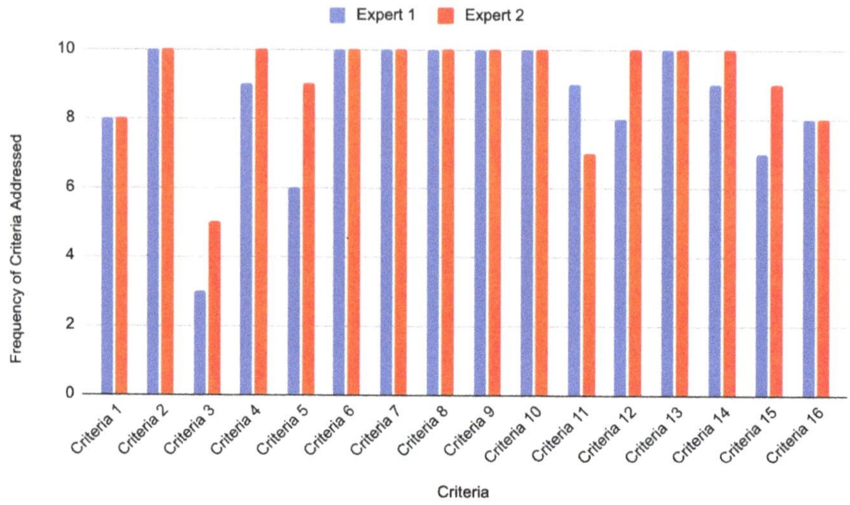

Figure 2. ChatGPT-3.5 frequency of criteria addressed.

3.4. *Estimated Complexity and Difficulty of Questions Generated by ChatGPT-3.5*

As demonstrated in Figure 3, expert 1 found one question very simple, five questions simple, two questions moderately complex, two questions complex, and no questions very complex. In contrast, expert 2 found three questions very simple, four questions simple, three questions moderately complex, and no questions complex or very complex.

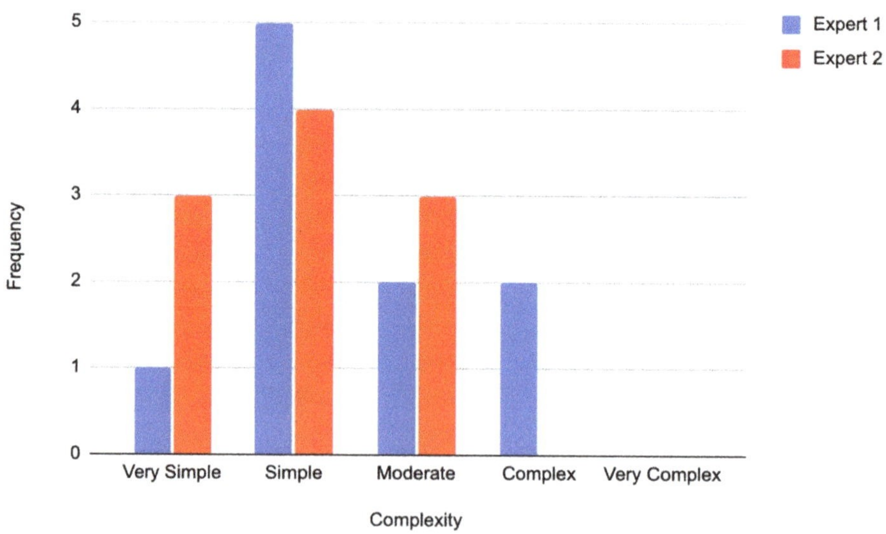

Figure 3. Complexity of questions by experts.

As depicted in Figure 4, expert 1 found four questions very easy, two questions easy, two questions moderately hard, two questions hard, and no questions very hard. In contrast, expert 2 found three questions very easy, four questions easy, three questions moderately hard, and no questions hard or very hard.

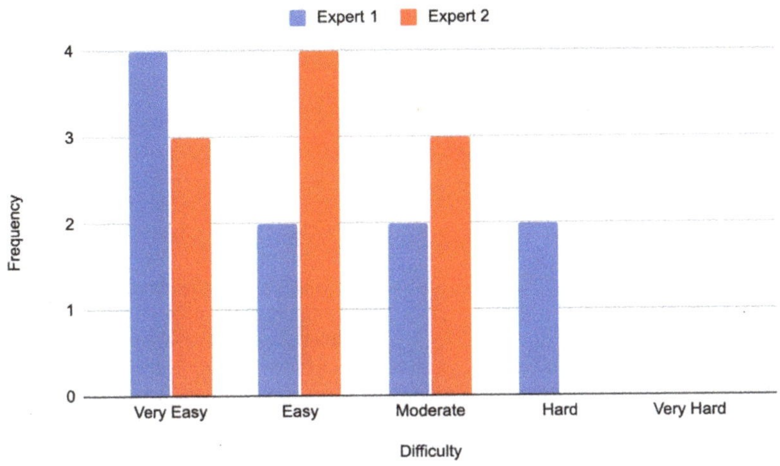

Figure 4. Difficulty of questions by experts.

4. Discussion

At face value, ChatGPT-3.5 provided remarkable results following the *NBME Item-Writing Guide* criteria [11], given the average score of 14.1 out of 16 (88.1%) between the two experts. However, there are significant improvements needed when thoroughly assessing the questions and answers. When the frequency of each of the criteria was evaluated, there was a trend in which criteria were missed more frequently compared with others. According to both experts 1 and 2, criterion 1, which assessed medical accuracy, was fulfilled by 8 out of 10 (80%) of the ChatGPT-generated questions. Thus, two questions contained medically inaccurate information. Given the importance of having the questions and answers contain medically accurate information, it is vital to ensure this criterion is always fulfilled. Having ChatGPT-3.5-generated questions that contain medically inaccurate information can be especially problematic when students prepare for USMLE exams. For example, when asked to evaluate the side effects of warfarin, ChatGPT-3.5 stated that thrombocytopenia is a side effect of warfarin and deemed that as the correct answer, when thrombocytopenia is not a side effect of warfarin [21]. This can lead to the student unknowingly making incorrect associations with drugs and adverse effects, such as abciximab actually causing thrombocytopenia, rather than warfarin [21]. Additionally, when the indications for metoprolol were assessed, ChatGPT-3.5 suggested that the indications for a patient with a history of myocardial infarction and heart failure be prescribed the beta-blocker for chronic stable angina and not hypertension. Although this indication can be true, without the patient's vitals, there is not enough information to decide between the provided answer choices of hypertension or chronic stable angina. Thus, this question is medically inaccurate.

The ability of ChatGPT to provide factually inaccurate information is potentially due to a phenomenon coined "*hallucinations*". "Hallucinations" are defined as the generation of probable statements that include inaccurate information. These "hallucinations" can be due to the multitude of datasets it is trained on and the mixing up of facts [22,23]. ChatGPT-3.5 has the potential to provide this medical information but needs to ensure it is always accurate in providing accurate medical information when generating NBME-standard clinical vignettes, answer choices, and explanations for each answer choice. Thus, having an AI system that is dedicated to the healthcare industry, which can provide medical diagnoses, as well as disseminate accurate medical information, can be highly beneficial for medical students, physicians, and patients alike [24].

According to expert 1, criterion 3 was fulfilled by 3 out of 10 (30%) ChatGPT-3.5-generated questions, and 4 out of 10 (40%) according to expert 2. This criterion was the most frequently missed criterion of the 16 criteria. This criterion assessed the ability of ChatGPT-3.5 to apply foundational medical knowledge, rather than basic recall. Additionally, another frequently missed criterion was criterion 5, which is the ability to answer the question without looking at the multiple-choice options. According to expert 1, 6 out of 10 (60%) questions, and according to expert 2, 9 out of 10 (90%) questions, fulfilled criterion 5. In addition to the questions assessing basic recall, the questions can be answered without multiple-choice options. Furthermore, this constitutes most of the questions as *"pseudo-vignettes"*. A pseudo-vignette is defined as a vignette that does not require the need for the clinical information provided to answer the question and, rather, tests basic recall of material [25]. For example, the following are some of the questions in which a clinical vignette was provided and asked the reader to answer the following: "Norepinephrine acts on which of the following receptors to exerts its vasoconstrictive effects?", "What is the primary mechanism of action of albuterol?", "What is the primary mechanism of action of metformin in the treatment of diabetes?", and "Which of the following side effects is most likely associated with the use of norethindrone?". It is evident that these questions can be answered without any other clinical information and are testing basic recall rather than the ability to apply medical knowledge. Given the low frequency of criterion 3 being followed, we further assessed the complexity and difficulty of the generated questions and answers. According to expert 1, 6 out of 10 (60%) questions were graded as either very simple or simple, and according to expert 2, 7 out of 10 (70%) questions were graded as either very simple or simple. When assessing difficulty, expert 1 rated 6 out of 10 (60%) questions as either very easy or easy, and expert 2 rated 7 out of 10 (70%) questions as either very easy or easy. Thus, this allows us to conclude that the majority of questions are too simple and too easy for USMLE Step preparation.

According to expert 1, criterion 11 was fulfilled by 9 out of 10 (90%) ChatGPT-3.5-generated questions, and 7 out of 10 (70%) according to expert 2. Questions missing this criterion provided alternative cues in a grammatical sense that prompted examinees to eliminate any answer choice options that did not fit the cues given. An example of this was seen when ChatGPT was asked to provide an NBME question evaluating the indication for cyclobenzaprine, where the patient in the clinical vignette presented with both acute lower back pain and muscle spasms. This provided a cue to the examinee by stating two different clinical problems needed to be fulfilled by the medication prescribed, which left the option "acute musculoskeletal pain with muscle spasms" as the only viable option, which was correct. Picking up on subtle cues like this that are not necessarily explicit may still provide guidance that does not necessarily evaluate the examinee's proficiency in the material, reducing the quality of the question. According to expert 1, criterion 12 was fulfilled by 8 out of 10 (80%) ChatGPT-3.5-generated questions, and 10 out of 10 (100%) according to expert 2. Providing grouped or exhaustive answer choices can cause the examinee to immediately negate all other option choices, leading to only the grouped answer choices. The example that was provided in criterion 11 also violated criterion 12, as it provided both "acute exacerbation of chronic obstructive pulmonary disease (COPD)" and "acute musculoskeletal pain with muscle spasms" as answer choices, with the latter being the correct answer choice. With these two answer choices being grouped together as acute conditions, the other answer choices were quickly able to be eliminated. To provide NBME-standard questions that can accurately evaluate the examinee's knowledge of the given pharmacological concepts, ChatGPT must be able to provide at least five answer choices that can be evaluated thoroughly to test the examinee's understanding of the material.

According to expert 1, criterion 15 was fulfilled by 7 out of 10 (70%) ChatGPT-3.5-generated questions, and 9 out of 10 (90%) according to expert 2. Repeating words or phrases within the clinical vignette and giving multiple-choice options can cue the examinee to determine the correct answer without accurately reflecting their proficiency in the material. For example, when asked to generate a question about the side effects of norethindrone, ChatGPT wrote within the clinical vignette that the patient reported breast tenderness and then provided breast tenderness as a correct answer choice. Providing keywords within the clinical vignette and answer choice negates the question's ability to evaluate the examinee's understanding of norethindrone and only evaluates their ability to dissect the clinical vignette. Lastly, according to both expert 1 and expert 2, criterion 16 was fulfilled by 8 out of 10 (80%) ChatGPT-3.5-generated questions. Criterion 16 assigns importance to keeping key terms balanced if key terms are used within the answer choices. When asked to generate the adverse effects of warfarin, ChatGPT provided both thrombocytopenia and heparin-induced thrombocytopenia, which could lead to all other option choices being immediately negated. If it is important to provide key terms within the choice options, it is important to provide a balancing of the terms throughout all the choice options to ensure the examinee is not able to remove certain choices due to the lack of keywords.

In terms of estimated question difficulties, the experts' ratings diverged. This could be due to limited calibration or the fact that it is very challenging to estimate the difficulty of a question for students.

While discussing the capabilities of AI and what improvements need to be made to make it a reliable source for NBME question generation, it is important to consider that AI is constantly evolving, updating, and improving its knowledge base [4]. With that being said, a recent ChatGPT update now provides the opportunity to provide an alternative output if the initial output was unsatisfactory to the user. Lastly, AI can be highly variable, and may not give the same output every time, despite the fixed input.

Future studies should employ a larger expert panel and implement a more comprehensive calibration exercise with more diverse and context-rich examples to assess a greater number of questions. Additionally, the criteria established for evaluating questions generated by ChatGPT should undergo scrutiny by an expert panel to identify any gaps and potentially incorporate additional criteria.

Furthermore, future research should investigate how OpenAI's new models, ChatGPT-4 and ChatGPT-4 Turbo, perform compared with ChatGPT-3.5 in generating questions that follow the NBME guidelines [11]. Given the more advanced processing of ChatGPT-4 and ChatGPT-4 Turbo, it can give insight into the updated capabilities of AI software. In addition, future research should also include comparing the capabilities of other AI models, such as Google's AI model Google Gemini and Facebook's AI model Llama 3, with those of ChatGPT in creating NBME-standardized questions. Comparing the similarities and differences between the various AI models can provide more insight into the advantages of each AI model in medical education.

The results of our study suggest that ChatGPT-3.5 has the potential to generate NBME-style questions, but there are significant limitations related to the depth of knowledge tested. These findings align with previous research, which highlighted that while AI models can emulate human-like question generation, their depth of clinical understanding remains limited [9]. This observation can be explained through the lens of cognitive load theory, which suggests that effective learning and assessment require engaging learners in complex, higher-order thinking tasks [26–28]. Our results show that ChatGPT-3.5 tends to favor questions that test recall rather than application or analysis, reflecting its reliance on pattern recognition over true clinical reasoning.

Furthermore, our study's findings raise important questions about the suitability of AI for medical education. According to constructivist learning theory, effective education should not only convey factual information but also facilitate the application of knowledge in real-world scenarios [29,30]. The tendency of ChatGPT-3.5 to generate "pseudo-vignettes", as identified in our analysis, suggests a gap between AI-generated content and the needs of complex, case-based learning environments advocated by constructivist principles.

These results have practical implications for medical educators, indicating that while AI tools like ChatGPT-3.5 can support question generation, they should be complemented with expert oversight to ensure the development of questions that engage critical thinking. Future research should explore ways to enhance the model's capacity to generate questions that align with theories of cognitive complexity, such as Bloom's Taxonomy, which emphasizes the importance of creating questions that test analysis, synthesis, and evaluation. By doing so, we can better integrate AI-generated content into medical education in a manner that promotes deeper learning and prepares students for clinical practice.

Proposed Evaluation Framework for Future Implementation of AI in Exam Generation.

Given the results of our study, which identified several shortcomings of ChatGPT-3.5, including hallucinations and the tendency to produce oversimplified questions, it is crucial to adopt a comprehensive, multi-stage evaluation framework for the future implementation of AI in exam question generation. This framework aims to enhance the reliability, accuracy, and educational value of AI-generated content, particularly for high-stakes assessments like the USMLE. We suggest the following steps:

- Initial automated screening: Implement AI-based tools such as the Google Knowledge Graph API, the Wolfram Alpha API, or the MedGPT to perform an initial quality check of the generated content. This stage would identify potential inaccuracies, inconsistencies, or superficial questions that do not meet established standards, flagging them for further review.
- Expert review process: Involve a panel of three to five domain-specific experts, such as pharmacologists and medical educators, to thoroughly assess the generated questions. This expert review would evaluate the medical accuracy, clinical relevance, level appropriateness, and adherence to item-writing standards (such as the NBME guidelines), ensuring that the questions align with the depth and complexity required for medical exams [11].
- Integration of specialized medical knowledge bases: Use external databases such as UpToDate, PubMed, or other clinical guidelines to cross-reference the generated content for factual accuracy. Incorporating these knowledge bases would help validate medical accuracy and ensure that the AI's knowledge aligns with the latest developments in current clinical practice.
- Iterative feedback loop: Create an iterative process where expert feedback is used to refine the AI-generated questions. This would involve adjusting prompts, question structures, or explanations, followed by re-evaluation until the content reaches a satisfactory level of quality and complexity.
- Comparison using bootstrapping methods: Recent studies suggested applying bootstrapping techniques to evaluate exam questions [31]. Bootstrapping could be used to compare the psychometric characteristics of AI-generated questions with instructor-written ones, analyzing factors such as the size of confidence intervals, reliability, and question difficulty.
- Pilot testing with medical students: Conduct small-scale pilot testing of AI-generated questions with medical students. This step would assess the perceived difficulty and educational value of the questions in real exam conditions, providing direct feedback on how well the questions prepare students for actual exams like the USMLE.

By adopting this multi-stage evaluation framework, future AI-generated questions can be fine-tuned to not only meet NBME standards but also foster critical thinking and higher-order reasoning among medical students. This approach addresses the limitations of current AI models while maximizing their potential as an educational tool.

However, a key consideration for future research is the emphasis on generating questions that test higher-level medical knowledge rather than relying predominantly on basic recall. While our study has demonstrated ChatGPT-3.5's ability to produce questions that meet many NBME criteria, a notable area for improvement is the focus on deeper analytical and reasoning skills. Higher-order questions challenge learners to apply their knowledge in complex clinical scenarios, which is essential for the development of critical thinking skills in medical education. Future research should explore prompt adjustments and evaluation processes that can guide AI models to create more sophisticated clinical vignettes. This would help ensure that the generated questions not only align with NBME standards but also effectively test learners' ability to synthesize and apply knowledge in a clinical context.

5. Conclusions

Based on the scores received, the ChatGPT-3.5-generated questions seem to satisfy the NBME guidelines [11]. However, when thoroughly going through the questions, the questions are not up to par with other Step exam material resources. ChatGPT-3.5 provided oversimplified questions and overuse of repeated words in the clinical vignette and answer choices that allow an individual to answer the question without any medical knowledge. Our data support the need for AI software that is specifically trained on medical and scientific information.

The high fulfillment rates for criteria 2, 6–10, and 13 suggest that these criteria likely involve straightforward and clear rules. It seems that ChatGPT can consistently follow and apply these types of rules. For instance, avoiding complex multiple-choice options (criterion 6) or using consistent answer-choice formats (criterion 9) are structural elements that AI can reliably adhere to. This finding highlights the strength of ChatGPT in following well-defined, rule-based guidelines that do not require deep contextual understanding. In a related vein, the lower fulfillment rates of 4/10 for criterion 3 (applying foundational knowledge) suggest that ChatGPT struggled with applying foundational medical knowledge rather than simple recall. This criterion requires a deeper understanding of medical concepts and their application in various contexts, which is challenging for an AI model primarily trained on text data without practical experience. This finding indicates a significant gap in ChatGPT's ability to create questions that go beyond basic recall and test higher-order thinking skills.

With regard to criterion 1 (medical accuracy), the 8/10 fulfillment rate shows instances where ChatGPT provided medically inaccurate information. This could be due to "hallucinations", where the AI generates plausible-sounding but incorrect information. Ensuring medical accuracy is critical but challenging due to the vast and complex nature of medical knowledge. The fulfillment of criterion 5 (cover-the-option rule) was moderate (7.5/10 times). The "cover-the-option" rule requires questions to be answerable without seeing the options, which tests the examinee's true understanding of the material. This criterion was harder for ChatGPT to consistently meet, likely due to its reliance on generating plausible distractors rather than deeply understanding the question context.

The fulfillment rates of 8/10 and 7/10 for criteria 11 and 15 (avoiding grammatical and repetitive cues, respectively, highlight occasional lapses where questions contain grammatical or repetitive cues that could inadvertently guide examinees to the correct answer) points to the need for more sophisticated language-processing capabilities to avoid such subtle errors.

The high scores (15/16) in neurology, respiratory, and gastrointestinal areas suggest that ChatGPT's training data and its ability to generate questions for these specialties are particularly robust. These fields may have clearer, more standardized guidelines and well-documented clinical scenarios that the AI can emulate effectively.

The relatively lower scores in reproductive and musculoskeletal (12.5/16 and 13/16) areas may reflect more complex or nuanced clinical scenarios that are harder for the AI to accurately capture. Additionally, reproductive health often involves sensitive and varied patient factors, which may not be as well represented in the AI's training data.

Author Contributions: Conceptualization, M.S., W.A., T.H. and C.M.; methodology, C.M., M.S., T.H., M.R. and W.A.; validation, C.M., M.S. and W.A.; formal analysis, C.M.; investigation, C.M., M.S. and W.A.; resources, M.S., C.M. and W.A.; data curation, M.S., C.M. and W.A.; writing—original draft preparation, M.S., W.A. and C.M.; writing—review and editing, C.M., M.S. and W.A.; visualization, M.S., C.M. and W.A.; supervision, C.M.; project administration, C.M., M.S. and W.A. All authors have read and agreed to the published version of the manuscript.

Funding: This research received no external funding.

Data Availability Statement: The raw data supporting the conclusions of this article will be made available by the first and second authors on request.

Acknowledgments: The authors would like to extend their gratitude to Steve Wilson, who substantially contributed to the development of the design guidelines and provision of software expertise.

Conflicts of Interest: The authors declare no conflicts of interest.

References

1. Natalie; OpenAI Help Center. What Is ChatGPT? 2023. Available online: https://help.openai.com/en/articles/6783457-what-is-chatgpt (accessed on 20 October 2024).
2. Biswas, S. ChatGPT and the Future of Medical Writing. *Radiology* **2023**, *307*, e223312. [CrossRef] [PubMed]
3. Niles, R.; OpenAI Help Center. GPT-3.5 Turbo Updates. 2023. Available online: https://help.openai.com/en/articles/8555514-gpt-3-5-turbo-updates (accessed on 20 October 2024).
4. Davis, S.E.; Walsh, C.G.; Matheny, M.E. Open questions and research gaps for monitoring and updating AI-enabled tools in clinical settings. *Front. Digit. Health* **2022**, *4*, 958284. [CrossRef] [PubMed]
5. Openai.com. Language Models Are Few-Shot Learners. Available online: https://openai.com/research/language-models-are-few-shot-learners (accessed on 20 October 2024).
6. Ruby, D. ChatGPT Statistics for 2023: Comprehensive Facts and Data. Demandsage. 28 April 2023. Available online: https://www.demandsage.com/chatgpt-statistics/ (accessed on 20 October 2024).
7. Brandl, R. ChatGPT Statistics and User Numbers 2023—OpenAI Chatbot. Tooltester. 15 February 2023. Available online: https://www.tooltester.com/en/blog/chatgpt-statistics/#:~:text=diagrams,%20and%20illustrations (accessed on 20 October 2024).
8. Step 1 Content Outline and Specifications | USMLE. Available online: https://www.usmle.org/prepare-your-exam/step-1-materials/step-1-content-outline-and-specifications (accessed on 20 October 2024).
9. Gilson, A.; Safranek, C.W.; Huang, T.; Socrates, V.; Chi, L.; Taylor, R.A.; Chartash, D. How Does ChatGPT Perform on the United States Medical Licensing Examination? The Implications of Large Language Models for Medical Education and Knowledge Assessment. *JMIR Med. Educ.* **2023**, *9*, e45312. [CrossRef] [PubMed]
10. Scoring & Score Reporting | USMLE. Available online: https://www.usmle.org/bulletin-information/scoring-and-score-reporting (accessed on 20 October 2024).
11. Item-Writing Guide | NBME. Available online: https://www.nbme.org/item-writing-guide (accessed on 20 October 2024).
12. Antaki, F.; Touma, S.; Milad, D.; El-Khoury, J.; Duval, R. Evaluating the Performance of ChatGPT in Ophthalmology: An Analysis of Its Successes and Shortcomings. *Ophthalmol. Sci.* **2023**, *3*, 100324. [CrossRef] [PubMed]
13. Sallam, M. ChatGPT Utility in Healthcare Education, Research, and Practice: Systematic Review on the Promising Perspectives and Valid Concerns. *Healthcare* **2023**, *11*, 887. [CrossRef] [PubMed]
14. Deng, J.; Lin, Y. The Benefits and Challenges of ChatGPT: An Overview. *Front. Comput. Intell. Syst.* **2023**, *2*, 81–83. [CrossRef]
15. Johnson, K.B.; Wei, W.Q.; Weeraratne, D.; Frisse, M.E.; Misulis, K.; Rhee, K.; Zhao, J.; Snowdon, J.L. Precision Medicine, AI, and the Future of Personalized Health Care. *Clin. Transl. Sci.* **2021**, *14*, 86–93. [CrossRef] [PubMed]
16. Rajpurkar, P.; Chen, E.; Banerjee, O.; Topol, E.J. AI in health and medicine. *Nat. Med.* **2022**, *28*, 31–38. [CrossRef] [PubMed]
17. Paranjape, K.; Schinkel, M.; Nannan Panday, R.; Car, J.; Nanayakkara, P. Introducing Artificial Intelligence Training in Medical Education. *JMIR Med. Educ.* **2019**, *5*, e16048. [CrossRef] [PubMed]
18. Benoit, J. ChatGPT for Clinical Vignette Generation, Revision, and Evaluation. *medRxiv* **2023**. [CrossRef]
19. Ahn, C. Exploring ChatGPT for information of cardiopulmonary resuscitation. *Resuscitation* **2023**, *185*, 109729. [CrossRef] [PubMed]
20. OpenAI Platform. Available online: https://platform.openai.com/docs/guides/prompt-engineering/six-strategies-for-getting-better-results (accessed on 20 October 2024).
21. Warfarin: Drug Information. UpToDate. Available online: https://www-uptodate-com.huaryu.kl.oakland.edu/contents/warfarin-drug-information?search=warfarin&source=panel_search_result&selectedTitle=1~148&usage_type=panel&kp_tab=drug_general&display_rank=1 (accessed on 20 October 2024).
22. Shuster, K.; Poff, S.; Chen, M.; Kiela, D.; Weston, J. Retrieval augmentation reduces hallucination in conversation. *arXiv* **2021**, arXiv:2104.07567.
23. Tian, K.; Mitchell, E.; Yao, H.; Manning, C.D.; Finn, C. Fine-tuning language models for factuality. *arXiv* **2023**, arXiv:2311.08401.
24. Basu, K.; Sinha, R.; Ong, A.; Basu, T. Artificial Intelligence: How is It Changing Medical Sciences and Its Future? *Indian J. Dermatol.* **2020**, *65*, 365–370. [CrossRef] [PubMed]
25. Vanderbilt, A.A.; Feldman, M.; Wood, I.K. Assessment in undergraduate medical education: A review of course exams. *Med. Educ. Online* **2013**, *18*, 1–5. [CrossRef] [PubMed]
26. Mohiyeddini, C.; Loftus, S.F. Editorial: Medical education in uncertain times: Threats, challenges, and opportunities of COVID-19. *Front. Psychol.* **2024**, *15*, 1467070. [CrossRef] [PubMed] [PubMed Central]
27. Sweller, J. Cognitive load during problem solving: Effects on learning. *Cogn. Sci.* **1988**, *12*, 257–285. [CrossRef]

28. Taylor, T.A.H.; Kamel-ElSayed, S.; Grogan, J.F.; Hajj Hussein, I.; Lerchenfeldt, S.; Mohiyeddini, C. Teaching in Uncertain Times: Expanding the Scope of Extraneous Cognitive Load in the Cognitive Load Theory. *Front. Psychol.* **2022**, *13*, 665835. [CrossRef] [PubMed] [PubMed Central]
29. Piaget, J. *The Construction of Reality in the Child*, Cook, M., Translator; Basic Books: New York, NY, USA, 1954. [CrossRef]
30. Gopnik, A.; Meltzoff, A.N.; Kuhl, P.K. *The Scientist in the Crib: Minds, Brains, and How Children Learn*; William Morrow & Co.: New York, NY, USA, 1999.
31. Mohiyeddini, C. Enhancing exam question quality in medical education through bootstrapping. *Anat. Sci. Educ.* 2024; *early view*. [CrossRef]

algorithms

MDPI

Article

Fair and Transparent Student Admission Prediction Using Machine Learning Models

George Raftopoulos †, Gregory Davrazos † and Sotiris Kotsiantis *

Department of Mathematics, University of Patras, 26504 Rio, Greece; georaftop@sch.gr (G.R.); gdavrazo@upatras.gr (G.D.)
* Correspondence: sotos@math.upatras.gr
† These authors contributed equally to this work.

Abstract: Student admission prediction is a crucial aspect of academic planning, offering insights into enrollment trends, resource allocation, and institutional growth. However, traditional methods often lack the ability to address fairness and transparency, leading to potential biases and inequities in the decision-making process. This paper explores the development and evaluation of machine learning models designed to predict student admissions while prioritizing fairness and interpretability. We employ a diverse set of algorithms, including Logistic Regression, Decision Trees, and ensemble methods, to forecast admission outcomes based on academic, demographic, and extracurricular features. Experimental results on real-world datasets highlight the effectiveness of the proposed models in achieving competitive predictive performance while adhering to fairness metrics such as demographic parity and equalized odds. Our findings demonstrate that machine learning can not only enhance the accuracy of admission predictions but also support equitable access to education by promoting transparency and accountability in automated systems.

Keywords: fairmachine learning; ethical AI in education; student admission prediction

1. Introduction

Machine learning (ML) and artificial intelligence (AI) systems are transforming society and industries by automating critical decision-making processes, influencing areas such as criminal justice, healthcare, finance, and employment. These algorithms are increasingly scrutinized for potential biases and unfair outcomes, which, if unchecked, may harm vulnerable groups. For instance, the use of algorithms in criminal sentencing has disproportionately impacted marginalized communities, as seen with COMPAS, a recidivism prediction tool found to have higher false-positive rates for African Americans than for Caucasians [1–3]. Since then, researchers and practitioners are increasingly focused on developing methodologies that not only enhance the accuracy and efficacy of ML models but also promote fairness, accountability, transparency, and ethics (FATE). The 2022 review by Kaur et al. [4] offers a comprehensive analysis of principles and methods necessary to develop trustworthy artificial intelligence (AI) systems. The authors emphasized the critical aspects of transparency, fairness, accountability, and privacy, which are essential to build reliable AI technologies for high-stakes fields, including healthcare, justice, and education. They highlighted issues such as algorithmic bias, data privacy, and lack of explainability, proposing a framework that incorporates human-centered design and collaborative oversight throughout the AI lifecycle.

In the highly competitive landscape of student admissions, institutions face the challenge of evaluating candidates through a complex interplay of academic, professional, and personal attributes. Ensuring fairness and transparency in the admissions process is not only critical for maintaining institutional credibility but also for fostering diversity and equity. Traditional methods often rely on subjective criteria, leading to potential biases that can undermine these goals. Machine learning (ML) models offer a promising alternative by providing data-driven insights to predict admission outcomes while maintaining consistency and objectivity. However, concerns about the interpretability and fairness of these models remain paramount, particularly in sensitive applications like admissions.

A widely debated approach to achieving fairness in machine learning models is the apparent removal of sensitive or protected attributes (fairness through unawareness). Some researchers argue that including these attributes (fairness through awareness [5]) can help address and correct structural disparities by explicitly accounting for them in the model. However, others caution that incorporating such variables risks reinforcing existing biases, as the model may inadvertently use them in a way that perpetuates discrimination [1,6,7].

Addressing fairness in ML involves defining, measuring, and mitigating bias, but this is challenging due to the trade-offs between fairness metrics and other model performance objectives. The research community explore various approaches such as pre-processing data adjustments (e.g., class balancing techniques), in-processing constraints during model training (e.g., adversarial learning), and post-processing corrections to reduce bias and enhance the fairness of outcomes (e.g., group-aware threshold adaptation). These techniques seek to balance the goals of accuracy and fairness, as enhancing one can sometimes impair the other [1,2,7,8].

In particular, the education sector exemplifies the need for fairness in algorithmic decision-making. To build more equitable educational systems, it is essential to prioritize fairness. Pardo and Siemens [9] presented a framework of ethical principles to align learning analytics practices with legal and ethical standards. The authors in [10] provided an in-depth analysis of ethical guidelines for implementing artificial intelligence (AI) in K-12 education, focusing on children's unique needs and rights in educational settings. They explored how AI technologies offer significant benefits for learning while raising ethical concerns about children's rights, teacher welfare, and educational appropriateness. In their systematic review, Fu and Weng (2024) [11] explored ethical practices for implementing human-centered artificial intelligence in educational contexts. By analyzing empirical studies, they identified five key characteristics of responsible AI for education: fairness and equity, privacy and security, non-maleficence and beneficence, agency and autonomy, and transparency and intelligibility. Idowu in [12] provided a systematic literature review of recent advancements in mitigating such biases within educational algorithms used for tasks including student dropout prediction, performance analysis, and content recommendation. His study advocates for an inclusive fairness model that broadens the focus beyond gender and race to include other attributes like socioeconomic status and disability, ultimately guiding more equitable algorithm design in educational contexts.

Sahlgren's argument, as presented in [13], emphasizes the necessity of critically evaluating the tools used to measure and address algorithmic bias within educational settings. These tools, while intended to promote fairness, can unintentionally perpetuate existing inequalities by prioritizing narrowly focused technical solutions over comprehensive educational reforms. Researchers engaged in advancing fairness in AI must remain cognizant of this critique, ensuring that their approaches do not reinforce systemic inequities but instead contribute to meaningful and transformative change.

2. Literature Review

We present the subsequent review of the literature, organized into two sections. In the first section, we examine studies that apply machine learning models to student admissions. The second section focuses on research addressing fairness issues within the educational context.

2.1. Student Admissions Through Machine Learning Models

In their study, AlGhamdi et al. [14] utilized the publicly available "Graduate Admissions 2" dataset from Kaggle to develop an automated model for predicting postgraduate admission likelihood. The primary objective of this research was to assist prospective graduate students in identifying and targeting universities that align optimally with their academic profiles. The same dataset was employed by Goni et al. [15], with the distinction that these authors implemented a Deep Neural Network model for their analysis.

The publicly available dataset titled "Recommendation System for Graduate Level Universities in the United States" was utilized by Sridhar et al. [16]. In their study, the authors proposed a stacked ensemble model that demonstrated superior predictive performance compared to other machine learning models, including deep learning approaches, in estimating a student's likelihood of admission to specific universities.

The study by Wu and Wu [17] examined the influence of selection criteria on the admission outcomes of non-native English-speaking MBA applicants in China, specifically within the Shanghai International MBA Program. The findings indicate that traditional selection metrics may inadequately assess the essential skills required for success in programs conducted in a non-native language. Consequently, the authors advocate for incorporating machine learning techniques into the student selection process to enhance admissions accuracy and identify candidates with a higher potential for success.

The study by Assiri et al. [18] examined university admissions criteria in Saudi Arabia, with an emphasis on enhancing the process of student major selection through machine learning methodologies. The research analyzed factors such as high school GPA, General Aptitude Test (GAT) scores, and Academic Test (AT) scores, applying models including K-Nearest Neighbor (KNN), Decision Tree (DT), and Support Vector Machine (SVM) to classify students into appropriate academic majors.

Assiri et al. [19] investigated improvements in student admissions processes at Saudi Arabian universities by integrating data mining and machine learning techniques. The study critiqued traditional admissions metrics, such as GPA and general aptitude scores, noting that they often fail to match students with the most suitable majors, resulting in higher dropout rates. To address this, the authors introduced an adapted Jaccard similarity model that links high school course performance with success in specific fields of study. Their findings suggest that this data-driven, personalized admissions approach could better align students' skills with appropriate academic tracks.

In their study, Mridha et al. [20] investigated the use of machine learning models to predict the likelihood of graduate admissions for applicants to U.S. universities. By training the model on key admissions criteria, such as GRE and TOEFL scores, undergraduate GPA, and research experience, their approach offers students an automated tool to assess their admission prospects. This method seeks to minimize dependence on potentially biased human consultants and to facilitate a more efficient application decision-making process.

In their study, Ursan and Bucos [21] examined predictive analytics for graduate admissions in engineering programs at Politehnica University Timișoara, Romania. The authors developed a multi-class classification model to predict student admission outcomes based on candidates' undergraduate grades, preferences, and demographic data.

Sharma and Soni [22] proposed a machine learning-based approach to predict likelihood for postgraduate admissions for Indian students. Additionally, they deployed their model as an interactive R Shiny web application, providing a user-friendly interface that enables students to easily estimate their admission prospects.

The study by Li et al. [23] presents a comprehensive literature review on the application of predictive analytics in university admissions. The authors identified key research areas, including admission outcomes, academic performance, admission yield, admission likelihood, and appropriate field of study selection. Their findings emphasize the potential of predictive analytics to improve university admissions processes and highlight the need for further research at the intersection of predictive techniques and student retention strategies within higher education.

Zub et al. [24] introduced a novel two-stage ensemble model that combines Probabilistic Neural Networks (PNNs) and Support Vector Machines (SVMs) to predict admissions in higher education. The proposed model leverages PNNs to expand the dataset by estimating class probabilities and employs a stacking ensemble of SVMs with various kernel functions, using Logistic Regression as the meta-algorithm. The results indicate that this model outperforms existing machine learning methods in admission prediction accuracy.

In their study, VanBusum and Fang [25] applied machine learning models to predict student admissions outcomes at a large urban research university. Their findings indicate that these predictive models disproportionately affected under-represented groups.This research contributes critical insights into the ethical and practical challenges of implementing predictive analytics in admissions, emphasizing the need for bias mitigation to ensure fairness and equity across diverse student demographics.

Zhao and his colleagues [26] aimed to develop machine learning models to improve admissions predictions for two STEM graduate programs, with a particular focus on the role of letters of recommendation (LORs). Their methodology involved analyzing 717 applications and included data from structured application forms, resumes, and LORs. Feature extraction incorporated demographic data, academic credentials, GRE scores, and natural language processing (NLP) to evaluate LORs' sentiment and tone. The study's findings indicate that while LORs alone have limited predictive power, integrating LOR data with other applicant information significantly enhances model accuracy, underscoring the value of combining qualitative and quantitative data in admissions predictions.

From this brief literature review, study [25] is among the first to reveal significant biases related to gender, race, and first-generation status when machine learning models are applied to student admissions processes.

Marcinkowski et al. [27] presented a pivotal study emphasizing the necessity of addressing fairness concerns in algorithmic decision-making (ADM) within higher education. Their research examined perceptions of fairness in ADM as compared to human decision-making (HDM) in university admissions, using survey data collected from students at a major German university. Their findings indicate that ADM is perceived as fairer than HDM in terms of both procedural and distributive fairness. This study highlights the critical role of fairness in ADM, particularly in maintaining student trust and protecting institutional reputation.

The preceding literature review, while not conducted as a systematic one, reveals a significant gap in current research: there is a marked shortage of studies that rigorously investigate the integration of fairness-aware machine learning algorithms within student admissions processes. This absence of research suggests that the critical intersection of algorithmic fairness and admissions decisions remains underexplored, potentially leaving biases and inequities unaddressed in the deployment of machine learning systems in educational settings.

2.2. *(Un)Fairness in Educational Settings*

The review article by Memarian et al. [28] delved into the application of artificial intelligence (AI) in higher education and highlighted the growing ethical concerns regarding the morality of AI programs. Through a systematic review of 33 articles sourced from databases such as SCOPUS and Web of Science, the authors explored how fairness, accountability, transparency, and ethics (FATE) are defined and studied within this domain. Their analysis categorized definitions of FATE into descriptive and technical types, revealing notable patterns: fairness tended to have more descriptive definitions and was studied quantitatively, whereas ethics was predominantly approached through qualitative definitions and methodologies.

The adoption of machine learning systems has profoundly transformed workflows and decision-making across various industries, including education. However, these systems raise critical ethical issues, particularly regarding their fairness and the impact on diverse populations. Nga et al. [29] conducted a systematic mapping of fairness research in higher education, analyzing 63 primary studies published between 2002 and 2023. This comprehensive study identified key research themes, including traditional machine learning algorithms, sensitive variables such as gender and race, and diverse fairness definitions.

Bayer et al. [30] shed light on systemic inequalities in higher education, with a focus on the persistent 13% degree-awarding gap for Black, Asian, and Minority Ethnic (BAME) students, alongside disparities affecting other protected groups. Their study evaluated the effectiveness of prediction models in identifying at-risk students and explored whether disaggregating data by protected attributes to create subgroup-specific prediction models could enhance fairness. The findings indicated that existing models disproportionately benefited the majority group, and subgroup-specific models failed to improve either fairness or accuracy, underscoring the complexity of addressing systemic inequities through technical interventions alone.

Deho et al. [31] examined the role of sensitive attributes such as gender, race, and disability in learning analytics models used to predict student outcomes. Drawing on data from a three-year study at a major Australian university, the research found that including or excluding these attributes had limited impact on model accuracy or fairness. Using Explainable AI (XAI), the study demonstrated that the relevance of sensitive attributes varied across student cohorts and contexts. This nuanced finding highlights the inadequacy of simplistic approaches—such as excluding sensitive variables—for achieving fairness. The authors advocate for more sophisticated bias mitigation strategies tailored to specific contexts.

Sha et al. [32] investigated data biases and their correlation with machine learning (ML) model fairness in education, focusing on distribution bias and hardness bias across five predictive tasks. The study proposed two class-balancing techniques to improve fairness. The results showed that addressing data biases could significantly enhance fairness (up to 66%) with minimal trade-offs in predictive accuracy (less than 1%). This work underscores the importance of tackling biases at the data level to improve equitable outcomes.

Li et al. [33] introduced a Fair Logistic Regression (Fair-LR) algorithm designed to balance predictive accuracy and fairness. Fairness was evaluated using the Equalized Odds metric, which assesses consistency in type I (false positive) and type II (false negative) error rates across demographic groups. Experimental comparisons with traditional models, such as Logistic Regression (LR), Support Vector Machine (SVM), and Random Forest (RF), demonstrated that Fair-LR achieved comparable predictive accuracy while significantly improving fairness. This innovation offers a promising avenue for developing fairness-aware predictive models.

Nezami et al. [34] explored the impact of data imputation techniques on the fairness and performance of predictive models for college student success. Their findings revealed that imputation could inadvertently amplify bias, particularly when testing data align with historical distributions reflecting societal inequities. However, the study also highlighted the potential for bias mitigation through systemic reforms that equalize future data distributions. This dual emphasis on refining technical methodologies and addressing broader societal injustices underscores the multifaceted approach needed to enhance the fairness and reliability of AI models in education.

Collectively, these studies illustrate the complex interplay of technical, ethical, and societal factors in leveraging AI for higher education. They highlight the need for interdisciplinary approaches to address fairness and ethics comprehensively, integrating technical innovations with systemic reforms.

3. Materials and Methods

For the experiments, three datasets were used.

3.1. MBA Admission Dataset Description

The dataset used in the study comprises synthetic data generated from the Wharton Class of 2025's statistics. The dataset was obtained in a CSV format from the Kaggle website [35]. The dataset consists of 6194 cases (number of applicants) and eight input feature attributes while the output feature refers to the result of the admissions process:

- Gender: Applicant's gender (Male, Female);
- International: International student (TRUE/FALSE);
- GPA: Grade Point Average of the applicant (on 4.0 scale);
- Major: Undergraduate major (Business, STEM, Humanities);
- Race: Racial background of the applicant (e.g., White, Black, Asian, Hispanic, Other/null: international student);
- GMAT: GMAT score of the applicant (maximum 800 points);
- Work_exp: Number of years of work experience;
- Work_industry: Industry of the applicant's previous work experience (e.g., Consulting, Finance, or Technology);
- Admission: Admission status (Admit, Waiting List, Deny).

All of these admission criteria are fully aligned with those reported in research papers reviewed in [36]. From the above features, Gender, International, Major, Race, Work_industry, and Admission are considered to be categorical variables while the other features are considered to be numerical ones.

The imbalance ratio for this dataset is calculated using the formula below:

$$\text{Imbalance Ratio (IR)} = \frac{N_{\text{majority}}}{N_{\text{minority}}} = 5.77$$

where $N_{\text{majority}} = N_{\text{Admit}}$ and N_{minority} represent the number of samples in the majority and minority classes, respectively. Although the current problem involves multi-class classification, we assumed that students placed on the Waiting List for admission are closer to a positive outcome than a negative one. We selected to remove all the cases related to the Waiting List, and therefore we defined $N_{\text{minority}} = N_{\text{Deny}}$.

Based on the descriptive statistics for the categorical features presented in Table 1 and the calculation of the imbalance ratio (see above), it can be inferred that the dataset is an imbalanced one, necessitating appropriate remedial techniques. For the Work_Industry feature, we could merge different categories to different groups but we selected to remove this feature for the subsequent experiment.

Although the dataset is synthetic, the specific procedure or algorithm used to generate it remains unknown to us.

Table 1. Descriptive statistics of categorical features.

Feature	Category	Frequency	Percent (%)
Gender	Male	3943	63.66
	Female	2251	36.34
International	True	1842	30
	False	4352	70
Major	Business	2481	40.05
	STEM	1875	30.27
	Humanities	1838	29.67
Race	Asian	1147	18.52
	Black	916	14.79
	Hispanic	596	9.62
	White	1456	23.51
	Other	2079	33.56

Table 1. *Cont.*

Feature	Category	Frequency	Percent (%)
Work_Industry	Consulting	1619	26.14
	PE/VC	907	14.64
	Technology	716	11.56
	Nonprofit/Gov	651	10.51
	Investment Banking	580	9.36
	Financial Services	451	7.28
	Other	421	6.8
	Health Care	334	5.39
	Investment Management	166	2.68
	CPG	114	1.84
	Real Estate	111	1.79
	Media/Entertainment	59	0.95
	Retail	33	0.53
	Energy	32	0.52
Admission	Admit	900	14.53
	Waiting List	100	1.61
	Deny	5194	83.86

3.2. *Law School Dataset Description*

The Law School Dataset [37] was compiled from a 1991 survey conducted by the Law School Admission Council (LSAC) across 163 U.S. law schools. This dataset includes a variety of candidate information relevant to admissions decisions, such as undergraduate GPA, LSAT scores, demographic details, and socioeconomic backgrounds. The prediction tasks focus on determining whether a candidate would pass the bar exam or forecasting a student's first-year grade average. In this research, we will focus only on predicting whether a candidate will pass the bar exam. For our research purposes, we will use that dataset as curated by Dam Harvey [38]. This dataset is characterized by 12 features:

- 3 categorical (fulltime, fam_inc, tier);
- 3 binary (Gender, Race (White, Non-white), Pass_Bar);
- 6 numerical (decile1b, decile3, lsat, ugpa, zfygpa, zgpa).

For the Law School Dataset, the calculated imbalance ratio is 9.18, indicating a significant disparity between majority and minority outcomes. The gender ratio (men to women) is computed at 1.29, while the race ratio (White to Non-white) is 14.56, highlighting pronounced racial imbalances.

These ratios underscore the unique characteristics of the dataset, making it particularly well suited for research on fairness in educational settings, particularly in the context of university admissions. The imbalance ratio reflects the uneven distribution of the target variable, which can influence classification performance and necessitate careful model evaluation to avoid biased outcomes. Meanwhile, the gender and race ratios emphasize the importance of addressing demographic disparities to ensure equitable decision-making.

This dataset provides a valuable testbed for developing and evaluating algorithms and methodologies aimed at reducing bias, promoting fairness, and ensuring that admissions decisions are transparent and justifiable. It supports investigations into critical questions, such as the impact of systemic inequalities, the role of demographic features in predictive modeling, and the potential trade-offs between accuracy and equity in admissions processes.

3.3. *College Admission Dataset Description*

The College Admission Dataset [39], available on the Kaggle platform, provides information on admission outcomes, demographic data, and GRE and GPA scores for an unspecified college. While this dataset lacks thorough documentation, it serves our research objectives. This dataset is characterized by 7 features:

- 3 categorical (Race, SES, Rank);
- 2 binary (Gender, Admit);
- 2 numerical (GRE, GPA).

For this dataset, the calculated imbalance ratio is 2.15, indicating a modest disparity in the distribution of outcomes. The gender ratio (men to women) is 1.10, the race ratio is 1.18, and the socioeconomic status (SES) ratio is 1.08, reflecting relatively balanced representation across these protected features. Collectively, these metrics suggest that the dataset does not suffer from significant imbalances in any of the protected attributes.

3.4. *Performance Metrics*

The primary metrics commonly used in research papers for evaluating classification problems include accuracy, recall, precision, F1-score, and the Matthews correlation coefficient (MCC). Among these, MCC stands out as a robust and comprehensive performance metric. The Matthews correlation coefficient is particularly notable for its ability to provide a balanced evaluation of classification models, especially when dealing with imbalanced datasets. MCC takes values ranging from –1 (indicating completely incorrect classification) to 1 (indicating perfect classification), with 0 representing random guessing. Unlike metrics such as accuracy, which can be misleading in cases of class imbalance, or F1-score, which focuses on the harmonic mean of precision and recall, MCC accounts for all elements of the confusion matrix (true positives, true negatives, false positives, and false negatives). This comprehensive consideration makes MCC a more reliable indicator of a classifier's performance in challenging scenarios where one class dominates over the other(s). For this reason, MCC is often recommended over simpler metrics for scenarios where class imbalance is significant, as it provides a clearer picture of a model's capability to generalize across both majority and minority classes [40].

3.5. *Fairness Metrics*

Fairness metrics provide a quantitative framework to evaluate and mitigate biases in ML models. These metrics serve as tools to identify disparities across demographic groups, guide the development of fair algorithms, and enable transparency in model performance. However, the landscape of fairness metrics is complex, with trade-offs that arise when different notions of fairness conflict. In this subsection, we review the most commonly used fairness metrics found in the literature [1–3,7,8,41].

3.5.1. Selection Rate

The selection rate refers to the proportion of individuals from a 'sensitive' group (based on gender, race, etc.) who are selected as "positive" by the model. The selection rate for a specific group is defined in a mathematical way as:

$$\text{Selection Rate for each group} = \frac{\text{Number of individuals classified as Positive in the group}}{\text{Total number of individuals in the group}}$$

or using probability terminology

$$\text{Selection Rate for group A} = P(\text{positive outcome} \mid \text{group A})$$

For example, if gender is the protected attribute, we calculate the selection rates separately for males and females. A significant difference between these rates may indicate potential gender bias in the model's decision-making process.

3.5.2. Risk Difference

Risk difference measures the difference in the selection rate between two groups (e.g., male and female, if gender is the protected attribute). Demographic parity is the same as risk difference.

3.5.3. Risk Ratio (RR)

The risk ratio, also called relative risk, compares the ratio of the selection rates between two groups.

3.5.4. Disparate Impact

Disparate impact is the same as the risk ratio and is considered to be acceptable if it is less than 0.8. In a mathematical way, it is defined as:

$$\text{Disparate Impact} = \frac{P(\text{positive outcome} \mid \text{group B})}{P(\text{positive outcome} \mid \text{group A})} \leq \frac{4}{5}$$

3.5.5. Equal Opportunity Difference

The equal opportunity difference is defined as the difference in true positive rate (TPR) (also known as recall) between two groups. Mathematically, it is defined as follows for two groups, A and B:

$$\text{TPR} = \text{Recall} = \frac{\text{True Positives}}{\text{True Positives} + \text{False Negatives}}$$

$$\text{Equal Opportunity Difference} = |\text{TPR for Group A} - \text{TPR for Group B}|$$

It can be defined as the difference in false negative rate [42].

3.5.6. Equalized Odds

Equalized odds is defined as the condition in which the differences in both true positive rate (TPR) and false positive rate (FPR) among the groups defined by the protected attribute must be equal. Mathematically, it is defined as follows for two groups, A and B:

$$\text{TPR for Group A} = \text{TPR for Group B} \quad AND \quad \text{FPR for Group A} = \text{FPR for Group B}$$

4. Results

In this study, we conducted an evaluation of several machine learning models using three datasets: the MBA Admission Dataset, the Law School Dataset, and the College Admission Dataset. The results are categorized into two key aspects: performance metrics and fairness metrics. Our primary objective was to achieve an optimal balance between accuracy and fairness, acknowledging that a highly accurate model might still exhibit biases that disadvantage specific demographic groups. This dual focus is crucial for promoting equitable decision-making processes in sensitive applications like admissions. Tables 2–4 comprehensively present both performance and fairness metrics for each model applied to these datasets.

To streamline the machine learning workflow, we utilized PyCaret, an AutoML library that automates essential steps in the machine learning pipeline. PyCaret functions as a versatile wrapper for several foundational Python libraries, such as scikit-learn, enabling the seamless integration and efficient execution of tasks. This library offers an array of low-code features, including data preprocessing, model training and selection, hyperparameter tuning, performance evaluation, model comparison, result visualization, and model deployment [43,44]. The use of PyCaret not only accelerated the experimentation process but also ensured reproducibility and consistency across different datasets and models.

Our approach underscores the importance of leveraging automated tools to enhance efficiency while maintaining a rigorous analytical framework. The findings of this study contribute to the ongoing discourse on fairness in machine learning, demonstrating the practical application of AutoML tools in tackling complex problems at the intersection of technology and ethics.

Table 2. Performance and fairness metrics for ML models for MBA Dataset.

	Performance Measures							Fairness Measures			
Model	**Accuracy**	**AUC**	**Recall**	**Prec.**	**F1**	**Kappa**	**MCC**	**Selection Rate**	**Disp. Impact**	**TPR**	**FPR**
Naive Bayes	0.8357	0.8166	0.9262	**0.8862**	0.9057	**0.2677**	**0.2719**	0.823529	0.862745	0.869565	1
Ada Boost	0.8450	0.8404	0.9491	0.8788	0.9126	0.2389	0.2545	0.648649	0.648649	0.773585	1
Decision Tree	0.7974	0.6173	0.8731	0.8874	0.8801	0.2254	0.2261	0.621622	0.770461	0.622642	1
Extra Trees	0.8262	0.7907	0.9251	0.8776	0.9007	0.2074	0.2127	0.773585	0.850943	0.830189	1
Random Forest	0.8322	0.8265	0.9356	0.8761	0.9048	0.2036	0.2120	0.783784	0.862162	0.869565	1
Extreme Gradient Boosting	0.8260	0.8284	0.9328	0.8720	0.9014	0.1705	0.1781	0.702703	0.772973	0.777778	1
Logistic Regression	**0.8468**	0.8191	**0.9722**	0.8649	**0.9154**	0.1358	0.1707	**0.924528**	**0.935155**	**0.943396**	1
Light Gradient Boosting	0.8302	0.8355	0.9474	0.8661	0.9048	0.1307	0.1439	0.783784	0.851518	0.851852	1
Gradient Boosting	0.8424	**0.8482**	0.9743	0.8596	0.9134	0.0816	0.1088	0.830189	0.830189	0.925926	1

Table 3. Performance and fairness metrics for ML models for Law School Dataset.

	Performance Measures							Fairness Measures			
Model	**Accuracy**	**AUC**	**Recall**	**Prec.**	**F1**	**Kappa**	**MCC**	**Selection Rate**	**Disparate Impact**	**TPR**	**FPR**
Naive Bayes	0.8395	0.8452	0.8635	**0.9541**	0.9066	**0.3474**	**0.3706**	0.045113	0.052542	0.08	**0.497207**
Ada Boost	0.9088	0.8648	0.9803	0.9233	0.9510	0.3103	0.3424	0.631579	0.646093	**0.786667**	0.87013
Logistic Regression	**0.9097**	**0.8722**	**0.9840**	0.9213	**0.9516**	0.2932	0.3350	0.632743	0.642507	0.773333	0.904762
Gradient Boosting	0.9084	0.8697	0.9821	0.9214	0.9508	0.2912	0.3281	0.62406	0.635609	0.746667	0.874459
CatBoost	0.9053	0.8625	0.9789	0.9211	0.9491	0.2802	0.3112	0.631579	0.643051	0.733333	0.887446
Extreme Gradient Boosting	0.9010	0.8486	0.9714	0.9229	0.9465	0.2875	0.3063	0.631579	0.649165	0.693333	0.87013
Random Forest	0.9035	0.8518	0.9776	0.9203	0.9481	0.2683	0.2975	0.654135	**0.667364**	**0.76**	0.891775
Light Gradient Boosting	0.9029	0.8621	0.9768	0.9204	0.9477	0.2679	0.2956	0.606195	0.618453	0.733333	0.883117
Extra Trees	0.9013	0.8422	0.9740	0.9211	0.9468	0.2707	0.2931	0.616541	0.63135	0.733333	0.896104

Table 4. Performance and fairness metrics for ML models for College Admission Dataset.

	Performance Measures							Fairness Measures			
Model	**Accuracy**	**AUC**	**Recall**	**Prec.**	**F1**	**Kappa**	**MCC**	**Selection Rate**	**Disparate Impact**	**True Positive Rate (TPR)**	**False Positive Rate (FPR)**
Ada Boost Classifier	0.6964	0.6290	0.3250	**0.5965**	0.4037	**0.2222**	**0.2506**	0.045455	0.257576	0	0.5
Ridge Classifier	0.6929	0.6522	0.2250	0.5452	0.3087	0.1610	0.1893	0.045455	0.257576	**0**	0.214286
Logistic Regression	**0.6893**	**0.6528**	**0.2139**	0.6000	**0.3016**	0.1525	0.1947	0.045455	0.193182	0	0.214286
Linear Discriminant Analysis	0.6893	0.6533	0.2361	0.5467	0.3180	0.1624	0.1906	0.045455	0.193182	0	0.214286
Naive Bayes	0.6821	0.6590	0.3917	0.5060	0.4368	0.2221	0.2279	0.045455	0.154545	0.111111	0.571429

4.1. Experiments for MBA Dataset

Using the PyCaret library, we trained and evaluated several machine learning classifiers, including Naive Bayes, AdaBoost, Decision Tree, Extra Trees, Random Forest, Extreme Gradient Boosting (XGBoost), Logistic Regression, Light Gradient Boosting Machine (LightGBM), and Gradient Boosting. To address the issue of class imbalance inherent in the dataset, we employed Stratified k-Fold Cross-Validation with k = 10, ensuring that each fold maintained the same class distribution as the full dataset.

For performance evaluation, we used the metrics outlined in Section 3.4, ranking models in descending order based on the Matthews correlation coefficient (MCC). For fairness assessment, we employed metrics including selection rate, disparate impact, true positive rate (TPR), and false positive rate (FPR). In order to present the fairness metric results effectively, we opted to include only the worst-case scenarios for each combination of protected attributes (e.g., gender or race) in Table 2. Specifically, we reported the minimum values for metrics such as selection rate, disparate impact, and true positive rate (TPR), as well as the maximum value for the false positive rate (FPR). It is important to emphasize that the worst-case values for these fairness metrics do not necessarily occur within the same combinations of protected attributes but rather across different ones.

In analyzing classifier performance on the MBA Dataset, distinct strengths emerge for both the Naive Bayes and Logistic Regression models, reflecting their suitability for different classification objectives. The Naive Bayes model demonstrates a notable advantage in metrics such as precision (0.8862), Kappa (0.9057), and Matthews correlation coefficient (MCC, 0.2719). These metrics highlight the model's strengths in scenarios requiring precision and reliable differentiation between classes. Specifically:

- Precision indicates the model's effectiveness in minimizing false positives, critical for decision-making tasks where incorrect classifications can have significant consequences.
- Kappa reflects a high level of agreement between the predicted and actual classifications beyond random chance, underscoring the model's reliability.
- MCC, though moderate, provides a more nuanced measure of correlation between predictions and actual outcomes, considering class imbalance.
- These attributes make Naive Bayes particularly effective in applications where the cost of false positives is high, such as screening processes where the precision of classification outweighs the need for broader recall.

Logistic Regression, on the other hand, excels in metrics that emphasize a balanced and inclusive approach, including accuracy (0.8468), recall (0.9722), and F1-score (0.9154):

- High recall indicates the model's ability to identify nearly all true positives, minimizing false negatives—a critical requirement in contexts where inclusivity and sensitivity are paramount.
- F1-score, which harmonizes precision and recall, underscores the model's robust overall performance, balancing both the reduction of false positives and false negatives.
- Accuracy further supports its ability to deliver consistent, reliable classifications across the dataset.

These characteristics position Logistic Regression as an excellent choice for tasks where fairness and inclusivity are critical, such as admissions systems. By effectively balancing precision and recall, it ensures that opportunities are distributed equitably while minimizing the risk of overlooking qualified candidates.

Figure 1 presents the feature importance plot produced by the Logistic Regression model applied to the MBA Dataset. This plot illustrates the relative contributions of individual features to the model's predictive performance, shedding light on their impact and significance. By visualizing these contributions, we gain valuable insights into the factors which are most influential in shaping the model's outcomes. Such an analysis not only enhances interpretability but also facilitates a deeper understanding of the underlying data patterns and relationships. Moreover, it can guide feature selection and inform strategic decisions, ensuring a more robust and transparent modeling process.

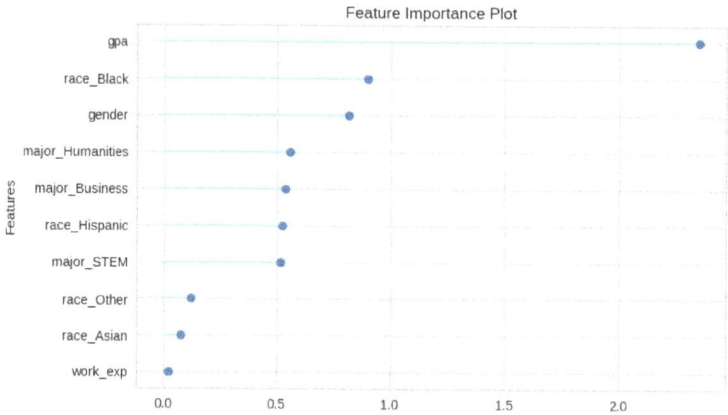

Figure 1. Feature importance of Logistic Regression for MBA Dataset.

In our pursuit of enhancing both model performance and fairness, we applied the Synthetic Minority Oversampling Technique (SMOTE) to address class imbalance and further balance the dataset. However, these efforts did not result in notable improvements across key performance metrics, including accuracy, precision, recall, F1-score, and Matthews correlation coefficient (MCC). Similarly, there was no discernible progress in fairness metrics, such as demographic parity and equalized odds.

To build on this, we explored ensemble techniques designed to harness the strengths of the top-performing models with respect to both accuracy and fairness. Specifically, we implemented hard voting and soft voting ensemble methods, which combine predictions from multiple classifiers to create a potentially more robust aggregated model. Unfortunately, these ensemble strategies also failed to deliver improvements in either performance or fairness metrics. This outcome suggests that the individual models may already be close to their optimal performance given the constraints imposed by the dataset.

These findings highlight the inherent challenges posed by the dataset's characteristics, including its class imbalance and demographic disparities. Traditional data balancing techniques, such as SMOTE, and model aggregation strategies, like ensemble methods, appear insufficient to overcome these limitations. This underscores the need for alternative approaches, such as advanced data augmentation, feature engineering, or fairness-aware optimization methods, to address the underlying challenges and enhance both predictive performance and fairness outcomes.

4.2. Experiments for Law School Dataset

Following exactly the same procedure as described earlier for the MBA Dataset, classifiers including Naive Bayes, AdaBoost, Logistic Regression, Gradient Boosting, CatBoost, Extreme Gradient Boosting, Random Forest, Light Gradient Boosting, and Extra Trees were trained and evaluated using the PyCaret library in Table 3.

In the Law School Dataset, the Naive Bayes model outperforms other classifiers on specific metrics, including precision (0.9541), Kappa (0.3474), and Matthews correlation coefficient (MCC, 0.3706). These results indicate that Naive Bayes excels at minimizing false positives while maintaining a moderate positive correlation between predicted and actual classifications. This performance makes it particularly effective in scenarios where precision is paramount, such as identifying true positives while avoiding over-classifying instances as positive incorrectly.

Conversely, Logistic Regression demonstrates consistently outstanding performance across a broader range of metrics, positioning itself as the most well-rounded classifier. It achieves high scores in accuracy (0.9097), Area Under the Curve (AUC, 0.8722), recall (0.9840), and F1-score (0.9516). These metrics highlight its capability to balance precision and recall effectively, ensuring high sensitivity to true positives while maintaining robust overall classification performance. This balance is especially critical in scenarios where the cost of false negatives is high, such as legal or educational contexts where missing a key outcome could have significant implications. Moreover, the model's simplicity, interpretability, and computational efficiency further enhance its appeal, making it an ideal choice for applications requiring both reliable performance and transparent decision-making.

Figure 2 visualizes the feature importance derived from the Logistic Regression model applied to the Law School Dataset. This plot reveals the relative contributions of each feature to the model's predictions, offering valuable insights into the primary factors influencing outcomes. Such analysis not only enhances our understanding of the dataset's underlying patterns but also informs strategic decision-making by identifying critical variables. These insights can be leveraged to refine data collection strategies, improve feature engineering, or guide interventions aimed at addressing key influences within the dataset.

Further efforts to enhance class balance using Synthetic Minority Oversampling Technique (SMOTE) and attempts to combine the strengths of top-performing models through ensemble methods (hard or soft voting) did not result in any measurable improvements in either performance or fairness metrics. This outcome suggests that the underlying structure of the dataset and the distribution of features may inherently limit the potential for gains through oversampling or ensemble strategies.

These findings emphasize the importance of tailoring model selection and optimization strategies to the specific characteristics of the dataset. While Naive Bayes and Logistic Regression each excel in different performance aspects, their limitations in addressing fairness and improving metrics through augmentation methods underscore the need for exploring alternative approaches.

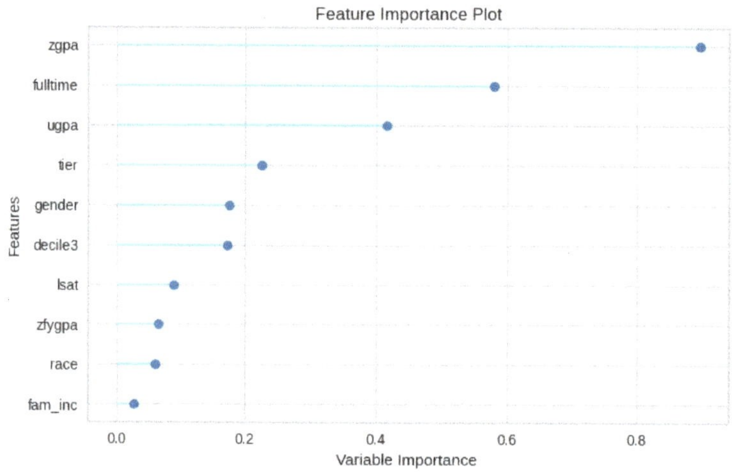

Figure 2. Feature importance of Logistic Regression for Law School Dataset.

4.3. *Experiments for College Admission Dataset*

Using the procedure outlined earlier, classifiers were trained and evaluated using the PyCaret library. The five top-performing models, based on the evaluation metrics, were Naive Bayes, AdaBoost, Logistic Regression, Ridge Regression, and Linear Discriminant Analysis. These classifiers demonstrated superior performance relative to others in the context of this dataset.

The results, summarized in Table 4, were ranked based on accuracy rather than MCC. This adjustment in ranking criteria reflects the balanced nature of the dataset, as the absence of significant imbalances diminishes the relevance of MCC as a primary performance metric. Accuracy is more indicative of classifier performance in balanced datasets and it also provides a more meaningful basis for classifier comparison.

For the fairness analysis, we considered only gender and race as protected attributes, deliberately excluding socioeconomic status from the evaluation.

The AdaBoost classifier achieved the highest accuracy (0.6964), marginally outperforming both the Ridge Classifier (0.6929) and Logistic Regression (0.6893). Additionally, AdaBoost exhibited the highest Matthews correlation coefficient (MCC) of 0.2506 and a Kappa value of 0.2222, closely followed by Naive Bayes in both metrics. Regarding the Area Under the Curve (AUC), Naive Bayes led with a score of 0.6590, surpassing both Logistic Regression (0.6528) and Linear Discriminant Analysis (LDA) (0.6533).

Naive Bayes also excelled in recall (0.3917) and F1-score (0.4368), with AdaBoost ranking second in these metrics (recall: 0.3250; F1-score: 0.4037). Interestingly, Logistic Regression achieved the highest precision (0.6000), narrowly beating AdaBoost. These results indicate that the top-performing classifiers were AdaBoost, Logistic Regression (and its variants), and Naive Bayes, showcasing complementary strengths across different performance metrics.

Beyond predictive performance, fairness-related metrics revealed nuanced insights. All models demonstrated identical worst-case selection rates of 0.0455. AdaBoost and the

Ridge Classifier shared the highest worst-case disparate impact (0.2576), although this value remains well below the typical fairness threshold of 0.8, suggesting potential challenges in equitable decision-making. Notably, Naive Bayes was the only model with a non-zero worst-case true positive rate (TPR) of 0.1111, indicating a relatively higher proportion of equitable positive predictions. However, this came at the cost of an increased false positive rate (FPR), highlighting a trade-off between fairness and precision.

Despite these differences, the overall performance metrics suggest that the classifiers do not significantly differ in terms of accuracy or fairness. Each model exhibits specific strengths and weaknesses, making their suitability context-dependent. For example, while AdaBoost delivers robust accuracy and balanced performance, Naive Bayes stands out for recall and fairness-related metrics. Logistic Regression offers the highest precision, ideal for applications prioritizing correct positive predictions.

If we were to select one of these classifiers, we would likely choose Naive Bayes as the most balanced option in terms of both performance and fairness metrics.

4.4. Graphical Representations of Classifier Performance Metrics

Figures 3 and 4 present graphical representations of Logistic Regression performance metrics, specifically analyzed across protected attributes such as gender and race, for the MBA and Law School Datasets, while Figure 5 presents the same information for the Naive Bayes classifier.

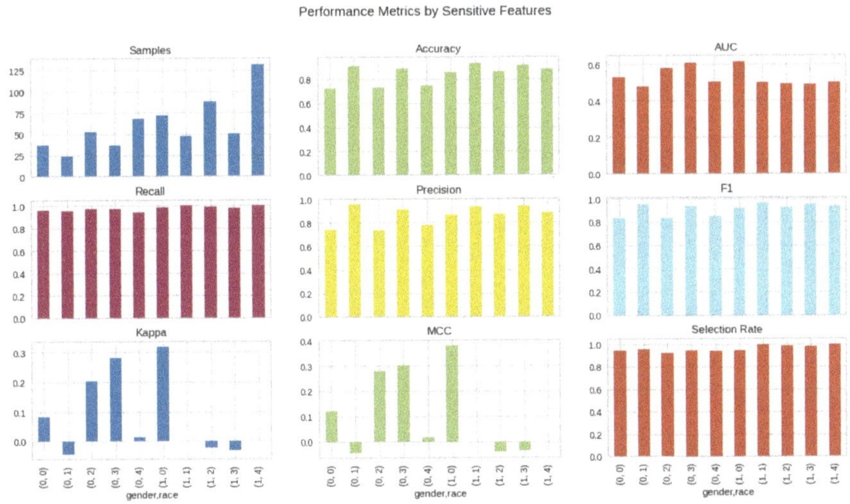

Figure 3. Logistic Regression performance metrics for MBA Dataset by sensitive features of gender and race.

In both MBA and Law School Datasets, Logistic Regression demonstrated strong fairness outcomes, making it a viable choice for equitable admissions predictions. For the MBA Dataset, this model achieved the highest selection rate of up to 0.9245 and disparate impact of up to 0.9352. Similarly, in the Law School Dataset, Logistic Regression maintained a selection rate of 0.6327 with a disparate impact of 0.6425, indicating a fairly consistent selection process across groups. These results collectively highlight Logistic Regression's ability to sustain relatively equitable treatment across different demographics, supporting its utility as a fairness-aware model in high-stakes educational admissions contexts. Although both datasets primarily focus on the admissions processes across various university programs, they share a common framework for building and evaluating machine learning classification models. Notably, Logistic Regression emerges as a standout performer, not only delivering high predictive performance but also demonstrating exceptional fairness metrics in the first two datasets.

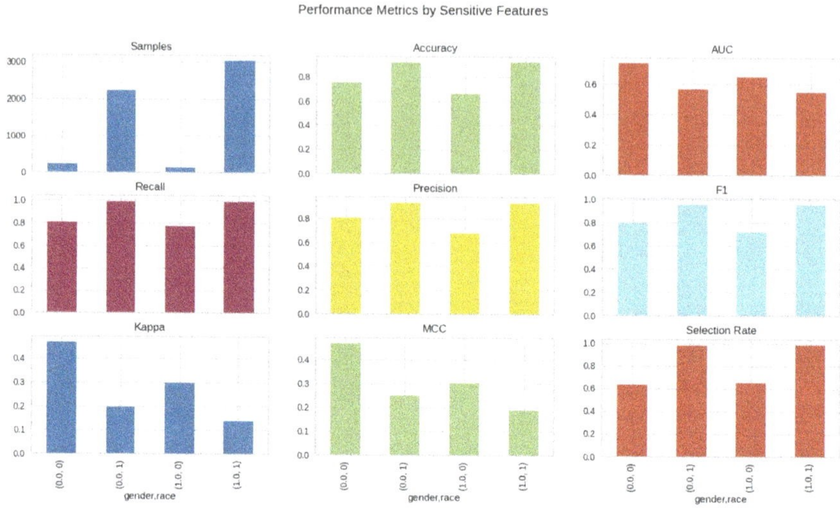

Figure 4. Logistic Regression performance metrics for Law School Dataset by sensitive features of gender and race.

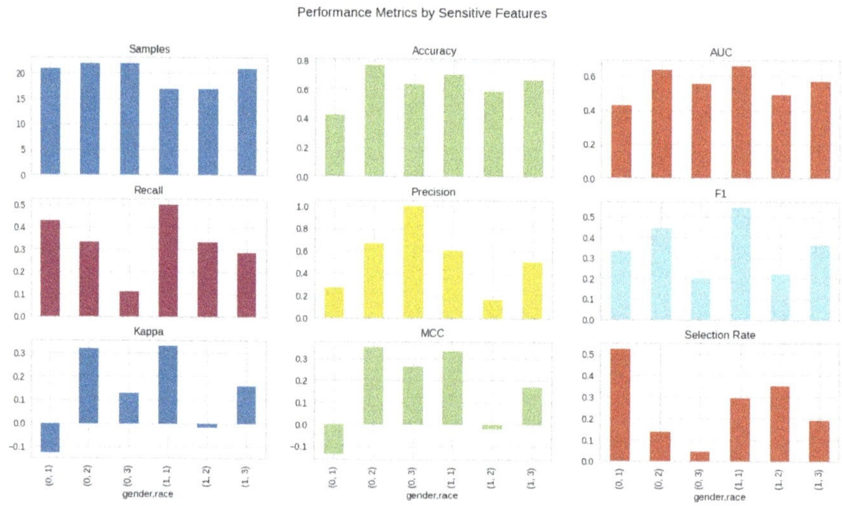

Figure 5. Naive Bayes performance metrics for College Admission Dataset by sensitive features of gender and race.

Although Logistic Regression emerges as the top choice in two out of three datasets, Naive Bayes consistently ranks second across all three datasets. This steady performance highlights its reliability as a balanced option, even if it does not achieve the top rank.

These findings highlight the importance of selecting classification models that align with both predictive goals and ethical requirements in sensitive domains like university admissions.

5. Discussion

In this study, we investigated the application of machine learning (ML) models to enhance fairness and transparency in predicting admission outcomes. Our analysis encompassed a range of ML algorithms, evaluating them not only on performance metrics such as accuracy, AUC, recall, precision, and F1-score but also on fairness metrics, including selection rate, disparate impact, true positive rate, and false positive rate. This dual evaluation ensured that predictive performance did not come at the expense of ethical and equitable considerations.

A particularly intriguing avenue for further exploration is the examination of whether certain classifiers, such as Logistic Regression or Naive Bayes, consistently demonstrate superior fairness across diverse datasets. To address this, experimental validation using an extensive set of benchmark datasets explicitly designed to assess fairness is essential. Such studies could offer valuable insights into the consistency and robustness of these classifiers with respect to fairness metrics across diverse contexts, highlighting potential limitations or biases stemming from variations in data distributions.

If empirical results substantiate the hypothesis that Logistic Regression or Naive Bayes are the most fair classifier in this domain, it would pave the way for an in-depth theoretical investigation. This could involve analyzing the algorithm's inherent characteristics, sensitivity to feature distributions, or interaction with fairness constraints. A theoretical framework could not only explain why these classifiers exhibits fairness advantages but also identify the conditions under which these advantages are sustained or compromised. These insights would enhance the model's generalizability and applicability in fairness-critical domains, thereby making a significant contribution to the broader discourse on fairness in machine learning.

Additionally, this study highlights the impact of dataset characteristics, such as class imbalance and demographic disparities, which pose significant challenges to achieving fairness and performance simultaneously. Traditional data balancing techniques and ensemble methods often fall short in addressing these issues effectively. Future research could explore advanced methodologies, such as cost-sensitive learning, fairness-aware algorithms tailored to specific domains, or innovative feature engineering approaches. These alternatives hold promise for achieving a more harmonious balance between performance and fairness, particularly in datasets with pronounced disparities. Furthermore, incorporating adaptive strategies, such as dynamic fairness constraints or adversarial debiasing, could offer new pathways for addressing persistent inequities in prediction outcomes. Collaboration with domain experts to integrate contextual fairness considerations into model development might also enhance the relevance and effectiveness of proposed solutions.

The findings of this study underscore the critical need for continued research in fairness-aware algorithms, particularly in domains where decisions have profound societal impacts, such as education, employment, and healthcare. While our analysis highlights the potential of existing fairness-aware approaches to mitigate biases, significant challenges remain in ensuring their effectiveness across diverse datasets and real-world scenarios. Future research could focus on developing algorithms that dynamically adapt to evolving fairness criteria and societal contexts, as well as integrating fairness considerations into more complex machine learning paradigms, such as deep learning and ensemble methods. Additionally, interdisciplinary studies that combine technical advancements with insights from social sciences and ethics could provide a more holistic understanding of fairness in algorithmic decision-making. Exploring how fairness-aware techniques can be extended beyond individual predictions to address systemic biases in datasets and broader workflows also represents a promising avenue. By advancing this field, researchers can contribute to building more equitable AI systems that align with societal values and ethical principles.

6. Conclusions

The findings suggest that ML models can be powerful tools for augmenting the admissions process, providing reliable, data-driven predictions that streamline decision-making and improve efficiency. However, the analysis also underscores the risks of embedding biases in these systems. Differences in model performance and fairness metrics reveal the potential for certain ML models to disadvantage specific applicant groups inadvertently. Notably, some models demonstrated high accuracy yet exhibited disparate impacts and significant variation in selection rates across demographic groups. These observations highlight the critical need to evaluate both performance and fairness comprehensively when deploying predictive systems in high-stakes applications like admissions.

Integrating fair and transparent ML models into higher education admissions holds transformative potential. These models can improve selection accuracy while promoting inclusivity and equity, helping ensure that opportunities are distributed more equitably among diverse applicant groups. By proactively addressing biases and advancing fairness, ML-driven approaches can contribute to a more balanced and representative student body. This shift not only aligns with ethical imperatives but also enhances institutional credibility and social responsibility.

Future research should focus on the development and evaluation of advanced fairness-focused algorithms, such as adversarial debiasing, fairness-aware regularization, and post hoc adjustment techniques, to mitigate biases more effectively. Exploring the potential of hybrid approaches that combine these techniques with traditional methods could yield even more robust solutions.

Investigating the interplay between algorithmic fairness and institutional policies is another critical area of exploration. Understanding how ML models interact with admissions criteria, affirmative action policies, and diversity initiatives can provide a roadmap for aligning technological advancements with societal and institutional values. This alignment is vital to ensure that ML systems do not inadvertently undermine broader equity goals.

Engaging stakeholders, including students, educators, policymakers, and advocacy groups, is also essential for ensuring that fairness-focused innovations are socially acceptable and reflective of higher education's ethical commitments. Such engagement could inform the design of ML systems, ensuring they address not only technical challenges but also the nuanced social dynamics of admissions.

Additionally, longitudinal studies are crucial to assess the broader impact of fair ML-driven admissions systems. These studies could measure long-term outcomes, such as student diversity, academic success, retention rates, and career achievements, offering a holistic understanding of these systems' efficacy. Such insights would be invaluable for refining algorithms and aligning them with the broader goals of educational equity and social mobility.

Fairness methods in machine learning have vast applicability beyond the education sector, with the potential to significantly impact a variety of critical domains. In hiring, fairness-aware algorithms can help mitigate biases in candidate selection, ensuring equal opportunities for individuals from diverse backgrounds. In the financial sector, these methods can promote equitable credit scoring and lending practices, addressing historical disparities that disadvantage under-represented groups. Healthcare is another domain where fairness can play a transformative role, from improving access to medical treatments to ensuring the unbiased allocation of scarce resources such as vaccines. Additionally, in the legal system, fairness-aware models can aid in reducing discrimination in areas like risk assessment for bail and sentencing. By tailoring fairness frameworks to address the unique challenges of each sector, these methods have the potential to enhance transparency, accountability, and inclusivity, ultimately fostering trust and promoting equity in decision-making processes across society.

Author Contributions: Conceptualization, G.R. and S.K.; methodology, G.R. and G.D.; software, G.R. and G.D.; validation, G.D.; formal analysis, G.D.; investigation, G.R.; resources, S.K.; data curation, G.D.; writing—original draft preparation, G.R. and G.D.; writing—review and editing, G.D. and S.K.; visualization, G.D.; supervision, S.K.; project administration, S.K.; funding acquisition, S.K. All authors have read and agreed to the published version of the manuscript.

Funding: This research received no external funding

Data Availability Statement: No new data were created

Conflicts of Interest: The authors declare no conflicts of interest.

References

1. Mehrabi, N.; Morstatter, F.; Saxena, N.; Lerman, K.; Galstyan, A. A Survey on Bias and Fairness in Machine Learning. *ACM Comput. Surv.* **2021**, *54*, 1–35. [CrossRef]
2. Pessach, D.; Shmueli, E. A Review on Fairness in Machine Learning. *ACM Comput. Surv.* **2022**, *55*, 1–44. [CrossRef]
3. Caton, S.; Haas, C. Fairness in Machine Learning: A Survey. *ACM Comput. Surv.* **2024**, *56*, 1–38. [CrossRef]
4. Kaur, D.; Uslu, S.; Rittichier, K.J.; Durresi, A. Trustworthy Artificial Intelligence: A Review. *ACM Comput. Surv.* **2022**, *55*, 1–38. [CrossRef]
5. Dwork, C.; Hardt, M.; Pitassi, T.; Reingold, O.; Zemel, R. Fairness through Awareness. In Proceedings of the 3rd Innovations in Theoretical Computer Science Conference, Cambridge, MA, USA, 8–10 January 2012; Association for Computing Machinery: New York, NY, USA, 2012; pp. 214–226.
6. Baker, R.S.; Hawn, A. Algorithmic Bias in Education. *Int. J. Artif. Intell. Educ.* **2022**, *32*, 1052–1092. [CrossRef]
7. Mangal, M.; Pardos, Z.A. Implementing Equitable and Intersectionality-Aware ML in Education: A Practical Guide. *Br. J. Educ. Technol.* **2024**, *55*, 2003–2038. [CrossRef]
8. Pessach, D.; Shmueli, E. Algorithmic Fairness. In *Machine Learning for Data Science Handbook: Data Mining and Knowledge Discovery Handbook*; Rokach, L., Maimon, O., Shmueli, E., Eds.; Springer International Publishing: Cham, Switzerland, 2023; pp. 867–886, ISBN 978-3-031-24628-9.
9. Pardo, A.; Siemens, G. Ethical and Privacy Principles for Learning Analytics. *Br. J. Educ. Technol.* **2014**, *45*, 438–450. [CrossRef]
10. Adams, C.; Pente, P.; Lemermeyer, G.; Rockwell, G. Ethical Principles for Artificial Intelligence in K-12 Education. *Comput. Educ. Artif. Intell.* **2023**, *4*, 100131. [CrossRef]
11. Fu, Y.; Weng, Z. Navigating the Ethical Terrain of AI in Education: A Systematic Review on Framing Responsible Human-Centered AI Practices. *Comput. Educ. Artif. Intell.* **2024**, *7*, 100306. [CrossRef]
12. Idowu, J.A. Debiasing Education Algorithms. *Int. J. Artif. Intell. Educ.* **2024**. [CrossRef]
13. Sahlgren, O. The Politics and Reciprocal (Re)Configuration of Accountability and Fairness in Data-Driven Education. *Learn. Media Technol.* **2023**, *48*, 95–108. [CrossRef]
14. AlGhamdi, A.; Barsheed, A.; AlMshjary, H.; AlGhamdi, H. A Machine Learning Approach for Graduate Admission Prediction. In Proceedings of the 2020 2nd International Conference on Image, Video and Signal Processing, Singapore, 20–22 February 2020; Association for Computing Machinery: New York, NY, USA, 2020; pp. 155–158.
15. Omaer Faruq Goni, M.; Matin, A.; Hasan, T.; Abu Ismail Siddique, M.; Jyoti, O.; Sifnatul Hasnain, F.M. Graduate Admission Chance Prediction Using Deep Neural Network. In Proceedings of the 2020 IEEE International Women in Engineering (WIE) Conference on Electrical and Computer Engineering (WIECON-ECE), Bhubaneswar, India, 26–27 December 2020; pp. 259–262.
16. Sridhar, S.; Mootha, S.; Kolagati, S. A University Admission Prediction System Using Stacked Ensemble Learning. In Proceedings of the 2020 Advanced Computing and Communication Technologies for High Performance Applications (ACCTHPA), Cochin, India, 2–4 July 2020; pp. 162–167.
17. Wu, X.; Wu, J. Criteria Evaluation and Selection in Non-Native Language MBA Students Admission Based on Machine Learning Methods. *J. Ambient Intell. Humaniz. Comput.* **2020**, *11*, 3521–3533. [CrossRef]
18. Assiri, B.; Bashraheel, M.; Alsuri, A. Improve the Accuracy of Students Admission at Universities Using Machine Learning Techniques. In Proceedings of the 2022 7th International Conference on Data Science and Machine Learning Applications (CDMA), Riyadh, Saudi Arabia, 1–3 March 2022; pp. 127–132.
19. Assiri, B.; Bashraheel, M.; Alsuri, A. Enhanced Student Admission Procedures at Universities Using Data Mining and Machine Learning Techniques. *Appl. Sci.* **2024**, *14*, 1109. [CrossRef]
20. Mridha, K.; Jha, S.; Shah, B.; Damodharan, P.; Ghosh, A.; Shaw, R.N. Machine Learning Algorithms for Predicting the Graduation Admission. In *Innovations in Electrical and Electronic Engineering. ICEEE 2022*; Mekhilef, S., Shaw, R.N., Siano, P., Eds.; Springer: Singapore, 2022; pp. 618–637.
21. Ursan, M.; Bucos, M. Predictive Analytics Models for Student Admission to Master Programs in Romania. In Proceedings of the 2022 International Symposium on Electronics and Telecommunications (ISETC), Timisoara, Romania, 10–11 November 2022; pp. 1–4.

22. Sharma, S.; Soni, H.K. An Approach for Predicting Admissions in Post-Graduate Programme by Using Machine Learning. In *Data, Engineering and Applications*; Sharma, S., Peng, S.-L., Agrawal, J., Shukla, R.K., Le, D.-N., Eds.; Springer Nature: Singapore, 2022; pp. 57–70.
23. Li, K.C.; Wong, B.T.-M.; Chan, H.T. Predictive Analytics for University Student Admission: A Literature Review. In *Blended Learning: Lessons Learned and Ways Forward*; Li, C., Cheung, S.K.S., Wang, F.L., Lu, A., Kwok, L.F., Eds.; Springer Nature: Cham, Switzerland, 2023; pp. 250–259.
24. Zub, K.; Zhezhnych, P.; Strauss, C. Two-Stage PNN–SVM Ensemble for Higher Education Admission Prediction. *Big Data Cogn. Comput.* **2023**, *7*, 83. [CrossRef]
25. Van Busum, K.; Fang, S. Analysis of AI Models for Student Admissions: A Case Study. In Proceedings of the 38th ACM/SIGAPP Symposium on Applied Computing, Tallinn, Estonia, 27–31 March 2023; Association for Computing Machinery: New York, NY, USA, 2023; pp. 17–22.
26. Zhao, Y.; Chen, X.; Xue, H.; Weiss, G.M. A Machine Learning Approach to Graduate Admissions and the Role of Letters of Recommendation. *PLoS ONE* **2023**, *18*, e0291107. [CrossRef]
27. Marcinkowski, F.; Kieslich, K.; Starke, C.; Lünich, M. Implications of AI (Un-)Fairness in Higher Education Admissions: The Effects of Perceived AI (Un-)Fairness on Exit, Voice and Organizational Reputation. In Proceedings of the 2020 Conference on Fairness, Accountability, and Transparency, Barcelona, Spain, 27–30 January 2020; Association for Computing Machinery: New York, NY, USA, 2020; pp. 122–130.
28. Memarian, B.; Doleck, T. Fairness, accountability, transparency, and ethics (FATE) in artificial intelligence (AI) and higher education: A systematic review. *Comput. Educ. Artif. Intell.* **2023**, *5*, 100152. [CrossRef]
29. Pham, N.; Hung, P.N.; Nguyen-Duc, A. Fairness for machine learning software in education: A systematic mapping study. *J. Syst. Softw.* **2025**, *219*, 112244. [CrossRef]
30. Bayer, V.; Hlosta, M.; Fernandez, M. Learning analytics and fairness: Do existing algorithms serve everyone equally? In *Artificial Intelligence in Education. AIED 2021*; Lecture Notes in Computer Science; Springer International Publishing: Cham, Switzerland, 2021; Volume 12749, pp. 71–75. [CrossRef]
31. Deho, O.B.; Joksimovic, S.; Li, J.; Zhan, C.; Liu, J.; Liu, L. Should Learning Analytics Models Include Sensitive Attributes? Explaining the Why. *IEEE Trans. Learn. Technol.* **2023**, *16*, 560–572. [CrossRef]
32. Sha, L.; Gašević, D.; Chen, G. Lessons from debiasing data for fair and accurate predictive modeling in education. *Expert Syst. Appl.* **2023**, *228*, 120323. [CrossRef]
33. Li, C.; Xing, W.; Leite, W. Using Fair AI to Predict Students' Math Learning Outcomes in an Online Platform. *Interact. Learn. Environ.* **2024**, *32*, 1117–1136. [CrossRef]
34. Nezami, N.; Haghighat, P.; Gándara, D.; Anahideh, H. Assessing Disparities in Predictive Modeling Outcomes for College Student Success: The Impact of Imputation Techniques on Model Performance and Fairness. *Educ. Sci.* **2024**, *14*, 136. [CrossRef]
35. MBA Admission Dataset, Class 2025. Available online: https://www.kaggle.com/datasets/taweilo/mba-admission-dataset/data (accessed on 10 December 2024).
36. Dakduk, S.; Malavé, J.; Torres, C.C.; Montesinos, H.; Michelena, L. Admission Criteria for MBA Programs: A Review. *Sage Open* **2016**, *6*. [CrossRef]
37. Le Quy, T.; Roy, A.; Iosifidis, V.; Zhang, W.; Ntoutsi, E. A Survey on Datasets for Fairness-Aware Machine Learning. *Wires Data Min. Knowl. Discov.* **2022**, *12*, e1452. [CrossRef]
38. Harvey, D. Law School Dataset. Available online: https://github.com/damtharvey/law-school-dataset (accessed on 1 December 2024).
39. Anup Pandey. College Admission Data Set. Available online: https://www.kaggle.com/datasets/pandanup/college-admission-data-set (accessed on 6 December 2024).
40. Chicco, D.; Jurman, G. The Advantages of the Matthews Correlation Coefficient (MCC) over F1 Score and Accuracy in Binary Classification Evaluation. *BMC Genom.* **2020**, *21*, *6*. [CrossRef]
41. Verma, S.; Rubin, J. Fairness Definitions Explained. In Proceedings of the International Workshop on Software Fairness, Gothenburg, Sweden, 29 May 2018; Association for Computing Machinery: New York, NY, USA, 2018; pp. 1–7.
42. Li, L.; Sha, L.; Li, Y.; Raković, M.; Rong, J.; Joksimovic, S.; Selwyn, N.; Gašević, D.; Chen, G. Moral Machines or Tyranny of the Majority? A Systematic Review on Predictive Bias in Education. In Proceedings of the LAK23: 13th International Learning Analytics and Knowledge Conference, Arlington, TX, USA, 13–17 March 2023; Association for Computing Machinery: New York, NY, USA, 2023; pp. 499–508.
43. Ali, M. Pycaret: An Open Source, Low-Code Machine Learning Library in Python, PyCaret Version 2.3.5. April 2020. Available online: https://www.pycaret.org (accessed on 1 December 2024).
44. Tolios, G. *Simplifying Machine Learning with PyCaret A Low-Code Approach for Beginners and Experts!*; Leanpub: Victoria, BC, Canada, 2022.

algorithms

MDPI

Article

Exploring Early Learning Challenges in Children Utilizing Statistical and Explainable Machine Learning

Mithila Akter Mim [1], M. R. Khatun [1], Muhammad Minoar Hossain [1,2], Wahidur Rahman [2,3] and Arslan Munir [4,*]

1 Department of Computer Science and Engineering, Bangladesh University, Dhaka 1000, Bangladesh; mithila.bu.75@gmail.com (M.A.M.); rokeya.khatun@bu.edu.bd (M.R.K.); minoar.hossain@bu.edu.bd (M.M.H.)
2 Department of Computer Science and Engineering, Mawlana Bhashani Science and Technology University, Tangail 1902, Bangladesh; wahidtuhin0@gmail.com
3 Department of Computer Science and Engineering, Uttara University, Dhaka 1230, Bangladesh
4 Department of Electrical Engineering and Computer Science, Florida Atlantic University, Boca Raton, FL 33431, USA
* Correspondence: arslanm@fau.edu

Abstract

To mitigate future educational challenges, the early childhood period is critical for cognitive development, so understanding the factors influencing child learning abilities is essential. This study investigates the impact of parenting techniques, sociodemographic characteristics, and health conditions on the learning abilities of children under five years old. Our primary goal is to explore the key factors that influence children's learning abilities. For our study, we utilized the 2019 Multiple Indicator Cluster Surveys (MICS) dataset in Bangladesh. Using statistical analysis, we identified the key factors that affect children's learning capability. To ensure proper analysis, we used extensive data preprocessing, feature manipulation, and model evaluation. Furthermore, we explored robust machine learning (ML) models to analyze and predict the learning challenges faced by children. These include logistic regression (LRC), decision tree (DT), k-nearest neighbor (KNN), random forest (RF), gradient boosting (GB), extreme gradient boosting (XGB), and bagging classification models. Out of these, GB and XGB, with 10-fold cross-validation, achieved an impressive accuracy of 95%, F1-score of 95%, and receiver operating characteristic area under the curve (ROC AUC) of 95%. Additionally, to interpret the model outputs and explore influencing factors, we used explainable AI (XAI) techniques like SHAP and LIME. Both statistical analysis and XAI interpretation revealed key factors that influence children's learning difficulties. These include harsh disciplinary practices, low socioeconomic status, limited maternal education, and health-related issues. These findings offer valuable insights to guide policy measures to improve educational outcomes and promote holistic child development in Bangladesh and similar contexts.

Keywords: child development; Bangladesh multiple indicator cluster surveys (MICS); machine learning; explainable AI; SHAP; LIME

1. Introduction

Children's learning capacities and psychological development are significantly influenced by the parenting practices and sociodemographic features in their environment. The impact of good relationships, engagement, and participation between parents and children on academic achievement is positive [1]. This engagement involves things like reading aloud to kids, guiding studies, and staying in touch with them, all of which are essential for

https://doi.org/10.3390/a18010020

creating a positive learning environment. The long-term effects of parenting practices such as friendly manners and flexibility significantly influence children's cognitive development and academic performance [2]. Furthermore, different racial and ethnic communities have distinct policies concerning the extent of parental engagement with children, which greatly impacts the growth and development of young children [3]. Sociodemographic factors, such as parental education level and socioeconomic status (SES), also significantly influence children's learning patterns. Moreover, the provision of mental and physical healthcare for children has a direct impact on their brain and cognitive development, highlighting the importance of home environments [4,5]. Additionally, households of higher SES generally enjoy superior access to educational resources and opportunities as well as good healthcare services, leading to enhanced learning outcomes for children [6]. Researchers are extensively exploring the influence of parenting styles, ensuring privilege, mental and physical care, and awareness of children's learning abilities.

Previous studies have demonstrated the application of a variety of methods in child development research. Researchers diagnose mental health problems and analyze parenting techniques to identify learning difficulties. Several research works have examined the application of machine learning (ML) algorithms to predict learning difficulties and variables influencing school-aged children's and college students' academic performance. To diagnose learning difficulties in kids, another study [7] used artificial neural network (ANN) and support vector machine (SVM) classifiers. The study emphasized the innovative application of ML to accurately identify learning disabilities. Researchers used supervised ML algorithms [8] to uncover the reasons behind college students' poor academic performance. That provides advice to help struggling students to do better. Additionally, researchers have used ML approaches to identify mental health issues in children and adolescents, including attention deficit hyperactivity disorder (ADHD) and depression. Multiple researchers [9,10] have employed ML models to forecast depression and ADHD in children, attaining superior classification accuracy and emphasizing the possibility of timely identification and remediation. Additionally, researchers [11] developed and evaluated ML-based prognosis tools to identify learning difficulties among students, aiming to improve early detection and intervention strategies. Furthermore, researchers used ML models to predict ADHD by analyzing prefrontal brain activity, underscoring the importance of neurophysiological data in diagnostic prediction [12]. Early detection is essential for prompt assistance and intervention in cases of autism spectrum disorder (ASD). ML techniques for early ASD detection have been the subject of several studies [13,14]. These studies used a variety of classifiers, including random forest (RF), logistic regression (LR), and support vector machine (SVM), to create precise prediction models based on physiological and behavioral data. The results imply that ML methods can improve the accuracy and effectiveness of ASD diagnosis.

Recent advancements in ML have significantly improved ASD detection by using SVM, and LR achieved 100% accuracy for children and 97.14% for adults, respectively, and ANN also showed promise, reaching 94.24% accuracy with optimized hyperparameters [15]. Additionally, a study analyzing toddlers using six classification models, including LR, reported a perfect accuracy score of 100% in ASD detection [16]. Beyond ASD detection, research has also examined the influence of parenting practices and other factors on children's development. Studies highlight that parenting style, gender, and socioeconomic background play a significant role in academic achievement, with authoritative parenting being particularly crucial for fostering successful educational outcomes [17]. Again, comparative studies have investigated the effectiveness of ML techniques in predicting children's educational activities compared to traditional methods [18,19]. These analyses highlight the benefits of ML algorithms for identifying important factors and improving prediction accuracy.

The Bangladesh Bureau of Statistics and UNICEF conducted the Multiple Indicator Cluster Surveys (MICS) in 2019. This survey collected a comprehensive dataset that includes information on child welfare, household characteristics, and parenting practices in Bangladesh [20]. Employing this information provides an opportunity to explore the multifaceted relationships between the sociodemographic characteristics, parenting styles, and educational achievement of Bangladeshi children, which can then be applied to similar studies. In addition, to analyze and forecast a wide range of outcomes regarding child development and education, ML approaches have become an increasingly powerful tool [21,22]. Researchers have the potential to use ML algorithms on the MICS 2019 dataset to gain valuable insights into the factors affecting children's learning skill comparisons. Moreover, they can apply these insights to shape interventions and policies that aim to enhance opportunities for children in Bangladesh.

The literature review shows how ML can predict academic performances, learning difficulties, mental health illnesses, and parenting styles in child development studies. These studies highlight the complicated relationship between individual, familial, and environmental influences on children. Our research is motivated by the critical need to address and understand challenges in early childhood development and education using advanced computational techniques. Our literature review revealed a research gap, as no previous studies have concentrated on identifying and forecasting the influencing factors for learning difficulties among Bangladeshi children. While ML has been widely used in child development studies in other countries, such as Oman, Australia, and the U.S., there has been limited exploration of early childhood learning outcomes in the Bangladeshi context. Our study addresses this gap by applying ML techniques to the MICS 2019 dataset, which uniquely captures the influence of sociodemographic factors, parenting styles, and children's learning abilities in Bangladesh. This research highlights the importance of leveraging local data to uncover insights specific to Bangladesh's context and social landscape, providing the foundation for targeted interventions. In addition to applying ML techniques, our study integrates explainable AI (XAI) methods like SHAP and LIME, which offer a novel transparent approach to understanding early childhood learning difficulties in Bangladesh. By incorporating XAI methods, our approach not only improves the interpretability of ML models but also identifies underlying causes of learning difficulties. These findings offer valuable insights for policymaking to improve early childhood education. The highlights of our objective are as follows:

- Employ statistical analysis to investigate the key factors influencing early learning among children under the age of five;
- Apply different ML models to forecast learning difficulties in children based on the selected features;
- Utilize XAI methods like SHAP and LIME to explain how different factors influence children learning difficulties. These insights will help guide policies to improve education and overall development in early childhood.

The rest of this paper is organized as follows. Section 2 provides a comprehensive overview of the materials and methods used in this study. It includes details about the dataset, statistical analysis, and ML algorithms that we employed and the criteria used for evaluating performance. Section 3 presents the results and discussion. Section 4 presents a comparison with previous works, while Section 5 concludes this study.

2. Materials and Methods

In this research, we investigated parenting practices and sociodemographic factors that influence children's learning skills using the MICS 2019 dataset. At first, we preprocessed the dataset to prepare it for statistical analysis and machine learning model fit. Afterward, we evaluated the results based on the performance parameters. Figure 1 shows the step-by-step process involved in analyzing the impact of various factors on children's learning abilities, starting from data collection and preprocessing, moving through specific analytical steps, and ending with an integrated analysis.

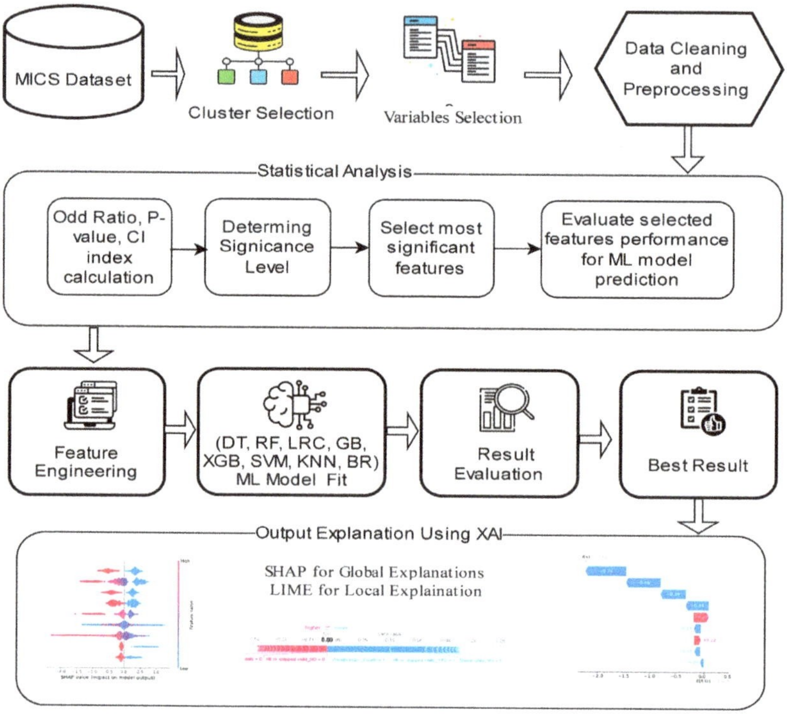

Figure 1. Workflow diagram for analyzing parenting practices and sociodemographic factors on children's learning abilities.

2.1. MICS Dataset

The Bangladesh Bureau of Statistics and the Ministry of Planning, with assistance from UNICEF, conducted the MICS 2019 in Bangladesh. The survey comprises clusters covering health, education, nutrition, water and sanitation, child health, and socioeconomic factors. The research population estimated several indicators on the status of children and women nationwide, in both urban and rural areas, in eight divisions and sixty-four districts. Initially, the total number of household samples was 64,000. The report BBS and UNICEF Bangladesh 2019 provides a comprehensive explanation of the survey methodology, which includes details on the calculation of the sample size. The dataset used in this research is publicly available from the MICS 2019, with permission from the UNICEF MICS team, and adheres to ethical standards, ensuring participant anonymity through de-identification and aggregation. To obtain access to the dataset initially, we had to obtain permission from the UNICEF MICS team. Thus, we sent them an email explaining our study plans, and in response, they gave us a link to access the dataset. Furthermore we addressed potential model biases by selecting features based on statistical relevance and employing

XAI techniques for transparency, fairness, and interpretability. This approach helps identify and mitigate biases, ensuring robustness in the findings.

2.2. Data Cleaning and Preprocessing

The MICS 2019 dataset encompasses various clusters with different domains. Among these, we chose the children's health (ch) dataset because it supported all the necessary domains for determining the learning skills of children under five years old. Initially, the dataset contained 24,686 samples with 346 features covering various sociodemographic, health, and behavioral aspects related to children and their families. However, not all features were directly relevant to understanding early childhood learning difficulties. Initially, data cleaning and preprocessing were performed to exclude irrelevant variables, such as identifiers and redundant features, as well as features with a high percentage of missing values. Then, we selected all possible features that linked to early childhood learning outcomes, such as parenting behaviors, maternal education, and child health metrics. We also focused on features that were most relevant to the target variable to ensure the inclusion. After careful consideration, we identified 19 features that demonstrated statistical significance, predictive power, and alignment with domain-specific knowledge. This process involved evaluating the importance of each feature, checking Pearson correlations, and of the most significant ones for model accuracy [23,24]. Subsequently, we removed samples with missing values in the target variable, resulting in a dataset of 14,058 samples. Further refinement involved dropping samples with "Don't know" or "No response" values, resulting in 14,044 samples. Furthermore, because addressing missing data points is critical for reliable model predictions, we employed different strategies to fill in missing values based on the feature data type [25]. For categorical features that represent non-numeric data, we filled missing values with the mode value. We imputed missing values for numerical features using the mean value. Afterward, duplicate entries were identified and removed from the dataset, resulting in a reduction to 13,821 unique samples. Next, we converted features with mixed or inconsistent data types to appropriate numerical formats (float, integer, or string) according to their intended meaning. Outliers, which can skew model results significantly, were identified and removed using the interquartile range (IQR) method [26]. Finally, we obtained a clean and well-organized dataset comprising 13,274 samples.

After repeated statistical analysis and data preprocessing, we chose the 10 most significant features out of 19. Table 1 describes the lists of selected variables or features. Out of 10 variables, 9 are independent variables, and 1 is a dependent variable. The independent variables include different factors related to the child, household, and parenting practices. The information collected includes numerical values like the child's weight (Child's_weight) and weight-for-age percentile (Weight_age_P). It also includes categorical variables that indicate disciplinary actions taken by parents (Took_away_privileges, Shook_child, Beat_hard, Called_dumb_lazy), the child's sex, wealth index quintile (Wealth_index), and the mother's education level (Mother's_education). The disciplinary action variables (Removed_privileges, Shook_child, Beat_hard, Called_dumb_lazy) represent different behaviors relevant to parenting practices. However, the dependent variable "Learning_skill" indicates whether or not the child has learning difficulties compared to other children of the same age. We combined these variables to create a comprehensive dataset to explore the child's learning difficulties based on the relationship between parenting practices, sociodemographic factors, and children's learning outcomes.

The MICS 2019 dataset is unbalanced because learning difficulties in children under five are relatively lower compared to those without such difficulties. This imbalance is a common characteristic of large-scale datasets dealing with minority outcomes, as such cases naturally occur less frequently. Factors like underreporting by parents, limited awareness of early developmental challenges, and disparities in access to health and education services further contribute to this imbalance. The implications of this imbalance have been recognized, and appropriate measures were considered to address its effects on analysis and predictions.

Table 1. Definition of variables or features list.

Independent Variables				
MICS Variables	**Variables**	**Description**	**Values**	**Data Type**
UCD2A	Removed_privileges	Took away privileges	YES, NO	Categorical
UCD2C	Shook_child	Shook child	YES, NO	Categorical
UCD2K	Beat_ hard	Beat child as hard as one could	YES, NO	Categorical
HL4	Sex	Sex	MALE, FEMALE	Categorical
windex5	Wealth_index	Wealth index quintile	Richest, Fourth, Second, Poorest, Middle	Categorical
welevel	Mother's_education	Mother's education	Higher secondary+, Primary, Secondary, Pre-primary or none	Categorical
UCD2H	Called_dumb_lazy	Called child dumb and lazy	YES, NO	Categorical
AN4	Child's_weight	Child's weight (kilograms)	1.1–35.8 kg	Numerical
WAP	Weight_age_P	Weight-for-age percentile	0.0–89.5	Numerical
Dependent Variables				
MICS variables	**Variable**	**Description**	**Values**	**Data Type**
UCF17	Learning_skill	Compared with children of the same age, child has difficulty learning things	NO DIFFICULTY, HAS DIFFICULTY	Categorical

Figure 2 presents six grouped bar charts comparing the count of children with and without learning difficulties across various categories. Blue bars represent children without learning difficulties, while red bars indicate children with learning difficulties. The charts show differences in experiences and demographics, highlighting factors and patterns that might contribute to learning difficulties.

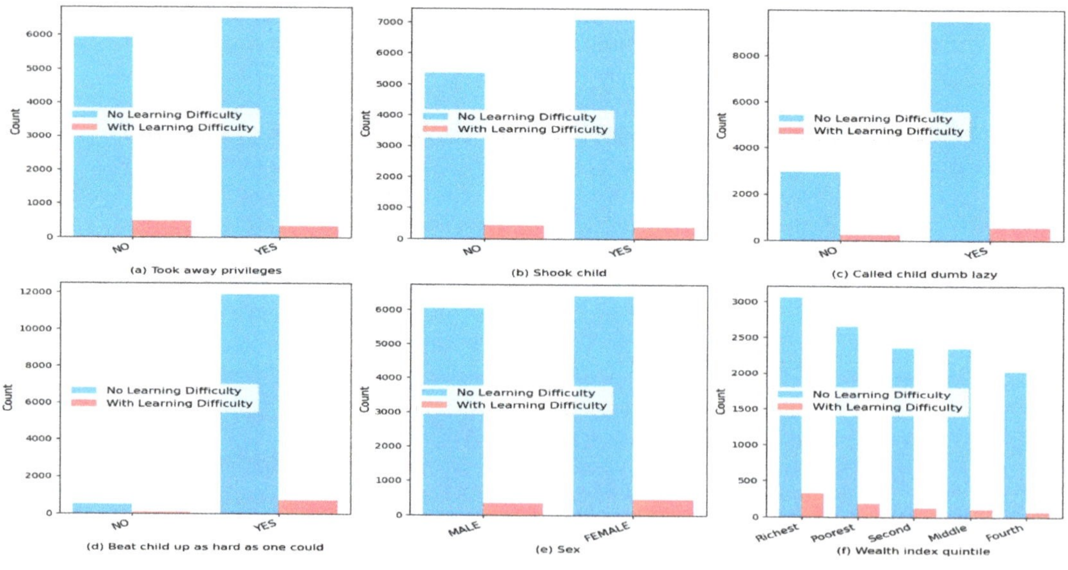

Figure 2. Analysis of categorical features.

The distribution of the variables Child's_weight and Weight_age_P was examined using density plots and boxplots to identify skewness, central tendencies, and outliers in Figure 3a,b. For Weight_age_P, the density plot revealed a highly right-skewed distribution, with values concentrated near zero and a long tail extending toward higher values. The boxplot confirmed this pattern, showing a narrow interquartile range (IQR) and numerous outliers above the upper whisker. To address this skewness and reduce the influence of outliers, a log transformation was applied, which stabilized variance and improved data symmetry. In contrast, the Child's_weight variable exhibited an approximately symmetric distribution, as seen in both the density plot and boxplot. The IQR captured most of the data, with the median centrally located. Although a few outliers were observed outside the whiskers, their impact on the overall distribution was minimal, and no transformation was required.

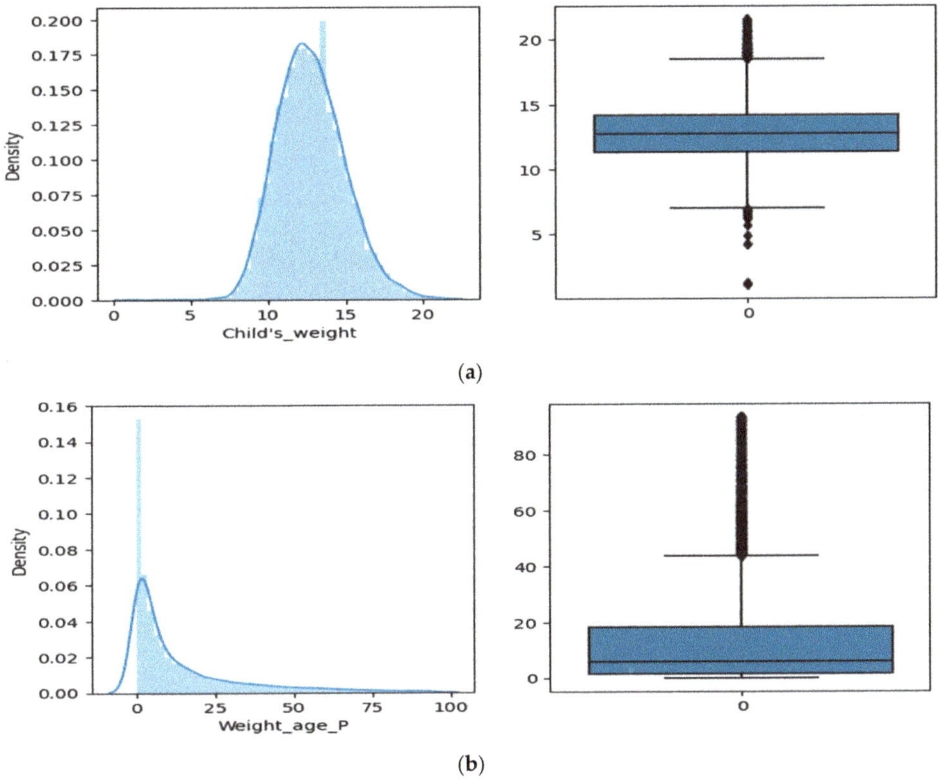

Figure 3. Analysis of numerical features (**a**) Child's_weight and (**b**) Weight_age_P.

2.3. Feature Importance

The Figure 4, derived using the RF model, highlights the most influential factors for prediction of Learning_skill. "Weight_age_P" and "Child's_weight" are the most significant features, showing the highest impact. "Mother's_education" and "Wealth_index" also contribute notably but to a lesser extent. Other factors such as "Sex", "Shook_child", "Called_dumb_lazy", "Removed_privileges", and "Beat_hard" show relatively lower importance in influencing the model's output.

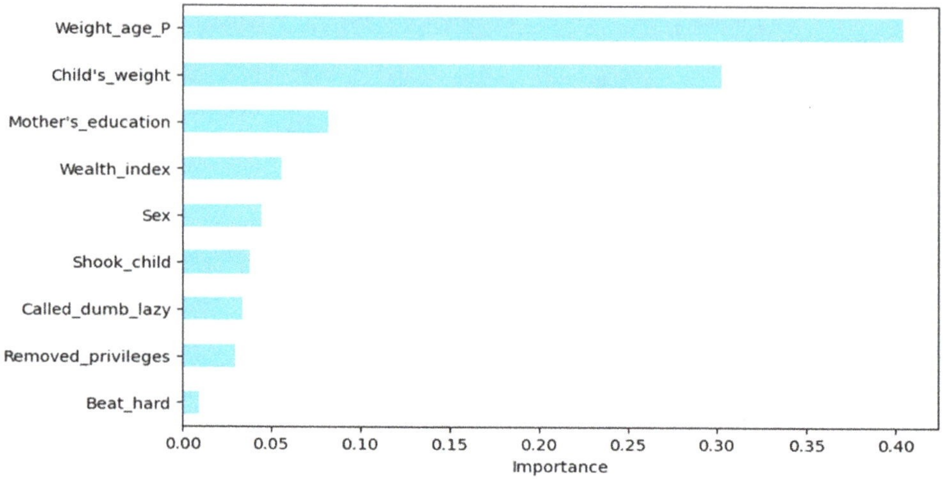

Figure 4. Feature importance for predicting learning skill.

2.4. Feature Engineering

Feature engineering is an important part of getting data ready for analysis and modeling. During this step, we used different methods to explore important patterns in data and make our predictions robust. First, we labeled or binned [27] the UCF17 feature, which encapsulates assessments regarding a child's learning difficulties. We carefully partitioned this categorical feature into two distinct classes: "NO DIFFICULTY" and "HAS DIFFICULTY", which provided a clear delineation for subsequent analysis. Furthermore, the categorical features were subjected to label encoding using a technique [28].

To prepare the data for fitting into an ML model, Table 2 displays the numerical representation of categorical variables. The table shows that we labeled features like taking away privileges, shaking or beating the child, and calling the child dumb or lazy with YES = 1 and NO = 2. In addition, we classified gender as follows: male is represented by the number 1, and female is represented by the number 2. The wealth index is coded on a scale of 1 to 5, with 1 representing the poorest and 5 representing the richest. The mother's education level is classified on a scale of 0 to 3, ranging from pre-primary or no education to higher secondary education. We also labeled the child's learning skills as NO DIFFICULTY = 0 and HAVE DIFFICULTY = 1.

Table 2. Numerical Labeling of Categorical Variables.

Variables	Assigned Numerical Values
Removed_privileges	YES = 1, NO = 2
Shook_child	YES = 1, NO = 2
Beat_hard	YES = 1, NO = 2
Sex	MALE = 1, FEMALE = 2
Wealth_index	Poorest = 1, Second = 2, Middle =3, Fourth = 4, Richest = 5
Mother's_education	Pre-primary or none = 0, Primary = 1, Secondary = 2, Higher Secondary = 3
Called_dumb_lazy	YES = 1, NO = 2
Learning_skill	NO DIFFICULTY = 0, HAVE DIFFICULTY = 1

Furthermore, to handle the problem of class imbalance in our target variable, we used a mix of techniques. We balanced the representation of different classes in our dataset by adding more samples to the minority class using SMOTE (Synthetic Minority

Oversampling Technique) and reducing the number of samples in the majority class with RandomUnderSampler [29,30]. This balancing made our analysis and modeling more reliable as well as helped to prevent any biases that might result from one class being more dominant than the others.

2.5. Statistical Measurements

In statistical analysis, understanding the relationship between variables depends upon several key metrics [31]. Together, the metrics odds ratio (OR), p-value, and 95% confidence interval (CI) provide a comprehensive framework for evaluating the strength, significance, and precision of the relationships observed in the data. The p-value is a statistical measure that indicates whether the relationship between an independent variable and whether the dependent variable is statistically significant. It helps to decide whether to reject the null hypothesis and thus plays a fundamental role in hypothesis testing. A low p-value (typically ≤ 0.05) indicates a significant association between the independent variable and the dependent variable. On the other hand, a high p-value (>0.05) indicates no significant association between the independent variable and the dependent variable. The OR is a crucial measure of association, indicating the odds of an event occurring in one group compared to another, whereas odds help to elucidate how likely an event is to happen compared to not happening. An OR greater than 1 indicates increased odds, an OR less than 1 indicates decreased odds, and an OR equal to 1 indicates no effect. The 95% CI further aids in understanding this precision. If the OR's 95% CI does not include 1, it suggests a significant effect of the independent variable on the dependent variable. If the 95% CI for an OR does not include 1, it suggests the result is statistically significant.

2.6. ML Models

Each ML model offers unique methodologies, algorithms, and mathematical formulations. We employed traditional machine learning models combined with ensemble techniques. A brief description of each model is presented below.

Decision trees (DT) are hierarchical structures that recursively split the data based on informative features at each node, aiming to maximize information gain or minimize impurity. At each node, the decision rule selects the attribute that best divides the data. The process continues until a stopping criterion is met, resulting in leaf nodes representing the final class predictions. The splitting criteria often include measures like Gini impurity or information gain [32].

Random forests (RF) are ensemble learning methods that aggregate predictions from multiple decision trees, each trained on random subsets of the data and features. By averaging or voting the predictions of individual trees, random forests improve generalization and reduce overfitting. Each decision tree in the forest operates independently, making predictions based on its subset of the data [33].

The logistic regression (LRC) model predicts the probability of the positive class using the logistic function. Logistic regression is a linear model used for binary classification, estimating the probability that an instance belongs to a particular class. The logistic function, also known as the sigmoid function, is used to map the output to a probability value between 0 and 1. The model's coefficients are estimated using maximum likelihood estimation [34].

K-nearest neighbors (KNN) is a non-parametric classification algorithm that makes predictions based on the majority class of its k nearest neighbors in the feature space. KNN is simple yet effective, as it relies on local information to classify instances. The predicted class for a new instance is determined by a majority vote or weighted vote of its nearest neighbors [35].

Gradient boosting (GB) is an ensemble learning method that sequentially builds a strong model by combining the predictions of weak learners, typically decision trees. Each new tree corrects the errors of the previous ones, resulting in a highly accurate ensemble model. The prediction of the ensemble is a weighted sum of the predictions of the individual weak learners [36].

Extreme gradient boosting (XGBoost) is a powerful ensemble learning method that utilizes gradient boosting to sequentially train decision trees and minimize a differentiable loss function. By iteratively adding weak learners, XGBoost improves the model's performance while reducing bias and variance. The objective function in XGBoost comprises a combination of a differentiable loss function and a regularizer term, which is optimized during training [37].

The hyperparameter settings used to optimize the performance of the ML models and achieve better accuracy are detailed in the Table 3 below.

Table 3. The values for hyperparameters tuning.

Classifier	Parameters
DT	Max_depth = 6
RF	n_estimators = 42 random_state = 42
LRC	random_state = 42
KNN	n_neighbors = 5, metric = minkowski, p = 2
GB	n_estimators = 100, learning_rate = 1.0, max_depth = 5
XGB	booster = gbtree, max_depth = 6, gamma = 0, min_child_weight = 1, subsample = 1.0, colsample_bytree = 1.0

These hyperparameter configurations were fine-tuned to achieve optimal performance. For instance, the max_depth parameter in DT and XGB prevents overfitting by limiting the tree depth, while the n_estimators in RF, GB, and bagging enhances predictive stability. Additionally, using random_state ensures reproducibility, and parameters like learning_rate and min_child_weight help balance model complexity and learning efficiency.

2.7. *Performance Metrics*

A confusion matrix is a valuable tool for evaluating the performance of a classification model by comparing the model's predicted outcomes with the actual outcomes [38]. It provides a detailed summary of prediction results, which is especially useful in scenarios with imbalanced classes or when different classification errors have varying consequences. By analyzing the matrix, we can gain insights into the types and frequencies of errors the model makes, aiding in understanding its overall performance. Figure 5 depicts the matrix, which includes key terms such as true positive (TP), true negative (TN), false negative (FN), and false positive (FP). Table 4 provides a summary of the performance measurement metrics used in this study. Accuracy represents the percentage of overall correct predictions, reflecting the model's ability to classify all cases correctly. Precision measures the rate of correct positive predictions among all predicted positive cases, indicating the model's reliability in identifying true positives. Recall highlights the percentage of correctly identified positive cases out of all actual positive cases, showcasing the model's sensitivity. Lastly, the F1-score combines precision and recall to provide a balanced measure of the classifier's precision and robustness, offering insight into the model's overall performance.

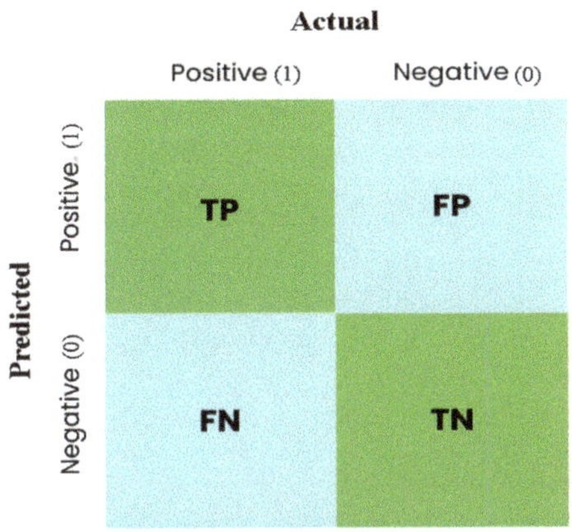

Figure 5. Format of confusion matrix.

Table 4. Description of performance measurement metrics:.

Metrics	Formula	Meaning
Accuracy	$\frac{TP+TN}{FP+TP+FN+TN} \times 100$	Rate of overall correct prediction
Precision	$\frac{TP}{TP+FP} \times 100$	Rate of correct positive predictions among all predicted positive cases
Recall	$\frac{TP}{TP+FN} \times 100$	Rate of correctly identified positive cases among all actual positive cases
F1-score	$2 \times \frac{Recall \times Precision}{Recall+Precision} \times 100$	Describe how precise and robust a classifier is

Receiver operating characteristic area under curve (ROC AUC): The ROC AUC is used to measure the area under the receiver operating characteristic (ROC) curve, which plots the true-positive rate (sensitivity) against the false-positive rate (1-specificity) for different threshold values [39]. It quantifies the model's ability to discriminate between positive and negative classes across all possible thresholds. The ROC AUC score ranges from 0 to 1, where a score closer to 1 indicates better model performance.

K-fold cross-validation: We use the K-fold cross-validation method to assess the performance and validity of an ML model [40]. We divide the dataset into k equal parts or folds. The model is then trained and validated k times, using a different fold as the validation set and the remaining K−1 folds as the training set. This process generates K performance scores, which are averaged to produce a single performance estimate. K-fold cross-validation helps reduce overfitting and efficient use of data. This method provides a robust evaluation by leveraging various data subsets for training and validation.

2.8. Explainable AI (XAI)

XAI is a field focused on making the decision-making processes of AI systems transparent and understandable to humans [41]. As AI models become more complex, particularly with the rise of deep learning, their internal workings can often appear as "black boxes", making it difficult to understand how they produce results. XAI seeks to demystify these processes, providing clear explanations that build trust and allow users to challenge or correct the decisions made by AI systems.

2.8.1. Shapley Additive Explanations (SHAP)

SHAP is a methodology based on cooperative game theory that assigns a unique value to each feature, known as the SHAP value [42]. This value represents the contribution of that feature to the model's prediction for a specific instance. SHAP is versatile, offering both global explanations, which provide insights into the overall behavior of the model across the entire dataset, and local explanations that clarify how individual features influence specific predictions. SHAP values are consistent, ensuring that the sum of contributions from all features matches the difference between the model's output for a given sample and the average output. While SHAP offers a comprehensive understanding of feature importance and interactions, it can be computationally intensive, particularly for complex models and large datasets.

2.8.2. Local Interpretable Model–Agnostic Explanations (LIME)

LIME is a methodology that provides localized explanations by approximating the behavior of a complex model around a specific prediction [43]. It works by generating perturbed versions of the original data point with slight modifications to feature values and then training a simple, interpretable model (such as linear regression) on these modified data. This simple model serves as a local approximation of the complex model's behavior in close proximity to the prediction. Any ML model can apply LIME, and its computational efficiency makes it suitable for real-time analysis. However, LIME's explanations are valid only within the local region around the specific prediction and may not generalize well to the entire model, as it assumes local linearity, which might not always hold true.

3. Result and Discussion

3.1. Statistical Analysis

We performed a logistic regression analysis on the dataset using Python's statistics models [44] and the smf.logit function. The model predicts the likelihood of having learning difficulties based on several independent variables, including categorical and numerical ones. After fitting the model, the model summary provides us with coefficients, p-values, OR, and CI. The interpretation of results involves understanding the impact of each independent variable on the likelihood of having learning difficulties. Table 5 displays each variable's p-value, OR, and 95% CI. Below is a detailed analysis of all variables to understand their impact:

- Took away privileges: Children who had privileges taken away are 1.490 times more likely to have learning difficulties compared to those who did not. This association is statistically significant ($p < 0.001$), with a confidence interval of 1.284 to 1.728, indicating a strong effect;
- Shook child: The odds of having learning difficulties are 1.260 times higher for children who were shaken compared to those who were not. This finding is statistically significant ($p = 0.002$), with a confidence interval of 1.086 to 1.462;
- Beat child as hard as one could: Children who were severely physically punished (beaten as hard as one could) have 2.265 times higher odds of learning difficulties compared to those who were not. This effect is highly statistically significant ($p < 0.001$), with a confidence interval of 1.776 to 2.888;
- Sex: Male children are 1.215 times more likely to have learning difficulties compared to female children. This effect is statistically significant ($p = 0.009$), with a confidence interval of 1.049 to 1.406;
- Wealth index and mother's education: Children from the poorest households are 2.612 times more likely to have learning difficulties compared to the richest households. The odds decrease with increasing wealth, remaining significant in the second and

middle quintiles but not in the fourth. Lower maternal education also increases the odds of learning difficulties, though not all levels are statistically significant;

- Called child dumb/lazy: The odds of learning difficulties for children who were called dumb or lazy are 1.077 times higher compared to those who were not, but this effect is not statistically significant ($p = 0.376$), with a confidence interval of 0.913 to 1.271;
- Weight-for-age percentile: The weight-for-age percentile does not show a statistically significant association with learning difficulties (OR = 1.000, $p = 0.963$), suggesting it has a negligible impact;
- Child's weight: Lower child weight is associated with slightly reduced odds of learning difficulties (OR = 0.954), and this effect is statistically significant ($p = 0.040$).

Table 5. Association between the dependent variable and independent variables.

Factors	Samples with No Learning Difficulty	Samples with Having Learning Difficulty	OR	*p*-Value	95% CI Interval	
					Low	High
Categorical						
Took away privileges						
NO (Reference)	5941	480	1			
YES	6516	337	1.490	0.000	1.284	1.728
Shook child						
NO (Reference)	5364	436	1			
YES	7093	381	1.260	0.002	1.086	1.462
Called child dumb lazy						
NO (Reference)	2955	244	1			
YES	9502	573	1.077	0.376	0.913	1.271
Beat child as hard as one could						
NO (Reference)	540	92	1			
YES	11,917	725	2.265	0.000	1.776	2.888
Sex						
FEMALE (Reference)	6418	465	1			
MALE	6039	352	1.215	0.009	1.049	1.406
Wealth index quintile						
Richest (Reference)	3064	331	1			
Poorest	2655	186	2.612	0.000	1.953	3.492
Second	2359	125	1.841	0.000	1.364	2.485
Middle	2351	108	1.401	0.033	1.027	1.911
Fourth	2028	67	1.275	0.128	0.933	1.743
Mother's education						
Higher secondary+ (Reference)	1493	138	1			
Pre-primary or none	3068	249	1.303	0.103	0.948	1.791
Primary	6130	358	1.216	0.188	0.909	1.627
Secondary	1766	72	1.110	0.449	0.848	1.452
Numerical	**Total samples**					
Weight-for-age percentile	13,274		1.000	0.963	0.994	1.006
Child's weight	13,274		0.954	0.040	0.912	0.998

The analysis highlights several key factors associated with learning difficulties in children. Disciplinary practices, such as taking away privileges, shaking, and severe physical punishment, significantly increase the odds of learning difficulties. Socioeconomic status plays a crucial role, with children from the poorest households being at a much higher risk, and lower maternal education also contributing to this increased likelihood. Additionally, male children are more likely to experience learning difficulties compared to females.

The heatmap shown in Figure 6 reveals a moderately strong positive correlation (0.663) between "Child's_weight" and "Weight_age_P", indicating that as a child's weight increases, their weight-for-age percentile also tends to rise. In contrast, both "Child's_weight" and "Weight_age_P" have weak negative correlations with "Learning_skill" (−0.030 and −0.032, respectively), suggesting that these physical growth indicators have a minimal relationship with the child's learning skills compared to others.

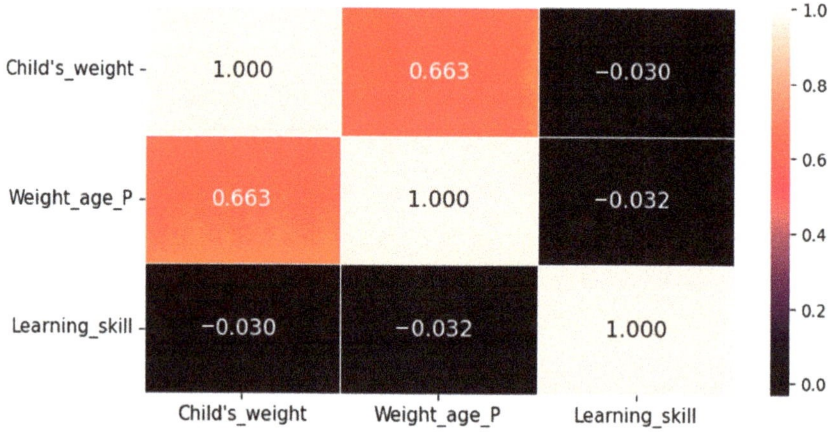

Figure 6. Correlation between child's weight, weight-for-age percentile, and learning skill compared to others.

3.2. ML Model Performance

These models were chosen to effectively capture the complex and multi-faceted nature of the dataset, which includes various socio-economic, health, and educational indicators relevant to learning difficulties. KNN was used for its simplicity and effectiveness in handling non-linear relationships within the dataset. LRC was chosen for its interpretability and ability to model linear relationships. DT and RF were selected for their flexibility in managing hierarchical data, while GB and XGB were employed to improve predictive accuracy through their iterative error-correcting process and capacity to handle complex interactions in the data. By utilizing these models, the study aimed to validate its findings across different ML algorithms, ensuring the robustness of the results within the context of the MICS 2019 dataset.

Figure 7 presents a comprehensive comparison of several machine learning algorithms applied to the MICS 2019 dataset for predicting child learning abilities. We evaluated the models using various performance metrics and assessed them through 10-fold cross-validation. Furthermore, we analyzed the performance metrics of various classification models to assess their effectiveness in predicting child learning difficulties. The DT model demonstrated moderate performance, with an accuracy of 0.70, precision of 0.67, and recall of 0.80, resulting in an F1-score of 0.73. In contrast, the KNN model showed better results with an accuracy of 0.86, a high recall of 0.97, and an F1-score of 0.87. LRC performed similarly across most metrics, with values around 0.69. The RF model performed well, achieving an accuracy of 0.91, precision of 0.89, recall of 0.93, and an F1-score of 0.91. GB and XGB yielded the best results, achieving exceptional performance metrics such as accuracy of 0.95, precision of 0.96–0.97, recall of 0.93, and an F1-score of 0.95. These models also had high NPV and ROC AUC scores of 0.93 and 0.95, respectively. This analysis suggests that GB and XGB are the most effective models for this application, outperforming other classifiers in nearly all metrics. The results show how well different ML models predict learning difficulties in children. It compares their performance using various measures that assess how accurately the models identify children with and without difficulties and how balanced their predictions are. RF, XGB, KNN, and GB perform very well, with results close to perfect, meaning they make highly reliable predictions and are good at correctly identifying both children with and without learning difficulties. In contrast, models like DT and LRC perform slightly less effectively. Their predictions are still useful but less consistent and accurate compared to the top-performing models.

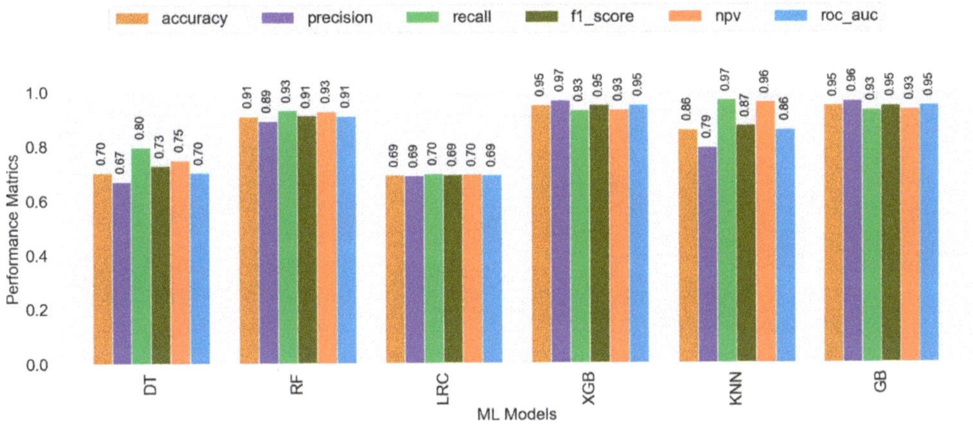

Figure 7. Performance metrics of various ML algorithms for predicting child learning difficulties.

The ML models in this study were trained on a workstation equipped with an Intel Core i3 CPU @ 2.3 GHz and 12 GB of RAM. Training times varied across models, reflecting their complexity and the chosen hyperparameters. The Table 6 shows that the DT model was the fastest, with a training time of 0.06 s and a testing time of 0.0007 s. Following DT, LRC had the best testing time at 0.0005 s, and XGB came next with a testing time of 0.0094 s. Other algorithms, while requiring more time, still provided valuable results with good accuracy and performance. These training times demonstrate the computational efficiency of each model within the constraints of the available resources, allowing for effective model evaluation and tuning without significant delays.

Table 6. Time Requirements for Training ML Models.

Models	Train_Time (s)	Test_Time (s)
DT	0.063787	0.000712
KNN	2.099552	0.037495
LRC	0.243012	0.00052
RF	2.256923	0.261399
GB	5.796678	0.011094
XGB	1.841549	0.009374

Furthermore, the Table 7 presents the performance metrics of the XGB model, evaluated using 1- to 10-fold cross-validation for predicting child learning difficulties. Each fold displayed consistent results, with high accuracy precision, recall, F1-score, NPV, and ROC AUC score. Overall, the table highlights the robust performance of the XGB model across multiple evaluation metrics.

Table 7. K-fold cross-validation performance metrics for XGB model predicting child learning difficulties.

K_Fold	Accuracy	Precision	Recall	F1_Score	npv	roc_auc
1_Fold	0.95	0.97	0.92	0.94	0.94	0.95
2_Fold	0.94	0.95	0.92	0.94	0.94	0.94
3_Fold	0.94	0.96	0.92	0.94	0.94	0.94
4_Fold	0.94	0.96	0.92	0.94	0.94	0.94
5_Fold	0.95	0.97	0.93	0.95	0.94	0.95
6_Fold	0.95	0.97	0.93	0.95	0.94	0.95
7_Fold	0.95	0.97	0.93	0.95	0.94	0.95
8_Fold	0.95	0.97	0.93	0.95	0.94	0.95
9_Fold	0.95	0.97	0.93	0.95	0.94	0.95
10_Fold	0.95	0.97	0.93	0.95	0.94	0.95

The confusion matrices in Figure 8 generated by the six different ML models DT, RF, LRC, KNN, GB, and XGB provide key insights into their effectiveness in predicting early child learning difficulties, where the outcomes are classified as either "NO DIFFICULTY" (0) or "HAS DIFFICULTY" (1). The XGB model stands out as a very good performer, with the highest number of true positives (1168) and true negatives (1208), coupled with the lowest number of false positives (36) and false negatives (79), indicating its high accuracy in identifying both children who have and those who do not have learning difficulties. Similarly, the GB model demonstrates strong performance, with slightly fewer true positives (1170), more true negatives (1212), and very few false positives (32), making it another reliable option. The RF model also performs well, with a favorable balance of true positives (1154) and true negatives (1100), though it has a moderate number of false positives (144) and false negatives (93), indicating some room for improvement in reducing misclassifications. The KNN model, despite its strong identification of true positives (1199), struggles with a higher number of false positives (324), making it less reliable in correctly identifying children without learning difficulties. The LRC, however, has a significant number of false negatives (397), posing a risk of under-detection. The DT model, with a substantial number of false positives (500), indicates a tendency to over-predict learning difficulties. Overall, XGB and GB emerge as the most effective models, offering the best balance between accurately predicting both classes and minimizing errors.

The ROC AUC curves in Figure 9 present a comparative analysis of six ML models applied to a dataset on child learning difficulties. The XGB and GB models, indicated by the orange and purple curves, respectively, both achieved the highest ROC AUC of 0.95, demonstrating their exceptional ability to differentiate between classes. The RF model, represented by the red curve, also performed well with an ROC AUC of 0.91, though it lagged slightly behind XGB and GB. In contrast, the DT, LRC, and KNN models, represented by blue, cyan, and green curves, respectively, each achieved an ROC AUC of 0.70, 0.69, and 0.86. This suggests that these models are less effective compared to the top-performing XGB, GB, and RF models. Overall, the analysis indicates that XGB and GB are the most effective models for predicting child learning difficulties, with RF following closely behind, while DT, LRC, and KNN exhibit lower classification performance.

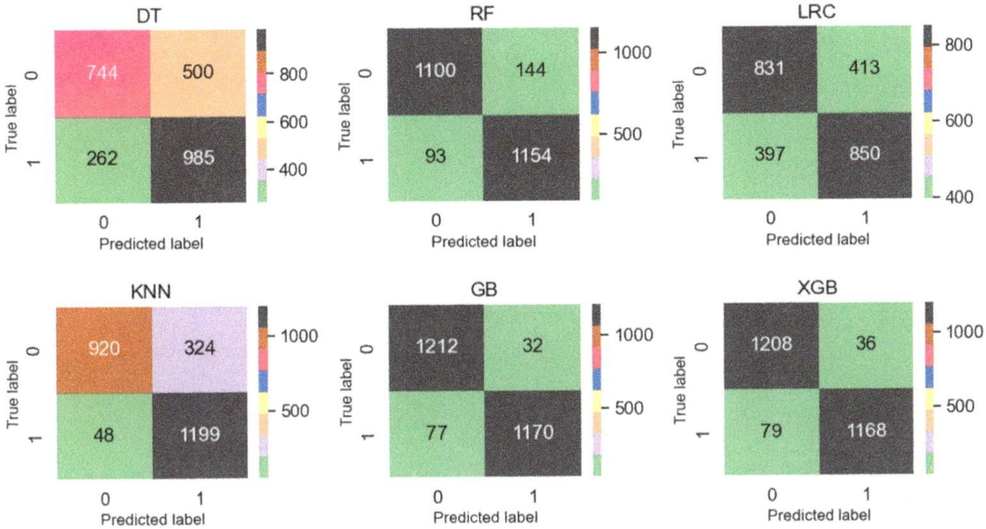

Figure 8. Confusion metrics for various machine learning algorithms for child learning difficulty prediction.

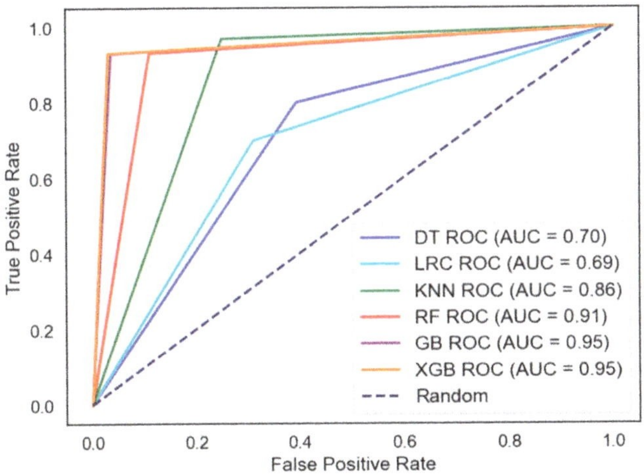

Figure 9. ROC AUC Curves for Various ML Algorithms for Child learning difficulties prediction.

3.3. SHAP Explanation

According to the ML model performance matrices, it is clear that the XGB and GB models perform best. Therefore, we utilized the XGB model in our XAI analysis to interpret the outputs based on the influence of the input features.

In Figure 10, the SHAP summary plot provides a detailed analysis of how various factors influence the probability of learning difficulties in children. Here, the negative SHAP value indicates the absence of learning difficulties, while the positive value indicates the presence of difficulties. The figure shows that removing privileges is a significant risk factor, increasing the probability of learning challenges. In contrast, a higher wealth index serves as a strong protective factor, reducing this risk by providing a more supportive environment for learning. Sex has a relatively smaller impact, suggesting that while gender differences exist, they are not as influential as socioeconomic factors. Negative behaviors, such as shaking the child, physical punishment (e.g., beating the child hard), and verbal abuse (e.g., calling the child dumb or lazy), are strongly associated with an increased likelihood of learning difficulties. These factors highlight the detrimental effects of harsh disciplinary actions on a child's cognitive development. On the other hand, higher levels of maternal education and better physical health indicators, such as a higher weight-for-age percentile and child's weight, act as protective factors, reducing the risk of learning difficulties. This emphasizes the importance of supportive environments in lowering the risk of learning difficulties and demonstrates how harmful negative behaviors and low socioeconomic status can be.

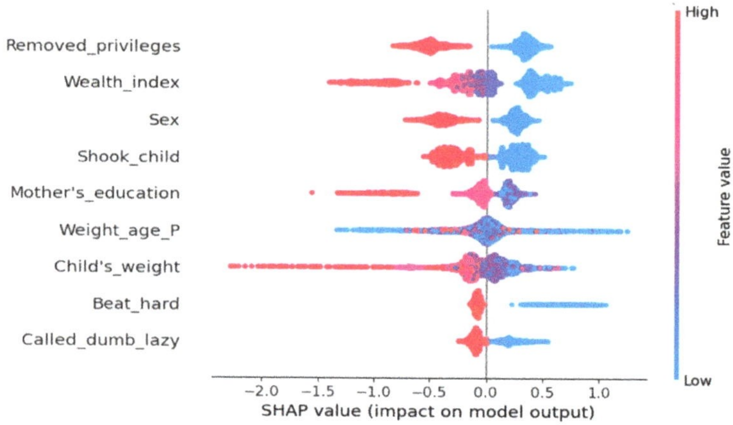

Figure 10. SHAP summary plot showing the influence of input features on children learning difficulties.

Furthermore, the SHAP waterfall plots reveal how various factors contribute to predicting the learning skill difficulties for two specific children. Both plots emphasize the strong influence of parenting practices, physical health, and socio-economic factors on the likelihood of learning difficulties in children.

In Figure 11, the model predicts a higher probability that the child has learning difficulties, as the output is f(x) = 1.229. The primary factors contributing to this prediction are the following:

- Beating hard (YES = 1) significantly increases the likelihood of learning difficulties (+0.51). Harsh physical punishment is strongly correlated with emotional and cognitive challenges in children (Beating or physically punishing a child is a crime punishable by law in many countries. Such abusive behavior has been proven to severely hinder a child's emotional, cognitive, and educational development, including their learning capabilities);
- Removal of privileges (YES = 1) adds positively to the prediction (+0.39), as this negative disciplinary action can affect a child's mental well-being and learning ability;
- Shaking the child (NO = 2) contributes negatively (−0.34), implying that the absence of shaking reduces the likelihood of learning difficulties;
- Sex (MALE = 1) increases the likelihood of difficulties (+0.2), indicating that male children may face a higher probability of learning issues in this dataset;
- Mother's education (Primary = 1) has a moderate positive influence (+0.18), showing that lower maternal education correlates with a higher risk of learning difficulties;

- Weight–age percentile (0.8) and called dumb/lazy (YES = 1) have smaller positive contributions (+0.12 and +0.1, respectively), indicating that poor physical health and verbal abuse contribute to learning difficulties;
- Child's weight (11.9) and wealth index (Second = 2) have minimal effects, with wealth index showing a slight negative impact (−0.02), suggesting that lower socio-economic status marginally increases learning difficulties.

Again, in Figure 12, the model predicts a lower probability of the child having learning difficulties, as the output is f(x) = −2.23. The primary factors contributing to this prediction are the following:

- Removed privileges (NO = 2) significantly reduce the likelihood of learning difficulties (−0.77). This suggests that not using this negative disciplinary tactic supports a positive outcome;
- Child's weight (13.6) and weight–age percentile (29.9) both have substantial negative contributions (−0.66 and −0.48, respectively), implying that good physical health strongly correlates with better cognitive outcomes;
- Shaking the child (NO = 2) also contributes negatively (−0.44), reinforcing that avoiding physical mistreatment reduces learning challenges
- Sex (MALE = 1) has a smaller positive impact (+0.28), suggesting that being male slightly increases the likelihood of learning difficulties, though its effect is less significant in this prediction;
- Called dumb/lazy (NO = 2) contributes negatively (−0.13), indicating that not verbally labeling the child helps reduce the likelihood of learning difficulties;
- Mother's education (None = 0) and wealth index (Second = 2) provide smaller positive and negative influences (+0.12 and −0.11, respectively), showing a marginal effect of socio-economic and educational factors;
- Beating hard (NO = 2) has a slight negative contribution (−0.07), suggesting that avoiding physical punishment supports lower chances of learning difficulties.

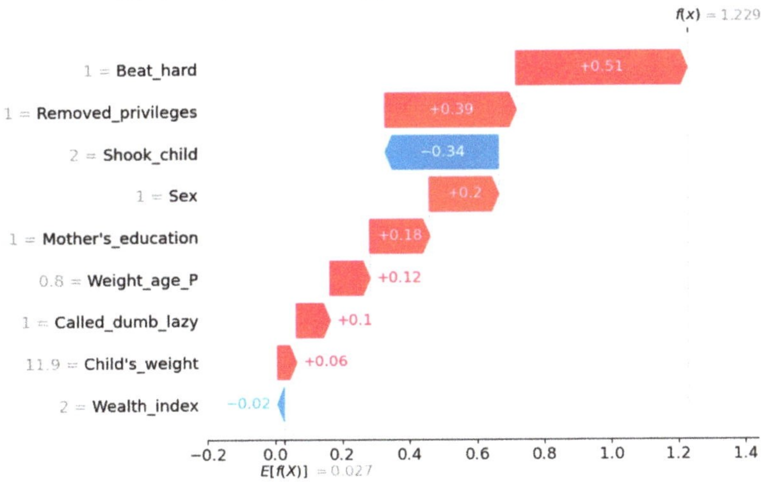

Figure 11. SHAP waterfall plot for predicting the presence of learning difficulties in a child.

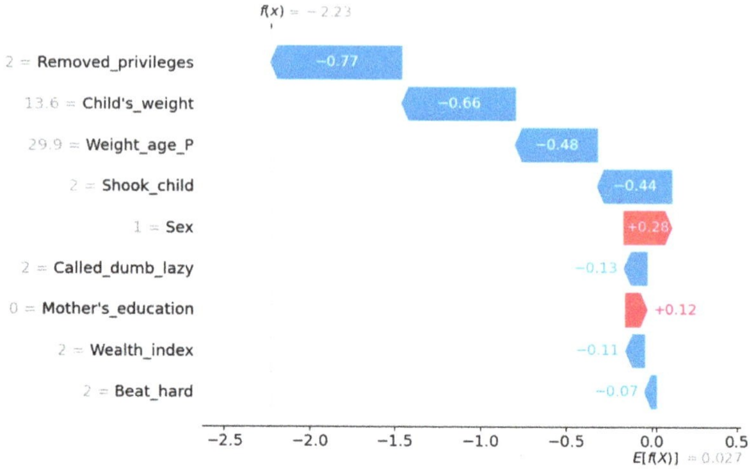

Figure 12. SHAP waterfall plot for predicting the absence of learning difficulties in a child.

3.4. LIME Explanation

The LIME plots offer a comprehensive explanation of the model's predictions on whether a child has learning difficulties based on various input features. These explanations, which were generated using the best-performing XGB model, emphasize the critical role of factors such as health, economic conditions, and parenting practices in predicting learning difficulties. They also identify areas that require improvement, especially in addressing factors that adversely affect a child's learning abilities.

In Figure 13, the model predicts a 0.93 probability that the child does not have learning difficulties. The primary factors contributing to this prediction are as follows:

- The factors of child's weight (14.30) and weight–age percentile (37.50) significantly influence the prediction that the child does not have learning difficulties. Higher values indicate good physical health, which is strongly associated with better cognitive development and learning capabilities;
- A higher wealth index (Richest = 5), which often provides access to better resources and educational opportunities, contributes to a lower likelihood of learning difficulties. This positive socio-economic status helps to minimize the negative impact of removing privileges (YES = 1), which otherwise increases the risk of learning difficulties;
- A lower level of maternal education (Primary = 1) is often associated with a higher likelihood of experiencing learning difficulties, which has some impact on the prediction;
- Negative parenting behaviors, such as shaking the child (YES = 1), increase the likelihood of learning difficulties. But beating hard (NO = 2) and calling the child dumb/lazy (NO = 2) indicate that the absence of severe physical punishment and abuse decreases the likelihood of learning difficulties;
- The factor Sex (FEMALE = 2) contributes to the prediction that female children have a lower probability of experiencing learning difficulties.

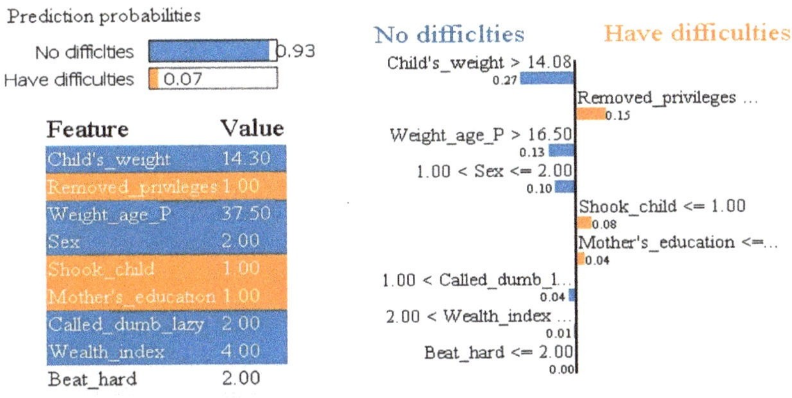

Figure 13. LIME plot explaining prediction of the absence of learning difficulties in a child.

Furthermore, in Figure 14, the model predicts with a high probability (1.00) that the child has learning difficulties. The key contributing factors to this prediction are as follows:

- The factors of the child's weight (11.28) and weight–age percentile (1.30) significantly contribute to the prediction of learning difficulties because the child's low weight and weight-for-age percentile suggest poor health, which is often associated with developmental challenges;
- The factors like removing privileges (YES = 1) along with wealth index (Poorest = 1) conditions are linked to a higher likelihood of learning difficulties;
- The mother's education (Primary = 1) factor slightly influences the prediction, as a lower level of maternal education is often associated with an increased risk of learning difficulties;
- The factor sex (FEMALE = 2) contributes to the "No difficulties" prediction in this case;
- Negative parenting behaviors: Shaking the child (NO = 2) and beating hard (NO = 2) slightly decreases the likelihood of learning difficulties, but calling the child dumb/lazy (YES = 1) contributes to the prediction of have difficulties, reinforcing the model's overall prediction.

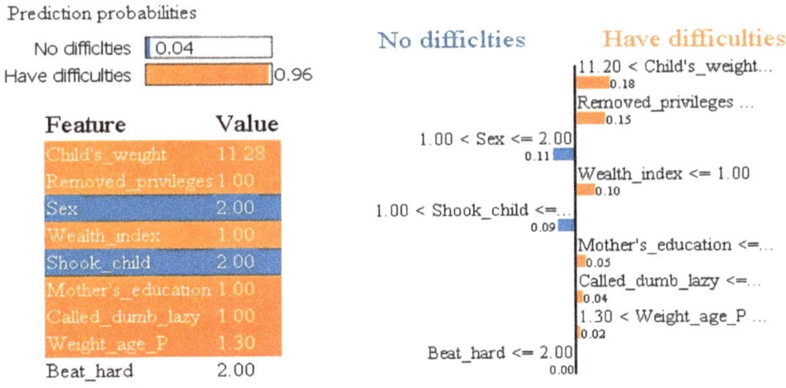

Figure 14. LIME plot explaining prediction of the presence of learning difficulties in a child.

4. Comparison with Other Works

This study compared its findings with research from Oman, Australia, and the U.S., focusing on early childhood learning outcomes. While previous studies used diverse datasets and methods, our approach uniquely applies the MICS 2019 dataset to the Bangladeshi context. Unlike prior research, which often lacked explainability, we integrated SHAP and LIME to enhance model interpretability. This comparison highlights our study's contribution to understanding learning difficulties through a region-specific lens, offering actionable insights for policymaking and education strategies.

Table 8 presents a detailed comparison of our work with other research studies, emphasizing methodologies, datasets, statistical applications of ML, and XAI techniques. The table highlights performance metrics like accuracy, precision, recall, and specificity to demonstrate the effectiveness of different approaches. Additionally, it outlines the integration of statistical ML and XAI tools, providing a comprehensive overview of how our work aligns with or advances existing research in the field.

One study explored factors impacting academic performance using statistical ML techniques, specifically the J48 algorithm, applied to a dataset of 6514 students over 11 years at a public university in Oman. The study achieved an accuracy of 82.4% but did not integrate any XAI methods or statistical explanations to interpret the results [8]. Another study applied ML to identify risk factors for ADHD in children using data from 45,779 participants in the 2018–2019 National Survey of Children's Health (NSCH). While logistic regression and eight ML classifiers were tested, the RF classifier stood out with an accuracy of 85.5% and an AUC of 0.94. However, the study focused only on statistical ML performance without employing XAI to explain the models [9].

Similarly, the study [10] predicted depression in children and adolescents using mental health and socio-environmental features from 6310 Australian participants (2013–2014). ML models like RF, XGB, DT, and Gaussian naive Bayes were used, with the RF model achieving 95% accuracy and 99% precision. Despite the robust performance, the study did not utilize XAI tools for model interpretability or statistical analysis of feature importance. Another research [11] evaluated ML techniques for predicting academic performance factors using data from 5084 students aged 10–17 in West Bank schools. Among the models tested (RF, ANN, SVM, DT, NB, and LR), LR achieved the best results with a sensitivity of 94.3%, specificity of 96.3%, and an AUC of 99.3%. However, no XAI techniques were used to explain the predictive factors.

In studies focused on autism spectrum disorder (ASD), research [15] analyzed data from 292 children and 704 adults using multiple ML algorithms. The ANN model achieved 94.24% accuracy and a high specificity of 95.05%, but no XAI methods were applied to interpret the findings statistically. Another study [16] focused on toddler ASD diagnosis, achieving a perfect performance of 100% accuracy, precision, recall, and F1-score using LR but without incorporating statistical analysis or XAI tools.

In contrast, our work integrated both statistical ML and XAI to identify key factors and predict learning difficulties in Bangladeshi children under five years of age. Using a refined dataset from MICS 2019, we employed ML algorithms like DT, LR, KNN, RF, XGB, and GB, alongside SHAP and LIME for interpretability. This combination allowed us to explain the significance of individual features statistically while enhancing the transparency of our models. The XGB classifier demonstrated superior performance, achieving 95% accuracy, 97% precision, 93% recall, 95% F1-score, 93% NPV, and an ROC of 95%. Our work not only matches or exceeds the performance metrics of prior studies but also provides a deeper understanding of the underlying factors through the integration of XAI, setting it apart from existing research.

Table 8. Summary of research outcomes.

Ref.	Findings	Data Source	ML Application	Statistical Analysis	XAI Uses	ML Performance
[8]	Identified factors impacting academic performance using ML algorithms	Data from 6514 students over 11 years at a public university in Oman	J48 algorithm	×	×	J48 achieved 82.4% accuracy
[9]	Identified risk factors for ADHD in children using ML classification	2018–2019 NSCH data from 45,779 children aged 3–17 years	Logistic regression and eight ML classifiers	✓	×	RF classifier achieved 85.5% accuracy, sensitivity of 84.4%, specificity of 86.4%, and AUC of 0.94
[10]	Predicted depression in children and adolescents using ML models	Australian child and adolescent responses from 6310 participants (2013–2014)	RF, XGB, DT, and Gaussian naive Bayes algorithms	×	×	RF model achieved 95% accuracy and 99% precision
[11]	Evaluated ML techniques for predicting academic performance factors	Data from 5084 students aged 10–17 in the West Bank	RF, ANN, SVM, DT, NB, and LR models	×	×	LR model achieved sensitivity of 94.3%, specificity of 96.3%, and AUC of 99.3%
[15]	Improved early ASD diagnosis using machine learning	Obtained from UCI Repository; 292 children and 704 adults	RF, KNN, XGB, SVM, DT, NB, LR, and ANN	×	×	ANN achieved 94.24% accuracy, precision 89.80% recall 92%, F1-score, 91%, specificity 95.05%, and AUC of 93.84%
[16]	Enhanced toddler ASD diagnosis using machine learning.	From UCI ML Repository; 1054 toddlers (12–36 months) via ASDTests app	SVM, RF, LR, DT, KNN, and NB	×	×	LR achieved 100% accuracy, 100% precision, 100% recall, and 100% F1-score
This work	Identified key factors and predicted learning difficulties in Bangladeshi children under 5 years old using ML models	Refined dataset of 13,274 samples and 19 features from MICS 2019	DT, LR, KNN, RF, XGB, GB algorithms, and SHAP and LIME explanations	✓	✓	XGB classifier achieved 95% accuracy, 97% precision, 93% recall, 95% F1-score, 93% NPV, and 95% ROC

5. Policy Implications

Figure 15 illustrates a structured framework that outlines a data-driven approach for predicting and addressing early childhood learning difficulties. It integrates family data collected by NGOs or health organizations, focusing on health, nutrition, family guidance, education, and socioeconomic status. Data were entered, processed, and analyzed through ML models to make predictions. XAI techniques were applied to identify key factors influencing learning difficulties, enhancing the interpretability of results. The identified learning gaps inform targeted policy implications and interventions, such as early childhood education, health services, parenting support, nutritional programs, and economic assistance. This framework provides actionable insights to address disparities and improve educational outcomes through informed policymaking.

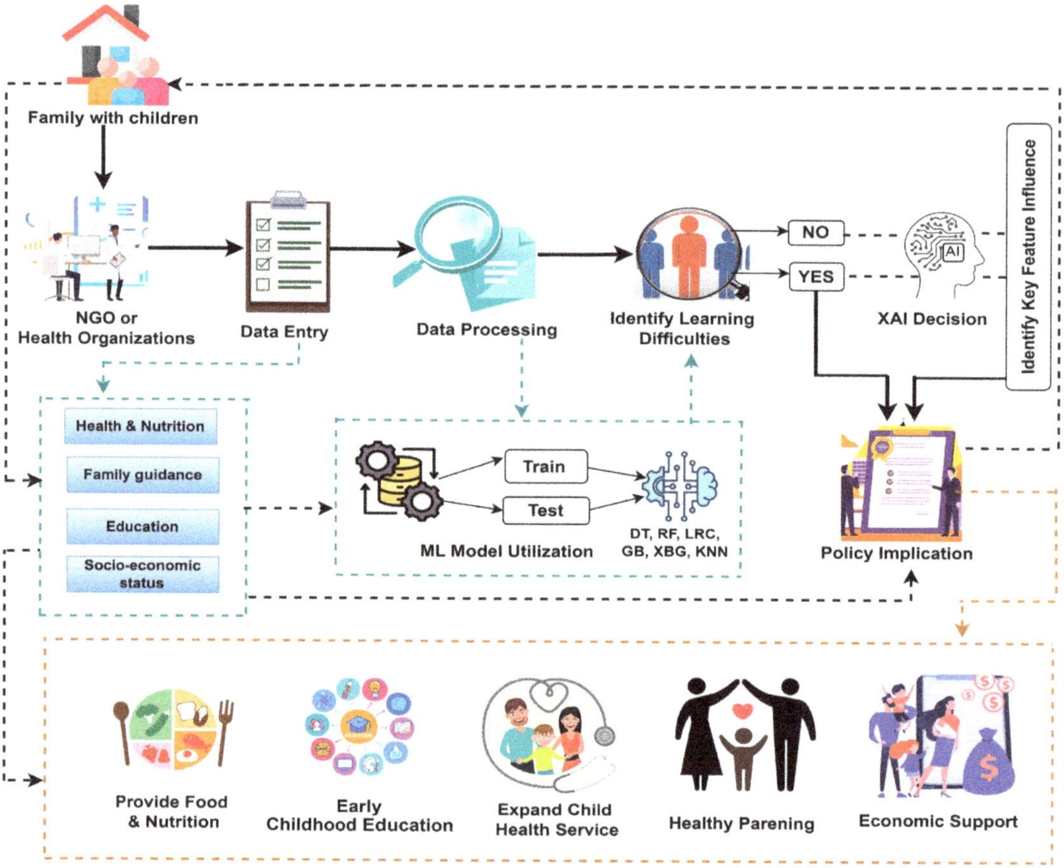

Figure 15. A data-driven framework for early childhood learning difficulties prediction and prevention policy implications.

The following steps will help in policy implications for addressing child learning disabilities:

- **Health and Nutrition Interventions:** To support children's health and development, it is essential to provide nutritional supplements or balanced meals to promote proper growth. Alongside this, organizing regular health check-ups and immunization drives helps prevent illnesses and ensures overall well-being. Additionally, educating parents on the importance of maintaining a healthy diet and hygiene creates a strong foundation for sustained child health;
- **Parenting Support:** Workshops should be conducted to raise awareness of early childhood care, provide counseling for behavioral issues, and encourage activities that strengthen parent–child bonds;
- **Education Enhancements:** Remedial or special education programs should be implemented to address the individual learning needs of children. At the same time, teachers should be trained in inclusive education practices and early detection of learning challenges, ensuring that resources are accessible for children with special needs;

- **Socio-economic Support:** Scholarships or financial aid should be provided to underprivileged families, and they should be linked to social welfare schemes to improve their living standards. This would be complemented by ensuring access to technology and learning aids in under-resourced communities, promoting equal opportunities for all children.

Generalizability and Limitations

This study, which uses the MICS 2019 dataset, provides useful insights into predicting early learning issues in children under the age of five years old. However, there are some limitations to consider. The use of self-reported data presents potential reporting biases. Guardians and parents might understate developmental issues due to cultural shame, a lack of understanding, or subjective impressions, hampering the dataset's credibility. Also, the dataset does not include all the important factors that can indicate learning difficulties, like family history, prenatal conditions, or socio-environmental factors. Furthermore, while the MICS dataset represents the Bangladeshi population, the socioeconomic and cultural diversity of other regions may restrict the findings' applicability to other populations. Despite these limitations, the proposed work demonstrates substantial potential for adaptation and application across other similar contexts (ASD, ADHD, etc.). By retraining and validating the models with region-specific data, the approach could be extended to address early learning challenges in diverse populations.

6. Conclusions

This study conducted both statistical and ML approaches to analyze the learning abilities of children under five years old, using the MICS 2019 dataset. The findings show that parental education, income, and parenting practices strongly affect children's learning outcomes. Additional factors contribute to learning difficulties, such as deprivation, intense physical punishment, and verbal reprimands. Socioeconomic factors exacerbate these issues, particularly urban living and poorer households. We then applied ML models to predict these difficulties and found that the GB and XGB classifiers performed best, achieving high accuracy, precision, recall, and F1-scores. Moreover, these findings underscore the importance of addressing socioeconomic disparities and improving parenting practices to reduce learning difficulties. Also, XAI techniques like SHAP and LIME provided more information about how different factors affect these predictions, which makes the results easier to understand and more open. The dataset may not have adequately captured some important variables, which is one of the study's limitations. Additionally, the findings are specific to Bangladesh and may not directly apply to other socio-economic and cultural contexts without further validation. Despite these limitations, the study emphasizes the importance of addressing socioeconomic disparities and promoting positive parenting practices to improve learning outcomes. The insights gained here can inform targeted policy interventions to reduce learning difficulties and foster comprehensive child development. In the future, researchers should focus on using longitudinal datasets to determine more factors to obtain a better picture of more complex factors, making sure that the results are valid to make them more useful.

Author Contributions: Conceptualization, M.A.M. and M.R.K.; methodology, M.M.H.; validation, M.A.M. and W.R.; formal analysis, M.R.K.; investigation, A.M.; resources, M.M.H.; writing—original draft preparation, M.A.M. and M.R.K.; writing—review and editing, A.M.; visualization, M.R.K.; supervision, M.M.H. and A.M.; funding acquisition, A.M. All authors have read and agreed to the published version of the manuscript.

Funding: This research received no external funding.

Institutional Review Board Statement: Not applicable.

Data Availability Statement: The source of dataset is mentioned in Section 2.1.

Conflicts of Interest: The authors declare no conflicts of interest.

References

1. López-Torres, L.; Hidalgo-Montesinos, M.D. Parental involvement and children's academic achievement: A meta-analysis. *Front. Psychol.* **2020**, *11*, 206.
2. Turney, K.; Kao, G. Parental involvement and academic achievement: A meta-analysis. *Soc. Forces* **2023**, *84*, 841–876.
3. Cabrera, N.J.; Hofferth, S.L.; Chae, S. Patterns and predictors of father-infant engagement across race/ethnic groups. *Early Child. Res. Q.* **2022**, *43*, 44–58. [CrossRef]
4. Han, W.J.; Ruhm, C.J. Maternal nonstandard work schedules and child cognitive outcomes. *Child Dev.* **2024**, *95*, 394–403 [CrossRef] [PubMed]
5. Liu, D.; Diorio, J.; Tannenbaum, B.; Caldji, C.; Francis, D.; Freedman, A.; Meaney, M.J. Maternal care, hippocampal glucocorticoid receptors, and hypothalamic-pituitary-adrenal responses to stress. *Science* **2023**, *277*, 1659–1662. [CrossRef] [PubMed]
6. Driessen, J. Socioeconomic status and parenting. In *The Encyclopedia of Child and Adolescent Development*; Hupp, S., Jewell, J., Eds.; John Wiley & Sons, Inc.: Hoboken, NJ, USA, 2016; pp. 1–8.
7. Englund, M.M.; Luckner, A.E.; Whaley, G.J.L.; Egeland, B. Children's achievement in early elementary school: Longitudinal effects of parental involvement, expectations, and quality of assistance. *J. Educ. Psychol.* **2020**, *96*, 723–730. [CrossRef]
8. Al-Alawi, L.; Al Shaqsi, J.; Tarhini, A.; Al-Busaidi, A.S. Using Machine Learning to Predict Factors Affecting Academic Performance: The Case of College Students on Academic Probation. *Educ. Inf. Technol.* **2023**, *28*, 12407–12432. [CrossRef] [PubMed]
9. Maniruzzaman, M.; Shin, J.; Hasan, M.A.M. Predicting Children with ADHD Using Behavioral Activity: A Machine Learning Analysis. *Appl. Sci.* **2022**, *12*, 2737. [CrossRef]
10. Haque, U.M.; Kabir, E.; Khanam, R. Detection of child depression using machine learning methods. *PLoS ONE* **2021**, *16*, e0261131. [CrossRef]
11. Qasrawi, R.; VicunaPolo, S.; Al-Halawa, D.A.; Hallaq, S.; Abdeen, Z. Predicting School Children Academic Performance Using Machine Learning Techniques. *Adv. Sci. Technol. Eng. Syst. J.* **2021**, *6*, 8–15. [CrossRef]
12. Yasumura, A.; Omori, M.; Fukuda, A.; Takahashi, J.; Yasumura, Y.; Nakagawa, E.; Koike, T.; Yamashita, Y.; Miyajima, T.; Koeda, T.; et al. Applied Machine Learning Method to Predict Children With ADHD Using Prefrontal Cortex Activity: A Multicenter Study in Japan. *J. Atten. Disord.* **2017**, *24*, 2012–2020. [CrossRef]
13. Akter, T.; Khan, M.I.; Ali, M.H.; Satu, M.S.; Uddin, M.J.; Moni, M.A. Improved Machine Learning based Classification Model for Early Autism Detection. In Proceedings of the 2nd International Conference on Robotics, Electrical and Signal Processing Techniques (ICREST), Dhaka, Bangladesh, 5–7 January 2021. [CrossRef]
14. Vakadkar, K.; Purkayastha, D.; Krishnan, D. Detection of Autism Spectrum Disorder in Children Using Machine Learning Techniques. *SN Comput. Sci.* **2021**, *2*, 386. [CrossRef]
15. Rasul, R.A.; Saha, P.; Bala, D.; Karim, S.R.U.; Abdullah, I.; Saha, B. An evaluation of machine learning approaches for early diagnosis of autism spectrum disorder. *Healthc. Anal.* **2024**, *5*, 100293. [CrossRef]
16. Shambour, Q. Artificial Intelligence Techniques for Early Autism Detection in Toddlers: A Comparative Analysis. *J. Appl. Data Sci.* **2024**, *5*, 1754–1764. [CrossRef]
17. Ali, N.; Ullah, A.; Khan, A.M.; Khan, Y.; Ali, S.; Bakhtawar; Khan, A.; Din, M.U.; Ullah, R.; Khan, U.N.; et al. Academic performance of children in relation to gender, parenting styles, and socioeconomic status: What attributes are important. *PLoS ONE* **2023**, *18*, e0286823. [CrossRef]
18. Vasiou, A.; Kassis, W.; Krasanaki, A.; Aksoy, D.; Favre, C.A.; Tantaros, S. Exploring Parenting Styles Patterns and Children's Socio-Emotional Skills. *Children* **2023**, *10*, 1126. [CrossRef] [PubMed]
19. Armstrong, R.; Symons, M.; Scott, J.G.; Arnott, W.L.; Copland, D.A.; McMahon, K.L.; Whitehouse, A.J.O. Predicting Language Difficulties in Middle Childhood From Early Developmental Milestones: A Comparison of Traditional Regression and Machine Learning Techniques. *J. Speech Lang. Hear. Res.* **2018**, *61*, 1926–1944. [CrossRef] [PubMed]
20. Bangladesh Bureau of Statistics (BBS); UNICEF. *Bangladesh Multiple Indicator Cluster Survey 2019: Final Report*; BBS and UNICEF: Dhaka, Bangladesh, 2019.
21. Bhuvaneswari, K.; Kanimozhi, G.; Shanmuganeethi, V. Prediction of student learning difficulties and performance using regression in machine learning. *Distance Educ. E-Learn.* **2023**, *11*, 2455–2460.
22. Wu, T.K.; Huang, S.C.; Meng, Y.R. Evaluation of ANN and SVM classifiers as predictors to the diagnosis of students with learning disabilities. *Expert Syst. Appl.* **2008**, *34*, 1846–1856. [CrossRef]
23. Heinze, G.; Wallisch, C.; Dunkler, D. Variable selection-A review and recommendations for the practicing statistician. *Biom. J.* **2018**, *60*, 431–449. [CrossRef]

24. Pryke, A.; Mostaghim, S.; Nazemi, A. Heatmap visualization of population based multi objective algorithms. In Proceedings of the Evolutionary Multi-Criterion Optimization: 4th International Conference, EMO 2007, Matsushima, Japan, 5–8 March 2007; Proceedings 4. Springer: Berlin/Heidelberg, Germany, 2007; pp. 361–375.
25. Little, R.J.A.; Rubin, D.B. *Statistical Analysis with Missing Data*, 3rd ed.; John Wiley & Sons: Hoboken, NJ, USA, 2019. [CrossRef]
26. Johnson, M.; Davis, E. A Comparative Study of Outlier Detection Algorithms for Data Cleansing. *Data Sci. J.* **2021**, *20*, 1–15. [CrossRef]
27. Witten, I.H.; Frank, E.; Hall, M.A.; Pal, C.J. *Data Mining: Practical Machine Learning Tools and Techniques*, 4th ed.; Morgan Kaufmann: Burlington, MA, USA, 2016.
28. Hastie, T.; Tibshirani, R.; Friedman, J. *The Elements of Statistical Learning: Data Mining, Inference, and Prediction*; Springer: Berlin/Heidelberg, Germany, 2009.
29. Chawla, N.V.; Lazarevic, A.; Hall, L.O.; Bowyer, K.W. (Eds.) SMOTEBoost: Improving prediction of the minority class in boosting. In *European Conference on Principles of Data Mining and Knowledge Discovery*; Springer: Berlin/Heidelberg, Germany, 2003.
30. Guo, X.; Yin, Y.; Dong, C.; Yang, G.; Zhou, G. On the class imbalance problem. In Proceedings of the 2008 ICNC'08 Fourth International Conference on Natural Computation, Jinan, China, 18–20 October 2008.
31. James, G.; Witten, D.; Hastie, T.; Tibshirani, R. *An Introduction to Statistical Learning*; Springer: New York, NY, USA, 2013; Volume 112.
32. Zhang, L. Using Decision Tree Classification Algorithm to Predict Learner Outcomes. *J. Educ. Data Sci.* **2023**, *7*, 45–60.
33. Breiman, L. Random forests. *Mach. Learn.* **2001**, *45*, 5–32. [CrossRef]
34. Hosmer, D.W., Jr.; Lemeshow, S.; Sturdivant, R.X. *Applied Logistic Regression*; John Wiley & Sons.: Hoboken, NJ, USA, 2013.
35. Cover, T.; Hart, P. Nearest neighbor pattern classification. *IEEE Trans. Inf. Theory* **1967**, *13*, 21–27. [CrossRef]
36. Friedman, J.H. Greedy Function Approximation: A Gradient Boosting Machine. *Ann. Stat.* **2001**, *29*, 1189–1232. [CrossRef]
37. Chen, T.; Guestrin, C. XGBoost: A Scalable Tree Boosting System. In Proceedings of the 22nd ACM SIGKDD International Conference on Knowledge Discovery and Data Mining, San Francisco, CA, USA, 13–17 August 2016; pp. 785–794.
38. Townsend, J.T. Theoretical analysis of an alphabetic confusion matrix. *Percept. Psychophys.* **1971**, *9*, 40–50. [CrossRef]
39. Park, S.H.; Goo, J.M.; Jo, C.H. Receiver operating characteristic (ROC) curve: Practical review for radiologists. *Korean J. Radiol.* **2004**, *5*, 11. [CrossRef] [PubMed]
40. Aghbalou, A.; Sabourin, A.; Portier, F. On the bias of K-fold cross-validation with stable learners. Proceedings of The 26th International Conference on Artificial Intelligence and Statistics. *Proc. Mach. Learn. Res.* **2023**, *206*, 3775–3794.
41. Arrieta, A.B.; Díaz-Rodríguez, N.; Del Ser, J.; Bennetot, A.; Tabik, S.; Barbado, A.; García, S.; Gil-López, S.; Molina, D.; Benjamins, R.; et al. Explainable Artificial Intelligence (XAI): Concepts, taxonomies, opportunities and challenges toward responsible AI. *Inf. Fusion* **2020**, *58*, 82–115. [CrossRef]
42. Roshan, K.; Zafar, A. Utilizing XAI technique to improve autoencoder based model for computer network anomaly detection with shapley additive explanation (SHAP). *arXiv* **2021**, arXiv:2112.08442. [CrossRef]
43. Gramegna, A.; Giudici, P. SHAP and LIME: An evaluation of discriminative power in credit risk. *Front. Artif. Intell.* **2021**, *4*, 752558. [CrossRef]
44. MICS | unicef. Retrieved from Survey. 2019. Available online: https://mics.unicef.org/surveys?display=card&f[0]=region:2521&f[1]=datatype:0&f[2]=year:2019 (accessed on 22 November 2024).

algorithms

MDPI

Article

AI-Enhanced Design and Application of High School Geography Field Studies in China: A Case Study of the Yellow (Bohai) Sea Migratory Bird Habitat Curriculum

Binglin Liu [1,2,†], Weijia Zeng [1,†], Weijiang Liu [3,†], Yi Peng [4,*] and Nini Yao [5,*]

[1] School of Geography and Planning, Nanning Normal University, Nanning 530001, China; dg1827018@smail.nju.edu.cn (B.L.); 15272121639@163.com (W.Z.)
[2] Key Laboratory of Environment Change and Resources Use in Beibu Gulf, Ministry of Education, Nanning Normal University, Nanning 530001, China
[3] College of Engineering, City University of Hong Kong, Hong Kong 99077, China; lliuweiji2-c@my.cityu.edu.hk
[4] School of Geographical Sciences, Southwest University, Chongqing 400715, China
[5] Department of Architecture and Built Environment, University of Nottingham, Ningbo 315154, China
* Correspondence: py210083@email.swu.edu.cn (Y.P.); saxny1@nottingham.edu.cn (N.Y.)
† These authors contributed equally to this work.

Abstract

China's Yellow (Bohai) Sea bird habitat is an important ecological region. Its unique ecology and challenges provide rich resources for research and study. Our course design concept is supported by AI technology, and improves students' abilities through innovative functions such as dynamic data support, personalized learning paths, immersive research and study experience, and diversified evaluation mechanisms. The course content revolves around the "human–land coordination concept", including pre-trip thinking, research and study during the trip, and post-trip exhibition learning, covering regional cognition, remote sensing image analysis, field investigation, and protection plan display activities. ERNIE Bot participates in optimizing the learning path throughout the process. The course evaluation system starts from the three dimensions of "land to people", "people to land", and the "coordination of the human–land relationship", adopts processes and final evaluation, and uses ERNIE Bot to achieve real-time monitoring, data analysis, personalized reports, and dynamic feedback, improving the objectivity and efficiency of evaluation, and helping students and teachers optimize learning and teaching. However, AI has limitations in geographical research and study, such as insufficient technical adaptability, the influence of students' abilities and habits, and the adaptation of teachers' role changes. To this end, optimization strategies such as improving data quality and technical platforms, strengthening student technical training, enhancing teachers' AI application capabilities, and enriching AI functions and teaching scenarios are proposed to enhance the application effect of AI in geographical research and promote innovation in educational models and student capacity building.

Keywords: AI; geography research course; evaluation system; human–land coordination concept

1. Introduction

In recent years, the rapid development of AI technology has brought unprecedented changes to the field of education [1]. With the support of cutting-edge technologies, such as

https://doi.org/10.3390/a18010047

generative AI, natural language processing (NLP), and educational data mining, the traditional teaching model has gradually been replaced by a digital and intelligent educational ecosystem [2]. In recent years, the Ministry of Education has repeatedly emphasized the deep integration of information technology in the field of education, and has proposed to give full play to the potential of AI in curriculum design, teaching evaluation, and resource management to meet the needs of students' personalized learning and all-round development [3]. These policies have pointed out the direction for AI-enabled education and have provided a theoretical basis and technical support for the innovation of specific subject teaching [4]. The application of AI technology in education is not a sudden rise, but the result of long-term exploration [5]. From early online learning platforms to today's intelligent teaching systems, AI has gradually penetrated into all aspects of education [6]. For example, AI-based learning management systems can dynamically analyze students' learning behaviors and generate personalized learning paths [7]; educational chatbots can instantly answer students' questions inside and outside the classroom and provide efficient interaction [8]. This intelligent teaching method with generative AI as the core can not only improve the efficiency of educational resource utilization, but also meet the diverse and personalized learning needs of students [9]. However, although AI technology has been widely used in many fields of education, its application in geography education is still insufficient [10]. As a subject that is both scientific and practical, high school geography involves complex spatiotemporal data analysis, ecosystem simulation, and dynamic research on regional human–land relationships [11]. The traditional teaching model emphasizes teaching geographical theory in class, and students learn through textbooks and test their results through examinations [12]. However, this one-way transmission model makes it difficult for students to truly understand the complexity of "human–land relationships", especially the connotation of "human–land coordination", a core aspect of geographical literacy [13]. Geographical education urgently needs a more efficient and participatory teaching model, and the introduction of AI technology provides the possibility of achieving this goal [14].

A geography study tour is an innovative education model that combines theory with practice. It brings students from the classroom into real geographical situations and allows them to experience the dynamic changes in geographical phenomena and the relationship between people and land [15]. Since the Ministry of Education issued the "Opinions on Promoting Study Tours for Primary and Secondary School Students" in 2016, study tours have gradually become an important part of basic education [16]. In particular, the promulgation of the "Geography Curriculum Standards for Ordinary High Schools" in 2017 further clarified the important role of geography study tours in cultivating students' core literacy [17]. Study tours can not only help students understand the complex relationship between the natural and social environment, but also cultivate students' ability to solve practical geographical problems and environmental protection awareness through hands-on practice [18]. In the implementation of geography study tours, the "human–land coordination concept" as the key objective of the core literacy of the geography subject has a particularly prominent educational value [19]. The "human–land coordination concept" refers to the harmonious development attitude and concept that humans should uphold when dealing with the relationship with the natural environment [20]. This core literacy emphasizes students' understanding of the interaction between the natural environment and human activities, and cultivates students' ability to solve practical problems in complex geographical situations [21]. Numerous studies have shown that geography study tours are of great significance for improving students' geographical practical ability and comprehensive literacy [16]. For example, some studies focus on the organization and implementation of study tours, emphasizing that through field trips students can gain a deep understanding of the natural and human geographical environments and enhance their perceptual understanding of geographical knowledge [11,12]. Some scholars have explored the positive role of study tours in cultivating students' regional cognition and geographical practical ability and have found that students can better master geographical survey methods and improve their ability to observe and analyze geographical phenomena during field research [20]. However, there are still some shortcomings in the traditional geography study tour course research. On the one hand, the course design often lacks systematicity and scientificity, relies too much on teacher experience, and finds it difficult to meet the diverse needs of students. On the other hand, the evaluation system is not perfect, focusing more on the students' knowledge mastery, and ignoring the comprehensive evaluation of students' thinking ability, innovation ability, "human–land coordination", and other core aspects of literacy [21]. In addition, in terms of teaching methods, traditional methods are mostly used in a manner that is lacking in terms of the effective use of modern information technology, and it is difficult to fully stimulate students' interest and initiative in learning. These shortcomings restrict the further development of geography study tour courses and also highlight the need to introduce new technologies for innovation [22].

Integrating AI technology into geography study tours provides a new idea for the innovation of this teaching model [23]. The advantages of AI technology lie in its powerful data processing capabilities and personalized learning support [14]. In geography study tours, AI can empower teaching through data visualization and dynamic analysis, personalized learning support, and real-time feedback and evaluation [14]. Through the above methods, AI-enabled geography study tours can help students analyze geographical phenomena and the relationship between people and land from multiple perspectives, and can help improve their comprehensive thinking and innovation capabilities [24]. In addition, the introduction of AI has greatly reduced the burden on teachers in the process of course design and implementation, allowing them to focus more on achieving teaching goals [25].

We integrated AI technology into a high school geography research course and used the generative AI (ERNIE Bot) developed by Baidu in China to explore how to use AI to empower traditional teaching models. The Yellow Sea (Bohai) Sea migratory bird habitat in China is an important node on the East Asia-Australasian migratory bird flyway with extremely high ecological value. However, the region has long faced ecological challenges such as wetland degradation and biodiversity decline. In this context, the goal of geography research travel is not only to help students understand the urgency of wetland protection, but also to enable students to participate in data analysis and ecological decision-making in real time through the support of AI technology. We aim to explore the specific application of AI technology in course design, implementation and evaluation by building an AI-driven geography research travel model. The following content of this article will be developed around the following: Section 2 introduces the research area and design concepts, explains the significance and challenges of the Yellow Sea (Bohai Sea) migratory bird habitat, and the principles of AI-based course design, such as using ERNIE Bot to integrate the "human-land coordination concept" under the principle of problem-oriented, to provide a framework for teaching. Section 3 talks about AI-assisted course design, including course goals such as using AI to improve students' various abilities, course content from the three dimensions of "human-land coordination concept", combining a variety of activity tools to optimize learning paths, and help students explore and innovate. Section 4 builds an evaluation system, based on the three dimensions of "human-land relationship", details process and final evaluation, and the role of AI in it, to achieve objective, efficient, personalized and dynamic evaluation, and to help optimize teaching. Section 5 analyzes the limitations of AI application, such as problems in technology, students, and teachers, and proposes optimization strategies, such as building a data platform to improve the effect. Section 6 summarizes the results, emphasizes the effect of AI-supported course design and the significance of the evaluation system, outlines the innovation points and practical significance, and looks forward to the prospects of AI application.

2. Study Area and Design Concept

2.1. Study Tour Project Area

China's Yellow Sea (Bohai) Sea migratory bird habitat is an important node in the field of global ecological protection, located in the center of the East Asia-Australasian Migratory Bird Flyway [26]. This area is famous for its unique natural ecological environment and rich biodiversity, providing a key place for many endangered species to live, reproduce and migrate [27]. As an important part of the world's natural heritage, the ecological protection of the Yellow Sea (Bohai) Sea migratory bird habitat is not only of global significance, but also an important support for regional economic and social development [28].

As shown in Figure 1, China's Yellow (Bohai) Sea migratory bird habitat covers coastal areas such as Yancheng, Jiangsu, which are famous for their rich tidal wetland resources. It has large-scale intertidal mudflats and is one of the largest wetlands in East Asia. Every year, more than 2 million migratory birds stop, forage, or breed on this migration route, including rare species such as red-crowned cranes and black-headed gulls. These migratory birds not only rely on wetland resources here, but also play a vital role in global biodiversity conservation. Wetlands are a core component of migratory bird habitats and an important part of the Earth's ecosystem. However, due to human activities such as reclamation, industrial development, and pollution, the area and ecological functions of the Yellow (Bohai) Sea wetlands have declined significantly in the past few decades. In recent years, through international cooperation and policy promotion, the protection of China's Yellow (Bohai) Sea migratory bird habitats has achieved remarkable results, which provides students with a realistic and vivid case to understand the relationship between humans and land.

Figure 1. Location and overview of the Yellow Sea (Bohai Sea) migratory bird habitat in Yancheng, China.

The ecological protection of the Yellow (Bohai) Sea migratory bird habitats provides rich teaching resources and practical opportunities for geography research. During the research activities, students can observe the habitat behavior of migratory birds through field visits to the wetland environment and understand the dynamic changes in the wetland ecosystem. In addition, the conflict between wetland protection and development is also an important geographical issue, which can guide students to think about how to balance the relationship between economic development and ecological protection, thereby deepening their understanding of the "coordination of humans and land".

2.2. Design Concept

The "coordination of humans and land" is the key objective of the core literacy of geography, emphasizing the harmonious coexistence of human activities and the natural environment [29]. In high school geography teaching, the traditional classroom model makes it difficult for students to truly experience the complexity of the interaction between nature and humans, while geography study tours provide a new teaching method [30]. When designing study courses, integrating the "coordination of humans and land" into the teaching objectives and helping students internalize this concept through specific activities is the core challenge of course design [31].

We proposed a research-based course design concept supported by AI technology, as shown in Table 1. The core of this design concept is to integrate the problem situation setting, learning the resource optimization and dynamic feedback mechanism in the research-based process through the empowerment of AI, so as to maximize the teaching effect. Compared with traditional research-based design, the addition of ERNIE Bot has brought a lot of innovation to course design.

Table 1. Comparison of innovative functions and applications of AI technology in geographical research.

Category	AI Technology Capabilities	Specific Applications
Dynamic data support	Process and analyze complex geographic data in real time to provide students with dynamic learning resources.	1. Analyze wetland ecological changes and migratory patterns of migratory birds. 2. Generate ecological change models based on historical data to help students predict future trends.
Personalized learning paths	Provide personalized learning topic recommendations and adjust task difficulty and content based on student feedback.	1. Students can choose learning topics based on their interests (e.g., migratory bird ecology or wetland protection). 2. Adjust task content in real time to meet the learning needs of different students.
Immersive study experience	Generate virtual study scenarios and support student data analysis and conclusion generation in real time.	1. Generate a 3D wetland model in the pre-trip stage to help students familiarize themselves with the characteristics of the area. 2. Provide real-time data analysis support during the in-service stage to accelerate students' understanding and application of collected data.
Diversified evaluation mechanism	Quantitatively evaluate student performance and generate learning reports to improve learning strategies.	1. Quantitatively evaluate students' knowledge, practical ability, and innovative thinking. 2. AI-generated reports help students and teachers improve their learning processes and strategies.

2.3. Design Principles

To achieve the above innovations, this course design follows the following principles:

1. Problem-oriented: Driven by real ecological problems, guide students to conduct in-depth discussions on the conflict between wetland protection and development. Set up a multi-level problem chain through the ERNIE Bot dialog box, gradually guide students from phenomenon observation to data analysis, and finally propose solutions.

2. Task-driven: Design a variety of learning tasks in the course, such as remote sensing image analysis, bird migration data processing, etc., and use ERNIE Bot's image and document reading functions to support students in completing tasks.

3. Interactive learning: Enhance students' participation and interactivity in the learning process through ERNIE Bot's chatbot and virtual assistant.

4. Collaborative learning: Guide students to work in groups, use ERNIE Bot to share data and assign tasks, and complete complex learning tasks in a team.

By integrating AI technology into geographical research design, students can not only deepen their understanding of the "human–land coordination concept", but also improve their abilities in many aspects in practice. The first is analytical ability. With the help of AI, students can extract key information from large amounts of data and form scientific judgments. The second is innovation ability. The ecological simulation supported by ERNIE Bot allows students to explore multiple possible solutions and cultivate their creative thinking. Finally, it is about action. After the study, the protection plans and practical suggestions proposed with the assistance of ERNIE Bot help to transform the learning results into practical actions.

3. Geography Research Course Design Assisted by AI

3.1. Course Objectives

The introduction of AI technology has brought unprecedented innovation momentum to geography research courses [32]. It not only promotes the transfer of knowledge, but also provides new perspectives and methods for the cultivation of students' abilities. Through the deep involvement of AI, this course aims to improve students' geographical practice ability, systematic thinking and innovation ability, and enhance their awareness of sustainable development [33]. First, the course will use ERNIE Bot to help students collect, analyze, and visualize data, thereby improving their ability to use geographical tools. For example, in the process of formulating and optimizing ecological protection plans, ERNIE Bot will assist students in completing specific tasks, helping them to improve their understanding and application of geographical phenomena and data processing in actual operations. Secondly, the course encourages students to develop systematic thinking and innovation capabilities [3]. With the help of ERNIE Bot to analyze the dynamic changes in the relationship between humans and land in wetland ecosystems, students will think about problems from a holistic perspective, understand complex ecological processes, and propose innovative ecological management plans on this basis [34]. In addition, the scenario simulation and decision support tools provided by ERNIE Bot will stimulate students' innovative potential when facing real problems [25]. Finally, the course is committed to cultivating students' awareness of sustainable development [26]. Through the dynamic feedback mechanism and situational learning assisted by ERNIE Bot, students will deeply understand the importance of sustainable development while exploring the complex relationship between wetland protection and human development. During the task implementation and evaluation process, students will be guided to think about the harmonious coexistence of humans and nature, thus forming a comprehensive understanding of ecological protection and rational use of resources.

3.2. Course Content

Based on the core geographical literacy of "the view of human–land coordination", the course content is developed in three dimensions: "land to people", "people to land" and "human–land coordination". Combined with various practical activities such as field observation, data collection, and ecological monitoring, students can explore the relationship between people and the environment in real situations and propose solutions to practical problems with innovative thinking. The design of the research and study program follows the three major links of pre-trip thinking, on-trip research and study, and post-trip learning, ensuring that students can systematically and deeply master the course content in terms of the learning of theoretical knowledge, participation in practical activities, and reflection and summary. Each module is deeply integrated with AI technology to optimize students' learning path and task completion effect. The specific tasks of each link are carried out through a variety of activities and tools, such as maps, remote sensing images, and data analysis tools, so that students can explore the ecological value of China's Yellow (Bohai) Sea migratory bird habitat from multiple perspectives, and think about and innovate on its existence in combination with human activities. The on-trip research and study link is the core part of the course. Through field investigation activities in China's Yellow (Bohai) Sea migratory bird habitat, students can personally experience the interaction between humans and nature and explore the complexity of wetland ecosystems in dynamic changes. The specific content design of the specific study tour course is shown in Table 2.

Table 2. Course design for the study tour to the Yellow Sea (Bohai Sea) bird habitat in China.

Modules	Activity Topics	Place	Activity Content	How to Get Involved with AI	Design Intent
Thinking before going	Regional cognition and background analysis	Classroom	1. Use AI-generated dynamic maps and wetland models to learn about migratory bird routes and wetland change history.	1. ERNIE Bot generates dynamic maps and wetland models, providing intuitive learning resources.	Guide students to understand the dynamic changes in wetland ecology and its global conservation significance, laying the foundation for subsequent field investigations.
			2. Use educational chatbots to answer questions related to ecological protection and sort out the relationship between wetlands and migratory bird ecosystems.	2. ERNIE Bot's chatbot supports students in answering questions and supplementing knowledge in real time.	
	Remote sensing images and environmental monitoring	Classroom	1. Students use AI-assisted remote sensing images to compare changes in wetland area over different eras.	1. ERNIE Bot processes remote sensing images over multiple time periods and generates wetland change trend maps in real time.	Cultivate students' ability to analyze geographic information and help them understand the driving factors of wetland ecological changes.
			2. Use AI to analyze the specific impact of human activities on wetland ecology.	2. ERNIE Bot automatically identifies key impact points of human activities (such as industrial development and tourism) on the ecosystem.	
Study on the Go	From the edge to the center: the return of the Chinese elk and the harmony between people and the land	Chinese Elk Park	1. Students use AI to collect data such as temperature, humidity, and air pressure to analyze the differences in natural conditions in elk habitats.	1. ERNIE Bot analyzes the data collected by students in real time and presents the correlation between natural conditions and ecological behaviors.	Help students intuitively understand the importance of the natural environment to the survival of species, and explore the dynamic changes in the relationship between humans and land through actual data.
			2. Using AI-generated ecological data, students study the impact of human activities on the habitat of elk.	2. ERNIE Bot generates a dynamic model of human activities and habitat suitability to assist students in drawing conclusions.	
	Green Ocean: Construction of Forest Ecosystem and Human–Land Relationship	Huanghai National Forest Park	1. Using AI-supported environmental measurement tools, students measure ecological data such as soil moisture in different zones and distribution of vegetation communities.	1. ERNIE Bot analyzes students' soil moisture and vegetation distribution data in real time, and automatically generates a visual report on the relationship between environmental factors and ecosystems.	Guide students to understand the impact of human activities on forest ecology through data and behavioral records, and explore how to achieve sustainable use of forest resources.
			2. Record the impact of tourist behavior and forest management measures on ecological balance, and use AI to generate a report on the ecological impact of behavior.	2. ERNIE Bot identifies visitor behavior data and provides automatic analysis and management optimization suggestions for ecological disturbance.	

Table 2. *Cont.*

Modules	Activity Topics	Place	Activity Content	How to Get Involved with AI	Design Intent
	Migratory bird paradise: practice of ecological balance and sustainable development	Tiaozini Wetland	1. Students use telescopes to record the behavioral characteristics of migratory birds, and AI helps to count population data and analyze its changing trends.	1. ERNIE Bot processes the migratory bird observation data uploaded by students and generates a dynamic analysis report on population size and behavioral characteristics.	Through observation and data analysis, students can understand the dynamic relationship between human activities and the natural environment and propose ecological protection strategies for sustainable development.
			2. Use AI to simulate the impact of different development or protection measures on wetland ecosystems and propose a balance between protection and development.	2. ERNIE Bot's ecological simulation tool generates an ecological impact prediction model based on the scenarios input by students, supporting students in optimizing strategy design.	
Post-trip learning	Ecological protection plan display	Classroom	1. Student teams present wetland protection plans, including data analysis results and innovative suggestions.	1. ERNIE Bot generates group data analysis reports to quantitatively evaluate the scientific nature of student solutions.	Guide students through the complete path from data to decision-making, and cultivate innovation capabilities and awareness of sustainable development.
			2. AI evaluates the scientificity and innovation of the solution, generates feedback reports, and provides optimization directions.	2. ERNIE Bot provides improvement suggestions based on ecological theory to support students in further optimizing their solutions.	
	Community Outreach and Environmental Action	Community	1. Students make environmental protection posters or videos, and AI helps to proofread the scientificity and logic of the content.	1. ERNIE Bot reviews the scientific validity of students' promotional content and provides optimization suggestions.	Transform students' learning outcomes into practical actions and enhance their sense of social responsibility and leadership.
			2. Use AI interactive platforms to promote wetland protection concepts, record community feedback and generate data reports.	2. ERNIE Bot analyzes community feedback data and automatically generates campaign impact assessment reports to support improvements in subsequent environmental protection actions.	

4. Evaluation System

The evaluation system plays a vital role in the design of research and study courses. Its core goal is to comprehensively evaluate students' ability performance in all aspects of the entire research and study process, including knowledge mastery, practical ability, innovative thinking, and the degree of understanding of the core concept of "human–land coordination" [27]. In the design of this research and study course, we adopted three core evaluation dimensions: "land to people", "people to land", and "human–land coordination" [35]. Each dimension reveals the interaction between human activities and the natural environment from different perspectives, and can help students deepen their understanding of the core geographical literacy of "human–land coordination" in real geographical contexts. The following is a brief description of each dimension and its important role in geographical research and study.

The impact of "land on people": This dimension focuses on the impact of the natural environment on human activities, helping students understand how the natural environment affects human survival, development, and social activities through factors such as climate, topography, and biodiversity. During the study process, students understand the importance of wetland resources to migratory birds and human production and life through field observations and data analysis. This dimension can cultivate students' sensitivity to the natural environment and its constraints, enhance their understanding of regional geographical characteristics, and help students understand the profound impact of nature on humans from the perspective of ecosystem functions [36].

Impact of "people on land": This dimension focuses on how human activities affect the natural environment, especially the changes in the ecosystem caused by human activities such as agriculture, industry, and tourism development. Through field visits to migratory bird habitats, students can intuitively understand the negative impacts of human activities on wetland ecosystems (such as pollution and habitat destruction) as well as positive ecological restoration measures. This dimension cultivates students' ability to analyze and evaluate the long-term impact of human activities on the natural environment, stimulates their ability to explore sustainable development paths, and enhances their environmental awareness and sense of responsibility [37].

"Human–land relationship coordination": This dimension explores how to promote human economic and social development and achieve harmonious coexistence between humans and nature while maintaining ecological balance. Through data analysis and group discussions, students propose innovative solutions between wetland protection and community development, such as the development of ecotourism and wetland restoration plans. This dimension helps students comprehensively consider the complex relationship between humans and the environment, exercises their dialectical thinking and innovation ability, and cultivates students to propose coordination strategies that take into account both ecological protection and social development [38].

In order to achieve the course objectives, the evaluation system of this course is divided into two parts: process evaluation and final evaluation. Through the deep support of the intelligent tool ERNIE Bot, dynamic monitoring and accurate feedback are ensured [33]. AI technology plays a key role in this process. First, it provides an accurate evaluation basis through real-time data analysis. AI can analyze students' data collection, task completion, and teamwork performance in research and study activities in real time; quantify students' performance; and generate core data for process evaluation. These data can not only reflect students' immediate performance in the course, but also provide an important basis for subsequent learning strategy adjustments [39]. Secondly, AI generates personalized learning reports based on students' performance in the tasks. These reports not only summarize students' strengths, but also accurately identify their shortcomings and provide practical suggestions for improvement [34]. Through these personalized reports, students can understand their learning progress more clearly and take more targeted measures to improve themselves [40]. Finally, AI also provides students with real-time interactive feedback through a dynamic feedback system [41]. This system can help students intuitively understand their learning effects and shortcomings, further optimize their learning paths, and ensure that they can achieve better growth and improvement in research and study activities [42].

4.1. Process Evaluation

Process evaluation aims to record students' performance in research and study activities, including knowledge mastery, practical operation ability, teamwork, and depth of thinking [43]. Through this evaluation, students can reflect on their performance in the task after each activity and adjust their learning strategies in a timely manner [44].

As shown in Table 3, with the help of ERNIE Bot's real-time monitoring and data analysis, the evaluation system is more accurate and efficient. During the study activities, the migratory bird data, soil moisture, and other information collected by students will be analyzed in real time by ERNIE Bot to generate a visual data report. ERNIE Bot will also track the completion of students' tasks and quantify their performance. After each activity, ERNIE Bot will automatically generate a phased feedback report covering the advantages and improvement directions of the group and individuals, providing students with continuous growth support.

Table 3. Study tour process evaluation table.

Evaluation Dimensions	Evaluation Project	Evaluation Criteria	AI Analysis Support
Knowledge Mastery	Wetland ecosystem and migratory bird habitat	Whether students can accurately understand the dynamic changes in wetland ecosystems and the ecological significance of migratory bird migration.	ERNIE Bot evaluates students' depth of understanding of ecosystem and migratory bird data based on their answers and data analysis results.
	Forest ecosystem and the impact of human activities	Can students analyze the environmental factors of forest ecology and the ecological impacts of human activities?	ERNIE Bot quantifies students' ability to process soil moisture and vegetation distribution data and generates charts for display.
Practical Operation	Data collection and processing capabilities	Whether students can correctly use instruments (such as telescopes and soil moisture meters) to complete data collection and use AI to process data.	ERNIE Bot detects the accuracy and completeness of data collection and generates real-time feedback.
	Simulation of ecological models and predictive capabilities	Can students use AI to generate ecological simulation models and make predictive conclusions?	ERNIE Bot evaluates the scientificity of students' models and the rationality of their predictions, and quantifies the accuracy of the simulation parameters used.
Teamwork	Task division and collaboration	Whether students have clear division of roles in group work and whether they can effectively communicate and collaborate with team members to complete tasks.	ERNIE Bot analyzes the efficiency and contribution ratio of team collaboration by recording task submission time and discussion records.
Depth of thinking	Data analysis and reflection	Can students draw scientific conclusions based on data and make suggestions for improvement based on reflection?	ERNIE Bot automatically analyzes students' data reports, marks logical loopholes and provides directions for improvement.

4.2. Summative Evaluation

The summative evaluation is used to comprehensively assess students' overall performance throughout the research and study course, including knowledge mastery, skill improvement, and the understanding and application of the core literacy of 'human–land coordination', as well as individual and group achievements and learning attitudes [34]. The summative evaluation not only includes individual student performance, but also integrates the group performance and the students' final project results. The summative evaluation form combines research and study reports, research and study manuals, photographic works, and other forms to ensure the comprehensiveness of the evaluation system. AI helps quantify students' comprehensive performance in this process and generates accurate personalized learning reports [41]. During the evaluation process, ERNIE Bot will summarize and analyze students' task data, program design and presentation, and generate personalized learning reports [42]. As shown in Table 4, by quantifying the overall performance of the group, ERNIE Bot will also compare the innovation and scientificity of the programs of different groups [43]. In addition, ERNIE Bot combines students' knowledge mastery, practical results, and innovative thinking to generate a comprehensive score to comprehensively evaluate students' performance [44].

Table 4. Summative evaluation.

Evaluation Dimensions	Evaluation Project	Evaluation Criteria	AI Analysis Support
Knowledge Application	Analysis and application of wetland and migratory bird data	Can students accurately explain the results of data analysis in their presentations and explain the phenomena using theories?	ERNIE Bot analyzes the accuracy and logic of the data used in the presentation and assesses the depth of students' integration of theory and practice.
	A balanced approach to ecological protection and development	Can students design feasible plans that take into account both ecological protection and economic development, and clearly express their scientific basis?	ERNIE Bot quantifies the innovations in the solution and generates targeted improvement suggestions.
Practical results	Data analysis and visualization	Can students complete analysis based on the collected data and create dynamic maps or charts?	ERNIE Bot detects the scientificity and completeness of charts and provides visual improvement directions.
	Model design and prediction capabilities	Can students use AI to generate ecological prediction models and verify their rationality?	ERNIE Bot analyzes model parameters and evaluates the accuracy and scientificity of predictions.
Teamwork	Group task division and results integration	Whether the team can efficiently complete the division of tasks and integrate the presentation to form systematic results.	ERNIE Bot counts team members' task participation and contribution ratios to evaluate the efficiency of team collaboration.
Innovative thinking	Ecological protection innovation	Whether students can propose innovative strategies in their plans and provide theoretical and data support.	ERNIE Bot identifies the innovative points in the solution and provides optimization directions.

4.3. AI Evaluation Summary and Feedback

After each research activity, a discussion session will be set up to encourage students to reflect on their performance through self-evaluation and mutual evaluation, and summarize their learning gains under the guidance of teachers [45]. The content of the discussion will cover the students' shortcomings and improvement points in practical operations, as well as their progress in thinking depth and innovation [36]. The teacher will provide written feedback after the discussion to help students further improve the research effect [35]. As shown in Table 5, in the entire evaluation process, AI not only undertakes the tasks of data analysis and report generation, but also helps students and teachers optimize the learning process through real-time feedback and personalized suggestions.

The evaluation system is deeply empowered by AI technology, which not only improves the objectivity and efficiency of evaluation, but also realizes personalized and dynamic feedback support. Under the guidance of AI, students can understand their own learning strengths and weaknesses and optimize their learning paths; teachers can adjust their teaching strategies through accurate evaluation data, and ultimately improve the effectiveness and quality of the entire research course.

Table 5. The multi-dimensional role of AI in evaluation summary and feedback.

Functional Category	Specific Content	The Role of AI Support
Generate personalized learning reports	1. Summarize students' knowledge, practical ability and innovative program design, generate personalized learning reports, and mark problems and strengths.	ERNIE Bot points out errors in the processing of migratory bird data in the data analysis report and provides directions for improvement.
		ERNIE Bot quantifies the innovativeness of solution designs and provides more scientific optimization suggestions.
Real-time dynamic feedback	1. In the process of evaluation, students can view the task completion progress and analysis results in real time.	Through ERNIE Bot's interactive feedback system, students can intuitively understand their performance and shortcomings in each aspect.
	2. In summative evaluation, generate suggestions in real time based on the presentation content to support student learning improvement.	ERNIE Bot provides dynamic progress and improvement suggestions for task completion to enhance the targeted nature of learning.
Improved learning paths	1. Based on students' comprehensive performance, recommend personalized learning improvement plans to help students make up for their shortcomings.	ERNIE Bot recommends more detailed data analysis guidance content to students with weaker performance.
	2. Provide more challenging tasks for high-performing students.	ERNIE Bot provides high-performing students with more complex ecological protection problem tasks and cultivates advanced analytical and problem-solving skills.

4.4. *Test and Effect Evaluation*

4.4.1. Process Test

The process test aims to comprehensively and dynamically monitor the development of students' abilities and knowledge mastery during the course study through a variety of test forms and high-frequency assessments, discover students' learning strengths and weaknesses in a timely manner, and provide a basis for personalized learning support and teaching strategy adjustments. The specific test content is shown in Table 6.

Table 6. Process test content.

Test Category	Specific Test Content	Test Format	Scoring Subject and Method
Knowledge mastery test	Knowledge on wetland ecosystem and migratory bird habitat	Weekly online quiz (5 multiple-choice questions, 3 short-answer questions, 2 analytical questions)	ERNIE Bot is evaluated based on answering questions and data analysis results, for teachers to refer to
	Knowledge on forest ecosystems and the impact of human activities	Group discussion and report every two weeks	Teachers grade students based on discussion performance (participation, accuracy, and depth of ideas) and presentation content
Practical skills test	Data collection and processing capabilities practice	After the field investigation, data will be collated and analyzed and a report will be submitted	ERNIE Bot is scored based on data accuracy, completeness, and analysis rationality
	Simulation ecological model and predictive capability practice	Use tools to build models and predict ecological change trends	Teachers and ERNIE Bot jointly evaluate the scientific nature of the model, the rationality of the prediction, and the ability to apply knowledge tools

Table 6. *Cont.*

Test Category	Specific Test Content	Test Format	Scoring Subject and Method
Teamwork ability test	Task division and collaboration observation	During each group activity, the teacher observes and ERNIE Bot records	Teachers make observations and ERNIE Bot analyzes team collaboration efficiency and other scores based on records.
	Teamwork project assessment	Monthly teamwork project presentation and evaluation (with the participation of other groups and teachers)	Other groups, teachers, and ERNIE Bot will rate based on project goals, division of labor, collaboration, results, etc.
Depth of thinking test	Data analysis and reflection report	Write a report after completing data collection and analysis	ERNIE Bot analysis report logic, depth and reflection effectiveness rating
	Problem-solving and Creative thinking challenges	Set questions from time to time and discuss solutions in groups	Teachers and ERNIE Bot evaluate the innovation, feasibility, flexibility, and depth of thinking of the solution

4.4.2. Summative Test

The summative test focuses on the comprehensive evaluation of the comprehensive learning outcomes achieved by students after the completion of the entire research course, and considers students' mastery of course content, ability improvement level, and understanding and practical ability in terms of core literacy from multiple dimensions, such as knowledge application, practical results, and overall team performance, to determine whether students have achieved the expected goals of the course. The specific content is shown in Table 7.

Table 7. Summative test content.

Test Category	Specific Test Content	Test Format	Scoring Subject and Method
Comprehensive test on knowledge application	Research results report and defense	After the course, the group will present and defend their research	Teachers grade the reports based on accuracy, logic, depth, and the degree of "coordination between humans and land". ERNIE Bot helps analyze the data.
	Study manual and knowledge summary assessment	Check the study manual and personal knowledge summary	Teachers grade the construction and deepening of the knowledge system based on the comprehensive accuracy, depth of knowledge understanding, and degree of integration with practice in the manual. ERNIE Bot assists in data analysis.
Comprehensive evaluation of practical results	Field investigation results display and evaluation	Present field investigation materials and analyze and propose solutions	Teachers grade the data based on the quality of the data, scientific analysis, and feasibility of the solution, and ERNIE Bot helps analyze the data
	Evaluation of innovative practice works	Submit innovative practice works (posters, videos, plans, etc.)	Teachers evaluate from multiple dimensions such as innovation, scientificity, practicality, and artistry, and ERNIE Bot helps analyze the rationality of data application, etc.

Table 7. *Cont.*

Test Category	Specific Test Content	Test Format	Scoring Subject and Method
Overall team performance evaluation	Quality assessment of team project results	Comprehensive evaluation of team projects (publicity activities, protection program implementation, etc.)	Teachers conduct field visits, community feedback surveys, and project report scoring, and ERNIE Bot assists in data analysis
	Team member growth and development analysis	Compare the performance of team members before and after the course, and analyze the role of collaboration in individual growth	Teachers conduct comprehensive evaluation based on observation and students' self-evaluation and peer evaluation, and ERNIE Bot assists in data analysis

4.4.3. Test Results Before and After the Course

1. Knowledge mastery. In the test of wetland ecosystems and migratory bird habitats, at the beginning of the course, the average score of students was about 60 points, the correct rate of multiple-choice questions was about 60%, the answers to short-answer questions were relatively brief, and the analytical questions generally lacked depth. As the course progressed, after multiple knowledge tests and learning activities, the average score in the middle of the course increased to about 75 points, the correct rate of multiple-choice questions increased to 80%, the short-answer questions were able to explain the principles in more detail, and the analytical questions began to be analyzed in depth with actual cases. At the end of the course, the average score reached more than 85 points, the correct rate of multiple-choice questions stabilized at more than 90%, the answers to short-answer questions were accurate and in-depth, and the analytical questions were able to comprehensively and deeply analyze the complex relationship between wetland ecological changes and migratory bird habitat changes. In the group discussion and report on the knowledge of forest ecosystems and the impact of human activities, at the beginning of the course, students had low participation, superficial views, and an insufficient ability to integrate and apply knowledge, with an average score of about 65 points. After a series of learning and practical activities, the students' participation in the course was significantly improved in the middle of the course. They were able to put forward some valuable ideas, and their ability to integrate and apply knowledge was enhanced. The average score increased to about 80 points. At the end of the course, the students were active in the discussion, able to deeply analyze the relationship between forest ecosystems and human activities, and could use the knowledge they learned to put forward reasonable protection and development suggestions, with an average score of more than 90 points.

2. Practical operation ability. In the practice of data collection and processing ability, at the beginning of the course, students had major problems in the accuracy of data collection, such as large errors in the statistical number of migratory birds and inaccurate soil moisture measurements. Data processing was also relatively unfamiliar, and the average score was only about 50 points. With the increase in the number of practices and the real-time guidance of ERNIE Bot, the accuracy of the students' data collection increased to more than 80% in the middle of the course, and they were able to skillfully use tools for data processing, with an average score of about 75 points. At the end of the course, the accuracy of the students' data collection reached more than 95%, and they were able to efficiently and accurately complete data processing and analysis, with an average score of more than 90 points. In the practice of simulating ecological models and predictive ability, at the beginning of the course, the models constructed by students had many scientific problems, the prediction results were unreasonable, and the average score was about 45 points. With the deepening of learning and the proficiency of the ERNIE Bot simulation tool,

the scientificity and predictive rationality of the model in the middle of the course were significantly improved, and the average score increased to about 70 points. At the end of the course, students were able to build a more complex and scientific ecological model, and the prediction results were highly reliable, with an average score of more than 85 points.

3. Teamwork ability. In the task division and collaboration observation, at the beginning of the course, some teams had problems such as unreasonable task allocation and poor communication among members, and the team collaboration efficiency was low, with an average score of about 60 points. After the guidance of teachers and the running-in of multiple team activities, the team collaboration situation in the middle of the course was significantly improved, the task division was more reasonable, the communication was smoother, and the average score increased to about 80 points. At the end of the course, the team members cooperated well and were able to complete the tasks efficiently, with an average score of more than 90 points. In the evaluation of teamwork projects, at the beginning of the course, the group projects had problems such as unclear goals and insufficient innovation in results, with an average score of about 65 points. With the improvement of teamwork ability and the cultivation of innovative thinking, the quality of the mid-course projects improved significantly, with clear goals and certain innovation in results, and the average score increased to about 85 points. At the end of the course, the group projects performed well in terms of goal achievement, innovative design, and results presentation, with an average score of more than 95 points.

4. Depth of thinking. In the data analysis and reflection report, at the beginning of the course, the logic of the student report content was poor, the reflection was not in-depth, and the improvement measures were not targeted, with an average score of about 55 points. As the course progressed, students gradually learned to analyze data in depth, their logical thinking ability was enhanced, their reflection was more profound, and their improvement measures were operational. The average score in the middle of the course increased to about 75 points. At the end of the course, students were able to write high-quality data analysis and reflection reports, with a high level of thinking depth and logic, and an average score of more than 90 points. In the problem solving and innovative thinking challenges, at the beginning of the course, the solutions proposed by students were relatively conventional, lacked innovation, and their thinking was not flexible enough, with an average score of about 50 points. After many challenges and much learning, students began to propose some novel solutions in the middle of the course, their thinking flexibility improved, and the average score increased to about 70 points. At the end of the course, students were able to propose innovative and feasible solutions to complex geographical problems, and their thinking depth and innovation ability were significantly improved, with an average score of more than 85 points.

5. Comprehensive test of knowledge application. In the report and defense of research results, the average score after the end of the course reached 88 points. In their reports, students were able to accurately apply geographical knowledge, deeply analyze the relationship between the Yellow Sea (Bohai Sea) migratory bird habitat ecosystem and human activities, and clearly explain the application of the "human–land coordination concept" in actual cases. For example, when explaining the relationship between wetland protection and the economic development of surrounding communities, they were able to use geographical principles to propose reasonable coordination plans. During the defense of their research, students were able to accurately answer questions raised by experts, showing a deep understanding and proficient application of knowledge. In the evaluation of the study manual and knowledge summary, the average score was 90 points. The students' study manuals were detailed and accurate, not only containing the key points of geographical knowledge, but also recording the observations and thoughts during the field investigation.

The personal knowledge summary can systematically sort out the knowledge learned during the study, deeply understand the connection between geographical concepts and principles, and reflect the construction and deepening of the knowledge system.

6. Comprehensive evaluation of practical results. In the display and evaluation of field investigation results, the average score was 92 points. The field investigation materials presented by the students are rich and detailed, and can accurately reflect the current situation and problems of wetland and forest ecosystems. The analysis of the data is in-depth and scientific. For example, by comparing photos of migratory bird habitats in different periods, the causes of ecological changes are accurately analyzed, and targeted protection measures are proposed. The solutions are highly feasible. For example, the proposed wetland ecological restoration plan combines local actual conditions and takes into account multiple factors such as ecology, economy, and society. In the evaluation of innovative practice works, the average score was 90 points. The students' innovative practice works were outstanding in terms of innovation. For example, some propaganda posters used unique perspectives and creative techniques to attract the audience's attention to ecological protection issues; the ecological protection plan proposed a novel ecotourism model that takes into account ecological protection and economic development. The scientificity and practicality of the works have also been recognized by experts. For example, the construction of the ecological prediction model conformed to scientific principles and can provide reference for actual decision-making.

7. Evaluation of the overall performance of the team. In the quality evaluation of the team project results, the average score was 95 points. In the ecological protection community publicity activities, the team effectively raised the ecological protection awareness of community residents through various forms (such as holding lectures, distributing publicity materials, organizing field experiences, etc.), and the participation in the activities was high, which was highly recognized by the community. In the implementation of the migratory bird habitat protection plan, the team was able to formulate detailed plans based on actual conditions and effectively implement them, achieving significant ecological protection results, such as an increase in the number of migratory birds and improvements in the habitat's ecological environment. In the analysis of the growth and development of team members, it was found that team members had significantly improved in terms of knowledge mastery, practical operations, and thinking patterns. For example, students who originally had a weak foundation in geography knowledge were able to skillfully use knowledge to solve practical problems through team collaboration and learning; the collaboration and communication skills among members were greatly exercised, forming a good team atmosphere, and promoting the all-round development of individuals.

4.4.4. Student Feedback on AI-Enabled Teaching Methods

1. Improved learning interest. More than 90% of the students said that the application of AI technology makes the learning process more vivid and interesting. For example, the 3D wetland model generated by ERNIE Bot made them feel as if they were there, enhancing their intuitive feeling of the geographical environment and thus stimulating their interest in learning. Students generally believe that the personalized learning path provided by AI can meet their different needs, allowing them to choose learning content according to their interests. For example, students interested in migratory bird ecology could explore related knowledge in depth, which improved their autonomy and enthusiasm for learning.

2. Improved learning efficiency. About 85% of the students reported that the powerful functions of AI tools for data processing and analysis have greatly saved time. When processing a large amount of migratory bird observation data and wetland ecological monitoring data, ERNIE Bot can quickly and accurately complete the analysis, helping

them to obtain valuable information in a timely manner, thereby improving learning efficiency. The real-time feedback mechanism is highly praised by students. In total, 75% of the students said that during the practical operation, ERNIE Bot could immediately point out problems and provide improvement suggestions, enabling them to adjust their learning strategies in time and avoiding wasting time in the wrong direction.

3. Improved perception of ability. In total, 95% of the students believe that their practical operation ability has been significantly improved through AI-enabled research courses. When using AI-assisted instruments for data collection and processing, they not only mastered advanced technical means, but also learned how to combine data with actual geographical phenomena for analysis, improving their practical hands-on ability. About 90% of the students feel that their innovative thinking ability has been exercised. With the support of virtual research scenarios and ecological simulation tools provided by AI, they were able to try different solutions and cultivate innovative awareness and innovation ability.

4. Overall evaluation of teaching methods. More than 95% of students are satisfied or very satisfied with the AI-enabled geographical research travel teaching method. They believe that this teaching method breaks the limitations of traditional teaching, allowing them to better understand and apply knowledge in real geographical situations, while cultivating a variety of abilities, which has a positive role in promoting their learning and growth.

5. Limitations of and Optimization Strategies for AI-Driven High School Geography Research Design

The application of AI in high school geography research and study provides great potential for the innovation of teaching models. However, in practice, AI-driven geography research and study design also faces some limitations that cannot be ignored. These limitations involve both technical bottlenecks and difficulties in teaching implementation and resource allocation. Therefore, exploring these limitations and proposing optimization strategies are of great significance to further improving the application effect of AI in geography research and study.

5.1. Limitations of AI in High School Geography Research

1. Insufficient technical adaptability

AI technology can achieve data analysis, dynamic feedback, and personalized support in geographical research and study, but its effectiveness is highly dependent on high-quality data input and the support of technical platforms. In ecological monitoring and geographic information system (GIS) applications, real-time updated data are particularly needed. However, in some remote areas, environmental data may be missing or inaccurate [46]. This problem is particularly prominent in the context of rural revitalization. Rural primary schools in some areas may face the problem of incomplete data collection, which affects the application effect of AI systems. For example, in the study activities of migratory bird habitats in the Yellow (Bohai) Sea, wetland ecological monitoring data may not cover all key nodes, which directly leads to certain deviations in the ecological model predictions generated by AI [47]. In this way, although AI can process and analyze large amounts of data, if there are loopholes or errors in the basic data, the final analysis results may be inaccurate, thus affecting students' understanding of and practice in the ecosystem.

In addition, the use of AI technology is highly dependent on the internet and high-performance devices [35]. In research and study activities, students need to access and operate AI through internet connections and advanced devices, but in some cases where the network is unstable or the equipment is in poor condition, all functions in the research and study design may not be realized. This technical dependence limits the widespread application of AI in different regions and schools, especially in some resource-scarce regions, where the advantages of AI technology in education may not be fully utilized.

2. Differences in students' abilities and learning habits

Although AI technology can support personalized learning, its application effect is still affected by students' basic abilities and learning habits [48]. Some students may lack the necessary data analysis skills or have insufficient understanding of AI, which may limit their participation and learning effects in research and study activities [3]. In particular, when operating AI, students of different abilities may face different difficulties [49]. For example, in the process of ecological model design and data visualization, some students may not fully understand the generated results, which affects their in-depth understanding and practical application of the learning content [50].

In addition, some students are overly dependent on AI-generated feedback, which may weaken their ability to think independently and practice [51]. Although AI can provide rapid analysis and feedback, over-reliance on AI may lead to students' lack of independent problem-solving ability, which in turn affects their critical thinking and innovation ability [52].

3. Transformation and adaptation of teachers' roles

The introduction of AI technology has placed higher demands on the role of teachers. Teachers not only need to master traditional teaching skills, but also need to be familiar with the operation and application of AI technology and be able to effectively guide students to use AI to complete tasks [53]. However, some teachers may face challenges in adapting and applying technology, especially in highly technical aspects such as data analysis and model design [54]. The existence of technical barriers means that the depth of teachers' understanding of AI directly affects the effectiveness of teaching design [50]. If technical training is insufficient, teachers may find it difficult to fully utilize the functions of AI, which will affect students' learning experience and the overall effect of research and study activities.

At the same time, the deep involvement of AI has also posed new challenges to the role of teachers. In traditional teaching, teachers are often in a dominant position, but the introduction of AI may weaken this dominance and give more control over learning to students and technology [44]. In this context, finding a balance between technical support and teaching guidance, taking advantage of AI while retaining the leading role of teachers, has become an important issue. This requires teachers to not only be users of AI, but also become a bridge between students and technology, redefining their roles and responsibilities in the context of AI-assisted teaching [10].

5.2. Optimization Strategy

In view of the above limitations, we propose the following optimization strategies to further improve the application effect of AI in geographical research design.

1. Improve data quality and technology platforms

To ensure the integrity and real-time nature of the data, a regional ecological data sharing platform can be established to cooperate with scientific research institutions and government departments. For example, cooperation with the Yellow (Bohai) Sea Bird Conservation Organization to obtain more accurate migratory bird data. This will not only help improve the accuracy of the AI model, but also promote the coordinated development of ecological protection and scientific research. At the same time, in order to support the smooth progress of research and study activities, it is necessary to provide a stable internet environment and high-performance equipment, especially in remote areas. Considering the special conditions in these areas, the application of portable devices and offline functions is particularly important, can effectively ensure the smooth development of research and study activities, and can continue to collect and analyze data even in an unstable network environment.

2. Strengthen students' technical training

During the pre-trip thinking stage, special training on the use of AI should be introduced to ensure that students master basic data processing and model operation skills. This will help students use AI more confidently in research and study activities, thereby improving learning efficiency and task completion. At the same time, in order to adapt to the differences in the abilities of different students, tiered teaching can be designed to provide basic and challenging task options. In this way, students can choose appropriate tasks to participate in according to their ability levels, which can ensure that students with weaker basic abilities can also obtain an effective learning experience, and sufficient challenges for students with higher abilities can be provided, stimulating their innovative thinking and interest in in-depth exploration. This tiered design helps to enhance each student's sense of participation and accomplishment.

3. Improve teachers' AI application capabilities

In order to improve teachers' AI application capabilities, systematic AI technology application training can be provided to teachers, covering GIS operations, ecological model construction, dynamic data analysis, and other aspects. This will help teachers better master the use of AI and improve their technical application capabilities in teaching. At the same time, in order to reduce the technical burden on teachers, an AI teaching assistant system can be introduced to assist teachers in task assignment, data analysis, and feedback report generation. With the support of AI teaching assistants, teachers can focus more on teaching design and student guidance, improve teaching efficiency and effectiveness, and ensure the smooth application of AI technology in the classroom.

4. Enrich AI functions and teaching scenarios

In order to stimulate students' interest in learning, personalized learning resource recommendation options can be provided to students. For example, relevant case studies and the latest scientific research results in the field of ecological protection can be provided so that students can be exposed to richer and more cutting-edge knowledge. This can not only enhance students' interest in the subject, but can also help them better understand practical applications and scientific research trends.

At the same time, AI technology can be combined with other disciplines (such as biology, environmental science, etc.) to design interdisciplinary tasks. This interdisciplinary integration approach helps to improve students' comprehensive literacy and cultivate their systematic thinking and ability to solve complex problems. By combining knowledge and skills from different fields, students can not only master AI technology, but can also have a deeper understanding of the connection and application between disciplines, thereby improving their comprehensive learning ability and innovation ability.

5.3. Application Prospects After Optimization

Through the above optimization strategies, the application of AI in geographical research will be more efficient and comprehensive. On the basis of mastering AI, students can complete tasks more confidently and propose scientific and innovative solutions. Personalized learning resource recommendations and hierarchical task design will greatly enhance students' sense of participation and achievement, and inspire their active exploration spirit in ecological protection and geographical research. At the same time, the role of teachers has transformed from a simple knowledge transmitter to a guide for the use of AI and a feedback analyst of the learning process. With the help of AI, teachers can perform data analysis and student performance evaluation more efficiently, provide more targeted guidance and support, and improve teaching effectiveness. Based on high-quality data and optimized AI functions, geographical research courses can be expanded to more ecological scenarios, cover a wider range of subject knowledge, dynamically update course content, and cultivate students' more comprehensive subject literacy and sustainable development awareness. This innovative course model supported by AI not only improves learning efficiency and teaching quality, but also promotes the transformation of the education model and promotes students to master the ability to solve real problems in practice.

6. Conclusions

With the continuous development of AI technology in the field of education, we focused on its exploration in the design and application of high school geography study and research. Taking the China Yellow (Bohai) Sea migratory bird habitat study and research course as an example, we have achieved a series of significant results.

First, in terms of design concept, we used AI (ERNIE Bot) as a support, integrated the problem situation setting, the learning resource optimization and the dynamic feedback mechanism, and formed an innovative research and study course design concept. By providing dynamic data support, personalized learning paths, immersive research and study experiences, and a diversified evaluation mechanism, it significantly improves students' learning experience and ability training.

Secondly, in terms of course content, we focused on the "coordination of people and land", covering pre-trip thinking, on-trip research, and post-trip learning. In each link, with the help of a variety of practical activities and tools, such as field investigations, data collection, ecological monitoring, maps, remote sensing images, and data analysis tools, AI technology is deeply integrated to optimize students' learning paths and task completion results.

Subsequently, we established an evaluation system based on the three dimensions of "land to people", "people to land" and the "coordination of human–land relationships" to comprehensively evaluate students' performance in terms of knowledge mastery, practical ability, innovative thinking, and understanding of the "coordination between people and land".

With the help of ERNIE Bot, process evaluation and final evaluation are intelligentized. In the process evaluation, the students' data collection, task completion, and teamwork performance were monitored in real time, and visual data reports and phased feedback reports were generated; in the final evaluation, the task data, program design, and presentation were summarized and analyzed, and personalized learning reports and comprehensive scores were generated. This not only improves the objectivity and efficiency of evaluation, but also provides personalized and dynamic feedback support to students and teachers, effectively optimizing learning and teaching strategies.

In general, we have provided a brand-new teaching model for high school geography education, organically combining traditional geographical research with modern AI technology, breaking the limitations of traditional teaching, and providing practical reference for the innovative development of geography teaching.

Author Contributions: Conceptualization, B.L., Y.P. and N.Y.; methodology, B.L. and W.Z.; software, B.L. and W.L.; formal analysis, B.L. and W.L.; investigation, B.L. and W.Z.; resources, B.L. and Y.P.; data curation, B.L. and N.Y.; writing—original draft preparation, B.L. and Y.P.; writing—review and editing, B.L. and W.L.; visualization, B.L.; supervision, N.Y. and W.L.; project administration, B.L. and N.Y.; funding acquisition, B.L. All authors have read and agreed to the published version of the manuscript.

Funding: This research was funded by the Nanning Normal University Demonstration Modern Industrial College (No. 6020303891920), Nanning Normal University Characteristic Undergraduate College Construction and College Teaching Quality and Reform Engineering Project—Undergraduate Education and Teaching Key Project (No. 6020303891924), Nanning Normal University Doctoral Research Startup Project (No. 602021239447).

Data Availability Statement: The original contributions presented in this study are included in the article. Further inquiries can be directed to the corresponding author(s).

Conflicts of Interest: The authors declare no conflicts of interest.

References

1. Pedro, F.; Subosa, M.; Rivas, A.; Valverde, P. Artificial Intelligence in Education: Challenges and Opportunities for Sustainable Development. 2019. Available online: http://repositorio.minedu.gob.pe/handle/20.500.12799/6533 (accessed on 21 November 2024).
2. Sun, Q. The Functional Mechanism, Practical Challenges and Path Selection of Artificial Intelligence Empowering the Innovation of Ideological and Political Education Mode for College Students. *High. Educ. Res.* **2024**, *10*, 81–84+89. [CrossRef]
3. Woodruff, A.; Shelby, R.; Kelley, P.G.; Rousso-Schindler, S.; Smith-Loud, J.; Wilcox, L. How knowledge workers think generative ai will (not) transform their industries. In Proceedings of the CHI Conference on Human Factors in Computing Systems, Honolulu, HI, USA, 11–16 May 2024.
4. Bit, D.; Biswas, S.; Nag, M. The Impact of Artificial Intelligence in Educational System. *Indo Am. J. Pharm. Res.* **2024**, *11*, 419–427. [CrossRef]
5. Cai, Y.; Fang, X. Analysis of the Hotspots and Trends of Foreign Artificial Intelligence Education Research. *Contin. Educ. Res.* **2023**, *10*, 56–62.
6. Mishra, A. *Scalable AI and Design Patterns: Design, Develop, and Deploy Scalable AI Solutions*; Springer Nature: Berlin/Heidelberg, Germany, 2024.
7. Paek, S.; Kim, N. Analysis of worldwide research trends on the impact of artificial intelligence in education. *Sustainability* **2021**, *13*, 7941. [CrossRef]
8. Chen, L.; Chen, P.; Lin, Z. Artificial intelligence in education: A review. *IEEE Access* **2020**, *8*, 75264–75278. [CrossRef]
9. Bin Salem, I. Integrating artificial intelligence in personalized learning: A future-oriented approach to enhance student engagement and achievement. *Int. J. Post Axial Futur. Teach. Learn.* **2024**, *2*, 111–119.
10. Rakuasa, H. Integration of Artificial Intelligence in Geography Learning: Challenges and Opportunities. *Sinergi Int. J. Educ.* **2023**, *1*, 75–83. [CrossRef]
11. Kerski, J.J. The implementation and effectiveness of geographic information systems technology and methods in secondary education. *J. Geogr.* **2004**, *102*, 165–174. [CrossRef]
12. Goldstein, D.; Alibrandi, M. Integrating GIS in the middle school curriculum: Impacts on diverse students' standardized test scores. *J. Geogr.* **2013**, *112*, 118–128. [CrossRef]
13. Bodzin, A.M.; Anastasio, D. Using web-based gis for earth and environmental systems education. *J. Geosci. Educ.* **2006**, *54*, 169–178. [CrossRef]
14. Hwang, G.-J.; Yang, L.-H.; Wang, S.-Y. A concept map-embedded educational computer game for improving students' learning performance in natural science courses. *Comput. Educ.* **2013**, *69*, 47–58. [CrossRef]
15. Henning, J.E. Beyond Action and Cognition: The Role of Awareness and Emotion in Experiential Learning. *J. Philos. Educ.* **2023**, *79*, 77.
16. Ministry of Education. Opinions on Promoting Study Tours for Primary and Secondary School Students. Ministry of Education of the People's Republic of China. 2 December 2016. Available online: https://www.moe.gov.cn/srcsite/A06/s3325/201612/t20161219_292354.html (accessed on 21 November 2024).
17. Ministry of Education of the People's Republic of China. *Compulsory Education Geography Curriculum Standards (2022 Edition)*; Beijing Normal University Press: Beijing, China, 2022.
18. Chen, Z.; Klahr, D. All other things being equal: Acquisition and transfer of the control of variables strategy. *Child Dev.* **1999**, *70*, 1239–1250. [CrossRef]
19. Kerski, J.J. The role of GIS in Digital Earth education. *Int. J. Digit. Earth* **2008**, *1*, 23–34. [CrossRef]
20. Bednarz, S.W.; van der Schee, J. Europe and the United States: The implementation of geographical information systems in secondary education in two contexts. *Technol. Pedagog. Educ.* **2006**, *15*, 5–19. [CrossRef]
21. Albert, W.S.; Golledge, R.G. The use of spatial cognitive abilities in geographical information systems: The map overlay operation. *Trans. GIS* **1999**, *3*, 193–206. [CrossRef]

22. Doering, A.; George, V. An investigation of the use of real-time, authentic geospatial data in the K-12 classroom. *J. Geogr.* **2008**, *106*, 217–225. [CrossRef]
23. Favier, T.T.; van der Schee, J.A. Exploring the characteristics of an optimal design for inquiry-based geography education with Geographic Information Systems. *Comput. Educ.* **2012**, *58*, 874–883. [CrossRef]
24. Gilmartin, P.P.; Patton, J.C. Comparing the sexes on spatial abilities: Map-use skills. *Ann. Assoc. Am. Geogr.* **1984**, *74*, 310–329. [CrossRef]
25. Marsh, M.; Golledge, R.; Battersby, S.E. Geospatial concept understanding and recognition in G6–College students: A preliminary argument for minimal GIS. *Ann. Assoc. Am. Geogr.* **2007**, *97*, 280–297. [CrossRef]
26. Kali, Y.; Orion, N.; Eylon, B.S. The effect of knowledge integration activities on students' perception of the earth's crust as a cyclic system. *J. Res. Sci. Teach.* **2003**, *40*, 656–684. [CrossRef]
27. Hattie, J. *Visible Learning: A Synthesis of over 800 Meta-Analyses Relating to Achievement*; Routledge: London, UK, 2008.
28. Liu, B.; Wu, H.; Zhang, Z.; Wei, G.; Wang, Y.; Zheng, J.; Ji, X.; Jiang, S. Recent evolution of the intertidal sand ridge lines of the Dongsha shoal in the modern radial sand ridges, east China. *Int. J. Environ. Res. Public Health* **2021**, *18*, 1573. [CrossRef] [PubMed]
29. Higuchi, H. Bird migration and the conservation of the global environment. *J. Ornithol.* **2012**, *153*, 3–14. [CrossRef]
30. Rutten, R.; Boekema, F. Regional social capital: Embeddedness, innovation networks and regional economic development. *Technol. Forecast. Soc. Chang.* **2007**, *74*, 1834–1846. [CrossRef]
31. Cheng, A.S.; Monroe, M.C. Place-based education: A model for integrating human and natural geography in the classroom. *J. Geogr.* **2017**, *116*, 117–125.
32. Falk, J.H.; Dierking, L.D. *The Museum Experience Revisited*; Left Coast Press: Walnut Creek, CA, USA, 2017.
33. Stevenson, R.B.; Brody, M. *Place-Conscious Education: Reimagining Learning Through the Local*; Harvard Education Press: Cambridge, MA, USA, 2019.
34. Chassignol, M.; Khoroshavin, A.; Klimova, A.; Bilyatdinova, A. Artificial Intelligence trends in education: A narrative overview. *Procedia Comput. Sci.* **2018**, *136*, 16–24. [CrossRef]
35. Woolf, B.P. AI grand challenges for education. *AI Mag.* **2013**, *34*, 66–84. [CrossRef]
36. Colucci-Gray, L.; Camino, E.; Barbiero, G.; Gray, D. From scientific literacy to sustainability literacy: An ecological framework for education. *Sci. Educ.* **2006**, *90*, 227–252. [CrossRef]
37. Fan, Y.; Chen, J.; Shirkey, G.; John, R.; Wu, S.R.; Park, H.; Shao, C. Applications of structural equation modeling (SEM) in ecological studies: An updated review. *Ecol. Process.* **2016**, *5*, 1–12. [CrossRef]
38. Pienaar, E.F.; Lew, D.K.; Wallmo, K. Are environmental attitudes influenced by survey context? An investigation of the context dependency of the New Ecological Paradigm (NEP) Scale. *Soc. Sci. Res.* **2013**, *42*, 1542–1554. [CrossRef]
39. Cao, F.; Jian, Y. The Role of integrating AI and VR in fostering environmental awareness and enhancing activism among college students. *Sci. Total. Environ.* **2023**, *908*, 168200. [CrossRef] [PubMed]
40. Crompton, H.; Burke, D. Artificial intelligence in higher education: The state of the field. *Educ. Technol. J.* **2023**, *3*, 1–15. [CrossRef]
41. Mousavi, S.A.; Schmidt, M.; Squires, V.; Wilson, K. Assessing the effectiveness of student advice recommender agent (SARA): The case of automated personalized feedback. *Int. J. Artif. Intell. Educ.* **2021**, *31*, 603–621. [CrossRef]
42. Wang, C.; Pastore, F.; Goknil, A.; Briand, L.C. Automatic generation of acceptance test cases from use case specifications: An nlp-based approach. *IEEE Trans. Softw. Eng.* **2020**, *48*, 585–616. [CrossRef]
43. Huang, J.; Wei, Y.; Zhang, L.; Chen, W. Evaluating generative artificial intelligence in answering course –related open questions: A pilot study. In Proceedings of the 2024 International Symposium on Educational Technology (ISET), Macau, Macao, 29 July–1 August 2024; pp. 64–69.
44. Gao, R.; Merzdorf, H.E.; Anwar, S.; Hipwell, M.C.; Srinivasa, A. Automatic assessment of text-based responses in post-secondary education: A systematic review. *Comput. Educ. Artif. Intell.* **2024**, *6*, 100206. [CrossRef]
45. Damasevicius, R. From Trivial Answers to Critical Questions: Transforming Education with AI-Driven Inquiry Scenarios. In *Teaching and Assessment in the Era of Education 5.0*; IGI Global: Hershey, PA, USA, 2024; pp. 173–193.
46. Himeur, Y.; Rimal, B.; Tiwary, A.; Amira, A. Using artificial intelligence and data fusion for environmental monitoring: A review and future perspectives. *Inf. Fusion* **2022**, *86–87*, 44–75. [CrossRef]
47. Almasri, F. Exploring the impact of artificial intelligence in teaching and learning of science: A systematic review of empirical research. *Res. Sci. Educ.* **2024**, *54*, 977–997. [CrossRef]
48. Wang, X.; Xu, X.; Zhang, Y.; Hao, S.; Jie, W. Exploring the impact of artificial intelligence application in personalized learning environments: Thematic analysis of undergraduates' perceptions in China. *Humanit. Soc. Sci. Commun.* **2024**, *11*, 1–10. [CrossRef]
49. Romero, C.; Ventura, S. Data mining in education. *Wiley Interdiscip. Rev. Data Min. Knowl. Discov.* **2013**, *3*, 12–27. [CrossRef]
50. Khreisat, M.N.; Khilani, D.; Rusho, M.A.; Karkkulainen, E.A.; Tabuena, A.C.; Uberas, A.D. Ethical Implications of AI Integration. *Educ. Decis. Mak. Syst. Rev.* **2024**, *30*, 8521–8527. [CrossRef]
51. Rizvi, S. Revolutionizing Student Engagement: Artificial Intelligence's Impact on Specialized Learning Motivation. *Int. J. Adv. Eng. Res. Sci.* **2023**, *10*, 27–31. [CrossRef]

52. Milberg, T. *The Future of Learning: How AI Is Revolutionizing Education 4.0. World Economic Forum*; World Economic Forum: Cologny Switzerland, 2024.
53. Anderson, J. *Understanding Cultural Geography: Places and Traces*; Routledge: London, UK, 2021.
54. Malik, G.; Tayal, D.K.; Vij, S. An analysis of the role of artificial intelligence in education and teaching. In *Recent Findings in Intelligent Computing Techniques: Proceedings of the 5th ICACNI 2017*; Springer: Singapore, 2019; Volume 1.

algorithms

MDPI

Article

Advancing AI in Higher Education: A Comparative Study of Large Language Model-Based Agents for Exam Question Generation, Improvement, and Evaluation

Vlatko Nikolovski [1], Dimitar Trajanov [1,2] and Ivan Chorbev [1,*]

1 Faculty of Computer Science and Engineering, "Ss. Cyril and Methodius" University in Skopje, 1000 Skopje, North Macedonia; vlatko.nikolovski@finki.ukim.mk (V.N.); dimitar.trajanov@finki.ukim.mk (D.T.)

2 Department of Computer Science, Metropolitan College, Boston University, Boston, MA 02215, USA

* Correspondence: ivan.chorbev@finki.ukim.mk

Abstract

The transformative capabilities of large language models (LLMs) are reshaping educational assessment and question design in higher education. This study proposes a systematic framework for leveraging LLMs to enhance question-centric tasks: aligning exam questions with course objectives, improving clarity and difficulty, and generating new items guided by learning goals. The research spans four university courses—two theory-focused and two application-focused—covering diverse cognitive levels according to Bloom's taxonomy. A balanced dataset ensures representation of question categories and structures. Three LLM-based agents—VectorRAG, VectorGraphRAG, and a fine-tuned LLM—are developed and evaluated against a meta-evaluator, supervised by human experts, to assess alignment accuracy and explanation quality. Robust analytical methods, including mixed-effects modeling, yield actionable insights for integrating generative AI into university assessment processes. Beyond exam-specific applications, this methodology provides a foundational approach for the broader adoption of AI in post-secondary education, emphasizing fairness, contextual relevance, and collaboration. The findings offer a comprehensive framework for aligning AI-generated content with learning objectives, detailing effective integration strategies, and addressing challenges such as bias and contextual limitations. Overall, this work underscores the potential of generative AI to enhance educational assessment while identifying pathways for responsible implementation.

Keywords: large language models; AI in higher education; automated exam question generation; exam question alignment; retrieval-augmented generation; knowledge graphs; explanation quality; domain-limited materials

1. Introduction

The emergence of large language models (LLMs) has generated significant enthusiasm in higher education due to their demonstrated ability to generate and analyze text, thereby potentially transforming academic tasks ranging from content creation to academic assessment. The authors in [1,2] acknowledge this potential of LLMs to transform higher education. Despite the promising opportunities that LLMs offer to streamline teaching and engage students, their deployment in educational settings, such as exam question generation, poses substantial challenges in terms of alignment, reliability, and fairness [3].

Unlike many general-purpose applications where broad knowledge is an advantage, university courses are built on carefully curated content—such as instructor-prepared notes, concise lecture summaries, and tailored presentations, and are particularly sensitive to even slight discrepancies or biases in AI-generated content. Such misalignment can undermine academic integrity and significantly affect student performance. This specificity demands that any AI-generated exam questions not only be accurate and clear but also align precisely with course objectives, maintain appropriate difficulty levels, and uphold strict standards of fairness.

A number of studies have reviewed the evolutionary potential of AI in education [1,4] and have examined automated question generation techniques and evaluations [5–7]. Existing studies tend to focus on broad trends or isolated tasks without critically examining the specific challenges that arise when integrating LLMs into the domain of academic assessment. In particular, prior research has rarely addressed the dual need for (i) ensuring that generated questions are rigorously aligned with course objectives and pedagogical standards, and (ii) providing interpretable justifications for the AI's decisions. This lack of a holistic framework means that, even when automated question generation appears technically sound, educators are left uncertain about the quality, fairness, and contextual relevance of the output.

In response to these gaps, our study proposes a comprehensive methodological framework specifically tailored for higher education. Our approach centers on three interrelated tasks:

1. Alignment Evaluation —assessing how accurately an existing exam question reflects a course's learning objectives.
2. Question Improvement—refining suboptimal exam questions to enhance clarity, specificity, and appropriate difficulty.
3. New Question Generation—creating entirely new exam questions that conform to intended learning outcomes.

These tasks are applied across multiple university courses that span both theory-oriented and application-oriented domains and cover various cognitive levels as delineated in Bloom's Taxonomy [8].

On top of this, our framework integrates a meta-evaluation layer that is supervised by human experts. In this setup, a specialized LLM that is augmented by rigorous human oversight assigns ground-truth scores and evaluates the quality of explanations underlying each AI agent's decision. This dual-level evaluation not only enables robust comparisons among different AI architectures (VectorRAG, VectorGraphRAG, and a Fine-Tuned LLM), but also produces detailed explanations that help identify sources of potential biases and/or misalignment. By offering detailed, empirically validated insights, our study contributes a set of best practices and actionable guidelines for the responsible and context-aware integration of AI in academic assessments.

Our goal is not to compete solely on the generation of quality metrics but rather to ensure that LLM-based agents are finely tuned to the specific demands of higher education, safeguarding academic integrity and enhancing assessment effectiveness. Ultimately, our work is designed to serve as a meticulous guide for educators and technology developers. It ensures that AI implementations are not only evaluated on traditional quality metrics but are also carefully aligned with the unique demands of higher education, thereby safeguarding academic integrity and supporting effective teaching and learning outcomes.

By addressing these specific gaps, the lack of targeted evaluation on alignment, the absence of human-supervised meta-assessment, and the limited discussion of actionable guidelines, our study tends to enhance both academic insights and the practical implementation of responsible, context-aware AI in higher education.

2. Related Work

The recent expansion of AI applications in education has led to a diverse body of research, ranging from general analyses to domain-specific implementations. However, a deeper examination reveals critical gaps that our study aims to address, with a focus on developing best practices for AI-enabled assessment.

2.1. AI in Education: Overviews and Trends

A number of comprehensive studies have been concluded towards exploring AI's broad potential in higher education. The authors in [9] provide a meta-systematic review that calls for heightened ethical standards, interdisciplinary collaboration, and methodological rigor in deploying AI. In addition, the authors in [1,4] further discuss how AI, and LLMs in particular, are reshaping educational landscapes by enhancing content creation and personalization, while [10] presents a systematic review in science education that highlights AI's capacity for personalized feedback and automated assessments while underscoring privacy and bias concerns. Moving towards practical implementation, the authors in [11] investigated the usage of knowledge graphs (KGs) to enhance curriculum alignment and employability outcomes, while the authors in [12] presented recommender systems as an AI tool that can personalize resource suggestions by accounting for learner preferences.

Despite these valuable conclusions, these studies tend to discuss general trends without analyzing the challenges of aligning AI outputs with the specific curricular objectives of university courses. Moreover, while discussions on AI integration in learning management systems [13] and ethical frameworks [14–16] have raised important issues of bias and transparency, they generally lack a rigorous, multi-dimensional evaluation framework that focuses on providing concrete, task-specific guidelines that address exam question generation, evaluation, and alignment.

2.2. LLM-Based Exam Question Generation

Several studies have explored the automated generation of exam questions using LLMs. The authors in [5] provided one of the initial insights into automated exam content creation, implying that the research on question generation predominantly employed syntax-based or template-driven methods. More recent studies have leveraged state-of-the-art LLMs—such as GPT-3, GPT-4, and T5—to generate a wide array of question types. For instance, the authors in [17] demonstrated that few-shot prompt engineering with ChatGPT4 models can be effective for generating reading comprehension questions, while the authors in [18] demonstrated the application of LLMs to create multiple-choice questions for computing courses. Although these studies showcase the technical feasibility of automated question generation, they often evaluate the generated questions on isolated quality metrics without a deeper analysis of alignment with course objectives or the provision of human-understandable explanations. Our work distinguishes itself by systematically assessing alignment and improvement tasks and by quantifying performance variations across different course types.

Other research efforts have sought to refine question generation by integrating domain-specific strategies. The authors in [19] introduced a method that fine-tunes LLMs in accordance with Bloom's Taxonomy to generate questions across various cognitive levels, and the authors in [20] incorporated knowledge graphs to improve domain specificity in cybersecurity education. Specialized approaches, such as domain-adapted training on scientific texts, demonstrate the scalability of QG methods [7,21], and modular QG pipelines that separate question stem generation from distractor formulation further enhance reliability [22,23]. Furthermore, an AI–educator workflow for generating math multiple-choice questions was presented in [24], while distractor quality through topic modeling was presented in [25] or ontology-based methods presented in [26]. Some recent work evaluates ChatGPT-generated assessments in probability and engineering statistics, noting mismatches in scoring schemes and inadequate coverage of higher-level cognitive domains [27]. Another study validates multi-task learning techniques for producing high-quality question–answer pairs in diverse subjects [28]. Yet, these studies typically consider question generation as a stand-alone task, rather than as part of an integrated framework that includes post-generation evaluation and iterative improvement.

2.3. *Improving and Evaluating Automated Content*

In addition to generation, a number of studies have sought to enhance the quality of AI-produced questions. For example, the authors in [29,30] highlight the role of prompt engineering and teacher feedback in improving question quality. Additionally, retrieval-augmented approaches have been used to reduce factual errors [20], while reinforcement learning has shown promise in refining AI-generated feedback [31]. Ontology-based approaches appear especially effective in conceptual domains like biology [26]. Large datasets such as SQuAD [32] have served as benchmarks for reading comprehension and question-answering, guiding the development and evaluation of LLM-driven generation. Even though these studies contribute important techniques for improving output quality, they rarely combine these methods into a unified evaluation framework that improves the content and the reasoning behind it.Our framework introduces a meta-evaluator, supervised by domain experts, which not only scores questions on multiple dimensions (such as alignment, clarity, and fairness) but also offers explanation quality ratings. This dual approach allows us to identify where and why certain agents may be biased or misaligned, a gap largely overlooked in prior research.

2.4. *Alignment with Curriculum and Learning Objectives*

Many studies have acknowledged the importance of aligning educational content with curriculum standards. Knowledge graphs have been used to map course content to industry-required skills by the authors in [11], and personalized tutoring systems have demonstrated the benefits of tailoring educational resources to individual learning trajectories explored in [12,33]. However, these approaches primarily focus on content recommendation rather than on ensuring that exam questions accurately reflect curricular goals. Our work directly addresses this shortfall by systematically evaluating alignment as a distinct task within our comprehensive framework.

2.5. *Automated Grading and Feedback Mechanisms*

Automated grading has evolved from simple scoring algorithms to more sophisticated, LLM-based methods that aim to replicate human grading, presented in [34–36]. While these studies demonstrate promising techniques for reducing grading workloads and increasing consistency, they often lack transparency; few provide detailed explanations for the assigned scores. This opacity makes it difficult to diagnose and correct biases in the grading process—a critical limitation that our meta-evaluation layer is specifically designed to overcome.

2.6. *Ethical Considerations: Fairness and Bias in AI-Assisted Education*

Ethical considerations, particularly regarding fairness and bias, are the center of discussions on AI in education. Various studies have outlined various fairness metrics [15] and ethical frameworks [13,14,16] aimed at guiding the responsible use of AI tools. Despite the fact that these contributions are essential, they often stop at general recommendations without addressing the detailed, practical challenges of implementing such frameworks in exam question generation and evaluation. Our framework explicitly incorporates human oversight to ensure that even subtle biases are identified and corrected, thereby ensuring that the AI outputs meet the high standards required in academic assessments.

2.7. Current Research Gaps and Our Contributions

Despite considerable progress across these areas, significant gaps remain. Most existing research addresses individual components—such as question generation, grading, or feedback—in isolation, without offering a comprehensive framework that integrates these elements under a unified evaluative rubric. Moreover, there is a notable lack of systematic guidelines that consider both the technical quality and the pedagogical alignment of AI-generated exam questions, especially in the context of higher education where even minor errors can have severe consequences.

To overcome these gaps, our study introduces a multi-purpose AI framework that:

- Proposes a three-task framework (Alignment Evaluation, Question Improvement, and New Question Generation) that reflects real-world academic assessment needs.
- Incorporates a human-supervised meta-evaluator to provide both numerical scores and detailed explanations.
- Utilizes mixed-effects modeling to rigorously quantify agent performance and isolate sources of bias or misalignment.
- Offers a set of best practices and actionable guidelines for educators and developers seeking to integrate LLMs into higher-education assessments.

While the previous work has provided an important groundwork in both automated question generation and AI in education, our study bases its uniqueness in its meticulous, multi-dimensional evaluation of LLM-based agents, to offer practical, actionable guidelines for educators seeking to implement responsible, context-aware AI in their assessment processes. By addressing the specific needs of higher education, where even minor misalignment can have severe impacts, we provide a framework that is not only scientifically rigorous but also practically valuable for safeguarding academic integrity and enhancing learning outcomes.

3. Materials and Methods

This section presents a comprehensive methodological framework that aims to systematically explore how large language models (LLMs) can evaluate, refine, and generate exam questions in a higher-education context. Figure 1 provides an overview of the complete workflow, beginning with the processing of partially condensed course materials and concluding with a structured comparative analysis of different LLM-based agents. In addition, our approach aims not only to assess these approaches from a purely statistical standpoint but also to provide guidelines and best practices for safely and effectively adopting AI in academic assessments. By acknowledging that most university courses in our dataset rely on distilled materials, such as instructor-curated notes, slides, and condensed summaries, our framework is designed to handle the alignment sensitivities and domain-specific constraints that characterize real-world higher education settings.

We pay special attention to how the nature of distilled course materials (versus entire textbook chapters), the design of retrieval-augmented databases, and supervised fine-tuning all interact to ensure precise alignment with learning objectives. Human experts play a crucial role throughout this pipeline, validating data pre-processing steps, monitoring potential biases, and supervising the meta-evaluator.

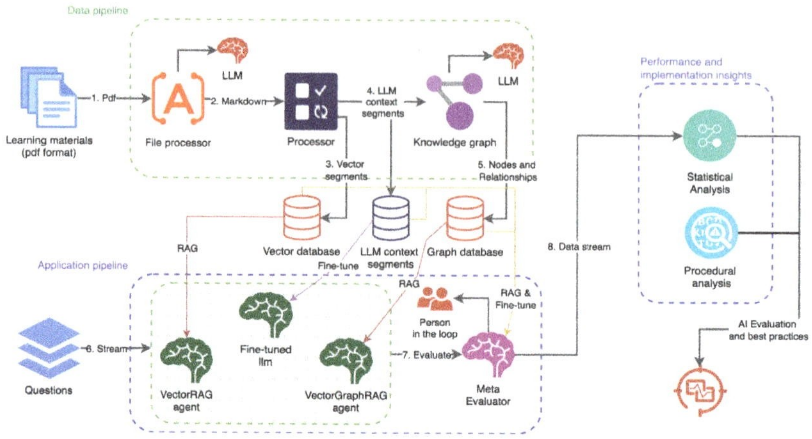

Figure 1. Schematic illustration of the workflow pipeline. Figure created using diagrams.net [37].

3.1. Workflow Pipeline Overview

Figure 1 shows the global process in three interconnected layers: the Data Pipeline, the Application Pipeline, and the Performance and Implementation Insights. Each layer builds upon the outputs of the previous one, creating a unified framework for generating, refining, and evaluating exam questions. Ultimately, the Performance and Implementation Insights identifies the best-performing agent configurations and best practices under varied pedagogical conditions.

3.1.1. Data Pipeline

The pipeline begins with converting original course materials (such as PDF slides and notes) into an enhanced Markdown format, producing structured and consistent text for subsequent processing. A central Processor then cleans, chunks, and embeds the text into two complementary forms: (i) smaller segments optimized for vector databases and hybrid (dense + sparse) retrieval [38], and (ii) larger segments aligned with an LLM context window. From these enriched materials, a customized knowledge graph is constructed to capture key conceptual relationships. In parallel, a Fine-Tune Processor compiles a domain-specific dataset from the processed text, enabling the fine-tuning of a baseline LLM on course-relevant content.

3.1.2. Application Pipeline

Three distinct agents leverage these prepared resources. The VectorRAG agent utilizes a vector database to retrieve contextually relevant passages before generating or scoring questions [39]. The VectorGraphRAG agent adds a knowledge-graph layer to model interlinked concepts for improved retrieval [40], while the Fine-Tuned LLM agent employs a pre-trained model refined on curated question data [41]. An agent evaluator orchestrates the three core tasks (see Section 3.3), while a Meta Evaluator assigns ground-truth scores and explanation-quality ratings. Human experts oversee the meta-evaluation to safeguard correctness and alignment with course goals.

3.1.3. Performance and Implementation Insights

The final layer consolidates numerical scores, textual justifications, and any expert-driven corrections into a comprehensive dataset for analysis. Primary and secondary statistical analyses are then applied to examine how each agent's performance varies by question type, Bloom's level, course category, and other factors. This includes linear mixed-effects models that account for correlations within the same question and specialized secondary analyses (e.g., self-reflection accuracy, over-/under-grading). These models help identify the most effective agent configurations under diverse pedagogical conditions.

3.2. Datasets

This study relies on three primary datasets: (1) Course Materials, (2) Exam Questions and (3) Fine-Tuning Datasets. By combining both theoretical and application-oriented resources from four university-level courses (Data Science, Web Design, Integrated Systems, and Operating Systems), the data collection process ensures a robust representation of each course's objectives and content.

3.2.1. Course Materials and Processing

Faculty and teaching assistants provided official documents such as lecture notes, slides, textbook excerpts, coding examples, laboratory guides, and supplementary readings. These materials, carefully curated to align with academic standards, capture both foundational theories and practical insights. The resulting corpus allows LLM-based agents to retrieve or generate exam questions that accurately reflect course-level learning outcomes.

These materials were initially converted from PDF and slide formats into Markdown by leveraging a multi-modal LLM [42] that could handle text blocks, embedded images, and tables. To ensure correctness and clarity, human reviewers supervised and corrected the resulting Markdown files, particularly focusing on accurate handling of diagrams, special characters, and spacing inconsistencies. Next, each Markdown file was chunked into segments with a maximum of 1000 characters and a maximum token count of 1024. The chunking process was guided by logical structures, such as whole topics or paragraphs, ensuring that splits preserved meaningful context. This threshold was established through an iterative process with human supervision, where different chunk sizes were tested and evaluated to balance retrieval efficiency, context retention, and minimizing partial overlaps between content blocks. The established threshold offered a practical balance: it minimized partial overlaps between content blocks yet retained enough context for meaningful retrieval.

Ultimately, these segments were embedded into a Qdrant [43] vector database for dense retrieval. In parallel, a domain-specific semantic knowledge graph was constructed in Neo4j [44]. The knowledge-graph layer mainly focuses on linking relevant entities and topics, but its detailed architecture is beyond the scope of this study and is described in a separate publication.

3.2.2. Exam Questions and Processing

Table 1 shows the distribution of the original exam questions, a wide range of open-ended (essay-style) questions spanned across different cognitive levels according to Bloom's taxonomy [8] and categorized by question design into: single-step questions—generally require students to address one primary concept or task; and multi-step questions—involve multiple, interlinked sub-tasks or a sequence of reasoning steps. These items reflect theory-oriented or application-oriented course content. Instructors contributed an initial set of questions, particularly single-step ones, which were further expanded through generative strategies. Using a fine-tuned LLM (detailed in Section 3.4), three variant forms of each original single-step item were created, each emphasizing different alignment aspects of the course materials. A second cycle then added multi-step questions by integrating vector-based and graph-based content, producing two new multi-step variations per original question. These added variations exhibited deliberately asymmetric alignments (one strongly matched vector-based content but loosely aligned with graph-based materials, and the other the reverse), thus probing how each LLM architecture handles partially overlapping or conflicting retrieval cues.

Table 1. Number of original exam questions across question categories, designs, and course characteristics.

Course Name	Course Category	Question Category	Question Design	Count
Data Science	Application-Oriented	Application-Based	Multi-Step	126
			Single-Step	189
		Creation and Evaluation	Multi-Step	126
			Single-Step	189
		Knowledge-Based	Multi-Step	126
			Single-Step	189
Integrated Systems	Theory-Oriented	Application-Based	Multi-Step	174
			Single-Step	261
		Creation and Evaluation	Multi-Step	174
			Single-Step	261
		Knowledge-Based	Multi-Step	174
			Single-Step	261
Operating Systems	Theory-Oriented	Application-Based	Multi-Step	232
			Single-Step	348
		Creation and Evaluation	Multi-Step	234
			Single-Step	351
		Knowledge-Based	Multi-Step	234
			Single-Step	351
Web Design	Application-Oriented	Application-Based	Multi-Step	276
			Single-Step	414
		Creation and Evaluation	Multi-Step	276
			Single-Step	414
		Knowledge-Based	Multi-Step	276
			Single-Step	414

Once aggregated, these original and generatively varied items served as inputs for the three tasks executed by each LLM-based agent. In Tasks 2 and 3, the agent itself generates two new questions (an improved question and an entirely new one), effectively increasing the total number of question-based responses well beyond the original items shown in Table 1. After discarding 37 invalid responses that did not meet minimum quality or consistency checks, the final dataset for this study included 3605 valid agent responses (covering Tasks 1, 2, and 3 across all conditions). The final exam-question dataset therefore encompassed both human-curated items and partially augmented versions. This balanced dataset supported robust evaluation of each LLM agent's ability to score, refine, and generate questions. Example questions are given in the Appendix A.2.

3.3. Core Tasks and Two-Part Evaluations

The study's experimental design encompassed three main tasks, each requiring two outputs from the agent: a numeric score (1–10) and a concise textual explanation. This approach ensures that an agent's performance can be evaluated not only on quantitative measures (e.g., alignment or clarity) but also on the reasoning reflected in its justifications.

Task 1 (Alignment Evaluation) has agents receive an existing exam question and evaluate its alignment with course objectives. They provide numeric ratings (e.g., concept coverage, specificity/relevance, and accuracy/correctness) and a textual rationale. Comparisons with ground-truth scores reveal where the agent might over- or under-grade alignment.

Task 2 (Question Improvement) asks agents to take a "suboptimal" exam question and propose an improved version, assigning scores for criteria such as alignment, clarity, fairness, or difficulty. This tests the agent's ability to refine prompts while adhering to curricular standards and is a practical scenario for real-world educational revision.

Task 3 (Question Generation) instructs agents to create a new question at a given Bloom's level and self-score it on alignment, clarity/fairness, difficulty, and originality. This tests the agent's capacity to synthesize novel items that remain pedagogically sound and balanced in complexity.

3.4. LLM Agents and Architectures

Three distinct LLM-based agents were developed for the study: VectorRAG, VectorGraphRAG, and a Fine-Tuned LLM. Each agent performs the same three tasks, alignment evaluation, question improvement, and new question generation, but is equipped with a unique approach to retrieving and processing domain-specific information.

3.4.1. VectorRAG

This agent is a retrieval-augmented model that queries the Qdrant [43] vector database to identify the most relevant text segments from the embedded course materials. Once these relevant context chunks are retrieved (e.g., top-5 or top-20, depending on the experimental setting), they are fed into a language model that uses Google Gemini 2.0 [42] as its backbone to produce a final output for alignment scores, improved questions, or newly generated questions.

3.4.2. VectorGraphRAG

This agent extends the retrieval-augmented approach by incorporating a knowledge graph (Neo4j [44]). In addition to standard vector retrieval, this agent leverages relationships stored in the knowledge graph, such as conceptual links or sentiment edges, to enrich its context. This approach is particularly useful for multi-step questions or cases where cross-topic reasoning is needed. The final text output is generated by the same backbone language model as VectorRAG [42] but is grounded by the graph-based insights.

3.4.3. Fine-Tuned LLM

The Fine-Tuned LLM is a specialized model built on top of Meta-Llama-3.1-8B [45]. It was refined using supervised fine-tuning (SFTTrainer) on a custom dataset derived from the course materials and exam questions. In an initial attempt (Fine-Tuned LLMv1 [46]), the model's outputs did not meet the quality criteria set by human reviewers. Consequently, the fine-tuning datasets were cleaned, noise was removed, and domain-distilled samples were added—resulting in a second version (Fine-Tuned LLMv2). This updated model (named vlada22/Meta-Llama-3.1-8B-Instruct-finki-edu-4courses) [47] was approved by human experts based on consistency, alignment with course concepts, and clarity.

Below is a high-level summary of the fine-tuning parameters used for the second version. Two main configurations (v1 and v2) differed in learning rate, epoch count, and batch size, among other settings. Both leveraged QLoRA and LoRA-based training modules, focusing on the query, key, value, and projection components of the model:

- **Configuration v1:**
  - `learning_rate` = 3×10^{-4}, `num_train_epochs` = 3, `per_device_train_batch_size` = 4

  Lower batch sizes and fewer epochs.
- **Configuration v2:**
  - `learning_rate` = 2×10^{-4}, `num_train_epochs` = 5, `per_device_train_batch_size` = 128

  Larger batch sizes, more epochs, and a carefully curated dataset.

Through human-in-the-loop experimentation, Fine-Tuned LLM v2 was ultimately selected for the final experiments due to its superior alignment and generation quality.

3.5. Meta Evaluator, Human Oversight, and Score Integration

A specialized **Meta Evaluator**, implemented as GPT4o [48] with strict evaluation policies, assigns ground-truth (reference) scores for each subdimension in Tasks 1–3 by referencing the original course materials. It also reviews each agent's justifications and produces a rating for explanation quality, emphasizing coherence, factual integrity, and logical clarity. Human experts resolve domain-specific nuances to ensure that all finalized ground-truth scores accurately reflect the intended learning objectives. Task 1 comparisons rely on an absolute error metric between the agent's subgrades and the meta-evaluator's ground-truth, whereas Tasks 2 and 3 treat the meta-evaluator's subgrades as *true* for measuring how closely the agent's improved or newly generated question aligns with course standards. The structured dataset ultimately captures all numeric outputs (agent and meta scores) plus explanation-quality ratings, providing a transparent record of agent performance and justifications across a range of question types.

Senior faculty members and domain experts from each course oversaw all critical stages, from data pre-processing (Markdown conversion, chunking, question selection) to the final meta-evaluation. Their role was to (1) review the correctness and fairness of auto-generated or refined questions, (2) validate the performance of the Fine-Tuned LLM during the iterative SFT process, and (3) supervise the meta-evaluator's final scoring to mitigate biases and address any missing context. The final meta scores (averaged or sub-dimensional) were thus the product of LLM-based evaluation plus domain-expert supervision, ensuring both consistency and reliability.

3.6. Data Parsing and Final Dataset Preparation

Once each LLM agent (VectorRAG, VectorGraphRAG, Fine-Tuned LLM) completed its assigned tasks, providing alignment scores, improved questions, and newly generated items, these outputs were consolidated into a single dataset. During this process, multiple versions of both the agent outputs and the meta-evaluation were created to refine quality and ensure final decisions were based on robust data:

- **Agents1 (Version 1)**—VectorRAG with a top-20 retrieval setting, VectorGraphRAG with top-50, and Fine-Tuned LLM v1 (the initial fine-tuned model).
- **Agents2 (Version 2)**—VectorRAG with top-5 retrieval, VectorGraphRAG with top-20, and Fine-Tuned LLM v2 (the improved fine-tuned model).
- **Meta_auto**—The "raw" outputs of the meta-evaluator (LLM-based) when scoring Agents2 responses.
- **Meta_human**—The final ground-truth dataset after human experts supervised and corrected the meta-evaluator's judgments from Meta_auto.

In the first version (Agents1) dataset, a preliminary human review of these outputs identified several issues with alignment, clarity, and difficulty, leading the team to conclude that they were insufficient for final analysis. To address these shortcomings, both the retrieval parameters and the fine-tuning process were refined. In the second version (Agents2) dataset, human experts conducted another review of the outputs and deemed them acceptable for statistical modeling and further study.

Following the collection of Agents2 responses, a Meta Evaluator was employed to produce meta_auto dataset: initial "ground-truth" scores generated automatically by an LLM-based system. However, because the study implies rigorous human supervision to mitigate biases or factual inaccuracies, domain experts manually examined and corrected the meta_auto outputs, creating a final reference dataset known as meta_human.

Consequently, meta_human represents the combined product of automated scoring and expert oversight.

With Agents2 outputs serving as the primary agent-based dataset and meta_human as the authoritative set of ground-truth evaluations, several comparative analyses were performed. This multi-stage workflow ensured that each iteration of data collection and evaluation was systematically validated, ultimately enabling robust conclusions about agent performance, fairness, and real-world applicability of the proposed LLM-based exam-question framework.

The final datasets (agents1, agents2, meta_auto, and meta_human) contain 3605 valid agent and meta responses, encompassing both original question evaluations and newly generated items.

3.7. *Statistical Modeling and Analysis*

After producing a final dataset from the Agents2 outputs and matching them to the Meta_human ground truth, several targeted analyses were performed to evaluate agent performance, detect biases, and validate the system's real-world applicability. The following subsections outline each analytical step in a structured but narrative style.

3.7.1. Main Analysis (Mixed-Effects Model)

A primary goal was to quantify how accurately each agent (VectorRAG, VectorGraphRAG, and Fine-Tuned LLM v2) performed across the three tasks (alignment evaluation, question improvement, and new question generation) under varying instructional contexts. To achieve this, a linear mixed-effects model (LMM) was fitted for each task. The model accounted for repeated measures on the same question by incorporating random intercepts, thereby mitigating potential correlations. Agent type, course orientation, question design, question category, and explanation-quality subdimensions were entered as fixed effects.

In Task 1, the outcome variable consisted of absolute alignment errors between the agent's subgrades and the Meta_human reference. For Tasks 2 and 3, the outcome was the Meta_human subgrade assigned to the improved or newly generated questions (e.g., averaged scores for alignment, clarity, difficulty, and originality). By including the same set of fixed effects in these models, the study systematically examined the circumstances under which particular agents excelled or struggled and assessed the impact of explanation clarity on overall performance.

3.7.2. Self-Reflection and Over-/Under-Grading

An additional focus was on the consistency between an agent's self-assessment and the external ground truth. In Tasks 2 and 3, each agent scored its own outputs for alignment or clarity, among other dimensions, and these self-scores were then compared with the Meta_human reference. The difference between the two scores revealed whether the agent tended to overestimate or underestimate its own quality.

In Task 1, a signed-error approach was taken by comparing the agent's alignment subgrades (concept coverage, specificity/relevance, accuracy/correctness) with the Meta_human scores, thereby highlighting any systematic over-grading or under-grading patterns. These self-reflection and over-/under-grading measures helped identify calibration gaps that could affect downstream decisions if agents were used unsupervised.

3.7.3. Bias Identification and Removal (Meta_auto vs. Meta_human)

To assess the robustness of the meta-evaluator itself, a bias analysis compared its initial automated assessments (Meta_auto) against the expert-supervised ground truth (Meta_human). The same Agents2 responses were used in both sets of evaluations, facilitating a clear measurement of discrepancies. Wilcoxon signed-rank and error distribution analyses were applied to ascertain whether the automated evaluator displayed systematic biases for particular question designs or content domains. Where biases were detected, human supervision played a crucial corrective role, providing adjustments to the meta-evaluator's evaluation policies. This process underscored the advantages of a hybrid system that combines LLM-based automation with expert oversight in high-stakes academic settings.

3.7.4. Real-World Validation on 100 Human-Created Exam Questions (Task 1)

To evaluate the practical applicability of the proposed framework, a set of 100 human-created exam questions was compiled. These questions were specifically chosen to be theory-oriented (course_category), application-based (question_category), and multi-step (question_design), reflecting a more complex examination style. The best-performing agent, as identified by the earlier analyses, was then used to evaluate the alignment of these questions with the intended course objectives under Task 1 only. Subsequently, human experts assigned comparable alignment scores to each of the same 100 questions, forming a basis for a direct comparison. A paired t-test and Bland–Altman analysis were conducted to assess whether the agent's alignment evaluations significantly differed from human judgments. If the differences are minimal and not statistically significant, it would indicate that the system's reliability extends to real exam scenarios.

3.8. *Workflow Implementation and Data Availability*

All workflow modules were implemented in Python (version 3.12). Data cleaning and organization utilized pandas [49], with statsmodels [50] supporting the mixed-effects analyses. Retrieval and knowledge-graph components were managed by LangChain [51], gte-Embegginds model based on [52], Qdrant [43], and Neo4j [44]. The VectorRAG and VectorGraphRAG agents used Google Gemini 2.0 [42], and the Fine-Tuned LLM relied on Meta-Llama-3.1-8B-Instruct-finki-edu-4courses [47]. The Meta Evaluator was GPT4o [48], supplemented by human experts to ensure alignment with genuine course standards. Appendix A.2 (Table A4) shows example questions generated by agents for Task 3.

The dataset includes both human-generated exam questions, which represent the actual question pool for the courses, and LLM-generated questions. Since the human-generated questions are actively used for student assessment, they cannot be published. However, all data generated by LLMs—including questions, course materials, fine-tuning datasets with the code for the actual fine-tuning, datasets produced by agents (Agents1 and Agents2), and meta-evaluation datasets with human supervision (Meta1 and Meta2), along with the analysis code, will be shared on the project's GitHub repository (v1.0.0) [53] after acceptance, in accordance with the journal's data-sharing guidelines.

3.9. *Methodological Synthesis and Alignment with Research Objectives*

Overall, this methodology integrates (i) a data pipeline that enriches course materials; (ii) an application pipeline in which three LLM-based agents evaluate, refine, and create exam questions; and (iii) a meta-evaluation layer that produces ground-truth and explanation-quality scores. The resulting dataset supports a mixed-effects framework capable of capturing agent, task, and question-level variations. By enforcing transparent scoring rubrics and explicit justifications, the study directly addresses its core goals: to measure alignment with course objectives, compare retrieval-based and fine-tuned LLMs, and determine whether high-quality justifications correlate with more reliable self-scoring or improved question quality.

Beyond these immediate research outcomes, the approach serves as a comprehensive guideline and set of best practices for educators and developers aiming to responsibly integrate AI into higher education. It addresses crucial considerations such as fairness, bias mitigation, domain-specific requirements, and the necessity of human oversight.

By adopting the methodological steps outlined in this study, educators and developers can deploy LLM-based question generation and evaluation tools with greater confidence, ensuring both pedagogical integrity and equitable student assessment.

4. Results

This section presents the findings from all experimental and analytical procedures described in Section 3.7. It begins with an overview of the final dataset and initial visualizations, followed by the core mixed-effects models for Tasks 1, 2, and 3. Furthermore, additional analyses are presented, including self-reflection and over-/under-grading, bias identification in meta-evaluation, and real-world validation on new questions.

4.1. Main Analysis (Mixed-Effects Model)

For all tasks, each agent's explanation quality was scored (1–10) on each relevant subdimension. This led to 108,150 long-format records (3605 questions × 3 agents × 10 task-subdimensions for tasks 1, 2 and 3). Figure 2 shows the Task 1 distributions of averaged absolute errors (lower is better), while Figure 3 shows Tasks 2 and 3 averaged meta scores (higher is better). These initial visualizations provide a preliminary overview before turning to mixed-effects models.

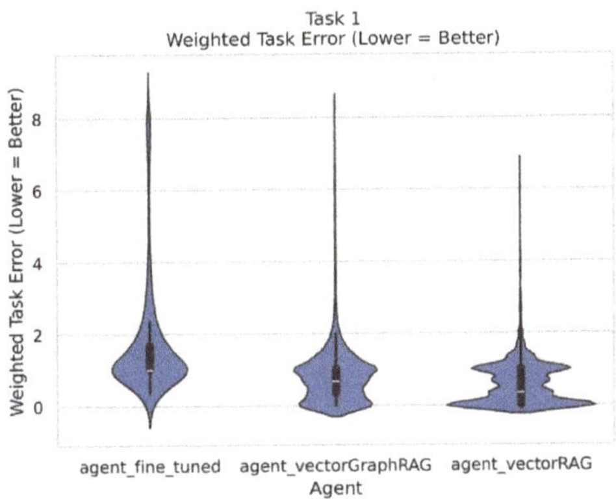

Figure 2. Task 1—distributions of averaged absolute errors (lower is better).

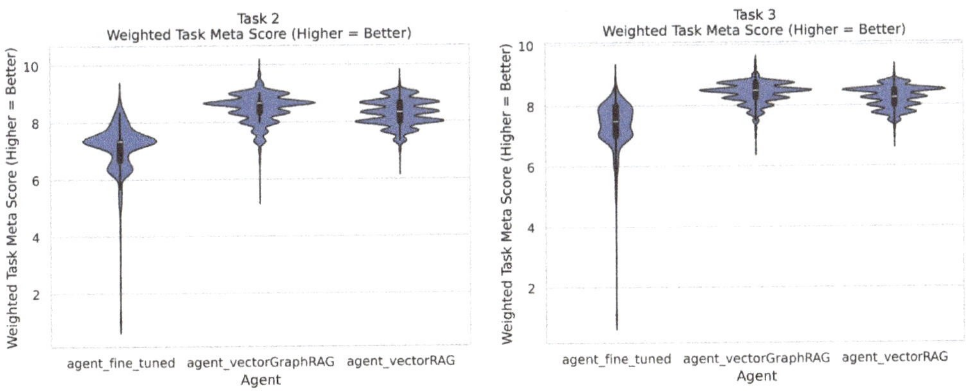

(a) (b)

Figure 3. Violin plots illustrating each agent's performance across the three tasks: (**a**) Task 2—distribution of averaged meta scores (higher is better). (**b**) Task 3—distribution of averaged meta scores (higher is better).

4.1.1. Mixed-Effects Modeling and Large-Output Tables

A linear mixed-effects model (LMM) was employed for each task to account for the nested data structure. Every question (question_id) can generate multiple observations (one for each agent, each subgrade, etc.), leading to potentially correlated residuals within the same question. Including $(1 \mid \text{question\_id})$ adds a random intercept for each question, thereby allowing each question to have its own baseline level. This approach reduces bias from unobserved question-level factors (such as difficulty, style, or intrinsic complexity) that could otherwise inflate residuals and obscure true agent or design effects.

The choice of LMM over simpler ANOVA or OLS arises from several considerations:

- **Repeated Measures on the Same Questions**: Each question is seen by multiple agents, so scores from the same question are not independent.
- **Varying Baseline**: Distinct questions may be inherently "easier" or "harder" to align, improve, or recreate, making a random intercept beneficial.
- **Complex Interactions**: Agents interact with question design (single-step vs. multi-step), question category (application, knowledge, or creation/evaluation), and course orientation (application vs. theory), potentially at different slopes.

Hence, the LMM properly captures these within-question correlations and estimates fixed effects for agent, design, category, course orientation, and explanation-quality subdimensions.

Each fitted model can easily produce 20–30 (or more) fixed-effect coefficients due to main effects, interactions, and explanation-quality dimensions. To maintain clarity, full tables with standard errors, *z* scores, *p*-values, and confidence intervals are placed in Appendix A.1 (Tables A1–A3). Summaries of critical effects and forest plots appear in the main text to highlight the most relevant findings. This strategy ensures both accessibility (concise narrative) and reproducibility (complete details in the Appendix A).

4.1.2. Task 1: Alignment Evaluation of Exam Questions

In Task 1, each agent and the meta-evaluator graded the same original question on three subgrades: Concept Coverage (CC), Specificity/Relevance (SR), and Accuracy/Correctness (AC). The alignment quality is captured by the Averaged_Task_Error:

$$\text{Averaged\_Task\_Error} = \frac{1}{3}\Big(\,|\, S_{\text{meta,CC}} - S_{\text{agent,CC}}| + |\, S_{\text{meta,SR}} - S_{\text{agent,SR}}| + |\, S_{\text{meta,AC}} - S_{\text{agent,AC}}|\,\Big). \tag{1}$$

A lower averaged absolute error indicates closer alignment with the meta-evaluator. The mixed model includes agent, question design (single-step vs. multi-step), question category (application-based, knowledge-based, or creation/evaluation), course category (application-oriented vs. theory-oriented), and the agent's explanation-quality subgrades (concept_coverage, specificity_relevance, accuracy_correctness). A random intercept for each question captures unobserved variability:

$$\begin{aligned} \text{Averaged\_Task\_Error} \sim\ & C(\text{agent}) \times C(\text{question\_design}) \\ & + C(\text{agent}) \times C(\text{question\_category}) \\ & + C(\text{agent}) \times C(\text{course\_category}) \\ & + \text{expl\_quality\_concept\_coverage} \\ & + \text{expl\_quality\_specificity\_relevance} \\ & + \text{expl\_quality\_accuracy\_correctness} \\ & + (1 \mid \text{question\_id}). \end{aligned} \tag{2}$$

Key Insights from the Model

Figure 4 illustrates the fixed effects as point estimates with 95% confidence intervals. The intercept (0.619) represents the fine-tuned LLM under baseline conditions (multi-step, application-based, application-oriented, and mean explanation quality). Single-step design significantly increases error by +0.937. VectorGraphRAG (+0.503) and VectorRAG (+0.215) both raise baseline error, but they also display large negative interactions with single-step (−1.271 and −1.134, respectively), indicating they can partially or fully offset the disadvantage of simpler tasks. Explanation-quality subgrades are strongly significant (e.g., specificity_relevance = −0.431), suggesting that stronger justifications reduce alignment errors by up to 0.4 or 0.5 points.

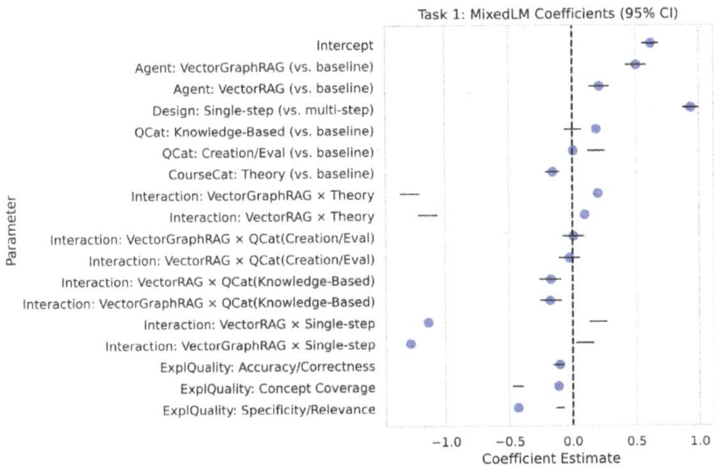

Figure 4. Forest plot of the Task 1 model's fixed-effect estimates with 95% confidence intervals. Negative coefficients reduce the predicted averaged absolute error, while positive coefficients increase it.

Overall, the fine-tuned LLM often achieves relatively low error in multi-step contexts, but VectorRAG or VectorGraphRAG can be more competitive if questions are single-step or if they provide higher-quality explanations in key sub-dimensions such as specificity/relevance.

4.1.3. Task 2: Exam Question Improvement

For Task 2, each agent improved the original question, and the meta-evaluator scored the result on three subgrades: Alignment with Objectives, Clarity, and Appropriate Difficulty (1–10 each). The Averaged_Task_Meta_Score is computed as

$$\text{Averaged\_Task\_Meta\_Score} = \frac{1}{3}\left(S_{\text{meta,align}} + S_{\text{meta,clarity}} + S_{\text{meta,difficulty}}\right). \quad (3)$$

Higher values reflect better improvements, from the meta-evaluator's perspective. The LMM for Task 2 includes similar predictors and a random intercept:

$$
\begin{aligned}
\text{Averaged\_Task\_Meta\_Score} \sim\ & C(\text{agent}) \times C(\text{question\_design}) \\
& + C(\text{agent}) \times C(\text{question\_category}) \\
& + C(\text{agent}) \times C(\text{course\_category}) \\
& + \text{expl\_quality\_alignment\_with\_objectives} \\
& + \text{expl\_quality\_clarity} \\
& + \text{expl\_quality\_appropriate\_difficulty} \\
& + (1 \mid \text{question\_id}).
\end{aligned} \tag{4}
$$

Key Insights from the Model

Figure 5 shows the forest plot. The intercept is 7.812, indicating the fine-tuned LLM's predicted meta score under baseline conditions (multi-step, application-based, application-oriented) with mean explanation quality. VectorRAG (+0.234) and VectorGraphRAG (+0.193) have higher baseline scores than the fine-tuned under these conditions, but they also have negative interactions with single-step (−0.200 and −0.186, respectively). Explanation-quality subgrades again exhibit large, significant coefficients (e.g., expl_quality_alignment_with_objectives = +0.349), each adding nearly 0.3–0.4 points to the final meta score when above average.

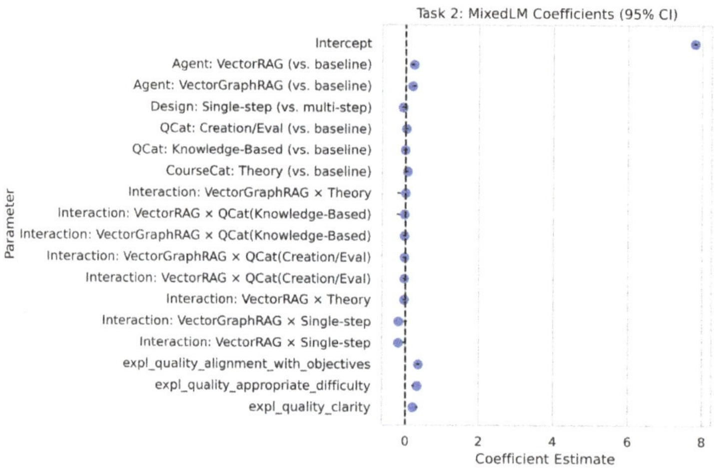

Figure 5. Forest plot of the Task 2 model's fixed-effect estimates with 95% confidence intervals. Positive coefficients increase the predicted averaged meta score, while negative coefficients reduce it.

Under average explanation quality, VectorRAG often achieves top averaged meta scores (reaching or surpassing 8.0) in multi-step, application-oriented improvements. The fine-tuned LLM can, however, catch or exceed those scores in theory-oriented tasks or when it delivers especially strong explanation quality (e.g., high clarity or appropriate difficulty).

4.1.4. Task 3: New Exam Question Generation

In Task 3, each agent produced a new question in the same Bloom's category, evaluated on four subgrades: Alignment, Clarity, Difficulty, and Originality (1–10 each). The Averaged_Task_Meta_Score is

$$
\text{Averaged\_Task\_Meta\_Score} = \frac{1}{4}\left(S_{\text{meta,align}} + S_{\text{meta,clarity}} + S_{\text{meta,difficulty}} + S_{\text{meta,originality}}\right). \tag{5}
$$

Higher scores indicate more suitable or creative question generation. The mixed-effects model follows the same pattern:

$$\begin{aligned} \text{Averaged\_Task\_Meta\_Score} \sim\ & C(\text{agent}) \times C(\text{question\_design}) \\ & + C(\text{agent}) \times C(\text{question\_category}) \\ & + C(\text{agent}) \times C(\text{course\_category}) \\ & + \text{expl\_quality\_alignment\_with\_objectives} \\ & + \text{expl\_quality\_clarity} \\ & + \text{expl\_quality\_appropriate\_difficulty} \\ & + \text{expl\_quality\_originality} \\ & + (1 \mid \text{question\_id}). \end{aligned} \tag{6}$$

Key Insights from the Model

Figure 6 indicates that the fine-tuned LLM's baseline intercept is 7.969. Although single-step tasks slightly reduce scores (−0.087), VectorRAG starts slightly above baseline in multi-step tasks (+0.030) but experiences a negative single-step interaction (−0.050). VectorGraphRAG is essentially near the fine-tuned baseline (−0.002), benefiting from large explanation-quality coefficients such as originality = +0.336. It can thus close or exceed gaps if it provides particularly creative or clear justifications.

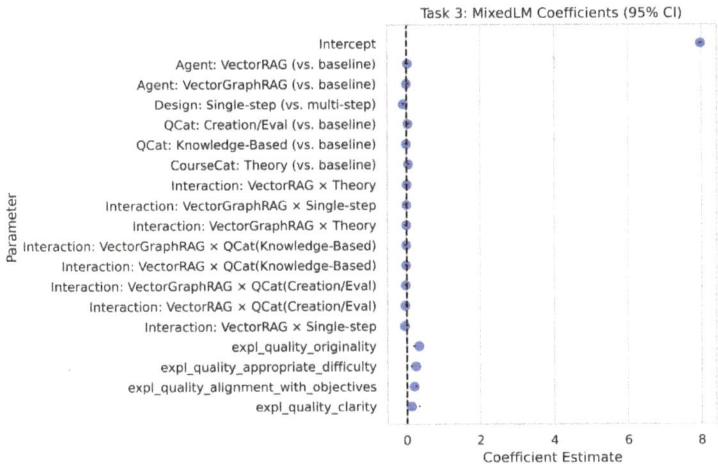

Figure 6. Forest plot of the Task 3 model's fixed-effect estimates with 95% confidence intervals. Positive coefficients raise the predicted averaged meta score, whereas negative coefficients reduce it.

The fine-tuned LLM generally excels in multi-step, theory-oriented tasks, whereas VectorRAG often thrives in application-oriented contexts. VectorGraphRAG tends to be more sensitive to explanation-quality subgrades, especially originality, allowing it to narrow or overcome baseline disadvantages.

4.2. Self-Reflection Analysis in Tasks 2 and 3

Each agent in Tasks 2 and 3 not only received a meta-evaluator score but also assigned its own self-score to the improved or newly generated question. A Self-Reflection Error was then computed as follows:

$$\text{Self-Reflection Error} = S_{\text{agent, self}} - S_{\text{meta, truth}}, \tag{7}$$

where a positive value indicates overestimation (agent scoring itself higher than the meta standard), and a negative value indicates underestimation. Figure 7 displays the observed distributions for these errors in Tasks 2 and 3.

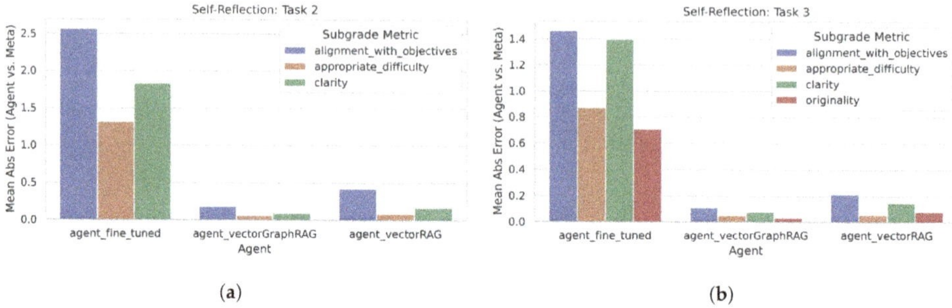

Figure 7. Self-reflection error distributions for Tasks 2 and 3. (**a**) Task 2: difference between agent's self-score and meta-evaluator ground truth. (**b**) Task 3: corresponding differences for newly generated questions.

Analyses reveal that the Fine-Tuned LLM systematically overestimates its performance by around +1.3 to +1.5 points, whereas VectorRAG and VectorGraphRAG hover near +0.1 to +0.2. This discrepancy suggests that, while fine-tuned LLM has strong generation capabilities, it may not be well-calibrated in judging its own improvements or new question quality.

4.3. Over-/Under-Grading Analysis in Task 1

Although Task 1 primarily uses absolute alignment errors, a signed perspective identifies whether agents consistently over-grade or under-grade certain items. The Signed Error in each dimension is

$$\text{Signed Error}(\text{dim } i) = S_{\text{agent},i} - S_{\text{meta},i}, \quad (8)$$

where a positive value indicates over-grading (the agent gave higher subgrades than the meta-evaluator) and a negative value indicates under-grading. Figure 8 visualizes mean signed errors in Task 1 across Concept Coverage, Specificity/Relevance, and Accuracy/Correctness, grouped by agent and question type.

In Task 1, the fine-tuned LLM tends to over-grade concept coverage for certain categories by $\sim$+1.3–1.4, consistent with its self-reflection bias in later tasks. VectorRAG has a mild positive bias in creation/evaluation questions, while VectorGraphRAG sometimes underestimates accuracy/correctness. These patterns reinforce the need for a meta-evaluator to mitigate systematic biases.

4.4. Bias Identification (Meta_auto vs. Meta_human)

An additional analysis was conducted to showcase how the automated meta-evaluator (Meta_auto) compared to the human-supervised reference (Meta_human), thereby revealing potential biases and the extent to which expert oversight can mitigate them. Specifically, the final dataset was merged to include both the Meta_auto and Meta_human scores for the same items, then grouped by key attributes: task, agent, question_category, question_design, and course_category. Within each group, the difference was computed separately for grading-related scores (e.g., alignment or improved question quality) and for explanation quality subdimensions, by using this formula:

$$\text{diff} = (\text{meta\_human} - \text{meta\_auto}) \quad (9)$$

After calculating mean and median differences, the Wilcoxon signed-rank test was used to determine whether these distributions significantly deviated from zero, indicating a systematic gap between the automated evaluator and the human reference. Tables in Appendix A.3 (Tables A5–A7) show that, for many combinations of task and agent, the p-values are extremely small (often lower than 10^{-20}), signifying that Meta_auto and Meta_human consistently differ in their evaluations. In some cases, such as fine-tuned under Task 2 or Task 3, the difference is notably negative, suggesting the human experts tended to provide lower numeric scores than the automated system. On the contrary, the positive mean differences for VectorGraphRAG indicate that Meta_human often rated these outputs higher than Meta_auto evaluations.

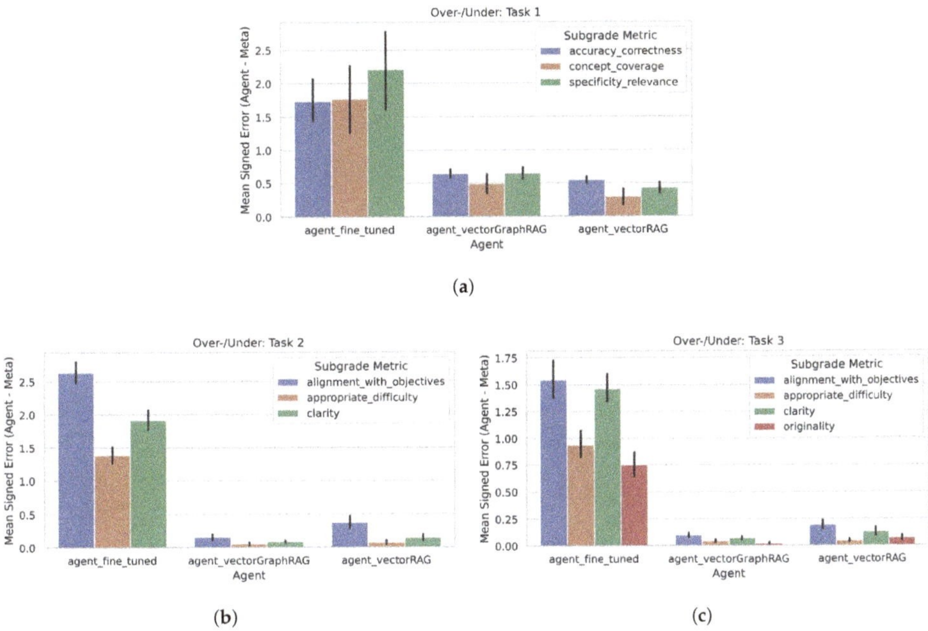

Figure 8. Agent under-/over-grading patterns across the three tasks: (**a**) Task 1 signed errors, (**b**) Task 2 agent self-scoring vs. meta-evaluator, and (**c**) Task 3 self-scoring vs. meta-evaluator.

These trends apply both to the grading/score dimension (alignment or improved/new question quality) and to explanation quality metrics. Notably, for some agent–task combinations, the Wilcoxon test shows large effect sizes, implying that the discrepancy is not sporadic but rather systematic. This underscores the necessity of human intervention, especially when tasks require nuanced judgments of clarity, correctness, or originality. Figure 9 illustrates how the differences cluster around negative or positive values depending on the agent and task, reinforcing that the automated meta-evaluator, though helpful, may overestimate or underestimate certain dimensions.

Overall, these results confirm that the Meta Evaluator (Meta_auto) introduces measurable biases in both grading and explanation scores, varying by agent type and question attributes. Human supervision (Meta_human) plays a crucial role in correcting systematic misalignment, especially in high-stakes educational contexts. By identifying where and why biases appear, future iterations of the meta-evaluation system can incorporate targeted calibrations or fine-tuning strategies to narrow the gap between automated judgments and expert assessments.

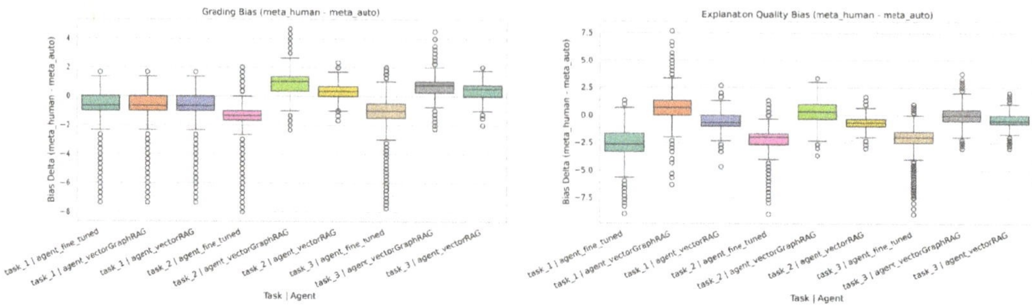

(a) (b)

Figure 9. Meta evaluator identified bias: (**a**) Grading Bias—Negative values indicate that human evaluators scored lower than the automatic meta evaluator, while positive values indicate higher human scores. Each box summarizes the distribution of bias across all questions in that category. (**b**) Explanation Quality Bias—A negative distribution means human evaluators found lower explanation quality relative to the automatic meta evaluation, and a positive distribution means higher human ratings. Each box represents the variability in bias across multiple questions in the corresponding task–agent grouping.

4.5. Real-World Validation on 100 Human-Created Exam Questions (Task 1)

To assess the framework's practical utility beyond the experimental conditions, a set of 100 human-authored exam questions was assembled. Each question fell under the theory-oriented course category, was application-based in Bloom's taxonomy, and had a multi-step design. The recommended agent, identified in earlier sections based on the mixed-effects modeling and subsequent evaluations, was applied to these questions for Task 1. A panel of human experts likewise scored each question's alignment (averaging concept coverage, specificity/relevance, and accuracy/correctness), thereby generating a reference for comparison.

Table 2 presents the key findings, including a paired t-test of the agent's average scores against the human scores, along with Bland–Altman statistics. The mean difference ($\approx$0.23) points) is relatively small, and the p-value ($\approx$0.1224) indicates **no statistically significant difference** in overall mean scores. This suggests that, on average, the agent's alignment evaluations are comparable to those of human experts.

Table 2. Paired t-test and Bland–Altman summary for the 100-question real-world validation set (Task 1).

Statistic	Value
Number of Questions (N)	100
Mean Agent Score	6.88
Mean Human Score	6.65
Mean Difference (Agent–Human)	0.23
Std. Dev. of Difference	1.45
Upper Limit of Agreement (LoA)	3.08
Lower Limit of Agreement (LoA)	−2.62
Paired t-Statistic	1.56
p-Value	0.1224

Figure 10 provides a Bland–Altman plot, illustrating each question's difference (agent minus human) against the mean of the two scores. The "mean difference" (red dashed line) is centered slightly above zero, reflecting the 0.23-point bias. The "95% limits of agreement" (green dashed lines) span from (−2.62) to (3.08), suggesting that, while the agent occasionally overestimates or underestimates certain items, most points fall within a reasonable range of agreement.

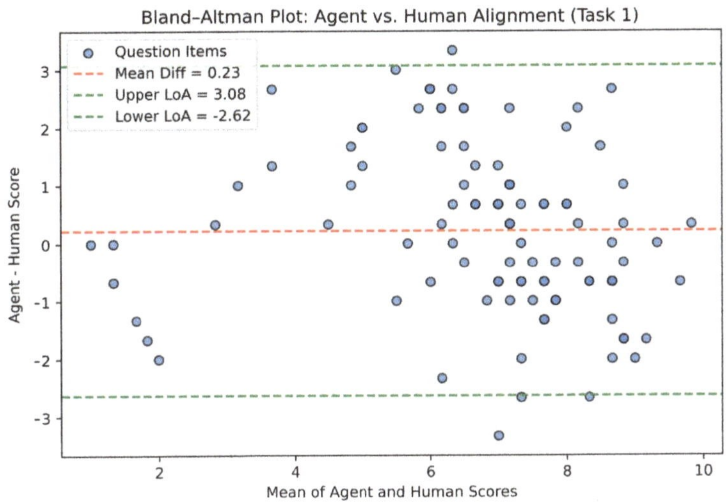

Figure 10. Bland–Altman plot for agent vs. human alignment on the 100-question validation set (Task 1). The center red line denotes the mean difference (0.23); the green lines define the 95% limits of agreement.

These results demonstrate that the discrepancies between the agent and the human experts are generally small and not statistically significant. While occasional outliers remain, the overall trend supports using this best-performing agent to autonomously assess alignment for multi-step, theory-oriented, application-based questions. In practice, instructor oversight continues to play a vital role, particularly for questions lying near the edges of the distribution. Nonetheless, the fact that the system's outputs do not systematically diverge from human judgments underscores the real-world viability of the proposed framework—indicating that it can be confidently deployed for large-scale alignment tasks while still allowing educators to perform final quality checks as needed.

4.6. Summary of Findings

No single agent dominates under every condition. The fine-tuned LLM often achieves lower error in multi-step, theory-oriented tasks, while VectorRAG excels in application-oriented tasks. VectorGraphRAG, although showing higher baseline error or lower baseline scores, can bridge the gap if it provides high explanation-quality subgrades (e.g., specificity/relevance in Task 1 or originality in Task 3).

Self-reflection Section 4.2 analysis indicates that the fine-tuned LLM overestimates its performance by more than +1 point, whereas VectorRAG and VectorGraphRAG remain closer to meta-evaluator judgments. Over-/under-grading Section 4.3 in Task 1 shows parallel biases, suggesting that calibration differences persist across tasks.

By adopting mixed-effects modeling with random intercepts for question_id, these analyses correctly account for within-question correlation, uncovering how agent-type, design, category, and explanation dimensions interact to influence alignment errors or meta scores. Full coefficient tables are in Appendix A.1, while the forest plots and predicted means presented here highlight the most influential terms and interactions.

5. Discussion

This study aimed to develop and evaluate a systematic framework and provide best practices for integrating large language models (LLMs) into higher-education exam-question design. Three primary tasks: (1) alignment evaluation of original questions, (2) question improvement, and (3) new question generation; were undertaken by three different LLM-based agents. Building on the detailed statistical models and numerical findings presented earlier, this discussion distills the core insights of each task into a cohesive narrative. It offers actionable guidance for selecting the most suitable agents under varying conditions and clarifies why these three LLM-based agents (VectorRAG, VectorGraphRAG, and a fine-tuned LLM) were studied, rather than more complex alternatives. This balanced approach emphasizes both the empirical robustness of the findings and their practical relevance, particularly within the delicate context of higher education, and derives best practices for real-world implementation.

5.1. Main Analysis: Alignment, Improvement, and Generation

The main analysis showcases each agent intrinsic strengths and limitations that deeply depend on the type of question, the nature of the course material, and the cognitive demands of the specific task.

5.1.1. Task 1 (Alignment Evaluation)

In this first task, each agent's subgrade of the original question was compared to a meta-evaluator's ground truth, and the discrepancy was measured via weighted absolute error. The fine-tuned LLM generally excelled in multi-step, theory-oriented contexts, especially for higher-level conceptual tasks. Conversely, VectorRAG tended to outperform others for single-step, application-oriented questions, leveraging retrieval-based augmentation. Although VectorGraphRAG started with a somewhat higher baseline error, it could partially close the gap when providing especially strong explanation-quality subgrades—for example, specificity/relevance or accuracy/correctness. Indeed, the regression coefficients indicated that a 1-point increase in specificity_relevance could reduce alignment error by up to 0.4 (e.g., −0.431 estimate), revealing the tangible impact of deeper, more precise justifications.

5.1.2. Task 2 (Question Improvement)

In this task, each agent generated an improved version of the original question, which the meta-evaluator scored on Alignment with Objectives, Clarity, and Appropriate Difficulty. The fine-tuned LLM tended to excel for theory-heavy or higher-level conceptual refinements, consistent with its domain-focused training. However, it was not always dominant in single-step, practical questions, where VectorRAG often delivered strong results—particularly in multi-step, application-oriented improvement scenarios. VectorGraphRAG's performance was close to the other agents, but it rarely occupied the top position unless it provided robust explanation-quality subgrades (alignment_with_objectives, clarity, appropriate_difficulty), each of which can raise the meta score by 0.2–0.3 points when above average.

5.1.3. Task 3 (New Question Generation)

For the final task, each agent created an entirely new question in the same Bloom's category, evaluated on Alignment, Clarity, Difficulty, and Originality. Much like Task 2, the Fine-Tuned LLM often led in theory-oriented or more complex, multi-step tasks. Meanwhile, VectorRAG excelled in application-oriented contexts where retrieval-based expansions offered practical authenticity. VectorGraphRAG generally showed moderate but steady performance, occasionally achieving higher scores when originality was strong (the regression estimate for originality, ≈+0.336, indicates a substantial positive impact). These results highlight the importance of well-substantiated creativity in pedagogical question design.

5.1.4. Guidelines for Agent Selection

Table 3 converts these findings into a practical reference. Each row captures an intersection of (i) Bloom's category (Knowledge-Based, Application-Based, Creation and Evaluation), (ii) question design (single-step or multi-step), and (iii) course orientation (theory-oriented or application-oriented). For each combination, the table identifies which agent tended to show higher performance in Task 1 (Alignment Evaluation), Task 2 (Question Improvement), and Task 3 (New Question Generation). When no consistent leader emerged, we note "All three agents performed similarly" to reflect minimal or inconsistent differences among the fine-tuned LLM, VectorRAG, and VectorGraphRAG.

Table 3. Observed performance patterns per task under each question category × question design × course category combination. "All three agents performed similarly" indicates no pronounced advantage for a single agent.

Question Category	Question Design	Course Category	Higher Performance (Task 1)	Higher Performance (Task 2)	Higher Performance (Task 3)
Knowledge-Based	Single-Step	Theory-Oriented	Fine-Tuned LLM	Fine-Tuned LLM	Fine-Tuned LLM
Knowledge-Based	Single-Step	Application-Oriented	VectorRAG	All three agents performed similarly *	All three agents performed similarly *
Knowledge-Based	Multi-Step	Theory-Oriented	Fine-Tuned LLM	Fine-Tuned LLM	Fine-Tuned LLM
Knowledge-Based	Multi-Step	Application-Oriented	All three agents performed similarly *	VectorRAG	VectorRAG
Application-Based	Single-Step	Theory-Oriented	Fine-Tuned LLM	Fine-Tuned LLM	Fine-Tuned LLM
Application-Based	Single-Step	Application-Oriented	VectorRAG	VectorRAG	VectorRAG
Application-Based	Multi-Step	Theory-Oriented	Fine-Tuned LLM	Fine-Tuned LLM	Fine-Tuned LLM
Application-Based	Multi-Step	Application-Oriented	All three agents performed similarly *	VectorRAG	VectorRAG
Creation and Evaluation	Single-Step	Theory-Oriented	Fine-Tuned LLM	Fine-Tuned LLM	Fine-Tuned LLM
Creation and Evaluation	Single-Step	Application-Oriented	VectorRAG	All three agents performed similarly *	All three agents performed similarly *
Creation and Evaluation	Multi-Step	Theory-Oriented	Fine-Tuned LLM	Fine-Tuned LLM	Fine-Tuned LLM
Creation and Evaluation	Multi-Step	Application-Oriented	All three agents performed similarly *	VectorRAG	VectorRAG

* Fine-Tuned LLM, VectorRAG, and VectorGraphRAG showed no significant or consistent difference in performance under those conditions.

While the Fine-Tuned LLM frequently exhibits strong performance in theory-oriented, multi-step tasks across all three tasks, VectorRAG tends to excel in application-oriented conditions for Tasks 2 and 3. Rows labeled "All three agents performed similarly" indicate that neither fine-tuned LLM nor VectorRAG nor VectorGraphRAG consistently outperformed the others, typically reflecting subtler differences that were not clearly resolved by the model predictions.

These findings suggest a task–agent matching approach, with a fine-tuned LLM for conceptual depth, VectorRAG for simpler application-based tasks, and VectorGraphRAG for cross-topic or multi-hop contexts. Certain agents perform better in specific scenarios because their design and training align differently with the nature of the question. The fine-tuned LLM, having absorbed domain-specific patterns from curated datasets, typically excels in multi-step theoretical tasks that require deeper conceptual reasoning. VectorRAG, which dynamically retrieves context from a vector database, tends to outperform others in practical or single-step prompts where references to real-world frameworks or coding snippets are essential. Meanwhile, VectorGraphRAG, enriched by a knowledge-graph layer, can handle multi-topic or cross-linked tasks effectively when it harnesses its graph-based insights and produces sufficiently cohesive explanations.

5.2. *Justification for Selecting These Three Agents*

Although more advanced LLMs and prompting techniques have emerged, the choice of VectorRAG, VectorGraphRAG, and a fine-tuned LLM was driven by higher education's unique needs for transparency, reliability, and domain specificity. Retrieval-augmented designs (VectorRAG, VectorGraphRAG) provide interpretable references to course content, which is often essential when validating the correctness or relevance of suggested improvements. Meanwhile, a fine-tuned LLM can specialize deeply in advanced theoretical or conceptual topics without incurring overfitting risks from large, unrelated corpora. VectorGraphRAG, though at times lagging in baseline conditions, can close gaps with high-quality subgrades. Moreover, the simpler retrieval approaches used here (rather than complex multi-hop or large-scale memory) facilitate easier deployment and maintenance within typical university infrastructures.

5.3. *Self-Reflection and Over-/Under-Grading Effects*

In Tasks 2 and 3, agents provided self-scores on their own question improvements or creations, revealing that the fine-tuned LLM systematically overestimated its quality by about +1 to +1.5 points relative to the meta-evaluator's ground truth. In contrast, VectorRAG and VectorGraphRAG hovered near +0.1 to +0.2, suggesting more self-awareness. Interestingly, this matches the over-/under-grading Section 4.3 findings in Task 1, where the fine-tuned LLM displayed a positive bias (e.g., inflating concept coverage by up to 1+ point), while the other two agents showed milder biases. Thus, the same calibration gaps that lead to over-grading in Task 1 resurface in self-reflection errors in Tasks 2 and 3, underscoring the importance of refining how LLMs judge and justify their own outputs if they are to be trusted for real-world educational use.

5.4. *Dual Grading System: Granular Scores and Justifications*

Across all tasks, each agent used a dual grading system that generated granular numeric sub-scores (e.g., alignment, clarity, correctness) alongside textual justifications. This dual-format output played a crucial role in the following:

- **Bias Detection**: The numeric scores enabled quantitative comparisons, while the explanations revealed how the agent arrived at each rating. Divergences, such as overinflated clarity scores or shallow justifications, were easier to spot.
- **Transparency and Accountability**: Instructors could see not just a final numeric grade but also the reasoning behind it, enabling more precise challenges or corrections.

- **Enhanced Objectivity**: By combining the objectivity of numeric sub-scores with the interpretability of human-readable justifications, the system fostered consistency across varying question categories and course types.

Overall, the dual scoring system added an important layer of insight, improving the detection of bias and reinforcing the trustworthiness of automated assessments.

5.5. Meta Evaluator as a Control Mechanism: Strengths and Limitations

A distinctive contribution of this research is the meta evaluator (Meta_auto), an automated system meant to assess agent outputs in parallel with expert-supervised scoring (Meta_human). Our results show that, while Meta_auto usefully flags questionable outputs, it can also exhibit systematic biases—occasionally overscoring the fine-tuned LLM or underscoring VectorGraphRAG explanations.

From a workflow perspective, a meta evaluator serves as an early warning system, revealing where an agent's sub-scores or explanations depart from expected norms. Educators can then focus on flagged items rather than manually re-checking every question. However, the meta evaluator itself requires careful prompt-engineering and tuning; routine human oversight remains essential, especially in high-stakes or conceptually complex scenarios.

5.6. Bias Evaluation and Sources of Discrepancy

Comparisons of Meta_auto and Meta_human revealed systematic positive or negative biases under specific agent–task conditions. The data reveal the following: (1) systematic over-scoring of the fine-tuned LLM – The meta evaluator appeared positively influenced by the more verbose or fluent style of the fine-tuned LLM, awarding it +1 to +3 points above human experts' ratings in many subgroups. This aligns with the fine-tuned LLM's self-reflection bias, indicating a synergy between the agent's own "confidence" and the meta-evaluator's preference for polished text; (2) Systematic under-scoring of retrieval-based agents – VectorRAG and VectorGraphRAG typically received lower automated scores than final human judgments, showing that factual correctness or concise referencing was underappreciated by the meta evaluator. Human experts generate increased scores based on actual content validity, reducing the negative gap.

When the magnitude of these biases exceeded 1.0–2.0 points on a 10-point scale, it underscored the need for targeted corrective strategies, such as revised meta-evaluator prompts or additional training data spotlighting robust justification. Our dual grading system (numeric plus explanation) proved especially helpful for identifying these anomalies, since the mismatch between numeric sub-scores and textual rationales became a clear signal for potential bias.

5.7. Real-World Validation: 100 New Questions

To confirm these patterns beyond controlled tests, we applied the best-performing agent to 100 real, instructor-created exam questions. The agent's alignment scores did not significantly differ from human expert ratings ($p \approx 0.12$), indicating it can effectively handle large-scale alignment tasks once biases are known and mitigated.

This finding underscores that our proposed framework, when carefully tuned and supervised, does not systematically deviate from human standards, boosting confidence in eventual large-scale adoption. Nevertheless, outliers remained, reiterating that full automation is neither recommended nor realistic, especially for high-stakes decisions or intricately nuanced questions.

5.8. Guidelines and Best Practices for Higher Education

Bringing together the insights from the analysis conducted in this study, along with the variety of practical trials for data processing and implementation, we propose a set of best practices for educators and developers:

- **Match LLM Architecture to Question Type**: Select the fine-tuned LLM for conceptually rich or multi-step tasks requiring deep alignment; use VectorRAG for simpler, application-heavy tasks with well-defined chunking and top-k retrieval; deploy VectorGraphRAG for contexts requiring cross-domain or knowledge-graph insights, ensuring it provides robust explanations.
- **Iterative Tuning and Data Curation**: Carefully adjust retrieval parameters (chunk size, top-k), monitor performance, and refine. Fine-tuning benefits from noise-free, domain-distilled datasets. Repeated cycles of training and expert feedback improve alignment and reduce hallucinations.
- **Leverage a Dual Grading System**: Mandate numeric sub-scores for transparency and comparative evaluation. Require textual justifications to reveal the basis for each score, facilitating bias detection and instructor trust. Repeatedly, we see that "better explanations = better scores." Require the AI to detail alignment decisions, clarity adjustments, or originality elements. This not only helps human reviewers pinpoint errors but also encourages the LLM to scrutinize its own logic more thoroughly.
- **Automated Meta Evaluation with Human Oversight**: While an automated meta-evaluator can drastically reduce instructor workloads, the bias tables prove that purely automated scoring is insufficient for high-stakes decisions. A best practice is to always have a final human check, while the meta evaluator should be used as a guard system that will flag potential discrepancies. Periodic random audits of the meta-evaluator's judgments can detect drift or emerging biases.
- **Monitor Agent Self-Reflection**: Agents vary in how accurately they self-score. The fine-tuned LLM often inflates its performance by +1 to +1.5 points. If an instructor uses these self-scores directly, students might see inflated question quality or misaligned difficulty levels. Pair self-reflection with external (meta or human) scoring to calibrate the agent's confidence over time.
- **Maintain Expert Oversight for High-Stakes Tasks**: Although the system can automate a large database of question alignment or generation, final accountability should remain with domain experts. We recommend an 80–20 model, with AI handling most items and experts focusing on random audits or flagged outliers, where this model will balance efficiency and educational precision.
- **Iterative Review and Calibration**: A continuous improvement cycle, ideally at semester boundaries, can keep the system aligned with evolving course objectives.

5.9. Limitations and Future Work

Despite the encouraging results, we note several certain limitations. Expert judgments, despite being thorough, retained elements of subjectivity, and the review process relied on the standards and norms of a single institution. Employing larger reviewer pools, multi-annotator consensus, or multi-institutional replication would help mitigate potential human-bias effects and increase generalizability. Partial real-world validation focused on Task1 with 100 newly created questions, leaving Tasks 2 and 3 to be tested more extensively and in a wider range of academic disciplines or question designs. This study also concentrated largely on text-centric, STEM-based courses; further exploration of humanities or social sciences, where interpretive or highly subjective items are common, could reveal different patterns of performance or bias.

Another limitation concerns the nature of the course materials themselves. The approach hinged on carefully curated lecture notes, slides, and condensed texts rather than raw, unstructured sources. If only dense textbooks or research articles were available, additional pre-processing or fine-tuning may be necessary. The meta-evaluator was similarly tied to a particular large language model and prompt design, so reproducing these results within different LLM ecosystems might introduce new biases or necessitate different calibration strategies. Scalability likewise presents challenges, as fine-tuning large models, maintaining knowledge graphs, and implementing real-time retrieval can require significant computational resources and specialized expertise—constraints that smaller institutions may find difficult to meet.

Finally, the absence of direct student feedback on AI-generated items leaves open questions about the effects on learner motivation, fairness perceptions, and actual educational outcomes. Future work could examine these dimensions by incorporating student perspectives, validating tasks beyond alignment (Tasks 2 and 3) at scale, exploring further refinements to the meta-evaluator prompts, and assessing the viability of more lightweight or distributed infrastructures. Furthermore, future work could also incorporate more sophisticated retrieval (e.g., multi-hop chaining, graph-based expansions, multi-modal models) or advanced multi-agent collaboration, provided that basic transparency and reliability standards are upheld. Such research would not only enrich the understanding of how these AI-driven tools function across diverse contexts but would also advance their integration into real-world academic environments.

6. Conclusions

This work set out to (i) investigate how large language models (LLMs) can evaluate, refine, and generate exam questions in higher education, (ii) establish guidelines and best practices for safely integrating AI into assessment workflows, and (iii) demonstrate the importance of a structured meta-evaluation layer to mitigate bias and maintain academic standards. By systematically analyzing three LLM-based agents (VectorRAG, VectorGraphRAG, and a fine-tuned LLM) across multiple question designs, Bloom's levels, and course orientations, this study revealed the following:

No single model is universally optimal: each agent excels under different conditions (e.g., theory-oriented, multi-step tasks vs. single-step, application-based tasks). A dual grading system of numeric scores and justifications provides transparency, effectively flags biases, and helps instructors pinpoint where alignment or explanation shortfalls occur. A meta evaluator with embedded guards and safety mechanisms can serve as a powerful control mechanism—identifying discrepancies in agent outputs, but itself requires routine human oversight to address systematic over or underestimation. The educational domain's high standards, originated from limited and often condensed course materials and the stakes of student assessment, demand that such AI-driven tools be meticulously tuned and regularly audited. Although a real-world test on newly crafted questions demonstrated the feasibility and accuracy of carefully configured AI agents, partial human supervision remains essential, especially when dealing with high-stakes or conceptually complex scenarios, to ensure that any questionable alignments or biases are quickly identified and corrected.

Taken together, these findings underscore the value of selective task–agent matching, iterative fine-tuning and retrieval design, and bias-aware monitoring as a comprehensive roadmap for adopting LLMs in higher-education assessment. By integrating these measures and incorporating partial human oversight through automated safety mechanisms, institutions can harness AI's potential to streamline question creation and evaluation without compromising the high-standards and the academic success.

Author Contributions: Conceptualization, V.N. and D.T.; methodology, V.N.; software, V.N.; validation, V.N., D.T. and I.C.; formal analysis, V.N.; investigation, V.N.; resources, I.C. and D.T.; data curation, V.N.; writing—original draft preparation, V.N.; writing—review and editing, V.N.; visualization, V.N.; supervision, I.C.; project administration, D.T.; funding acquisition, I.C. All authors have read and agreed to the published version of the manuscript.

Funding: This research received no external funding.

Data Availability Statement: The data presented in this study along with the source code, are available on request from the corresponding author. The data are not publicly available due to ongoing research.

Conflicts of Interest: The authors declare no conflicts of interest.

Appendix A

Appendix A.1

The following tables summarize the fixed effects from the mixed-effects regression models used to evaluate agent performance across three tasks in the study.

Table A1. Full fixed effects for Task 1 mixed-effects model (weighted absolute error).

Parameter	Estimate	SE	z	*p*-Value	95% CI (Lower–Upper)
Intercept (Fine-Tuned, multi-step, Appl.-Based, Appl.-Oriented)	0.619	0.033	19.009	<0.001	(0.555–0.682)
C(agent)[T.agent_vectorGraphRAG]	0.503	0.040	12.635	<0.001	(0.425–0.581)
C(agent)[T.agent_vectorRAG]	0.215	0.039	5.442	<0.001	(0.137–0.292)
C(question_design)[T.single_step]	0.937	0.030	30.757	<0.001	(0.877–0.996)
C(question_category)[T.Creation and Evaluation Questions]	0.006	0.033	0.178	0.859	(−0.059–0.070)
C(question_category)[T.Knowledge-Based Questions]	0.190	0.033	5.760	<0.001	(0.125–0.255)
C(course_category)[T.Theory-Oriented]	-0.158	0.027	−5.864	<0.001	(−0.211-−0.105)
C(agent)[T.agent_vectorGraphRAG]: C(question_design)[T.single_step]	−1.271	0.037	−34.209	<0.001	(−1.344-−1.199)
C(agent)[T.agent_vectorRAG]: C(question_design)[T.single_step]	−1.134	0.038	−30.029	<0.001	(−1.209-−1.060)
C(agent)[T.agent_vectorGraphRAG]: C(question_category)[T.Creation and Evaluation Questions]	0.007	0.042	0.175	0.861	(-0.075–0.090)
C(agent)[T.agent_vectorRAG]: C(question_category)[T.Creation and Evaluation Questions]	−0.025	0.042	−0.586	0.558	(−0.107–0.058)
C(agent)[T.agent_vectorGraphRAG]: C(question_category)[T.Knowledge-Based Questions]	−0.179	0.042	−4.249	<0.001	(−0.261-−0.096)
C(agent)[T.agent_vectorRAG]: C(question_category)[T.Knowledge-Based Questions]	−0.174	0.042	−4.132	<0.001	(−0.256-−0.091)
C(agent)[T.agent_vectorGraphRAG]: C(course_category)[T.Theory-Oriented]	0.202	0.034	5.897	<0.001	(0.135–0.269)
C(agent)[T.agent_vectorRAG]: C(course_category)[T.Theory-Oriented]	0.098	0.034	2.848	0.004	(0.030–0.165)
expl_quality_concept_coverage	−0.113	0.021	−5.411	<0.001	(−0.154-−0.072)
expl_quality_specificity_relevance	−0.431	0.020	−21.885	<0.001	(−0.470-−0.393)
expl_quality_accuracy_correctness	−0.102	0.016	−6.523	<0.001	(−0.132-−0.071)
Group Var (question_id)	0.122	0.012	–	–	–

Table A2. Full Fixed Effects for Task 2 Mixed-Effects Model (Weighted Meta Score).

Parameter	Estimate	SE	z	p-Value	95% CI (Lower–Upper)
Intercept (Fine-Tuned, multi-step, Appl.-Based, Appl.-Oriented)	7.812	0.016	481.715	<0.001	(7.780–7.844)
C(agent)[T.agent_vectorGraphRAG]	0.193	0.019	10.415	<0.001	(0.157–0.229)
C(agent)[T.agent_vectorRAG]	0.234	0.018	13.147	<0.001	(0.199–0.269)
C(question_design)[T.single_step]	−0.063	0.015	−4.341	<0.001	(−0.092–−0.035)
C(question_category)[T.Creation and Evaluation Questions]	0.024	0.017	1.446	0.148	(−0.009–0.057)
C(question_category)[T.Knowledge-Based Questions]	−0.004	0.017	−0.238	0.812	(−0.037–0.029)
C(course_category)[T.Theory-Oriented]	0.058	0.014	4.244	<0.001	(0.031–0.084)
C(agent)[T.agent_vectorGraphRAG]: C(question_design)[T.single_step]	−0.186	0.016	−11.782	<0.001	(−0.217–−0.155)
C(agent)[T.agent_vectorRAG]: C(question_design)[T.single_step]	−0.200	0.016	−12.519	<0.001	(−0.231–−0.169)
C(agent)[T.agent_vectorGraphRAG]: C(question_category)[T.Creation and Evaluation Questions]	−0.027	0.018	−1.488	0.137	(−0.062–0.008)
C(agent)[T.agent_vectorRAG]: C(question_category)[T.Creation and Evaluation Questions]	−0.031	0.018	−1.707	0.088	(−0.066–0.005)
C(agent)[T.agent_vectorGraphRAG]: C(question_category)[T.Knowledge-Based Questions]	−0.027	0.018	−1.474	0.140	(−0.062–0.009)
C(agent)[T.agent_vectorRAG]: C(question_category)[T.Knowledge-Based Questions]	−0.022	0.018	−1.248	0.212	(−0.058–0.013)
C(agent)[T.agent_vectorGraphRAG]: C(course_category)[T.Theory-Oriented]	0.003	0.015	0.176	0.861	(−0.026–0.032)
C(agent)[T.agent_vectorRAG]: C(course_category)[T.Theory-Oriented]	−0.037	0.015	−2.509	0.012	(−0.066–−0.008)
expl_quality_alignment_with _objectives	0.349	0.011	31.654	<0.001	(0.328–0.371)
expl_quality_clarity	0.204	0.008	25.088	<0.001	(0.188–0.220)
expl_quality_appropriate _difficulty	0.319	0.011	28.252	<0.001	(0.297–0.342)
Group Var (question_id)	0.068	0.009	–	–	–

Table A3. Full fixed effects for Task 3 mixed-effects model (weighted meta score).

Parameter	Estimate	SE	z	p-Value	95% CI (Lower–Upper)
Intercept (Fine-Tuned, multi-step, Appl.-Based, Appl.-Oriented)	7.969	0.015	541.833	<0.001	(7.940–7.998)
C(agent)[T.agent_vectorGraphRAG]	−0.002	0.016	−0.105	0.916	(−0.034–0.030)
C(agent)[T.agent_vectorRAG]	0.030	0.016	1.916	0.055	(−0.001–0.061)
C(question_design)[T.single_step]	−0.087	0.013	−6.746	<0.001	(−0.112–−0.062)
C(question_category)[T.Creation and Evaluation Questions]	0.036	0.015	2.446	0.014	(0.007–0.065)
C(question_category)[T.Knowledge-Based Questions]	−0.008	0.015	−0.547	0.584	(−0.037–0.021)
C(course_category)[T.Theory-Oriented]	0.048	0.012	4.026	<0.001	(0.025–0.072)
C(agent)[T.agent_vectorGraphRAG]: C(question_design)[T.single_step]	−0.003	0.014	−0.234	0.815	(−0.030–0.024)
C(agent)[T.agent_vectorRAG]: C(question_design)[T.single_step]	−0.050	0.014	−3.579	<0.001	(−0.077–−0.023)

Table A3. Cont.

Parameter	Estimate	SE	z	*p*-Value	95% CI (Lower–Upper)
C(agent)[T.agent_vectorGraphRAG]: C(question_category)[T.Creation and Evaluation Questions]	−0.022	0.016	−1.415	0.157	(−0.053–0.009)
C(agent)[T.agent_vectorRAG]: C(question_category)[T.Creation and Evaluation Questions]	−0.036	0.016	−2.269	0.023	(−0.067––0.005)
C(agent)[T.agent_vectorGraphRAG]: C(question_category)[T.Knowledge-Based Questions]	−0.008	0.016	−0.516	0.606	(−0.039–0.023)
C(agent)[T.agent_vectorRAG]: C(question_category)[T.Knowledge-Based Questions]	−0.015	0.016	−0.941	0.347	(−0.046–0.016)
C(agent)[T.agent_vectorGraphRAG]: C(course_category)[T.Theory-Oriented]	−0.004	0.013	−0.342	0.733	(−0.030–0.021)
C(agent)[T.agent_vectorRAG]: C(course_category)[T.Theory-Oriented]	0.011	0.013	0.845	0.398	(−0.014–0.036)
expl_quality_alignment_with _objectives	0.199	0.010	20.464	<0.001	(0.180–0.218)
expl_quality_clarity	0.126	0.007	17.052	<0.001	(0.112–0.141)
expl_quality_appropriate _difficulty	0.249	0.008	31.482	<0.001	(0.234–0.265)
expl_quality_originality	0.336	0.007	50.092	<0.001	(0.323–0.349)
Group Var (question_id)	0.054	0.009	–	–	–

Appendix A.2

Table A4. Sample questions generated by agents for Task 3 (Question Generation).

New Question
Explain the role of a data lake in storing and making dark data accessible for analysis. Describe how schema-on-read can help with analyzing unstructured dark data.
In the context of integrating data from multiple ERP systems into a unified data warehouse, how would you design a data modeling strategy that addresses the challenges of differing data semantics and metadata across systems to ensure the consistency, usability and analytical value of the integrated data?
Suppose a system has two resources, R1 and R2, each with a finite number of instances. Processes P1, P2, and P3 are competing for these resources. P1 holds an instance of R1 and requests R2; P2 holds R2 and requests R1; P3 holds an instance of R1 and requests another instance of R1. Illustrate a resource allocation graph for this scenario. How would you determine if this system is in a safe or unsafe state, and what minimal modification could prevent a deadlock in this specific scenario, assuming mutual exclusion is necessary?
For a web application using the "About Us" section as an example that requires quick access to main content while also allowing users to dive deeper into sub-pages without leaving the primary section, assess the trade-offs between a flat site structure versus a cascading one in terms of findability and the user's overall navigation experience within the section. Detail how the chosen architecture influences the site menu design and its maintenance.
Compare and contrast the effects of LASSO and Ridge regularization on model parameters in polynomial regression, considering their impact on model complexity, and provide a hypothetical scenario where you need to choose between them based on specific data characteristics to avoid overfitting.

Appendix A.3

Table A5. Grading bias across all categories (Task 1 only). *Legend:* ABQ = Application-based question; CEQ = Creation and evaluation question; KBQ = Knowledge-based question; AO = Application-oriented; TO = Theory-oriented; FT = Agent–fine-tuned; VGR = Agent–vectorGraphRAG; VR = Agent–vectorRAG.

Agent	Question Category	Question Design	Course Category	n	Mean Diff	Median Diff	p Value
FT	ABQ	multi_step	AO	400	−0.655833	−0.666667	1.98272×10^{-40}
FT	ABQ	multi_step	TO	397	−0.480269	−0.333333	1.4517×10^{-36}
FT	ABQ	single_step	AO	200	−0.98	−0.666667	4.31865×10^{-23}
FT	ABQ	single_step	TO	197	−0.974619	−0.666667	5.49911×10^{-24}
FT	CEQ	multi_step	AO	402	−0.536484	−0.666667	2.13293×10^{-39}
FT	CEQ	multi_step	TO	405	−0.553086	−0.666667	6.67326×10^{-40}
FT	CEQ	single_step	AO	197	−1.20643	−0.666667	1.04331×10^{-27}
FT	CEQ	single_step	TO	202	−0.978548	−0.666667	2.23348×10^{-24}
FT	KBQ	multi_step	AO	402	−0.687396	−0.666667	3.52073×10^{-46}
FT	KBQ	multi_step	TO	406	−0.598522	−0.666667	7.82425×10^{-43}
FT	KBQ	single_step	AO	199	−1.61642	−1	2.13189×10^{-27}
FT	KBQ	single_step	TO	197	−1.16751	−0.666667	9.71129×10^{-26}
VGR	ABQ	multi_step	AO	400	−0.655833	−0.666667	1.98272×10^{-40}
VGR	ABQ	multi_step	TO	397	−0.480269	−0.333333	1.4517×10^{-36}
VGR	ABQ	single_step	AO	200	−0.98	−0.666667	4.31865×10^{-23}
VGR	ABQ	single_step	TO	197	−0.974619	−0.666667	5.49911×10^{-24}
VGR	CEQ	multi_step	AO	402	−0.536484	−0.666667	2.13293×10^{-39}
VGR	CEQ	multi_step	TO	405	−0.553086	−0.666667	6.67326×10^{-40}
VGR	CEQ	single_step	AO	197	−1.20643	−0.666667	1.04331×10^{-27}
VGR	CEQ	single_step	TO	202	−0.978548	−0.666667	2.23348×10^{-24}
VGR	KBQ	multi_step	AO	402	−0.687396	−0.666667	3.52073×10^{-46}
VGR	KBQ	multi_step	TO	406	−0.598522	−0.666667	7.82425×10^{-43}
VGR	KBQ	single_step	AO	199	−1.61642	−1	2.13189×10^{-27}
VGR	KBQ	single_step	TO	197	−1.16751	−0.666667	9.71129×10^{-26}
VR	ABQ	multi_step	AO	400	−0.655833	−0.666667	1.98272×10^{-40}
VR	ABQ	multi_step	TO	397	−0.480269	−0.333333	1.4517×10^{-36}
VR	ABQ	single_step	AO	200	−0.98	−0.666667	4.31865×10^{-23}
VR	ABQ	single_step	TO	197	−0.974619	−0.666667	5.49911×10^{-24}
VR	CEQ	multi_step	AO	402	−0.536484	−0.666667	2.13293×10^{-39}
VR	CEQ	multi_step	TO	405	−0.553086	−0.666667	6.67326×10^{-40}
VR	CEQ	single_step	AO	197	−1.20643	−0.666667	1.04331×10^{-27}
VR	CEQ	single_step	TO	202	−0.978548	−0.666667	2.23348×10^{-24}
VR	KBQ	multi_step	AO	402	−0.687396	−0.666667	3.52073×10^{-46}
VR	KBQ	multi_step	TO	406	−0.598522	−0.666667	7.82425×10^{-43}
VR	KBQ	single_step	AO	199	−1.61642	−1	2.13189×10^{-27}
VR	KBQ	single_step	TO	197	−1.16751	−0.666667	9.71129×10^{-26}

Table A6. Grading bias (Task, Agent Only).

Task	Agent	n	Mean_Diff	Median_Diff	p-Value
task_1	agent_fine_tuned	3604	−0.773307	−0.666667	0
task_1	agent_vectorGraphRAG	3604	−0.773307	−0.666667	0
task_1	agent_vectorRAG	3604	−0.773307	−0.666667	0
task_2	agent_fine_tuned	3604	−1.38198	−1.33333	0
task_2	agent_vectorGraphRAG	3604	0.930725	1	0
task_2	agent_vectorRAG	3604	0.32242	0.333333	5.66181×10^{-190}
task_3	agent_fine_tuned	3604	−1.13596	−1	0
task_3	agent_vectorGraphRAG	3604	0.667037	0.75	0
task_3	agent_vectorRAG	3604	0.389637	0.5	1.62539×10^{-304}

Table A7. Explanation bias (Task, Agent Only).

Task	Agent	n	Mean_Diff	Median_Diff	p-Value
task_1	agent_fine_tuned	3604	−2.6428	−2.66667	0
task_1	agent_vectorGraphRAG	3604	0.732242	0.666667	1.90502×10^{-244}
task_1	agent_vectorRAG	3604	−0.528394	−0.666667	2.55173×10^{-271}
task_2	agent_fine_tuned	3604	−2.23372	−2	0
task_2	agent_vectorGraphRAG	3604	0.315113	0.333333	3.19784×10^{-82}
task_2	agent_vectorRAG	3604	−0.613578	−0.666667	0
task_3	agent_fine_tuned	3604	−2.03205	−2	0
task_3	agent_vectorGraphRAG	3604	0.0767897	0	8.9893×10^{-9}
task_3	agent_vectorRAG	3604	−0.44298	−0.5	4.00907×10^{-270}

References

1. Wang, S.; Xu, T.; Li, H.; Zhang, C.; Liang, J.; Tang, J.; Yu, P.S.; Wen, Q. Large language models for education: A survey and outlook. *arXiv* **2024**, arXiv:2403.18105.
2. Peláez-Sánchez, I.C.; Velarde-Camaqui, D.; Glasserman-Morales, L.D. The impact of large language models on higher education. *Front. Educ.* **2023**, *8*, 1392091.
3. Baierl, J.D. Applications of Large Language Models in Education: Literature Review and Implications. *arXiv* **2023**, arXiv:2307.10246.
4. Chen, L.; Chen, P.; Lin, Z. Artificial intelligence in education: A review. *IEEE Access* **2020**, *8*, 75264–75278. [CrossRef]
5. Kurdi, G.; Leo, J.; Parsia, B.; Sattler, U.; Al-Emari, S. A systematic review of automatic question generation for educational purposes. *Int. J. Artif. Intell. Educ.* **2020**, *30*, 121–204. [CrossRef]
6. Scaria, N.; Dharani Chenna, S.; Subramani, D. Automated Educational Question Generation at Different Bloom's Skill Levels Using Large Language Models: Strategies and Evaluation. In *Artificial Intelligence in Education*; Springer: Cham, Switzerland, 2024; pp. 165–179.
7. Bulathwela, S.; Muse, H.; Yilmaz, E. Scalable educational question generation with pre-trained language models. In *Artificial Intelligence in Education*; Springer: Cham, Switzerland, 2023; pp. 327–339.
8. Bloom, B.S.; Engelhart, M.D.; Furst, E.J.; Hill, W.H.; Krathwohl, D.R. *Taxonomy of Educational Objectives: The Classification of Educational Goals. Handbook I: Cognitive Domain*; David McKay Company: Philadelphia, PA, USA, 1956.
9. Bond, M.; Khosravi, H.; De Laat, M.; Bergdahl, N.; Negrea, V.; Oxley, E.; Pham, P.; Chong, S.W.; Siemens, G. A meta systematic review of artificial intelligence in higher education: A call for increased ethics, collaboration, and rigour. *Int. J. Educ. Technol. High. Educ.* **2024**, *21*, 4. [CrossRef]
10. Almasri, F. Exploring the impact of artificial intelligence in teaching and learning of science: A systematic review of empirical research. *Res. Sci. Educ.* **2024**, *54*, 977–997. [CrossRef]
11. Fettach, Y.; Ghogho, M.; Benatallah, B. Knowledge graphs in education and employability: A survey on applications and techniques. *IEEE Access* **2022**, *10*, 80174–80183. [CrossRef]
12. Bulathwela, S.; Pérez-Ortiz, M.; Yilmaz, E.; Shawe-Taylor, J. Power to the learner: Towards human-intuitive and integrative recommendations with open educational resources. *Sustainability* **2022**, *14*, 11682. [CrossRef]
13. Alotaibi, N.S. The Impact of AI and LMS Integration on the Future of Higher Education: Opportunities, Challenges, and Strategies for Transformation. *Sustainability* **2024**, *16*, 10357. [CrossRef]
14. Pamboris, A. The Impact of LLMs on Higher Education: Balancing Innovation with Ethics, Integrity, and Fairness. *Eloquence AI* 2024. Available online: https://eloquenceai.eu/the-impact-of-llms-on-higher-education-balancing-innovation-with-ethics-integrity-and-fairness/ (accessed on 27 December 2024).
15. Bouchard, D. An actionable framework for assessing bias and fairness in large language model use cases. *arXiv* **2024**, arXiv:2407.10853. Available online: https://arxiv.org/abs/2407.10853 (accessed on 22 February 2025).
16. University, A.S. Evaluation Framework Sets a New Benchmark for Ethical AI. *ASU News* 2024. Available online: https://tech.asu.edu/features/evaluation-framework-sets-new-benchmark-ethical-ai (accessed on 13 January 2025).
17. Lee, U.; Jung, H.; Jeon, Y.; Sohn, Y.; Hwang, W.; Moon, J.; Kim, H. Few-shot is enough: Exploring ChatGPT prompt engineering method for automatic question generation in english education. *Educ. Inf. Technol.* **2024**, *29*, 11483–11515. [CrossRef]
18. Tran, A.; Angelikas, K.; Rama, E.; Okechukwu, C.; Smith, D.H.; MacNeil, S. Generating multiple choice questions for computing courses using large language models. In Proceedings of the 2023 IEEE Frontiers in Education Conference (FIE), College Station, TX, USA, 18–21 October 2023; pp. 1–8.

19. Duong-Trung, N.; Wang, X.; Kravčík, M. BloomLLM: Large Language Models Based Question Generation Combining Supervised Fine-Tuning and Bloom's Taxonomy. In *Technology Enhanced Learning for Inclusive and Equitable Quality Education*; Springer: Cham, Switzerland, 2024; pp. 93–98.
20. Agrawal, G.; Pal, K.; Deng, Y.; Liu, H.; Chen, Y.C. CyberQ: Generating Questions and Answers for Cybersecurity Education Using Knowledge Graph-Augmented LLMs. *AAAI Conf. Artif. Intell.* **2024**, *38*, 23164–23172. [CrossRef]
21. Bhowmick, A.K.; Jagmohan, A.; Vempaty, A.; Dey, P.; Hall, L.; Hartman, J.; Kokku, R.; Maheshwari, H. Automating question generation from educational text. In *Artificial Intelligence XL*; Springer: Cham, Switzerland, 2023; pp. 437–450.
22. Lodovico Molina, I.; Švábenský, V.; Minematsu, T.; Chen, L.; Okubo, F.; Shimada, A. Comparison of Large Language Models for Generating Contextually Relevant Questions. In *Technology Enhanced Learning for Inclusive and Equitable Quality Education*; Springer: Cham, Switzerland, 2024; pp. 137–143.
23. Gonzalez, H.; Dugan, L.; Miltsakaki, E.; Cui, Z.; Ren, J.; Li, B.; Upadhyay, S.; Ginsberg, E.; Callison-Burch, C. Enhancing human summaries for question-answer generation in education. In Proceedings of the 18th Workshop on Innovative Use of NLP for Building Educational Applications (BEA 2023), Toronto, ON, Canada, 13 July 2023; pp. 108–118.
24. Lee, J.; Smith, D.; Woodhead, S.; Lan, A. Math Multiple Choice Question Generation via Human-Large Language Model Collaboration. *arXiv* **2024**, arXiv:2405.00864.
25. Shin, J.; Guo, Q.; Gierl, M.J. Multiple-choice item distractor development using topic modeling approaches. *Front. Psychol.* **2019**, *10*, 825. [CrossRef]
26. Stasaski, K.; Hearst, M.A. Multiple choice question generation utilizing an ontology. In Proceedings of the 12th Workshop on Innovative Use of NLP for Building Educational Applications, Copenhagen, Denmark, 8 September 2017; pp. 303–312.
27. Kwan, C.C.L. Exploring ChatGPT-Generated assessment scripts of probability and engineering statistics from bloom's taxonomy. In *Technology Enhanced Learning for Inclusive and Equitable Quality Education*; Springer: Singapore, 2023; pp. 275–286.
28. Ling, J.; Afzaal, M. Automatic question-answer pairs generation using pre-trained large language models in higher education. *Comput. Educ. Artif. Intell.* **2024**, *6*, 100252. [CrossRef]
29. Elkins, S.; Kochmar, E.; Serban, I.; Cheung, J.C. How useful are educational questions generated by large language models? In Proceedings of the International Conference on Artificial Intelligence in Education, Tokyo, Japan, 3–7 July 2023; pp. 536–542.
30. Maity, S.; Deroy, A. The future of learning in the age of generative ai: Automated question generation and assessment with large language models. *arXiv* **2024**, arXiv:2410.09576.
31. Scarlatos, A.; Smith, D.; Woodhead, S.; Lan, A. Improving the validity of automatically generated feedback via reinforcement learning. In Proceedings of the International Conference on Artificial Intelligence in Education, Recife, Brazil, 8–12 July 2024; pp. 280–294.
32. Rajpurkar, P. Squad: 100,000+ questions for machine comprehension of text. *arXiv* **2016**, arXiv:1606.05250.
33. Walkington, C.; Bernacki, M.L. Personalizing algebra to students' individual interests in an intelligent tutoring system: Moderators of impact. *Int. J. Artif. Intell. Educ.* **2019**, *29*, 58–88. [CrossRef]
34. Xie, W.; Niu, J.; Xue, C.J.; Guan, N. Grade Like a Human: Rethinking Automated Assessment with Large Language Models. *arXiv* **2024**, arXiv:2405.19694.
35. Ishida, T.; Liu, T.; Wang, H.; Cheung, W.K. Large Language Models as Partners in Student Essay Evaluation. *arXiv* **2024**, arXiv:2405.18632.
36. Elkins, S.; Kochmar, E.; Cheung, J.C.; Serban, I. How Teachers Can Use Large Language Models and Bloom's Taxonomy to Create Educational Quizzes. *arXiv* **2024**, arXiv:2401.05914. [CrossRef]
37. Diagrams.net. Online Diagram Software and Flowchart Maker. Available online: https://www.diagrams.net/ (accessed on 27 December 2024).
38. Łukawski, K. Hybrid Search Revamped—Building with Qdrant's Query API. *Qdrant Articles* 2024. Available online: https://qdrant.tech/articles/hybrid-search/ (accessed on 27 December 2024).
39. Lewis, P.; Perez, E.; Piktus, A.; Petroni, F.; Karpukhin, V.; Goyal, N.; Küttler, H.; Lewis, M.; Yih, W.T.; Rocktäschel, T.; et al. Retrieval-Augmented Generation for Knowledge-Intensive NLP Tasks. *Adv. Neural Inf. Process. Syst.* **2020**, *33*, 9459–9474.
40. Peng, B.; Zhu, Y.; Liu, Y.; Bo, X.; Shi, H.; Hong, C.; Zhang, Y.; Tang, S. Graph Retrieval-Augmented Generation: A Survey. *arXiv* **2024**, arXiv:2408.08921.
41. Bui, T.; Tran, O.; Nguyen, P.; Ho, B.; Nguyen, L.; Bui, T.; Quan, T. Cross-Data Knowledge Graph Construction for LLM-enabled Educational Question-Answering System: A Case Study at HCMUT. *arXiv* **2024**, arXiv:2404.09296.
42. Google. Introducing Gemini 2.0: Our New AI Model for the Agentic Era. 2024. Available online: https://blog.google/technology/google-deepmind/google-gemini-ai-update-december-2024/ (accessed on 13 January 2025).
43. Qdrant. Vector Search Engine and Database. 2023. Available online: https://qdrant.tech/ (accessed on 13 January 2025).
44. Neo4j, Inc. *Neo4j Graph Database Platform*; Neo4j, Inc.: San Mateo, CA, USA, 2023. Available online: https://neo4j.com/ (accessed on 13 January 2025).

45. Touvron, H.; Lavril, T.; Izacard, G.; Martinet, X.; Lachaux, M.A.; Lacroix, T.; Rozière, B.; Goyal, N.; Hambro, E.; Azhar, F.; et al. The Llama 3 Herd of Models. *arXiv* **2024**, arXiv:2407.21783.
46. Nikolovski, V. Meta-Llama-3.1-8B-Instruct-finki-edu-5c. 2024. Available online: https://huggingface.co/vlada22/Meta-Llama-3.1-8B-Instruct-finki-edu-5c (accessed on 10 February 2025).
47. Nikolovski, V. Meta-Llama-3.1-8B-Instruct-finki-edu-4courses. 2024. Available online: https://huggingface.co/vlada22/Meta-Llama-3.1-8B-Instruct-finki-edu-4courses (accessed on 13 January 2025).
48. OpenAI. Introducing GPT-4o and More Tools to ChatGPT Free Users. 2024. Available online: https://openai.com/index/gpt-4o-and-more-tools-to-chatgpt-free/ (accessed on 13 January 2025).
49. Pandas Development Team. Pandas: Python Data Analysis Library. 2023. Available online: https://pandas.pydata.org/ (accessed on 13 January 2025).
50. Seabold, S.; Perktold, J. Statsmodels: Statistical Models in Python. 2010. Available online: https://www.statsmodels.org/ (accessed on 13 January 2025).
51. LangChain. *Building Applications with LLMs Through Composability*; LangChain: San Francisco, CA, USA, 2023. Available online: https://python.langchain.com/ (accessed on 13 January 2025).
52. Zhang, X.; Zhang, Y.; Long, D.; Xie, W.; Dai, Z.; Tang, J.; Lin, H.; Yang, B.; Xie, P.; Huang, F.; et al. mGTE: Generalized Long-Context Text Representation and Reranking Models for Multilingual Text Retrieval. *arXiv* **2024**, arXiv:2407.19669.
53. Vlada22. Advancing AI in Higher Education. 2025. Available online: https://github.com/vlada22/advancing-ai-in-higher-education (accessed on 10 February 2025).

algorithms

MDPI

Article

A Scoring Algorithm for the Early Prediction of Academic Risk in STEM Courses

Vanja Čotić Poturić [1,2], Sanja Čandrlić [1] and Ivan Dražić [2,*]

1 Faculty of Informatics and Digital Technologies, University of Rijeka, 51000 Rijeka, Croatia; vcotic@uniri.hr (V.Č.P.); sanjac@uniri.hr (S.Č.)
2 Faculty of Engineering, University of Rijeka, 51000 Rijeka, Croatia
* Correspondence: ivan.drazic@uniri.hr; Tel.: +385-51-651-482

Abstract

Educational data mining (EDM) and learning analytics (LA) are widely applied to predict student performance, particularly in determining academic success or failure. This study presents the development of a scoring algorithm for the early identification of students at risk of failing science, technology, engineering, and mathematics (STEM) courses. The proposed approach follows a structured process: First, educational data are collected, processed, and statistically analyzed. Next, numerical variables are transformed into dichotomous predictors, and their relevance is assessed using Cramér's V measure to quantify their association with course outcomes. The final step involves constructing a scoring system that dynamically evaluates student performance over 15 weeks of instruction. Prospective validation of the model demonstrated excellent predictive performance (accuracy = 0.93, sensitivity = 0.95, specificity = 0.92), confirming its effectiveness in early risk detection. The resulting scoring algorithm is distinguished by its methodological simplicity, ease of implementation, and adaptability to different educational settings, making it a practical tool for timely interventions.

Keywords: educational data mining; learning analytics; academic risk prediction; scoring algorithm; Cramér's V; early intervention

1. Introduction

The early prediction of student success and academic risk has become a central focus in educational data mining (EDM) and learning analytics (LA), two rapidly evolving fields that leverage data-driven methodologies to enhance learning outcomes [1]. It can be said that EDM focuses more on techniques and methods, while LA is more about application. However, these differences are less noticeable as both fields evolve over time [2]. Predictive modeling has been widely applied in education, relying on academic performance indicators to evaluate the probability of success or failure of students [3].

Nabil et al. [4] performed a literature review on the prediction of student academic performance using different machine learning techniques and found that the grade point average (GPA) of students and the cumulative grade point average (CGPA) are the most common indicators used as predictive values to assess and predict student academic performance at the university level. Some studies emphasize the importance of including academic and non-academic factors such as motivational and self-regulation variables to improve the predictive power of the models [5,6].

In science, technology, engineering, and mathematics (STEM) education, research has shown that student interaction with the learning management system (LMS) provides valuable predictive insights. For example, Kittur et al. [7] emphasized that the amount of time students spend on various course components, such as tests and assignments, can be an indicator of the likelihood that they will successfully complete the course. Similarly, research by Cui et al. [8] showed that quiz and assignment scores, along with engagement metrics such as the frequency of LMS logins, are critical predictors of overall course performance. These findings suggest that early assessments and continuous monitoring of student engagement are critical for accurately identifying students who may struggle later in the semester.

Several studies have focused on developing their own prediction models tailored to specific educational contexts. One study by Caicedo-Castro presented "Course Prophet", a machine learning-based system to predict student failure in a course in numerical methods [9]. This model used students' grades in prerequisite courses and admission test scores as predictor variables, demonstrating the effectiveness of early intervention strategies based on predictive analytics. The study highlights the importance of using historical academic performance data to predict future outcomes, which is consistent with general trends in educational data mining. Similarly, Fahd and Miah [10] designed a Big Data Analytics System that utilizes LMS interaction data to identify at-risk students, highlighting the role of artificial intelligence (AI) driven engagement analysis in predicting student success. However, despite their high predictive accuracy, AI-based black-box models lack transparency, which remains a major barrier to their adoption in education [11,12]. Researchers argue for the need for interpretable models that not only perform well but also provide insight into their predictions, as this is crucial for promoting trust in sensitive areas such as education. Therefore, moving from black-box to more transparent models is essential in detecting at-risk students [13–15].

The timing of predicting student success is a critical aspect of educational intervention strategies. Theobald et al. [16] indicated that active learning strategies employed early in the course can help close achievement gaps, supporting the notion that early prediction is critical to student success. Furthermore, Refs. [17–19] indicated that early predictions can significantly impact student outcomes by allowing timely intervention. These findings underscore the critical role of early detection in supporting student success and the need for institutions to take proactive measures based on predictive analytics.

This study aims to develop a transparent scoring algorithm for early academic risk prediction, offering a balance between interpretability, predictive accuracy, and ease of implementation. This scoring system will be grounded in transparent and classical statistical methods—widely trusted by both researchers and educators—rather than relying on "black-box" approaches. The objective is to achieve a predictive accuracy comparable to that of advanced AI models while ensuring the interpretability and reliability of the underlying methodologies.

The proposed algorithm for early detection of student failure (as discussed in Section 5) is characterized by its simplicity, ease of understanding, and practical applicability, making it particularly suitable for educational institutions with limited resources. In contrast to complex machine learning models, the algorithm uses dichotomization of predictors to simplify data processing, while Cramér's V-measure ensures reliable selection of the most important predictors. Using the Youden index to determine risk thresholds, the algorithm enables an objective and transparent classification of students. By applying simple yet robust statistical techniques, the algorithm provides a dynamic, intuitive, and resource-efficient framework for proactive student support. The algorithm combines simple statistical methods into a dynamic system that is intuitive to use, robust in execution, and exceptionally practical to implement.

The remainder of this paper is structured as follows. First, Section 2 provides a brief overview of the state of the field. Section 3 details the materials and methods, while Section 4 introduces the predictor variables. Section 5 presents the results, focusing on the development of a scoring system and a corresponding algorithm designed as a predictive classification model to assess students' success or failure during each of the 15 weeks of classes. Section 6 discusses these findings, and Section 7 concludes the paper with recommendations for future research.

2. State of the Field

Recent research highlights the significant influence of learning motivation as a key predictor of academic success, while advances in LMS data analytics have created new opportunities for real-time performance monitoring. Leveraging insights about student motivational factors and interactions within LMS enables educators to take proactive measures and implement early intervention strategies. As academic institutions increasingly focus on improving retention rates and overall student success, early prediction models are emerging as important tools to identify at-risk students and develop targeted support mechanisms. While traditional prediction approaches have relied predominantly on statistical analysis, recent developments in machine learning (ML) have improved both the accuracy and adaptability of these models.

In STEM subjects, where the subject matter is often particularly challenging, motivation to learn plays a crucial role in academic performance. Studies have shown a strong correlation between higher levels of intrinsic motivation and better academic outcomes, suggesting that students who demonstrate greater engagement in STEM subjects are more likely to persevere despite challenges [20]. For example, Yeager et al. conducted a nationwide study showing that interventions aimed at promoting a growth mindset were effective in improving students' grades across different demographic groups, highlighting the important link between motivation and academic success [20]. Similarly, Daker et al. examined the negative effects of math anxiety, an issue closely linked to motivation, and emphasized its predictive role in STEM avoidance [21]. These findings underscore the need to develop targeted interventions that address both motivational barriers and academic difficulties and reinforce the importance of incorporating psychological factors into academic support systems to maximize their effectiveness.

The results of learning motivation analysis can be integrated with LMS interaction logs to provide comprehensive insights into student engagement and behavioral patterns, both of which are critical to academic success. Santos and Henriques emphasized that examining various aspects of student interactions within LMS platforms can reveal early indicators of risk that facilitate data-driven decision-making for the implementation of targeted interventions [22]. Furthermore, Akçapınar et al. developed an early warning system that utilizes eBook interaction logs to identify students at risk, demonstrating the potential of LMS data in establishing timely academic support mechanisms [23]. In addition, Osborne and Lang's research confirmed that LMS data can be effectively used to create predictive models that can identify at-risk students as early as the fifth week of the semester and achieve satisfactory predictive accuracy [24].

Statistical models, such as logistic regression, are often used to predict academic performance due to their simplicity and interpretability. For example, Zakopoulos et al. developed a binary logistic regression model to identify students at risk in blended learning environments. The independent variables included attendance, participation in online discussions, and the completion of assignments. The model achieved a reported predictive accuracy of 0.82, underscoring the importance of engagement metrics in identifying students who may struggle, consistent with the findings that passive participation does not effectively predict performance [25]. Yousafzai and Jamil examined the relationship between admission criteria and academic performance using correlation and regression analyses. The study demonstrated a significant relationship, reporting that metrics such as high school GPA and standardized test scores significantly correlated with college performance. This underscores the importance of using admission data as a predictive tool for academic success in higher education institutions [26]. While these models are effective in identifying key predictive factors, they struggle to capture the intricate, nonlinear relationships inherent in educational datasets, limiting their ability to fully account for the complexity of student achievement patterns.

In contrast, ML models have proven to be powerful tools for uncovering hidden patterns in data, as shown by the results of Akçapınar et al. who demonstrated the effectiveness of ML techniques in developing early warning systems to identify at-risk students [23]. Nabil et al. also emphasized that ML algorithms, especially deep neural networks, provide superior prediction accuracy by processing multidimensional datasets that traditional statistical methods may miss [4]. This capability is particularly important, as Mahboob et al. have shown, as early identification of at-risk students through ML-based approaches enables timely interventions that can significantly improve educational outcomes [27]. Sandoval et al. (2020) conducted a case study integrating neural networks and logistic regression to develop a model for predicting early dropout among college students. The model incorporated a number of predictors, including demographics, prior academic performance, and enrollment status, and achieved an accuracy of 0.87 and a sensitivity of 0.85 demonstrating its strong ability to identify at-risk students entering college [28]. Similarly, Mogavi investigated different methods for predicting dropout in STEM subjects, focusing on ML approaches to assess student engagement and academic performance. The study reported an accuracy of 0.90 with an area under the receiver operating characteristic curve (AUC-ROC) of 0.93, highlighting the effectiveness of ML models in predicting dropout risk based on historical academic data. The model took into account several indicators, including attendance records, number of assignments submitted, and exam performance [29]. In a more recent study, Won et al. developed a multimodal model for predicting dropout that combined structured data (e.g., GPA, attendance) with unstructured textual data from discussion forums and advising notes. By using a deep learning approach, the model achieved an accuracy of 0.92. This demonstrates the benefits of combining different data sources to improve predictive performance and capture the multifaceted nature of dropout risk [30].

3. Materials and Methods

This study is based on data collected from the LMS platform Merlin, an implementation of the open-source system Moodle (version 4.2). The dataset comprises user activity logs, quiz scores, overall course performance metrics, and responses to two questionnaires conducted in the first week of the course.

The first questionnaire evaluated students' prior mathematical knowledge based on three key indicators: high school mathematics grades and state matriculation examination results. The second questionnaire used the adapted academic motivation scale, translated and adapted into Croatian by G. Ribić [31]. This 24-item instrument measured six motivation factors, which encompassed three types of extrinsic motivation (external regulation, introjected motivation, and identified motivation) and three forms of intrinsic motivation (motivation for knowledge, achievement, and stimulation). The responses collected provided insight into students' academic backgrounds and motivational profiles, which were later analyzed in relation to their course performance.

Data collection was carried out in two phases. The first phase was a retrospective analysis based on data from the 2023/2024 academic year, which included 76 students enrolled in the compulsory course Mathematics 1 at the Faculty of Engineering, University of Rijeka. Among them, 26 students did not complete the course successfully. The second phase was a prospective analysis conducted on 70 students enrolled in the same course during the academic year 2024/2025. All records were anonymized prior to thhe analysis to ensure compliance with ethical standards and data protection regulations, thereby safeguarding student privacy.

The preprocessing phase included handling missing values and transforming independent variables for statistical analysis. In the retrospective dataset, students with missing data for any of the required variables were excluded from the analysis, resulting in a final dataset of 43 students for model evaluation.

Independent variables (as described in Section 4) were originally numeric and converted to categorical dichotomous variables. The optimal cut-off point for dichotomization was determined using the Youden index, ensuring a statistically robust separation between categories. The Youden index [32] is a measure of effectiveness that combines sensitivity and specificity and it is calculated as follows:

$$\text{Youden index} = \text{sensitivity} + \text{specificity} - 1\,.$$

Specificity is a measure of the correct identification of negative cases, while sensitivity is a measure of the correct identification of positive cases. The Youden index ranges from 0 to 1. A value close to 1 indicates high model efficiency in distinguishing students who will pass the course from those who will not.

The variable *Success* in the retrospective analysis was defined as a dichotomous variable, where *Success* = 1 indicated that the student passed the course, and *Success* = 0 indicated failure. In the prospective analysis, *Success* was based on passing the first mid-term exam. The prospective dataset from 2024/2025 did not require handling missing values, as all required data were available to all students. The preprocessing was performed using R version 4.3.3.

Pearson's chi-square test was used to identify the most relevant dichotomous predictors of *Success*. The Pearson chi-square test [33] is a statistical test used to determine whether there is a significant association between two categorical variables. It compares the observed frequencies (O) with the expected frequencies (E) to check if differences are due to chance. The value of the Pearson chi-square statistic (χ^2) is defined as follows:

$$\chi^2 = \sum \frac{(E_{ij} - O_{ij})^2}{E_{ij}}\,. \tag{1}$$

The LMS variables considered relevant on a weekly basis were those for which the corresponding p-value of Pearson's chi-square test was below the significance level of 0.05.

For each of the 15 weeks of teaching, the association between relevant variables and *Success* was quantified using Cramér's V coefficient. This measure provided insight into the effect size of the relationships between categorical predictors and student outcomes. Cramér's V coefficient [34] is based on the Pearson chi-square statistic, and its significance is determined based on the p-value of the Pearson chi-square test. Cramér's V coefficient is defined as follows:

$$V = \sqrt{\frac{\chi^2/n}{\min(k-1, r-1)}} \tag{2}$$

where

χ^2 is the value of the chi-square statistic;

n is the total number of observations;

k is the number of categories of one variable; and

r is the number of categories of the other variable.

Based on the results of Cramér's V measure, a scoring system was developed to predict student success, which represents the primary objective of this study.

Descriptive statistical techniques were used to summarize the data, including measures of central tendency (arithmetic mean and median) and dispersion (standard deviation and range). Frequency calculations and corresponding graphical representations were also included to provide a clearer overview of the dataset.

Model performance was evaluated using sensitivity, specificity, accuracy, and AUC-ROC. All statistical analyses were performed with R.

Students accessed Merlin from their personal computers, while researchers analyzed the data on a computer equipped with a 13th Gen Intel® Core™ i7-1360P processor (2.20 GHz, x64 architecture), manufactured by Intel Corporation, Santa Clara, CA, USA, 16.0 GB of installed RAM, and a 64-bit version of Windows 11 operating system.

4. Overview of the Variables Used in the Analysis

A clear understanding of the structure and assessment methods of the Mathematics 1 course is crucial for interpreting the variables used in this study.

The Mathematics 1 course is a compulsory first-year course at the Faculty of Engineering, University of Rijeka. The course is delivered through traditional in-person instruction for 15 weeks, with students attending three hours of lectures and three hours of exercises per week. In addition, students have access to the Mathematics 1 e-course via the LMS Merlin, which facilitates e-learning through the distribution of learning materials, communication tools, and online assessments. While the platform tracks student activity and generates descriptive reports, it does not offer predictive insights or personalized recommendations.

All exercise tasks in Merlin are stored as formulaic questions. This format allows for the use of global and local variables, enabling the generation of multiple versions of the same task. An example of a formulaic question code and two generated tasks can be found in Figure 1. On the left side of Figure 1, the code for creating a question is shown, containing variables (random and global) as well as the main question (i.e., the task text). On the right side of Figure 1, two different tasks generated from this code are displayed.

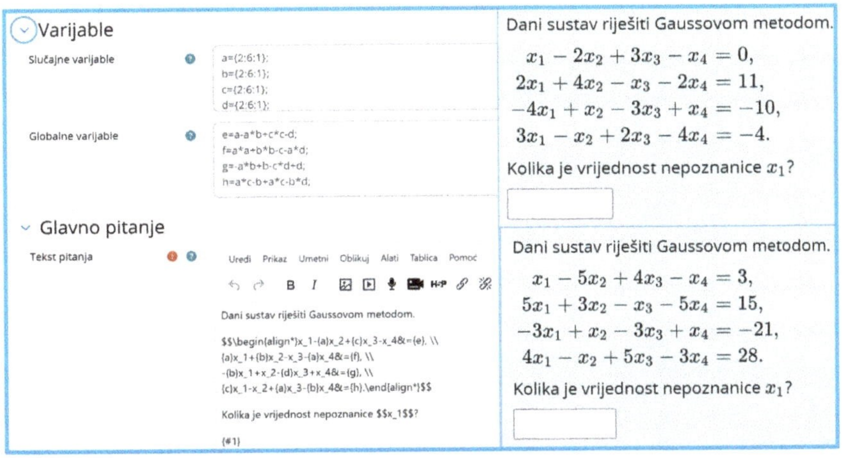

Figure 1. An example of a formulaic question in the learning management system (LMS) Merlin.

These tasks serve as the basis for weekly tests. Each week, students take a test during exercises and later have the opportunity to solve equivalent learning tests at home, where parameters differ, allowing them to practice and independently verify their acquired knowledge.

The maximum attainable score in the course is 100 points. Throughout the semester, three midterm exams are held, contributing to a total of 70 points. The first mid-term takes place in week 5, the second in week 11, and the third in week 16 (the first week after the end of classes). Students who accumulate at least 35 points during the semester qualify for the final exam, which carries an additional 30 points. To pass the course, a student must obtain at least 15 points on the final exam. If a student does not accumulate 35 points during the semester or does not reach the minimum passing score on the final exam, they receive a failing grade (F) and must retake the course.

The analysis in this study relies on a set of variables that capture different aspects of student participation, assessment performance, and learning activity within the Mathematics 1 course.

The variable *Number of learning tests* represents the total number of instances in which a student has completed a learning test in a given week, including repeated attempts. The variable *Maximum of learning tests* records the highest percentage of points a student achieved in a given week, providing insight into their highest performance during that period.

The descriptive statistical indicators for these variables per week are presented in Table 1. The table illustrates that students engage more actively in learning tests in the weeks preceding midterm exams. Their performance also improves during these periods, suggesting intensified preparation and focused study efforts.

Table 1. Descriptive statistical indicators for the variables *Number* and *Maximum of learning tests*.

Week	Number of Learning Tests		Maximum of Learning Tests	
	Mean (Std Dev)	Median (Min–Max)	Mean (Std Dev)	Median (Min–Max)
Week 1	0.14 (0.42)	0 (0–2)	0.08 (0.24)	0.00 (0.00–1.00)
Week 2	0.32 (0.59)	0 (0–2)	0.20 (0.35)	0.00 (0.00–1.00)
Week 3	0.50 (0.81)	0 (0–3)	0.26 (0.38)	0.00 (0.00–1.00)
Week 4	1.18 (1.78)	0 (0–9)	0.39 (0.42)	0.00 (0.00–1.00)
Week 5	0.13 (0.38)	0 (0–2)	0.08 (0.23)	0.00 (0.00–0.94)
Week 6	0.21 (0.72)	0 (0–4)	0.08 (0.24)	0.00 (0.00–0.92)
Week 7	0.20 (0.61)	0 (0–3)	0.05 (0.20)	0.00 (0.00–0.92)
Week 8	0.13 (0.47)	0 (0–3)	0.05 (0.19)	0.00 (0.00–0.94)
Week 9	0.13 (0.64)	0 (0–5)	0.04 (0.18)	0.00 (0.00–1.00)
Week 10	1.66 (2.73)	0 (0–17)	0.28 (0.35)	0.00 (0.00–0.95)
Week 11	0.30 (0.65)	0 (0–3)	0.07 (0.20)	0.00 (0.00–0.84)
Week 12	0.33 (1.09)	0 (0–8)	0.10 (0.26)	0.00 (0.00–1.00)
Week 13	0.11 (0.39)	0 (0–2)	0.05 (0.20)	0.00 (0.00–0.93)
Week 14	0.11 (0.42)	0 (0–3)	0.02 (0.11)	0.00 (0.00–0.71)
Week 15	3.54 (4.30)	1.5 (0–16)	0.38 (0.38)	0.40 (0.00–1.00)

Note: The weeks preceding midterm exams are highlighted in light blue.

The graphical representation of the arithmetic mean and the standard deviation for the variable *Number of learning tests* is shown in Figure 2 to visually illustrate the increased activity of the students in the weeks before the midterm exams.

High values of the arithmetic mean and the standard deviation in the weeks before the midterm exams (especially at the end of the semester) indicate increased activity of the students in solving the weekly tests as well as considerable differences in the number of attempts to solve these tests among the students.

In addition to the learning tests, course participants have access to additional practice tests within the Merlin e-course. These practice tests are also generated from a database of formulaic questions, allowing students to engage with a diverse set of problems and reinforce their understanding of the material.

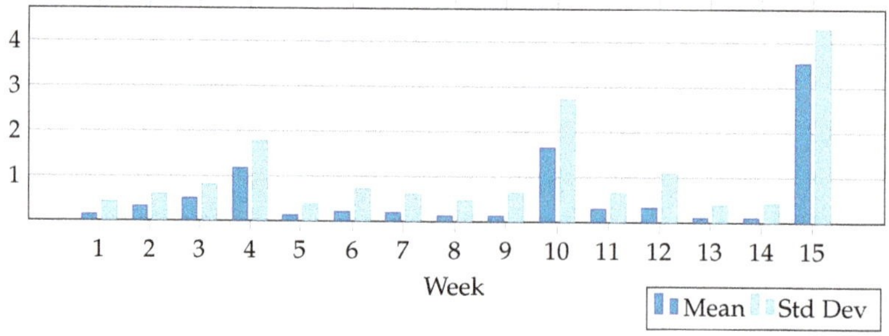

Figure 2. The graphical representation of the arithmetic mean and the standard deviation for the variable *Number of learning tests*.

The variable *Number of practice tests* represents the total number of times a student has completed a practice test in a given week, including repeated attempts for further reinforcement. The variable *Maximum of practice tests* records the highest percentage of points a student achieved in that week, reflecting their best performance in all completed practice tests.

The descriptive statistical indicators for these variables per week are presented in Table 2. The table indicates that students predominantly complete practice tests in the weeks leading up to midterm exams, mirroring the pattern observed with learning tests.

Table 2. Descriptive statistical indicators for the variables *Number* and *Maximum of practice tests*.

Week	Number of Practice Tests		Maximum of Practice Tests	
	Mean (Std Dev)	Median (Min–Max)	Mean (Std Dev)	Median (Min–Max)
Week 1	0.21 (0.72)	0 (0–4)	0.06 (0.20)	0.00 (0.00–1.00)
Week 2	0.24 (0.76)	0 (0–4)	0.09 (0.25)	0.00 (0.00–1.00)
Week 3	0.53 (1.21)	0 (0–5)	0.16 (0.33)	0.00 (0.00–1.00)
Week 4	2.26 (3.77)	0 (0–22)	0.32 (0.41)	0.00 (0.00–1.00)
Week 5	0.12 (0.43)	0 (0–2)	0.04 (0.16)	0.00 (0.00–0.86)
Week 6	0.28 (0.92)	0 (0–6)	0.08 (0.24)	0.00 (0.00–1.00)
Week 7	0.17 (0.60)	0 (0–3)	0.05 (0.18)	0.00 (0.00–0.92)
Week 8	0.11 (0.51)	0 (0–3)	0.03 (0.15)	0.00 (0.00–0.86)
Week 9	0.08 (0.36)	0 (0–2)	0.03 (0.14)	0.00 (0.00–0.86)
Week 10	1.49 (3.38)	0 (0–24)	0.21 (0.30)	0.00 (0.00–1.00)
Week 11	0.17 (0.55)	0 (0–4)	0.06 (0.20)	0.00 (0.00–0.86)
Week 12	0.33 (0.89)	0 (0–4)	0.06 (0.19)	0.00 (0.00–1.00)
Week 13	0.13 (0.44)	0 (0–3)	0.07 (0.24)	0.00 (0.00–1.00)
Week 14	0.07 (0.30)	0 (0–2)	0.01 (0.08)	0.00 (0.00–0.57)
Week 15	1.41 (2.88)	0 (0–16)	0.14 (0.28)	0.00 (0.00–1.00)

Note: The weeks preceding midterm exams are highlighted in light blue.

The graphical representation of the arithmetic mean and the standard deviation for the variable *Number of practice tests* is shown in Figure 3 to visually illustrate the increased activity of the students in the weeks before the midterm exams.

If we look at the weeks before midterm exams, we can see in Figure 3 that interest in solving practice tests decreases throughout the semester, with interest being the highest in the week before the first midterm exam and the lowest in the week before the last midterm exam.

Within the Merlin e-courses, students have access to lecture presentations used by the professor. They are encouraged to download these presentations and take notes to support their learning. The course material is structured so that different presentations are used in specific weeks: the first presentation covers weeks 1–3, the second covers weeks 4–6, the third covers weeks 7–9, the fourth covers weeks 10–12, and the fifth covers weeks 13–15.

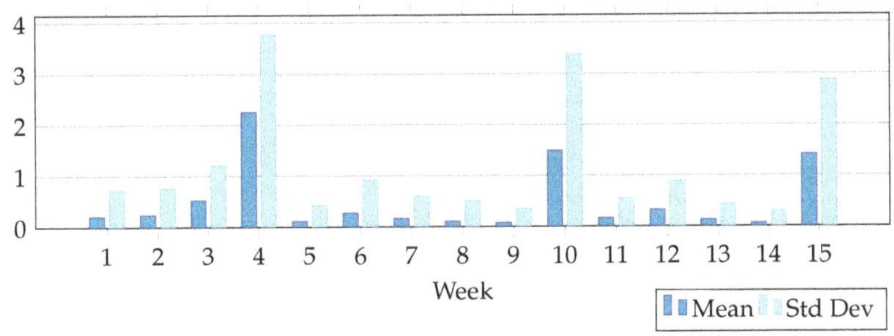

Figure 3. The graphical representation of the arithmetic mean and the standard deviation for the variable *Number of practice tests*.

The variable *Presentation* indicates whether a student has downloaded the presentation for the corresponding week. It takes the value 1 if the presentation was downloaded and 0 otherwise. For example, if a student downloads the first presentation in the second week, the variable *Presentation* would have the values (0, 1, 1) for the first three weeks.

Since *Presentation* is a dichotomous variable with only two possible values (0 and 1), its distribution across weeks is illustrated in Figure 4. The values of this variable are relatively uniform across the weeks analyzed, suggesting a consistent pattern of engagement with the materials provided.

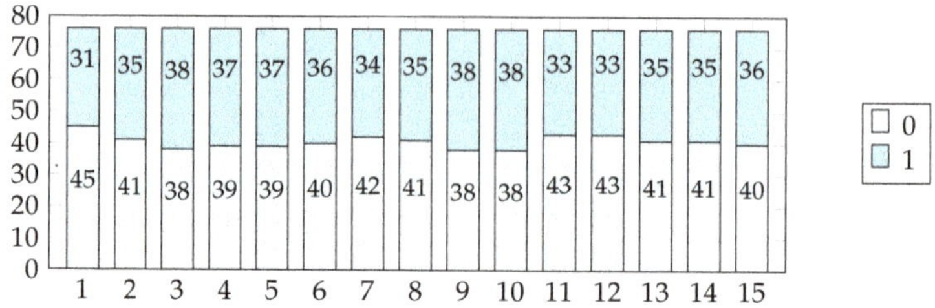

Figure 4. Graphical representation of the *Presentation* variable by week.

During the 2020/2021 academic year, lectures and exercises were conducted synchronously via remote access, and all exercise sessions were recorded. Based on these recordings, 15 video lessons were created and made available on Merlin, allowing students to access them as supplementary learning material.

The variable *Video* represents the number of times a student accessed video lessons in a given week, including all previously available lessons. The descriptive statistical indicators for the variable *Video* per week are presented in Table 3. The table indicates that students tend to watch video lessons more frequently in the weeks leading up to midterm exams. Additionally, exceptionally high maximum values are observed, probably due to the way Merlin logs activity, registering an interaction whenever a video is accessed, regardless of whether it is watched in its entirety or merely opened and closed.

During the semester, students can earn up to 70 assessment points through three midterm exams. The first midterm takes place in week 5, the second in week 11, and the third in week 16. The results of the third midterm were not included in the analysis, as they were obtained at the very end of the semester and are therefore not relevant for the development of an early identification system.

In addition to the midterms, students take four short bonus tests throughout the semester. These tests provide the opportunity to earn up to 5 additional points, helping students improve their midterm results. The bonus tests are administered at weeks 4, 7, 10, and 13.

Table 3. Descriptive statistical indicators for the variable *Video* by week.

Week	Mean (Std Dev)	Median (Min–Max)
Week 1	0.00 (0.00)	0 (0–0)
Week 2	0.00 (0.00)	0 (0–0)
Week 3	4.33 (11.24)	0 (0–51)
Week 4	23.92 (40.35)	4 (0–203)
Week 5	7.61 (21.33)	0 (0–152)
Week 6	3.75 (14.21)	0 (0–95)
Week 7	7.43 (17.19)	0 (0–96)
Week 8	2.18 (14.26)	0 (0–122)
Week 9	3.96 (22.42)	0 (0–193)
Week 10	24.51 (45.22)	0 (0–200)
Week 11	17.75 (46.06)	0 (0–342)
Week 12	8.50 (33.79)	0 (0–255)
Week 13	3.38 (12.17)	0 (0–72)
Week 14	8.57 (20.11)	0 (0–119)
Week 15	149.5 (227.67)	53 (0–1318)

Note: The weeks preceding midterm exams are highlighted in light blue.

The variables *Colloquium 1* and *Colloquium 2* denote the percentage of points obtained in the first and second midterm exams, respectively. The variables *Test 1*, *Test 2*, *Test 3*, and *Test 4* record the percentage of points earned in the corresponding bonus tests. Descriptive statistical indicators for these variables are presented in Table 4.

Table 4. Descriptive statistical indicators for the variables *Colloquium 1*, *Colloquium 2*, *Test 1*, *Test 2*, *Test 3*, and *Test 4*.

Week	Variable	Mean (Std Dev)	Median (Min–Max)
Week 4	*Test 1*	0.46 (0.38)	0.55 (0.00–1.00)
Week 5	*Colloquium 1*	0.72 (0.24)	0.80 (0.00–1.00)
Week 7	*Test 2*	0.11 (0.25)	0.00 (0.00–1.00)
Week 10	*Test 3*	0.11 (0.25)	0.00 (0.00–1.00)
Week 11	*Colloquium 2*	0.44 (0.25)	0.38 (0.00–0.94)
Week 13	*Test 4*	0.61 (0.45)	0.90 (0.00–1.00)

The results in Table 4 show that students performed significantly better on the first midterm exam (Mean = 0.72, Median = 0.80) compared to the second midterm exam (Mean = 0.44, Median = 0.38), indicating a decrease in performance as the semester progressed. Furthermore, while the first and last tests had relatively higher mean and median scores, intermediate tests show notably lower averages, suggesting that many students either did not attempt these tests or struggled to achieve points.

Data on previous mathematical knowledge, collected through a questionnaire, together with the corresponding variables, are presented in Table 5.

Table 5. Descriptive statistical indicators for the answers about the previous learning level.

Variable	Mean (Std Dev)	Median (Min–Max)
School grade	4.00 (0.55)	4.00 (2.30–5.00)
Matriculation grade	3.22 (0.70)	3.00 (2.00–5.00)
Matriculation percentage	0.64 (0.13)	0.65 (0.27–0.85)

The results of the motivation questionnaire, along with the corresponding variables, are presented in Table 6. However, encouraging student participation in these questionnaires proved challenging, resulting in a high rate of non-responses. Consequently, these variables introduced problems with missing data.

Table 6. Descriptive statistical indicators for the answers to the questions on study motivation.

Variable	Mean (Std Dev)	Median (Min–Max)
To know	4.74 (1.37)	4.75 (1.75–7.00)
Toward accomplishment	4.47 (1.74)	4.50 (1.00–7.00)
To experience stimulation	3.88 (1.57)	3.75 (1.25–7.00)
External regulation	5.62 (1.34)	6.00 (1.75–7.00)
Introjected	5.50 (1.33)	6.00 (1.75–7.00)
Identified	3.76 (1.84)	3.50 (1.00–7.00)

Table 6 shows that students exhibit the highest levels of motivation in external regulation (Mean = 5.62, Median = 6.00) and introjected motivation (Mean = 5.50, Median = 6.00), indicating that external pressures and internalized expectations significantly influence their academic engagement. In contrast, motivation to experience stimulation (Mean = 3.88, Median = 3.75) and identified motivation (Mean = 3.76, Median = 3.50) received the lowest scores, implying that fewer students are driven by personal identification with learning goals or the enjoyment of studying itself. The relatively high variability in responses, particularly in identified motivation (Std Dev = 1.84), suggests notable differences in how students perceive their reasons for academic effort.

5. Results

The Youden index is used to determine the threshold value c when converting a numerical variable into a dichotomous one. The value of c, for which the Youden index is the highest, represents the optimal threshold for distinguishing between negative and positive outcomes.

For example, if the variable *Colloquium 1*, which records the percentage of points obtained on the first midterm exam (ranging from 0% to 100%), is to be converted into a dichotomous variable that takes values 0 or 1, the optimal threshold (cut-off point) can be determined using the Youden index. All percentage values lower than the optimal threshold c will be assigned a value of 0, while all values equal to or greater than c will be assigned a value of 1.

For different threshold values $c \in [0\%, 100\%]$ of the percentage of points obtained on the first midterm exam, the numerical variable is transformed into a dichotomous variable. Then, for this independent dichotomous variable and the known values of the dependent dichotomous variable *Success*, the Youden index is calculated. The value of c for which the Youden index is the highest is the optimal threshold value for converting the numerical variable into a dichotomous one.

Table 7 presents several different threshold values for the variable *Colloquium 1* along with the corresponding Youden index values. The maximum Youden index value is achieved at a threshold of 0.82, making it the optimal threshold value for the variable *Colloquium 1*.

All values of the variable *Colloquium 1* that are less than 0.82 are assigned the value 0 ($n = 42$), while all other values are assigned the value 1 ($n = 34$), thus converting *Colloquium 1* into a dichotomous variable. Using this method, all numerical variables for each of the 15 weeks of teaching were converted into dichotomous variables and then used for further analysis.

To identify the most relevant predictors of student success, Pearson's chi-square test was applied to all dichotomous variables. A variable was considered significant if its associated p-value was below the threshold of 0.05.

Table 7. Different threshold values for the variable *Colloquium 1* along with the corresponding Youden index values.

Cut-Off	Sensitivity	Specificity	Youden Index
0.745	0.78	0.808	0.588
0.765	0.76	0.808	0.568
0.785	0.74	0.846	0.586
0.795	0.72	0.885	0.605
0.805	0.66	0.885	0.545
0.820	0.66	0.962	**0.622**
0.835	0.60	1.000	0.600
0.845	0.56	1.000	0.560
0.855	0.50	1.000	0.500
0.870	0.48	1.000	0.480

Note: The maximum Youden index and the corresponding cut-off value are shown in bold.

For example, the value of the Pearson chi-square statistic for the variable *Colloquium 1* is $\chi^2 = 26.71$ (according to expression (1)). The corresponding p-value is very small ($p < 0.001$), indicating a significant association between the variables *Colloquium 1* and *Success*. This suggests that *Colloquium 1* is a relevant variable for predicting the variable *Success*.

Table 8 presents the list of variables that met this criterion, organized by week, highlighting which aspects of student engagement and performance exhibit a statistically significant association with course success at different stages of the semester.

Of the 20 variables analyzed, 16 were identified as relevant and included in the subsequent analysis to develop the scoring system. The number of relevant variables fluctuated throughout the semester, with the fewest ($n = 7$) observed in the second week and the highest ($n = 15$) in the final week.

Following the identification of relevant variables, their association with course success was quantified using the Cramér's V coefficient. If, for example, we want to determine the value of Cramér's V coefficient for the variables *Colloquium 1* and *Success* (for which the chi-square statistic was previously calculated as $\chi^2 = 26.71$), the calculation, according to expression (2), is as follows:

$$V = \sqrt{\frac{\chi^2/n}{\min(\mathrm{k}-1,\mathrm{r}-1)}} = \sqrt{\frac{26.71/76}{\min(2-1,2-1)}} = \sqrt{0.351} = 0.593\,.$$

Table 9 presents the computed Cramér's V values for all significant variables throughout the weeks, indicating the strength of their relationship with the *Success* variable. Higher values suggest a stronger predictive influence on student performance.

Table 8. Relevant variables (predictors) by week.

Variable	1	2	3	4	5	6	7	8	9	10	11	12	13	14	15
School grade	✓	✓	✓	✓	✓	✓	✓	✓	✓	✓	✓	✓	✓	✓	✓
Matriculation percentage	✓	✓	✓	✓	✓	✓	✓	✓	✓	✓	✓	✓	✓	✓	✓
Toward accomplishment	✓	✓	✓	✓	✓	✓	✓	✓	✓	✓	✓	✓	✓	✓	✓
Introjected	✓	✓	✓	✓	✓	✓	✓	✓	✓	✓	✓	✓	✓	✓	✓
Identified	✓	✓	✓	✓	✓	✓	✓	✓	✓	✓	✓	✓	✓	✓	✓
Number of learning tests	✓			✓	✓		✓			✓					✓
Maximum of learning tests	✓		✓	✓	✓		✓			✓					✓
Number of practice tests	✓	✓	✓	✓			✓			✓					✓
Maximum of practice tests	✓	✓	✓	✓		✓	✓			✓					✓
Video							✓			✓				✓	✓
Presentation							✓	✓	✓		✓	✓			
Test 1				✓	✓	✓	✓	✓	✓	✓	✓	✓	✓	✓	✓
Test 2							✓	✓	✓	✓	✓	✓	✓	✓	✓
Test 4													✓	✓	✓
Colloquium 1					✓	✓	✓	✓	✓	✓	✓	✓	✓	✓	✓
Colloquium 2											✓	✓	✓	✓	✓
Count	9	7	8	10	9	8	14	9	9	13	10	10	10	11	15

Table 9. Values of the Cramér's V association coefficient between the relevant variables of the e-learning system and the variable *Success* by weeks.

Variable	**1**	**2**	**3**	**4**	**5**	**6**	**7**	**8**	**9**	**10**	**11**	**12**	**13**	**14**	**15**
School grade	0.362	0.362	0.362	0.362	0.362	0.362	0.362	0.362	0.362	0.362	0.362	0.362	0.362	0.362	0.362
Matriculation percentage	0.325	0.325	0.325	0.325	0.325	0.325	0.325	0.325	0.325	0.325	0.325	0.325	0.325	0.325	0.325
Toward accomplishment	0.393	0.393	0.393	0.393	0.393	0.393	0.393	0.393	0.393	0.393	0.393	0.393	0.393	0.393	0.393
Introjected	0.409	0.409	0.409	0.409	0.409	0.409	0.409	0.409	0.409	0.409	0.409	0.409	0.409	0.409	0.409
Identified	0.377	0.377	0.377	0.377	0.377	0.377	0.377	0.377	0.377	0.377	0.377	0.377	0.377	0.377	0.377
Number of learning tests	0.264	/	/	0.425	0.264	/	0.264	/	/	0.395	/	/	/	/	0.407
Maximum of learning tests	0.264	/	0.242	0.425	0.247	/	0.230	/	/	0.352	/	/	/	/	0.425
Number of practice tests	0.230	0.264	0.254	0.278	/	/	0.230	/	/	0.240	/	/	/	/	0.263
Maximum of practice tests	0.230	0.264	0.343	0.354	/	0.247	0.230	/	/	0.260	/	/	/	/	0.277
Video	/	/	/	/	/	/	0.378	/	/	0.254	/	/	/	0.388	0.482
Presentation	/	/	/	/	/	/	0.242	0.269	0.263	/	0.254	0.251	/	/	/
Test 1	/	/	/	0.404	0.404	0.404	0.404	0.404	0.404	0.404	0.404	0.404	0.404	0.404	0.404
Test 2	/	/	/	/	/	/	0.322	0.322	0.322	0.322	0.322	0.322	0.322	0.322	0.322
Test 4	/	/	/	/	/	/	/	/	/	/	/	/	0.361	0.361	0.361
Colloquium 1	/	/	/	/	0.593	0.593	0.593	0.593	0.593	0.593	0.593	0.593	0.593	0.593	0.593
Colloquium 2	/	/	/	/	/	/	/	/	/	/	0.503	0.503	0.503	0.503	0.503
Count	9	7	8	10	9	8	14	9	9	13	10	10	10	11	15
Sum	2.854	2.395	2.705	3.752	3.375	3.111	4.759	3.454	3.448	4.686	3.941	3.939	4.048	4.436	5.903

The results in Table 9 indicate that prior academic performance, particularly *School grade* (Cramér's V = 0.362) and *Matriculation percentage* (Cramér's V = 0.325), maintains a consistent association with course success throughout the semester. Among motivational factors, *Introjected motivation* (Cramér's V = 0.409) and *Motivation toward accomplishment* (Cramér's V = 0.393) exhibit the strongest relationships with student outcomes.

Regarding LMS activity, *Number of learning tests* and *Maximum of learning tests* show fluctuating but notable associations, particularly in the weeks preceding the assessments (e.g., week 4: Cramér's V = 0.425). *Colloquium 1* (Cramér's V = 0.593) and *Colloquium 2* (Cramér's V = 0.503) emerge as the strongest predictors, reinforcing the importance of early assessment performance in determining final success. The Sum of Cramér's V values per week suggests an increasing trend, peaking in week 15 (5.903), indicating a growing influence of these predictors as the semester progresses.

5.1. Development of the Predictive Model

The Cramér's V coefficient values from Table 9 were normalized by dividing each value by the total sum of Cramér's V coefficients for the corresponding week, then multiplying by 100 and rounding to the nearest whole number. This approach ensures that the relative contribution of each variable is proportionally represented within a standardized framework.

As a result, a weekly scoring system was developed, assigning coefficient-based weights to relevant activities for each of the 15 weeks (Table 10). Within this framework, a student can accumulate a maximum of 100 points per week, providing a structured and interpretable measure of engagement and performance across the semester.

Table 10. Scoring system of the coefficients of the relevant variables of the e-learning system by weeks.

Variable	**1**	**2**	**3**	**4**	**5**	**6**	**7**	**8**	**9**	**10**	**11**	**12**	**13**	**14**	**15**
School grade	13	15	13	10	11	12	8	11	11	8	9	9	9	8	6
Matriculation percentage	12	14	12	9	10	10	7	9	9	7	8	8	8	7	6
Toward accomplishment	14	16	15	10	12	13	8	11	11	8	10	10	10	9	7
Introjected	14	17	15	11	12	13	9	12	12	9	11	11	10	9	7
Identified	13	16	14	10	11	12	8	11	11	8	10	10	9	9	6
Number of learning tests	9	0	0	11	8	0	5	0	0	8	0	0	0	0	7
Maximum of learning tests	9	0	9	11	7	0	5	0	0	7	0	0	0	0	7
Number of practice tests	8	11	9	7	0	0	5	0	0	5	0	0	0	0	4
Maximum of practice tests	8	11	13	10	0	8	5	0	0	6	0	0	0	0	5
Video	0	0	0	0	0	0	8	0	0	5	0	0	0	9	8
Presentation	0	0	0	0	0	0	5	8	8	0	6	6	0	0	0
Test 1	0	0	0	11	12	13	8	12	12	9	10	10	10	9	7
Test 2	0	0	0	0	0	0	7	9	9	7	8	8	8	7	5
Test 4	0	0	0	0	0	0	0	0	0	0	0	0	9	8	6
Colloquium 1	0	0	0	0	17	19	12	17	17	13	15	15	15	14	10
Colloquium 2	0	0	0	0	0	0	0	0	0	0	13	13	12	11	9
Sum	100	100	100	100	100	100	100	100	100	100	100	100	100	100	100

For 43 students who completed both surveys and for whom data on all relevant activities in the LMS Merlin and the value of the *Success* variable were available, the number of points they achieved in each week was calculated. Then, for each week, the optimal cut-off point of the number of points for which the value of the Youden index is highest was determined. The optimal cut-off points for the sum of scores per week are shown in Table 11.

Table 11. Optimal cut-off points for the sum of scores per week.

Week	1	2	3	4	5	6	7	8	9	10	11	12	13	14	15
Cut-off	33	39	32	52	37	40	33	49	49	47	53	43	50	55	55

Based on these optimal cut-off points for the sum of scores for each week, the numeric variable is transformed into a dichotomous variable.

5.2. Development of the Prediction Algorithm

The scoring system is created at the end of the academic year when the values of the dependent variable, whether the student has passed or failed the course, are known. The described process of developing a scoring system that serves as a classification prediction model is illustrated by the flowchart in Figure 5. By following this process, teachers can create their own scoring system. They must independently determine the student activities in their course that they want to track and consider as potential predictor variables. The model is applicable to different courses and different activities within a course. Once teachers have established their scoring system, they can use it in subsequent academic years to predict student success in the course.

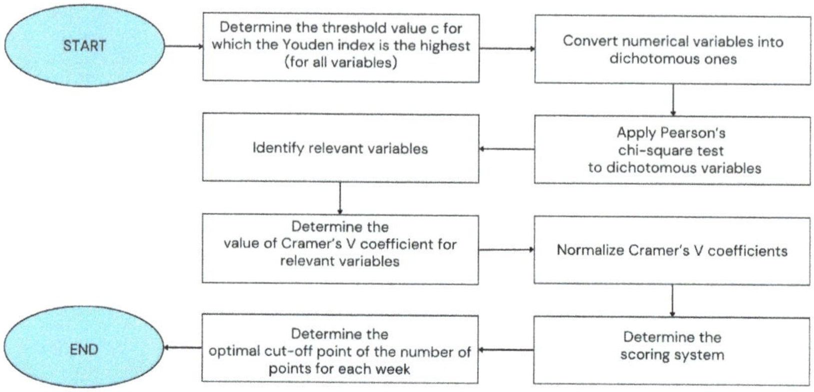

Figure 5. Flowchart of the designing scoring system.

The predictive model was designed as a weekly classification system to assess the likelihood that students will fail the course. The algorithm follows a structured process, as illustrated in Figure 6, ensuring that the predictions are continuously updated based on student engagement and performance data.

The process begins with the definition of the course settings, including the course structure, the grading policies, and key assessment milestones. The prediction variables are then determined, selecting relevant indicators such as attendance, participation, and self-reported engagement. These variables are collected through student surveys and activity logs.

Each week, the participation of students in the course activities is monitored, and based on their recorded participation a score is calculated. This score represents an aggregated measure of their academic performance and engagement up to that point. Students are then classified as "at risk" or "not at risk" based on a predefined cut-off threshold. If a student's score falls below this threshold, they are flagged as at risk of failing the course.

This score-based classification is then used to provide personalized feedback to students, helping them understand their current risk level and encouraging corrective action if necessary. By making students aware of their status early in the semester, the system enables timely interventions that can improve their performance.

The process repeats weekly, updating the predictions dynamically. The system runs until the final week of the semester, at which point the iterative predictions stop.

This predictive model allows educators to implement targeted pedagogical strategies (feedback to the students) in real time. In our prospective study, these strategies include the following:

- Individual consultation invitations, encouraging students to discuss their challenges and receive tailored guidance;
- The integration of motivational narratives within lectures to reinforce resilience and engagement; and
- The organization of group-based supplementary exercises, fostering peer learning and collaborative problem-solving.

Beyond direct interventions, predictive insights are also used to guide students toward specific learning resources. Based on their risk score, students are advised to review selected video lectures, attempt additional problem sets, or revisit fundamental concepts, ensuring that support is both personalized and actionable.

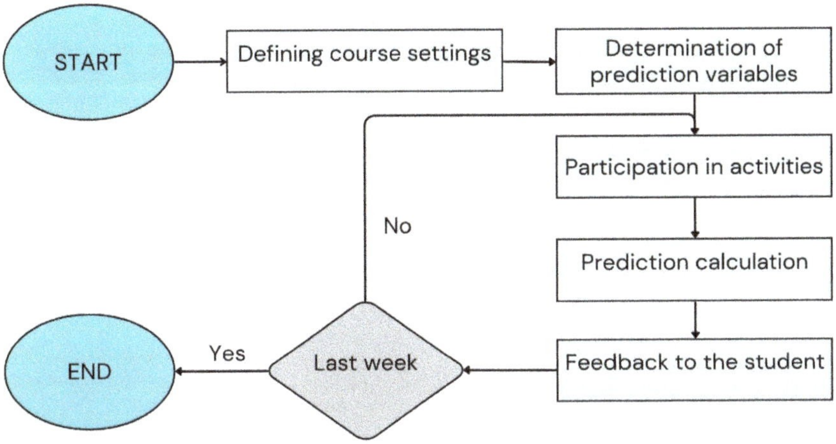

Figure 6. Flowchart of the predictive model used for student classification.

5.3. Retrospective Model Evaluation

To assess the performance of the predictive model, its predictions were compared with the true labels of the test dataset. Table 12 presents the accuracy, specificity, sensitivity, and AUC-ROC values for each of the 15 weeks of teaching.

Performance metrics indicate that the model maintained stable accuracy throughout the weeks, with consistently high sensitivity values, suggesting that it effectively identified students at risk of failing the course. The AUC-ROC values remained above 0.78 in all weeks, peaking at week 15 (0.89), indicating strong discriminatory power. In particular, sensitivity was highest in the initial weeks but exhibited a gradual decrease towards the final weeks, which could be attributed to evolving student engagement patterns over the semester.

Table 12. Performance metrics of the predictive model per week in the 2023/2024 academic year.

Week	Accuracy	Specificity	Sensitivity	AUC-ROC
Week 1	0.74	0.70	0.90	0.80
Week 2	0.72	0.67	0.90	0.78
Week 3	0.79	0.76	0.90	0.83
Week 4	0.81	0.76	1.00	0.88
Week 5	0.81	0.79	0.90	0.84
Week 6	0.81	0.79	0.90	0.84
Week 7	0.81	0.79	0.90	0.84
Week 8	0.77	0.73	0.90	0.81
Week 9	0.77	0.73	0.90	0.81
Week 10	0.81	0.82	0.80	0.81
Week 11	0.79	0.76	0.90	0.83
Week 12	0.86	0.91	0.70	0.80
Week 13	0.86	0.88	0.80	0.84
Week 14	0.81	0.79	0.90	0.84
Week 15	0.88	0.88	0.90	0.89

5.4. Prospective Model Evaluation

The system was evaluated a second time in the following academic year using data from 70 students attending the same course. Table 13 presents the accuracy, specificity, sensitivity, and AUC-ROC values of the predictive model for the first four weeks.

For this analysis, the outcome variable *Success* was determined based on the results of the students in the first colloquium. Students who scored below the passing threshold were classified as "at risk", while those who passed were classified as "successful". This definition aligns with the objective of identifying at-risk students early enough to allow timely intervention.

In the context of early identification of at-risk students, the performance metrics for week 4, the week preceding the first colloquium, are particularly revealing. The model achieved an accuracy of 93%, with both specificity (92%) and sensitivity (95%) reaching their highest levels. This suggests that by week 4, the model was able to reliably distinguish between students who were likely to pass and those at risk of failing, providing a strong basis for early intervention strategies.

A comparison between retrospective and prospective evaluations reveals differences in model performance across academic years. While the overall trend of high sensitivity and stable accuracy is consistent, week 4 of the prospective evaluation shows significantly higher predictive power. These differences and their possible causes are further analyzed in the Section 6.

Table 13. Performance metrics of the predictive model per week in the 2024/2025 academic year.

Week	Accuracy	Specificity	Sensitivity	AUC-ROC
Week 1	0.80	0.78	0.84	0.81
Week 2	0.77	0.75	0.84	0.79
Week 3	0.83	0.88	0.68	0.78
Week 4	0.93	0.92	0.95	0.93

Note: The week preceding first midterm exam is highlighted in light blue.

6. Discussion

The scoring system was designed based on 16 variables. A direct numerical comparison of the relationships between different prediction variables and their impact on student performance across studies is limited due to methodological differences. However, the result remains qualitatively the same; it is crucial to identify which variables are relevant predictors, regardless of the method used.

Prior academic performance—specifically *School grade* (*Cramér's V = 0.362*) and *Matriculation percentage* (*Cramér's V = 0.325*)—emerges as the strongest predictor. This aligns with the foundational nature of mathematics, where new concepts build upon previously acquired knowledge.

Motivational variables also played a crucial role, with both intrinsic (*Toward accomplishment, Cramér's V = 0.393)* and extrinsic components (*Introjected, Cramér's V = 0.409)* emerging as consistent predictors across all weeks. These findings align with previous research [5,6], confirming that motivation significantly influences engagement and persistence, making it an essential component of predictive modeling.

However, a key challenge in incorporating both academic and non-academic variables lies in their method of collection. Unlike the variables obtained directly through the LMS, these data were collected using two voluntary questionnaires. In particular, 43% of the students did not complete them, leading to missing data that could impact the reliability of the predictions. Missing responses may introduce selection bias, where students who voluntarily participate in surveys differ systematically from those who do not, potentially skewing model results.

To ensure the robustness of the model, it is essential to address this limitation. Educators should clearly communicate the purpose and benefits of the prediction model to students, emphasizing how their participation can lead to better support and intervention strategies. Actively encouraging students to complete both questionnaires in the first week of instruction is crucial to ensuring the reliability of predictions. Increasing response rates, for instance, by embedding surveys into early course activities, could further enhance prediction accuracy.

The variables that capture students' engagement in solving tasks throughout the semester (task engagement metrics: *Number of learning tests*, *Maximum of learning tests*, *Number of practice tests*, *Maximum of practice tests*) play a particularly significant role in predicting student outcomes. Our findings align with previous research [7,8], which also identified time spent on various course components, such as tests and assignments, along with quiz and assignment scores, as key predictors of overall course performance.

Specifically, these task engagement metrics emerge as significant predictors of *Success* in at least 6 out of 15 weeks. In contrast, variables *Video* and *Presentation* appear as relevant predictors in fewer weeks. This discrepancy may be attributed to the way LMS Merlin records these activities: The system records only whether an activity was accessed, lacking finer engagement metrics, such as time spent reviewing materials or depth of interaction, which may limit its predictive reliability. As a result, recorded engagement with these resources may not always reflect real learning activity, making them a less reliable predictor compared to interactive assessments such as tests and quizzes.

In line with [9], our study underscores the importance of using historical academic performance data to predict future outcomes. Student assessment activities throughout the semester (*Test 1*, *Test 2*, *Test 4*, *Colloquium 1*, *Colloquium 2*) consistently emerge as strong predictors of *Success* in all weeks following their completion (Cramér's V values between 0.322 and 0.593). These assessments represent critical intervention points. Identifying students with low performance early enables timely adjustments to instructional methods, including adaptive learning resources, targeted feedback, and structured peer support.

The scoring system was developed using classical statistical methods, with numerical variables transformed into categorical, dichotomous variables based on the Youden index, which optimally separates students at risk of failing from those predicted to succeed. The relationship between key variables and *Success* was quantified using Cramér's V coefficients, allowing us to assess the strength of the association between predictor variables and student performance.

Cramér's V and the Youden index were selected because of their suitability for the analysis of categorical data, the optimization of threshold values, and their practical interpretability in the field of education. Cramér's V quantifies the strength of association between nominal or ordinal variables and is therefore particularly suitable for assessing the relationship between early course performance indicators and final student outcomes. Unlike Pearson's correlation coefficient, which is designed for continuous variables and assumes a linear relationship, Cramér's V captures nonlinear dependencies and allows for easy interpretation of categorical predictors [34]. The Youden index has been used to establish optimal cut-off points for academic risk classification. While ROC curves provide a comprehensive assessment of classification performance by plotting sensitivity against specificity, they do not inherently define a single optimal threshold. The Youden index, on the other hand, directly identifies the threshold that maximizes both true-positive and true-negative rates, making it particularly effective for balancing sensitivity and specificity in early intervention strategies [32].

The resulting scoring system and its associated algorithm function as a predictive classification model, forecasting student *Success* throughout all 15 weeks of instruction. What distinguishes this model is its transparency, ease of interpretation, and practical applicability. While complex machine learning models may offer marginally higher predictive accuracy, this approach provides educators with direct insights into the contribution of each variable to student performance, making it particularly suited for educational interventions.

Our study builds on previous research [13–15], reinforcing the importance of interpretable models that not only achieve strong predictive performance but also offer actionable insights into their decision-making processes. By providing clear, interpretable predictions, this model enables instructors to implement proactive teaching strategies. For example, educators can use early warning indicators to tailor instructional pacing, design adaptive assignments, or introduce peer mentoring programs to support at-risk students.

The robustness of the model was evaluated in two phases: first in its development dataset and later in a new cohort where real-time interventions were introduced.

Evaluation of the original dataset demonstrated consistent performance across all weeks in identifying students at risk of failing Mathematics 1. With consistently high sensitivity, the model effectively flagged nearly all students who were genuinely at risk, aligning with the primary goal of the study. Specificity varied across weeks, occasionally flagging students as at risk when they were not. Future refinements could explore adaptive thresholds that dynamically adjust to student behavior trends, ensuring that interventions remain timely and precisely targeted. However, this trade-off is acceptable in this context, as the priority is to minimize false negatives, ensuring that no genuinely at-risk students go unnoticed. In an educational setting, identifying all at-risk students—even at the cost of a few false positives—is preferable to missing those who need support.

The consistently high AUC-ROC scores (above 0.80) confirm the model's strong discriminative power, indicating its robustness in distinguishing between at-risk and non-at-risk students even as engagement patterns fluctuate over the semester. This stability suggests that the model captures core behavioral trends that persist across different teaching weeks, maintaining stable predictive power regardless of minor variations in student engagement patterns.

Given this strong discriminative performance, we next examined whether real-time interventions could further enhance the model's effectiveness in guiding student behavior. The model was tested a second time using new data, now incorporating an intervention component. Each week, students received messages informing them of their scores and predicted risk of failing the course. Those identified as at risk also received targeted intervention messages with specific recommendations on how to improve their performance the following week.

As a result, performance metrics evolved over the first four weeks, reflecting the impact of these interventions. Students flagged as at-risk adjusted their behavior based on the feedback, leading to changes in their status over time. The most critical point of analysis is the fourth week, the week before the first colloquium, where the model demonstrated particularly high sensitivity (0.95). This is crucial as it ensures that almost all at-risk students are correctly identified and have the opportunity to take corrective action before a major assessment.

Our model achieves accuracy and AUC-ROC of 0.93 in the fourth week, performing as well as, or in some cases better than, other recently published models. For instance, Akçapınar et al. developed an early warning system to identify students at risk, with their model achieving its highest accuracy in the 3rd and 6th weeks, at 0.79 and 0.81, respectively [23]. Additionally, Osborne and Lang's research confirmed that LMS data can be effectively used to create predictive models capable of identifying at-risk students as early as the fifth week of the semester. Their model achieved an accuracy of 0.877, a sensitivity of 0.265, a precision of 0.601, a specificity of 0.973, and an AUC-ROC of 0.808 [24].

The model's effectiveness in early identification and intervention underscores its value as a proactive tool for improving student outcomes and reducing failure rates. These findings align with previous research [17–19], reinforcing the idea that early predictions can significantly influence student success by enabling timely and targeted interventions. Future implementations should examine how predictor variables may need to be adapted for different subjects, particularly those that rely on project-based learning or qualitative assessment rather than structured problem-solving and quantitative exams.

The comparison between retrospective and prospective evaluations demonstrates the model's adaptability across different student cohorts, further reinforcing its potential for broader application. While both evaluations confirmed high sensitivity and stable predictive power, key improvements emerged in the prospective evaluation, particularly when combined with an intervention component. The observed increase in early-stage accuracy and sensitivity suggests that students in the second cohort responded more actively to feedback, potentially due to greater awareness of their academic standing and the motivational effect of targeted intervention messages. These findings reinforce the importance of continuous monitoring and refinement of predictive models to ensure their effectiveness across different student cohorts. Future research should explore the model's applicability across diverse student populations and learning environments, particularly in assessing whether predictive improvements remain consistent across different institutional and curricular structures. Additionally, further studies should examine how refining the timing, frequency, and messaging of interventions can maximize student responsiveness and long-term academic outcomes.

This study has opened several avenues for future research, particularly in the refinement of the prediction model and its practical application. One promising direction is to restructure the course organization to highlight the milestones that have the greatest impact on early risk detection. Identifying these critical points could allow instructional strategies to be optimized and assessments to be aligned with key moments of student engagement.

In addition, developing comprehensive guidelines for educators could facilitate the implementation of educational interventions and ensure that support mechanisms are both timely and effective. While this study has demonstrated the predictive accuracy of the model, future research should investigate how different types of feedback affect student motivation and performance. Understanding the psychological and behavioral responses to predictive analytics could shed light on how students adjust to receiving regular assessments of their academic performance. In addition, it is important to explore the applicability of the model beyond STEM disciplines to determine whether similar indicators have predictive power in fields that rely on qualitative assessment rather than structured problem-solving.

Beyond student-centered implications, faculty acceptance of predictive systems remains an open question. Investigating how teachers perceive and integrate such models into their teaching practice could reveal barriers to adoption and identify strategies to improve user confidence and system usability. The ethical implications of predictive learning analytics, particularly the trade-offs between early intervention, student autonomy, and data privacy, also require further investigation.

Ultimately, the refinement of predictive models should go beyond accuracy metrics and focus on their broader implications for student learning, institutional practices, and educational equity. By answering these questions, future research can contribute not only to improving the detection of academic risk, but also to shaping a more adaptive, responsive, and ethical educational environment.

7. Conclusions

The proposed algorithm provides a practical and adaptable framework for the early detection of students at risk of failure, offering a balance between predictive accuracy, interpretability, and ease of implementation. Its simplicity, ease of implementation, and minimal computational requirements make it highly accessible to a broad spectrum of educational institutions, regardless of their technological infrastructure. The model's iterative weekly application allows for continuous monitoring and timely interventions, ensuring that students receive support before their performance declines significantly. Additionally, the integration of Cramér's V measure and the Youden index enables systematic predictor selection and the establishment of clear risk thresholds.

The analysis showed that the most influential predictors included prior academic performance, with Cramér's V values of 0.362 for grades and 0.325 for enrollment rates, as well as motivational factors, such as introjected motivation (0.409) and achievement motivation (0.393). Among the course engagement variables, weekly test performance and early assessments showed the highest predictive power, with Colloquium 1 and Colloquium 2 achieving Cramér's V values of 0.593 and 0.503, respectively. The Youden index was applied to determine optimal thresholds for risk classification, with weekly thresholds ranging from 32 to 55 points, as shown in Table 11. These scores provide an objective basis for early risk detection and enable timely and targeted interventions.

A key advantage of this approach is its methodological simplicity, relying on well-established statistical techniques that are widely accepted among educators. This increases the likelihood of adoption, particularly among senior instructors who may have reservations about more complex machine learning methods. Furthermore, the model combines objective indicators of prior knowledge, motivational characteristics, and student work habits, creating a holistic predictive model rather than relying solely on learning analytics from the LMS.

By structuring the model as an algorithm, its automation is straightforward, making it scalable for courses with large student enrollments. The model is also designed to accommodate weekly variations in student behavior, allowing educators to track changes over time and adjust interventions accordingly. A clear methodological framework is provided, making it adaptable to different courses, either through direct implementation or minor adjustments.

One of the most impactful aspects of the model is its intervention component, which enables educators to provide individualized support to at-risk students. The prospective analysis demonstrated that the model exhibited exceptionally high discriminative power in the week before the first major exam, ensuring that nearly all at-risk students were correctly identified in time for targeted interventions. The high sensitivity of the scoring system further guarantees that students in need of support are not overlooked.

Despite these strengths, some challenges remain. The relatively small sample size in this study was a limitation, although the prospective analysis indicated that this did not significantly affect the model's performance. Additionally, collecting motivational and non-LMS data proved challenging, as it required voluntary student participation, potentially impacting response rates. While the model can be integrated into existing LMS platforms, some degree of manual processing may be required, posing an implementation challenge for large-scale adoption. Lastly, although alternative statistical methods (e.g., logistic regression) could be explored for further refinement, the choice of simpler techniques was intentional, prioritizing interpretability and practical application.

The proposed model has already been successfully implemented in our prospective analysis, where it was directly applied to real teaching scenarios without modification. Through this implementation, we utilized previously described pedagogical interventions, including individual consultations, motivational components in lectures, targeted study recommendations, and structured peer-support activities. Given the universal nature of academic risk factors, we believe that this framework could be effectively applied to all STEM courses, provided that appropriate interventions are systematically integrated into the instructional process.

From a broader perspective, the model's meta-structure is highly adaptable across different courses and institutions. However, its implementation requires context-specific adjustments to align with institutional policies, such as the number of permitted assessments, methods of continuous evaluation, and ethical guidelines for data collection. While inherently designed for STEM disciplines, where structured assessment and standardized grading are prevalent, the model would require modifications for subjects involving laboratory work, such as chemistry, biology, or physics.

Beyond STEM fields, the model's applicability in humanities and social sciences necessitates further investigation. These disciplines often emphasize discussion-based instruction and essay-style assessments, differing significantly from the quantitative evaluation methods used in STEM. However, with adequate quantification of qualitative indicators, a similar predictive framework could potentially be developed for these fields, expanding the model's reach to a broader academic spectrum.

To enhance practical usability, efforts should focus on raising awareness among both students and faculty regarding the model's potential benefits. Continuous faculty training and student orientation sessions would facilitate its seamless integration into the educational workflow. Furthermore, greater automation of the predictive process would streamline its implementation, reducing the need for manual data handling and increasing accessibility for instructors.

The model should also undergo periodic validation and refinement, ensuring its continued relevance by incorporating new predictors as educational environments evolve. Additionally, adapting course structures to better align with data-driven insights—for example, refining assessment schedules to generate key performance indicators earlier in the semester—could further enhance its predictive accuracy and effectiveness in guiding interventions. Ultimately, the long-term success of this model depends not only on its statistical robustness but also on its integration into institutional practices. By fostering a culture of data-informed teaching, facilitating contextual adaptations, and maintaining continuous model evaluation, this approach has the potential to become an invaluable tool for academic risk detection and personalized student support.

Future work should focus on validating the algorithm's effectiveness across diverse datasets and educational systems, ensuring its scalability and adaptability. Expanding its applicability and refining its predictive capabilities will solidify its role as a scalable, data-driven solution for improving student retention, academic performance, and overall educational outcomes.

Author Contributions: Conceptualization, V.Č.P., I.D., and S.Č.; methodology, V.Č.P.; software, V.Č.P.; validation, V.Č.P., I.D., and S.Č.; formal analysis, V.Č.P.; investigation, V.Č.P.; resources, V.Č.P.; data curation, V.Č.P.; writing—original draft preparation, V.Č.P.; writing—review and editing, I.D. and S.Č.; visualization, V.Č.P.; supervision, I.D.; project administration, S.Č.; funding acquisition, S.Č. All authors have read and agreed to the published version of the manuscript.

Funding: This research was funded by the University of Rijeka, Croatia, grant number uniri-iskusni-drustv-23-236 (Development of an information system for early detection of failure among students in STEM subjects). The APC was funded by MDPI.

Data Availability Statement: The raw data supporting the conclusions of this article will be made available by the first author upon request.

Conflicts of Interest: The authors declare no conflicts of interest.

Abbreviations

The following abbreviations are used in this manuscript:

EDM	educational data mining
LA	learning analytics
STEM	science, technology, engineering, and mathematics
GPA	grade point average
CGPA	cumulative grade point average
LMS	learning management system
AI	artificial intelligence
ML	machine learning
AUC-ROC	area under the receiver operating characteristic curve

References

1. Siemens, G.; Baker, R. Learning analytics and educational data mining: Towards communication and collaboration. In Proceedings of the 2nd International Conference on Learning Analytics and Knowledge, Vancouver, BC, Canada, 29 April–2 May 2012.
2. Calvet Liñán, L.; Juan Pérez, A. Educational data mining and learning analytics: Differences, similarities, and time evolution. *Int. J. Educ. Technol. High. Educ.* **2015**, *12*, 98–112.
3. Brooks, C.; Thompson, C. Predictive modelling in teaching and learning. In *Handbook of Learning Analytics*, 2nd ed.; SoLAR, Lang, C., Siemens, G., Friend Wise, A., Gašević, D., Merceron, A., Eds.; Nature Publishing Group: London, UK, 2022; pp. 29–37.
4. Nabil, A.; Seyam, M.; Abou-Elfetouh, A. Prediction of Students' Academic Performance Based on Courses' Grades Using Deep Neural Networks. *IEEE Access* **2021**, *9*, 140731–140746.
5. Fan, Y.; John, S.; Singh, S.; Jovanović, J.; Gašević, D. A learning analytic approach to unveiling self-regulatory processes in learning tactics. In Proceedings of the LAK21: 11th International Learning Analytics and Knowledge Conference, Irvine, CA, USA, 12–16 April 2021; pp. 184–195.
6. Karabatak, S.; Yıldırım, Ö.; Karabatak, M. Evaluation of academic self-efficiency, community feeling, and academic achievement of students in the process of the COVID-19 pandemic by data mining techniques. *Fırat Univ. Muhendis. Bilim. Derg.* **2024**, *36*, 301–310. [CrossRef]
7. Kittur, J.; Bekki, J.; Brunhaver, S. Development of a student engagement score for online undergraduate engineering courses using learning management system interaction data. *Comput. Appl. Eng. Educ.* **2022**, *30*, 661–677.
8. Cui, Y.; Chen, F.; Shiri, A. Scale up predictive models for early detection of at-risk students: A feasibility study. *Inf. Learn. Sci.* **2020**, *12*, 97–116.
9. Caicedo-Castro, I. Course Prophet: A System for Predicting Course Failures with Machine Learning: A Numerical Methods Case Study. *Sustainability* **2023**, *15*, 13950. [CrossRef]
10. Fahd, K.; Miah, S.J. Designing and evaluating a big data analytics approach for predicting students' success factors. *J. Big Data* **2023**, *10*, 159.
11. Wang, Y.; Joe, H. OISE: Optimized Input Sampling Explanation with a Saliency Map Based on the Black-Box Model. *Appl. Sci.* **2023**, *13*, 5886. [CrossRef]
12. Hassija, V. Interpreting Black-Box Models: A Review on Explainable Artificial Intelligence. *Cogn. Comput.* **2024**, *16*, 45–74. [CrossRef]
13. Doshi-Velez, F.; Kim, P. Towards A Rigorous Science of Interpretable Machine Learning. *arXiv* **2017**, arXiv:1702.08608.
14. Ribeiro, M.T.; Singh, S.; Guestrin, C. "Why Should I Trust You?": Explaining the Predictions of Any Classifier. In Proceedings of the 22nd ACM SIGKDD International Conference on Knowledge Discovery and Data Mining, San Francisco, CA, USA, 13–17 August 2016.
15. Žlahtič, B. Transferring Black-Box Decision Making to a White-Box Model. *Electronics* **2024**, *13*, 1895. [CrossRef]
16. Theobald, E.J.; Hill, M.J.; Tran, E.; Agrawal, S.; Arroyo, E.N.; Behling, S.; Chambwe, N.; Cintrón, D.L.; Cooper, J.D. Active learning narrows achievement gaps for underrepresented students in undergraduate science, technology, engineering, and math. *Proc. Natl. Acad. Sci. USA* **2020**, *117*, 6476–6483. [PubMed]
17. Hamid, S.; Ismail, S.N.; Hamzah, M.; Malik, A.W. Developing engagement in the learning management system supported by learning analytics. *Comput. Syst. Sci. Eng.* **2022**, *42*, 336–350.

18. Maraza-Quispe, B.; Valderrama-Chauca, E.D.; Cari-Mogrovejo, L.H.; Apaza-Huanca, J.M.; Sanchez-Ilabaca, J. A predictive model implemented in KNIME based on learning analytics for timely decision making in virtual learning environments. *Int. J. Inf. Educ. Technol.* **2022**, *12*, 91–99.
19. Kite, J.; Schlub, T.E.; Zhang, Y.; Choi, S.; Craske, S.; Dickson, M. Exploring lecturer and student perceptions and use of a learning management system in a postgraduate public health environment. *E-Learn. Digit. Media* **2020**, *17*, 183–198. [CrossRef]
20. Yeager, D.S.; Hanselman, P.; Walton, G.M.; Murray, J.S.; Crosnoe, R.; Muller, C.; Tipton, E.; Schneider, B.; Hulleman, C.S.; Hinojosa, C.P.; et al. A National Experiment Reveals Where a Growth Mindset Improves Achievement. *Nature* **2019**, *573*, 364–369. [CrossRef]
21. Daker, R.J.; Gattas, S.U.; Sokolowski, H.M.; Green, A.E.; Lyons, I.M. First-Year Students' Math Anxiety Predicts STEM Avoidance and Underperformance Throughout University, Independently of Math Ability. *NPJ Sci. Learn.* **2021**, *6*, 17.
22. Santos, R.; Henriques, R. Predicting Student Performance From Moodle Logs in Higher Education: A Course-Agnostic Approach. In *Education and New Developments*; inScience Press: Lisbon, Portugal, 2023; Volume 2.
23. Akçapınar, G.; Hasnine, M.N.; Majumdar, R.; Flanagan, B.; Ogata, H. Developing an Early-Warning System for Spotting at-Risk Students by Using eBook Interaction Logs. *Smart Learn. Environ.* **2019**, *6*, 4. [CrossRef]
24. Osborne, J.; Lang, A. Predictive Identification of At-Risk Students: Using Learning Management System Data. *J. Postsecond. Stud. Success* **2023**, *2*, 108–126.
25. Zakopoulos, V.; Georgakopoulos, I.; Kossieri, E.; Kallivokas, D. Controlling attrition in blended courses by identifying students at risk: A case study on MS-Teams. *Int. J. Financ. Insur. Risk Manag.* **2021**, *11*, 57–68
26. Yousafzai, I.; Jamil, B. Relationship between admission criteria and academic performance: A correlational study in nursing students. *Pak. J. Med. Sci.* **2019**, *35*, 858. [CrossRef]
27. Mahboob, K.; Asif, R.; Haider, N.G. Quality enhancement at higher education institutions by early identifying students at risk using data mining. *Mehran Univ. Res. J. Eng. Technol.* **2023**, *42*, 120–136. [CrossRef]
28. Sandoval-Palis, I.; Naranjo, D.; Vidal, J.; Gilar-Corbi, R. Early dropout prediction model: A case study of university leveling course students. *Sustainability* **2020**, *12*, 9314 . [CrossRef]
29. Mogavi, R.H.; Ma, X.; Hui, P. Characterizing student engagement moods for dropout prediction in question pool websites. *Proc. ACM Hum.-Comput. Interact.* **2020**, *5*, 1–22. [CrossRef]
30. Won, H.S.; Kim, M.J.; Kim, D.; Kim, H.S.; Kim, K.M. University student dropout prediction using pretrained language models. *Appl. Sci.* **2023**, *13*, 7073. [CrossRef]
31. Ribić, G. Motivacija za Studij kod učEnika Srednjih šKola: Uloga Osnovnih Psiholoških Potreba i Identiteta, Diplomski Rad. Ph.D. Thesis, University of Rijeka, Rijeka, Croatia, 2016.
32. Youden, W.J. Index for rating diagnostic tests. *Cancer* **1950**, *3*, 32–35. [CrossRef]
33. Pearson, K. On the criterion that a given system of deviations from the probable in the case of a correlated system of variables is such that it can be reasonably supposed to have arisen from random sampling. *Lond. Edinb. Dublin Philos. Mag. J. Sci.* **1900**, *50*, 157–175. [CrossRef]
34. Cramér, H. *Mathematical Methods of Statistics*; Princeton University Press: Princeton, NJ, USA, 1946; pp. 367–369.

algorithms

MDPI

Article

Navigating Stakeholders Perspectives on Artificial Intelligence in Higher Education

Aleida Chavarria [1,*], Ramon Palau [2] and Raúl Santiago [3]

1 School of Social Sciences, Universidad Latina de Costa Rica, San José 11501, Costa Rica
2 Applied Research Group Education Technology, Universidad Rovira i Virgili, 43003 Tarragona, Spain; ramon.palau@urv.cat
3 Department of Educational Sciences, Universidad de La Rioja, 26006 Logroño, Spain; raul.santiago@unirioja.es
* Correspondence: aleida.chavarria@ulatina.cr

Abstract

As artificial intelligence (AI) becomes increasingly integrated into higher education, understanding perceptions across different demographic groups is essential for its effective implementation. This study examines attitudes toward AI among students, lecturers, and academic staff, considering factors such as gender, age, occupation, academic discipline, ethical concerns, and experience level. The findings indicate that while overall perceptions of AI in education are positive, concerns about ethics and uncertainty regarding its role persist. Gender and age differences in AI perceptions are minimal, though female students, educators, and individual in humanities disciplines express slightly higher ethical concerns. Teachers exhibit greater skepticism, emphasizing the need for transparency, ethical guidelines, and training to build trust. The study also highlights the influence of AI experience and perceptions. Frequent users tend to have a more positive outlook, whereas those with advance expertise engage with AI more selectively, suggesting a shift toward intentional and strategic use.

Keywords: artificial intelligence; higher education; ethics; emerging technologies; awareness; stakeholders' perception

1. Introduction

Artificial intelligence (AI) technologies are rapidly transforming the landscape of higher education, offering innovative learning opportunities and enhancing institutional operations through intelligent systems. When integrated thoughtfully, AI can enrich educational experiences while preserving the human connections vital to emotional and social development [1–3]. However, responsible implementation requires institutions to evaluate not only technical and administrative readiness but also the perceptions and concerns of the people affected, students, educators, and academic staff [4,5].

Existing literature has examined the ethical, pedagogical, and social implications of AI in education [6,7]. Studies have reported both enthusiasm and hesitation toward AI, citing issues such as data privacy, loss of human interaction, and the uncertainty of algorithmic systems [7,8]. Yet, many of these studies focus on either students or educators in isolation, without accounting for how factors like academic discipline, professional role, and AI experience level interact to shape attitudes. Moreover, research has primarily been concentrated in well-resourced or Anglophone contexts, leaving a gap in understanding how AI is perceived in diverse institutional and cultural environments.

This study addresses these gaps by examining the perceptions of AI across three key stakeholder groups, students, educators, and administrative staff, within a Latin America higher education institution, Universidad Latina. It considers how demographic variables (age, gender and discipline), professional roles, and AI experience influence attitudes and ethical concerns. It also distinguishes between frequent users and advanced experts of AI tools, revealing important patterns in how experience shapes engagement and trust. By offering a holistic, contextually grounded perspective, this study contributes to the design of equitable and ethically sound AI strategies for higher education. The study seeks to answer the following research questions:

1. What are the attitudes and perceptions of participants regarding the implementation of AI in higher education?
2. What are the ethical and social implications of implementing AI in higher education?
3. How do participants'demographic characteristics influence their perception on AI implementation?

Background Literature

The integration of artificial intelligence (AI) into higher education today explores its transformative potential, encompassing its applications in teaching, learning, and administrative processes, while addressing the ethical implications [9]. Contemporary definitions positions AI as the simulation of human cognitive functions by machines [10], with generative AI (GenAI) tools capable of producing original content from user prompts, becoming increasingly prevalent across disciplines [9,11]. These technologies promise personalization, efficiency, and innovation but simultaneously raise urgent concerns regarding ethics, equity, and the redefinition of pedagogical roles [12–14].

Studies by Al-Badi [15] and Al-Zahrani [3] have explored the dual nature of AI's potential in education, highlighting both its benefits and inherent limitation. Several studies report positive attitudes among students and faculty toward AI's capacity to enhance educational outcomes, promote accessibility, and support engagement and streamlining institutional processes [16–19]. Yet optimism is tempered by caution, issues such as data privacy, algorithmic opacity, threats to academic integrity, and the erosion of human-centered teaching practices continue as dominant themes in the literature [13,20]. These ethical and philosophical concerns have led to calls for greater transparency, clear regulatory frameworks, and professional development initiatives focused on algorithmic literacy [21].

Despite the growing body of research, several gaps remain. First, many studies are limited to either the student or faculty perspective, neglecting administrative staff and the institutional dimensions of AI integration. Second, demographic factors, such as age, gender, and academic discipline, are often considered in isolation rather than in intersectional terms. Furthermore, studies examined how a user's prior experience with AI influences not only their acceptance of the technology but also their ethical instance and trust in its application. Existing research also tends to reflect global North or Anglophone contexts, underrepresenting higher education institutions in Latin America, where infrastructural, cultural, and pedagogical variables may shape AI perceptions differently [22–26].

Transparency and explainability are crucial for responsible AI implementation [27]. This is, to have clear documentation of data collection, labels, and algorithms to ensure traceability, identify errors, and prevent future mistakes.

AI decisions impacting human lives must be communicated effectively, ensuring that all stakeholders fully understand them [28]. Autonomy in academic decision-making is key, emphasizing the need for AI-influenced decisions to be transparent, understandable, and fair. This transparency is essential for fostering trust in the educational system [29].

This study addresses these limitations by providing a multidimensional analysis of AI perceptions across three stakeholder groups, students, educators, and administrative staff, within a Latin American university context. By integrating demographic variables (age, gender and discipline) occupational roles, and AI experience levels, the research offers a holistic view of how attitudes, expectations, and ethical concerns converge in shaping AI's role in higher education. In doing so, it contributes to a more significant understanding of user diversity, intentionally in AI adoption, and the ethical frameworks necessary to support inclusive and sensitive technology integration.

2. Methods

In this study, a quantitative methodology was employed using a survey questionnaire to examine the implications for AI on higher education. The data collection regarding attitudes, perceptions, and experiences of students, educators, and administrative staff about AI in higher education used an online survey questionnaire.

The questionnaire developed by Al-Zahrani and Alasmari [3] was designed to examine various aspects of AI in higher education, with a strong Cronbach's alpha value of $\alpha = 0.96$. It was validated by educational technology experts in Saudi Arabia and subsequently reviewed by other professionals in technology education from Spain. Validation results in Costa Rica are presented in the Section 3.

The questionnaire's first section focused on participant demographics, including age, gender, occupation, education level, AI expertise, AI tools and services used, frequency of use, and purposed for using AI (Appendix A.1). The second section contained 32 items that asked participants' perspective on AI in higher education (Appendix A.2). These items explored attitudes and perceptions, AI's role in teaching and learning, ethical and social implications, and the future role.

Data was analyzed using SPSS software version 27, which includes Cronbach's alpha reliability to assess internal consistency. A descriptive analysis was implemented for various subscales. An independent sample *t*-test was also conducted to determine gender differences across the various subscales, as well as an ANOVA test to determine differences in perceptions of AI use in higher education based on participants' age group, current occupation, and disciplinary area. Reliability analyses were conducted for the subscales of the questionnaire on perceptions of AI use in higher education. The analyses indicate good levels of reliability, as shown in Table 1.

Table 1. Reliability statistics of the questionnaire on perceptions of AI use in higher education (N = 430).

Subscale	α De Cronbach
Attitudes and perceptions	0.89
Role of AI in the teaching-learning process	0.88
Ethical and social implications	0.84
Future role of AI	0.79
Total scale	0.93

Participants

The study involved 430 participants, randomly selected to ensure a representative sample from three distinct groups: students, teachers and administrative staff). The sampling strategy was intentionally designed to encompass individuals from diverse disciplines, providing a comprehensive range of perspectives and experiences related to the impact of AI in higher education.

The random sampling ensured that all participants were chosen entirely by chance, giving every individual in the population an equal opportunity to be selected. Its purpose was to minimize bias and provide a representative sample of the population. By including participants from varied roles within the institution, the study aimed to capture the multifaceted nature of attitudes and perceptions toward AI.

The questionnaire included a consent form, and participants clicked on the "accept" button to proceed with completing the instrument. A description and objective were presented at the beginning of the questionnaire, emphasizing the anonymity of the responses. Participants were also informed that the results would be used in general form and that their individual responses would remain confidential. The main sociodemographic characteristics of the sample, reflecting this diversity, are detailed in Table 2.

Table 2. Sample description.

Characteristics	Students		Teachers		Administratives		Total Sample	
	n	%	n	%	n	%	n	%
Gender								
Male	137	31.9	37	8.6	26	6	200	46.5
Female	161	37.4	44	10.2	25	5.8	230	53.5
Age								
Less than 25	177	41.2	1	0.2	0	0	178	41.4
25 to 34	74	17.2	13	3	10	2.3	97	22.6
35 to 44	35	8.1	17	4	10	2.3	62	14.4
45 to 54	10	2.3	32	7.4	17	4	59	13.7
55 or older	2	0.5	18	4.2	14	3.3	34	7.9
Academic level								
Bachelor	194	45.1	4	0.9	13	3	211	49.1
Licenciatura	98	22.8	32	7.4	13	3	143	33.3
Master	6	1.4	40	9.3	22	5.1	68	15.8
Doctorate	0	0	5	1.2	3	0.7	8	1.9
Disciplinary area								
Art, Design & Communication	56	13	6	1.4	4	0.9	66	15.3
Health Sciences	77	17.9	30	4.7	4	0.9	101	23.5
Business and Hospitality	47	10.9	10	3	11	2.6	68	15.8
Social Sciences	39	9.1	35	8.1	19	4.4	93	21.6
Engineering and Information Technology	79	18.4	10	2.3	13	3	102	23.7

3. Results

The results of the study offer a comprehensive analysis of participants' perceptions, attitudes, and experiences regarding the integration of AI in higher education. By examining various dimensions, including the role of AI in teaching and learning, its ethical implications and stakeholders' expectations for its future use, the finding provide a deeper understanding of AI's potential impact on academic settings.

Table 3 presents a descriptive analysis of different subscales related to perceptions of AI in higher education. The four subscales measure different aspects on how AI is viewed in this context.

The lowest mean score (3.65) for AI's role in the teaching-learning process suggests that there is some hesitation about how well AI can support education, which could be due to concerns about loss of human interactions, AI's effectiveness, or potential biases in AI tools.

A comparison between male and female respondents was performed with independent samples *t*-tests across various subscales. The analysis revealed no significant differences [12,16] in any of the subscales ($p > 0.05$). In all subscales, the p values were greater than 0.05, meaning that any differences between males and females were likely due to random variation rather than meaningful distinctions, as shown in Table 4.

Table 3. Descriptive analysis of subscales on perceptions of AI in higher education.

	M	DE	Min	Max
Attitudes and perceptions	3.86	0.806	1.00	5.00
Role of AI in the teaching-learning process	3.65	0.771	1.00	5.00
Ethical and social implications	4.23	0.615	1.13	5.00
Future role of AI	4.10	0.573	1.25	5.00

Table 4. Gender differences in subscales on perceptions of AI in higher education.

Subscale	Male		Female		T (428)	*p*	d
	M	DE	M	DE			
Attitudes and perceptions	3.89	0.928	3.83	0.68	0.86	0.389	0.08
Role of AI in the teaching-learning process	3.70	0.822	3.61	0.72	1.25	0.212	0.12
Ethical and social implications	4.18	0.645	4.26	0.59	−1.30	0.193	−0.13
Future role of AI	4.11	0.593	4.08	0.56	0.58	0.562	0.06

Additionally, several one-way ANOVA tests were conducted to examine differences in perceptions of AI use in higher education based on participants' age group, current occupation, and disciplinary area. Regarding age group (Table 5), the analyses revealed no significant differences across any of the subscales ($F_{4425} = 1.81$, $p = 0.127$ for the attitudes and perceptions subscale; $F_{4425} = 0.40$, $p = 0.81$ for the role of AI in the teaching-learning process; $F_{4425} = 1.82$, $p = 0.124$ for ethical and social implications, and $F_{4425} = 0.65$, $p = 0.625$ for the role of AI in the future).

Table 5. Differences in perceptions of AI use in higher education by age group.

Subscale	Less than 25		25–34		35–44		45–54		Más de 55		F(2,4)	*p*	η2
	M	DE	M	DE	M	DE	M	DE	M	DE			
Attitudes and perceptions	3.94	0.81	3.80	0.73	3.95	0.85	3.70	0.95	3.69	0.58	1.81	0.127	0.017
Role of AI in the teaching-learning process	3.69	0.82	3.64	0.68	3.61	0.79	3.65	0.81	3.52	0.63	0.40	0.809	0.004
Ethical and social implications	4.16	0.63	4.21	0.62	4.38	0.53	4.25	0.72	4.34	0.40	1.82	0.124	0.017
Future role of AI	4.12	0.54	4.06	0.58	4.14	0.63	4.11	0.65	3.97	0.48	0.65	0.625	0.006

For subscale attitudes and perceptions toward AI the means range from 3.69 (55+) to 3.95 (35–44), suggesting a slightly more positive attitude among younger age groups (especially under 25 and 35–44). The small effect size ($\eta^2 = 0.017$) indicates that age does not strongly influence general attitudes toward AI. Although younger individuals (under 25 and 35–44) seem slightly more optimistic about AI, the difference are not meaningful in a statistical sense.

At the role of AI in the teaching-learning process subscale, the means are fairly consistent across age groups, ranging from 3.52 (55+) to 3.69 (under 25). The smallest effect size in the table (($\eta^2 = 0.004$) suggests that age has almost no impact on views about AI's role in education. All age groups hold similar opinions on AI's role in teaching and learning with no strong generational divide.

For the ethical and social implications of AI subscale, the highest scores were from 35–44 (M = 4.38) and 55+ (M = 4.34), indicating that older individuals may be slightly more concerned about ethics than younger groups. While older respondents may place slightly more importance on ethical concerns, the difference in not significant enough to suggest a generational divide.

In the future role of AI subscale, scores are fairly high across all age groups, ranging from 3.97 (55+) to 4.14 (35–44). All age groups believe AI will play an important role in the future, with no major differences in optimism across generations.

Table 6 presents comparisons between students, educators, and administrative staff regarding their perceptions of AI in higher education. There are significant differences in the attitudes and perceptions subscale (F2427 = 3.87, p = 0.022). Post hoc analyses with Bonferroni corrections revealed that students (M = 3.92, SD = 0.78) scored significantly higher than faculty members (M = 3.65, SD = 0.79, p = 0.019), indicating that students hold more positive attitudes and perceptions toward AI compared to faculty. However, no significant differences were found between students and administrative staff (M = 3.81, SD = 0.91, p = 0.624) or between administrative staff and faculty (p = 0.490).

Table 6. Differences in perceptions of AI use in higher education by current occupation.

Subscale	Students		Teachers		Administratives		F(2427)	p	η^2
	M	DE	M	DE	M	DE			
Attitudes and perceptions	3.92 [a]	0.78	3.65 [a]	0.79	3.81	0.91	3.87	0.022 *	0.018
Role of AI in the teaching-learning process	3.67	0.79	3.50	0.70	3.78	0.73	2.47	0.086	0.011
Ethical and social implications	4.18	0.60	4.35	0.64	4.31	0.61	2.90	0.056	0.013
Future role of AI	4.11	0.55	4.08	0.56	4.14	4.05	0.712	0.755	0.001

Note. * $p < 0.05$, measures sharing [a] supscript indicate significant differences.

For the other subscales, no significant differences were observed; (F4427 = 2.47, p = 0.86 for the role of AI in the teaching-learning process; F4427 = 2.90, p = 0.056 for ethical and social implications; and (F4427 = 0.28, p = 0.755 for the role of AI in the future).

Regarding the disciplinary area (Table 7), the analyses revealed no significant differences across any of the subscales (F4425 = 1.02, p = 0.397 for the attitudes and perceptions subscale; F4425 = 0.85, p = 0.49 for the role of AI in the teaching-learning process; F4425 = 2.19, p = 0.069 for the ethical and social implications; and F4425 = 1.05. p = 0.383 for the role of AI in the future).

Table 7. Differences in perceptions of AI use in higher education by disciplinary area.

Subscale	Art, Design & Communication		Health Sciences		Business and Hospitality		Social Sciences		Engineering and Information Technology		F(2425)	p	η^2
	M	DE	M	DE	M	DE	M	DE	M	DE			
Attitudes and perceptions	3.93	0.70	3.86	0.73	3.86	0.83	3.72	0.80	3.94	0.92	1.02	0.397	0.009
Role of AI in the teaching-learning process	3.56	0.79	3.65	0.72	3.67	0.77	3.59	0.77	3.75	0.80	0.85	0.495	0.008
Ethical and social implications	4.37	0.61	4.20	0.59	4.20	0.51	4.30	0.61	4.11	0.70	2.19	0.069	0.020
Future role of AI	4.11	0.51	4.13	0.53	4.09	0.57	3.99	0.62	4.15	0.61	1.05	0.383	0.010

Finally, a bivariate correlation analysis was conducted between the subscales of perceptions of AI use in higher education and variables such as age, frequency or AI use, and AI experience. The analysis revealed significant relationships between age and both attitudes and perceptions (r = −0.10, p = 0.4) and ethical and social implications (r = −0.10,

$p = 0.03$), indicating that higher scores on these subscales are associated with younger participants.

Significant correlations were also found between AI experience and the subscales of attitudes and perceptions ($r = 0.31$; $p < 0.001$), the role of AI in the teaching-learning process ($r = 0.26$, $p < 0.001$), and the role of AI in the future ($r = 0.19$, $p < 0.001$), showing that greater experience with AI is linked to higher scores on these subscales. Additionally, a negative relationship was observed between AI experience and age ($r = -0.20$, $p < 0.001$), indicating that younger participants tend to have more AI experience.

The frequency of AI use was positively correlated with attitudes and perceptions ($r = 0.40$, $p < 0.001$), the role or AI in the teaching-learning process ($r = 0.35$, $p < 0.001$), and the role of AI in the future ($r = 0.31$, $p < 0.001$), suggesting that higher scores on these subscales are associated with more frequent AI use. However, a negative correlation was found between AI experience and frequency of use ($r = -0.60$, $p < 0.001$), indicating that greater AI experience is associated with less frequent use of AI.

4. Discussion

Overall, participants have positive perceptions of AI in higher education [3,12], as all mean values are above 3.5. However, the variability in responses (as reflected in the standard deviation) suggests that not everyone agrees on AI's role, especially in teaching and learning. Besides, the highest mean score (4.23) for ethical and social implications shows that issues like fairness, bias, and data privacy are important factors in AI adoption. This finding highlights the need for responsible AI policies that ensure equity and transparency in AI-driven education. To provide a comprehensive interpretation, the results should be discussed in relation to previous studies and the study's working hypotheses. Additionally, the broader implications of these findings warrant further exploration, including potential directions for future research.

Regarding AI's future role, the relatively high mean score (4.10) suggests that most respondents expect AI to become increasingly integrated into education, aligning with Mujtaba's [18] findings. However, the presence of lower minimum values indicates that not all participants share this optimism, with some expressing concern about the challenges AI may introduce. This variation in perspectives suggests that while AI's expansion in education is widely anticipated, skepticism remains regarding its implications.

Since gender differences are not significant [1,3], AI-related policies and educational strategies can be designed without major gender-based distinctions. Meanwhile, age appears to have a weak but notable relationship with AI perceptions. Younger individuals generally exhibit more positive attitudes toward AI, yet they also express significantly greater concerns regarding its ethical and social implications. This generational difference may reflect varying levels of awareness or differing perspectives on AI's social impact. Despite this, age does not strongly influence overall AI perceptions, although younger individuals 'critical stance of AI's ethical dimensions are worth further investigation.

Experience with AI emerges as a key factor of positive attitudes toward its role in higher education. Participants with more AI experience are more likely to recognize its value in learning and its future importance. Additionally, younger individuals tend to have greater AI exposure, which may contribute to their overall more favorable perceptions. Interestingly, while frequent AI users tend to have more positive attitudes toward AI in education and its future significance, those with greater AI experience report using it less frequently. This suggest that expertise may lead to more strategic or efficient AI usage rather than habitual reliance.

These findings contribute to the broader discourse of AI adoption in education, emphasizing the importance of ethical considerations, experience-driven perceptions, and demographic influences. Future research should further explore these dimensions, particularly the nuanced relationship between AI familiarity, critical awareness, and usage patterns, to inform more effective AI integration strategies in higher education.

5. Conclusions

As artificial intelligence continues to transform higher education, understanding how different groups perceive its role is essential for effective implementation. This study examined attitudes and perceptions toward AI across various demographics, including gender, age, occupation, and academic discipline, while also considering ethical concerns and experience levels.

Answering the first research question, findings indicate that while overall attitudes toward AI in higher education are generally positive, ethical concerns and uncertainty about its role in teaching and learning remain. The study highlights the complex relationship between age, experience, and AI perceptions. Younger individuals tend to be more critical of AI's ethical and social implications, as noted by Tamanna & Sinha [26]. However, their greater exposure to AI also cultivates a more positive outlook on its potential. Additionally, frequent AI users generally perceive AI more favorably, though those with advanced expertise tend to use it less frequently, suggesting that deeper knowledge leads to more deliberate and strategic utilization.

The second question refers to the ethical and social implications of AI implementation, the study suggests that AI policies in higher education can be designed without major gender or age-based distinctions. However, ethical concerns, especially among female students and educators in humanities disciplines, should be addressed. Teachers show more skepticism toward AI, emphasizing the need for transparency, ethical guidelines, and training to build trust and facilitate adoption. In line with Khatri & Karki [13], higher-education institutions should actively promote and enforce academic integrity policies to address stakeholders' concerns and ensure the responsible use of AI in classrooms.

While no significant differences were found across academic disciplines, humanities-based fields demonstrated slightly ethical and social concerns, whereas Engineering and IT students showed greater acceptance of AI in education than other occupation groups, but no significant differences exist in their perceptions of AI's role or future potential. Across academic disciplines, no statistically significant variations were found (all p-values > 0.05). However, humanities-based fields show a slightly higher level of ethical concern, while students in Engineering and IT exhibit greater acceptance of AI in education.

Regarding the last question regarding how demographic characteristics of participants influence their perception on AI, results show that gender differences in AI perceptions are minimal. While females exhibit slightly greater concern for ethical and social implications, and males show marginally higher confidence in AI's role and future potential, these differences are too small to be meaningful [13]. Similarly, age does not significantly influence perceptions of AI in higher education. Though older respondents (35–44 and 55+) express slightly greater ethical and social concerns, and younger participants (under 25 and 35–44) are marginally more optimistic about AI's educational role, these differences are statistically insignificant.

These findings emphasize the need for informed, balanced engagement with AI technologies across all demographics, ensuring ethical and social considerations. AI adoption in higher education institutions should be prioritized by having clear ethical guidelines and transparency to build trust and acceptance among stakeholders.

6. Limitations

As artificial intelligence continues to shape the landscape of higher education, it is essential to recognize the limitations of this study to ensure its ethical and effective integration into teaching and learning environments. This research primarily focuses on attitudes and perceptions, rather than actual outcomes of AI implementation in higher education. Consequently, it does not assess real-world effects of AI on the learning process.

Another limitation is that while the study explores faculty attitudes, it does not deeply examine how AI influences instructional design, pedagogical strategies, or faculty workload. Additionally, the research does not measure whether AI exposure correlates with improvements in academic performance, critical thinking, or student engagement, important variables that warrant further investigation.

7. Implications

Despite the valuable insights gained from this study, there are several implications that should be considered, which may affect the generalizability of the findings. For instance, higher education institutions should establish clear ethical guidelines for AI integration, addressing critical concerns such as fairness, bias, and data privacy in order to build institutional trust.

AI adoption should be discipline-sensitive, ensuring that its use aligns with subject-specific needs, particularly addressing ethical concerns raised by participants of this study. Furthermore, the study suggests a gap in AI experience, with younger and more experienced AI users exhibiting greater optimism. This points to the need for targeted AI training programs for older faculty members and students with less exposure to AI technologies.

The findings of this study open several avenues for future research, particularly in terms of pedagogical transformation and ethical practices. Future studies should track the long-term effects of AI adoption on teaching methodologies, student engagement, and academic outcomes to better understand its evolving role in education.

In closing, future research will be pivotal in exploring the complex interrelationship between AI, pedagogy, and ethical concerns. It is necessary to ensure that AI adoption in higher education is both effective and equitable, fostering environments that benefit all stakeholders.

Author Contributions: Conceptualization, A.C., R.P. and R.S.; Methodology, A.C., R.P. and R.S.; Validation, A.C., R.P. and R.S.; Formal analysis, A.C., R.P. and R.S.; Investigation, A.C., R.P. and R.S.; Resources, A.C., R.P. and R.S.; Writing—original draft preparation, A.C., R.P. and R.S.; Writing—review and editing, A.C., R.P. and R.S.; Supervision, R.P. and R.S. All authors have read and agreed to the published version of the manuscript.

Funding: This research received no external funding.

Data Availability Statement: The raw data supporting the conclusions of this article will be made available by the authors on request.

Acknowledgments: We would like to express our gratitude to all the participants and colleagues who provided valuable assistance and encouragement throughout this research.

Conflicts of Interest: The authors declare no conflicts of interest.

Appendix A

Appendix A.1

Instrument "Exploring the Impact of Artificial Intelligence on Higher Education: The Dynamics of Ethical, Social, and Educational Implications".

Table A1. Section 1: Demographic Characteristic.

Age	1. 24 or less 2. 25 to 34 3. 35 to 44 4. 45 or more
Gender	1. Male 2. Female
Current Occupation	1. Student 2. Faculty 3. Administrator
Education Level	1. Bachelor 2. Master 3. Ph.D.
Major	1. Medicine, engineering, or computer science 2. Literary, humanities, or education 3. Business, commerce, or law
Subjective AI Expertise	1. Low perceived expertise 2. Medium perceived expertise 3. High perceived expertise
Frequency of Usage	1. Rarely 2. Monthly 3. Weekly 4. Daily
AI Tools and Services *5 points Likert scale*	1. Face-recognition services used in mobile phones and some security cameras 2. Speech recognition such as Google Speech-to-Text and Microsoft Azure 3. AI-Chatting and research tools such as ChatGPT-4, Chatbots, Bing Chat 4. Google AI services including Google Cloud AI Platform and Products 5. AI-powered design and creativity tools such as Adobe Sensei, Adobe Lightroom, Luminar AI
Purpose of Usage *5 points Likert scale*	1. General Purposes 2. Entertainment Purposes 3. Educational Purposes 4. Research Purposes 5. Commercial purposes 6. e-Government Purposes
Negative Experiences *5 points Likert scale*	1. Technical issues during installation 2. Technical issues during usage 3. Usage difficulties 4. Financial costs 5. Privacy and security issues

Appendix A.2

Table A2. Section 2: Please indicate your level of agreement or disagreement with the following statements: 5 points Likert scale.

A: Attitudes and Perceptions towards the Use of AI in Higher Education
1. The use of AI in higher education has the potential to enhance the learning experience.
2. Integrating AI technologies in higher education can improve student outcomes.
3. AI technologies should be integrated into the curriculum to prepare students for the future workforce.
4. AI can assist in providing personalized feedback to students.
5. AI can improve access to educational resources and materials.
6. AI can help identify areas where students may need additional support.
7. AI has the potential to revolutionize the way higher education institutions operate.
8. AI technologies can help optimize administrative processes in higher education institutions.
B: Impact of AI on Teaching and Learning in Higher Education
9. AI technologies have positively influenced the teaching methods employed by faculty.
10. The use of AI in higher education has improved student engagement and participation.
11. AI technologies have facilitated personalized learning experiences for students.
12. AI can help automate administrative tasks, allowing faculty to focus more on teaching.
13. AI can provide real-time insights into student performance, allowing for timely interventions.
14. AI can help create adaptive learning environments tailored to individual student needs.
15. AI has the potential to improve the accessibility of higher education for diverse learners.
16. AI can support the development of critical thinking and problem-solving skills in students.
C: Ethical and Social Implications of AI in Higher Education
17. There are concerns about data privacy and security when using AI technologies in higher education.
18. The use of AI in higher education should be transparent and accountable.
19. AI algorithms should be designed to address potential biases and ensure fairness in higher education.
20. Ethical guidelines and regulations should be established to govern the use of AI in higher education.
21. AI should not replace human interaction and support in the educational process.
22. AI should be used responsibly to avoid exacerbating societal inequalities.
23. The use of AI in higher education should prioritize the ethical collection and use of student data.
24. AI technologies should be developed and used in a manner that respects student autonomy and agency.
D: Envisioning the Future Role of AI in Higher Education
25. AI will play a significant role in transforming teaching and learning in higher education in the future.
26. The future integration of AI in higher education should prioritize ethical considerations and human values.
27. AI technologies will create new opportunities for collaboration and interdisciplinary research in higher education.
28. AI can assist in developing personalized learning pathways for students.
29. AI can help predict and address students' individual learning needs.
30. AI can contribute to the development of intelligent tutoring systems.
31. AI has the potential to enhance the assessment and evaluation processes in higher education.
32. AI can support the development of lifelong learning skills in students.

References

1. Algahtani, T.; Badreldin, H.; Alrahed, M.; Alshaya, A.; Alghamdi, S.; Sleh, K.; Alowais, S.; Alshaya, O.; Rahman, I.; Al Yami, M.; et al. The emergent role of artificial intelligence, natural learning processing, and large language models in higher education and research. *Res. Soc. Adm. Pharm.* **2023**, *19*, 1236–1242. [CrossRef]
2. López-Villanueva, D.; Santiago, R.; Palau, R. Flipped Learning and Artificial Intelligence. *Electronics* **2024**, *13*, 3424. [CrossRef]
3. Al-Zahrani, A.; Alasmari, T. Exploring the impact of artificial intelligence on higher education: The dynamic of ethical, social and educational implications. *Humanit. Soc. Sci. Commun.* **2024**, *11*, 2–20. [CrossRef]
4. Babu, G.; Wooden, O. Strategic Transformation of Higher Education through Artificial Intelligence. *Adm. Sci.* **2023**, *13*, 2–20. [CrossRef]

5. Kuleto, V. Exploring Opportunities and Challenges of Artificial Intelligence and Machine Learning in Higher Education Institutions. *Sustainability* **2021**, *13*, 10424. [CrossRef]
6. Mouta, A.; Torrecilla-Sánchez, E.M.; Pinto-Llorente, A.M. Design of a future scenarios tookit for an ethical implementation of artificial intelligence in education. *Educ. Inf. Technol.* **2023**, *29*, 10473–10498. [CrossRef]
7. Holmes, W.; Iniesto, F.; Anastopoulou, S.; Boticario, J. Stakeholder Perspectives on the Ethics of AI in Distancie-Based Higher Education. *Int. Rev. Res. Open Distrib. Learn.* **2023**, *24*, 96–117. [CrossRef]
8. Manoj, N. Analyzing Stakeholder Feedback Using AI, Harrisburg University Dissertation and These. 2024. Available online: https://digitalcommons.harrisburgu.edu/dandt/8 (accessed on 25 February 2025).
9. McKinsey & Company. *How Technology Is Shaping Learning in Higher Education*; McKinsey & Company: Zurich, Switzerland, 2022.
10. Coursera. What is Artificial Intelligence? Definition, Uses, and Types. 2024. Available online: https://www.coursera.org/articles/what-is-artificial-intelligence (accessed on 11 December 2024).
11. Eke, D.O. ChatGPT and the rise of GenAI: Treat to academic integrity? *J. Responsible Technol.* **2023**, *13*, 100060. [CrossRef]
12. Haleem, A.; Javaid, M.; Singh, R.P. An era of ChatGPT as a significant futuristic support tool: A study on features, abilities and challenges. *BenchCouncil Trans. Benchmarks Stand. Eval.* **2022**, *2*, 100089. [CrossRef]
13. Khatri, B.B.; Karki, P.D. Artificial intelligence (AI) in higher education: Growing academic integrity and ethical concerns. *Nepal. J. Dev. Rural. Stud.* **2023**, *20*, 1–7. [CrossRef]
14. Popenici, S. The critique of AI as a foundation for judicious use in higher education. *J. Appl. Learn. Teach.* **2023**, *6*, 1–7. [CrossRef]
15. Al-Badi, A.; Khan, A.; Alotaibi, E. Perceptions of Learners and Instructors toward Artificial Intelligence in Personalized Learning. *Procedia Comput. Sci.* **2022**, *201*, 445–451. [CrossRef]
16. Jensen, L.; Buhl, A.; Sharma, A.; Bearman, M. Generative AI and higher education: A review of claims from the first months of ChatGPT. *Higher Education* **2025**, *89*, 1145–1161. [CrossRef]
17. Khan, S.; Mazhar, T.; Shahzad, T.; Khan, M.A.; Rehman, A.U.; Saeed, M.M.; Haman, H. Harnessing AI for sustainable higher education: Ethical considerations, operational efficiency, and future directions. *Discov. Sustain.* **2025**, *6*, 23. [CrossRef]
18. Mujtaba, B. Clarifying Ethical Dilemmas in Sharpening Students 'Artificial Intelligence Proficiency: Dispelling Myths about using AI tools in Higher Education. *Bus. Ethics Leadersh.* **2024**, *8*, 2520–6761. [CrossRef]
19. Omar, A.; Shaqour, A.Z.; Khlaif, Z.N. Attitudes of faculty members in Palestinian universities toward employing artificial intelligence applications in higher education: Opportunities and challenges. *Front. Educ.* **2024**, *9*, 1414606. [CrossRef]
20. Leoste, J.; Jogi, L.; Oun, T.; Pastor, I.; San Martín López, J.; Grauberg, I. Perceptions about the Future of Integrating Emerging Technologies into Higher Education—The Case of Robotics with Artificial Intelligence. *Computers* **2021**, *10*, 110. [CrossRef]
21. Lee, D.; Arnold, M.; Srivastava, A.; Plastow, K.; Strelan, P.; Ploeckl, F.; Lekkas, D.; Palmer, E. The impact of generative AI on higher education learning and teaching: A study of educators 'perspectives. *Comput. Educ. Artif. Intell.* **2024**, *6*, 100221. [CrossRef]
22. Bobrytska, V. Artificial intelligence (AI) in Ukrainian Higher Education: A Comprehensive Study of Stakeholder Attitudes, Expectations and Concerns. *Int. J. Learn. Teach. Educ. Res.* **2024**, *23*, 400–426. [CrossRef]
23. Chan, C.; Hu, W. Students 'voices on generative AI: Perceptions, benefits, and challenges in higher education. *Int. J. Educ. Technol. High. Educ.* **2023**, *20*, 4–15. [CrossRef]
24. García-Peñalvo, F. Inteligencia Artificial Generativa en la Educación Superior: Una Perspectiva de 360°. In *IFE Conference*; Universidad de Salamanca: Salamanca, Spain, 2024.
25. Jianzheng, S.; Xuwei, Z. Integration of AI with Higher Education Innovation: Reforming Future Educational Directions. *Int. J. Sci. Res.* **2024**, *12*, 1727–1731. [CrossRef]
26. Tamanna, M.; Sinha, B. A conceptual analysis of artificial intelligence (AI) on academic opportunities and challenges: A case study based on higher educational institutions in Bangladesh. *Qual. Assur. Educ.* **2025**, *33*, 218–236. [CrossRef]
27. Williams, R.T. The ethical implications of using generative chatbots in higher education. *Front. Educ.* **2024**, *8*, 1331607. [CrossRef]
28. Slimi, Z.; Carballido, B. Navigating the Ethical Challenges of Artificial Intelligence in Higher Education: An Analysis of Seven Global AI Ethics Policies. *TEM J.* **2023**, *12*, 590–602. [CrossRef]
29. Acuña, E.G. Fortalecimiento de la integridad académica a través de la IA. Estrategias de prevención del plagio en la Era Digital. *Areté Rev. Digit. Dr. Educ.* **2024**, *10*, 49–67. [CrossRef]

algorithms

MDPI

Systematic Review

ChatGPT in Education: A Systematic Review on Opportunities, Challenges, and Future Directions

Yirga Yayeh Munaye [1,*], Wasyihun Admass [2], Yenework Belayneh [1], Atinkut Molla [1] and Mekete Asmare [3]

1 Department of Information Technology, Injibara University, Injibara P.O. Box 40, Ethiopia; yenework.belayneh@inu.edu.et (Y.B.); atinkut.molla@inu.edu.et (A.M.)
2 School of Software Engineering, University of Science and Technology of China, Suzhou 215123, China; bywasyihun@gmail.com
3 Department of Electrical and Computer Engineering, Injibara University, Injibara P.O. Box 40, Ethiopia; mekete.asmare@inu.edu.et
* Correspondence: byyirga@gmail.com

Abstract

This study presents a systematic review on the integration of ChatGPT in education, examining its opportunities, challenges and future directions. Utilizing the PRISMA framework, the review analyzes 40 peer-reviewed studies published from 2020 to 2024. Opportunities identified include the potential for ChatGPT to foster individualized educational experiences, tailoring learning to meet the needs of individual students. Its capacity to automate grading and assessments is noted as a time-saving measure for educators, allowing them to focus on more interactive and engaging teaching methods. However, the study also addresses significant challenges associated with utilizing ChatGPT in educational contexts. Concerns regarding academic integrity are paramount, as students might misuse ChatGPT for cheating or plagiarism. Additionally, issues such as ChatGPT bias are highlighted, raising questions about the fairness and inclusivity of ChatGPT-generated content in educational materials. The necessity for ethical governance is emphasized, underscoring the importance of establishing clear policies to guide the responsible use of AI in education. The findings highlight several key trends regarding ChatGPT's role in enhancing personalized learning, automating assessments, and providing support to educators. The review concludes by stressing the importance of identifying best practices to optimize ChatGPT's effectiveness in teaching and learning environments. There is a clear need for future research focusing on adaptive ChatGPT regulation, which will be essential as educational stakeholders seek to understand and manage the long-term impacts of ChatGPT integration on pedagogy.

Keywords: ChatGPT in education; artificial intelligence; AI in pedagogy; AI-powered learning

1. Introduction

The rapid advancement of artificial intelligence (AI) has significantly transformed various sectors, including education. Among AI-driven tools, chat generative pre-trained transformer (ChatGPT), developed by OpenAI, has gained prominence due to its ability to generate human-like text, assist in tutoring, content creation, and interactive discussions, and support students and educators in diverse learning environments [1] with significant benefits, including personalized learning, automated assessments, and administrative efficiency. However, its integration into education also raises concerns regarding academic integrity, data privacy, AI biases, and its long-term impact on pedagogy [2].

Although the governance and ethical implications of ChatGPT in education remain underexplored [3], some researchers argue that AI could enhance critical thinking and engagement, while others warn of plagiarism risks, misinformation, and the erosion of teacher authority [4]. Additionally, disparities exist in institutional AI consistency in its use across educational settings [5]. To address these complexities, this study conducts a systematic review using the preferred reporting items for systematic reviews and meta-analyses (PRISMA) framework, evaluating ChatGPT's role in teaching, learning, governance, and policy challenges. By analyzing both its opportunities and risks, the study provides insights into best practices for responsible AI integration in education.

Despite its transformative potential, the integration of ChatGPT in education presents several critical challenges that require urgent attention. One of the most pressing concerns is that students increasingly rely on ChatGPT for assignments and assessments, raising risks of plagiarism and reduced critical thinking skills [6]. Educational institutions must establish clear guidelines to ensure AI is utilized as a learning aid rather than a substitute for independent intellectual engagement [7]. Another major challenge is bias and misinformation in AI-generated content. Since ChatGPT is trained on vast datasets, it can sometimes produce inaccurate, misleading, or biased responses, which may reinforce harmful stereotypes and misinform students [8]. To mitigate this risk, continuous refinement of AI models and AI literacy programs is necessary, equipping students with critical evaluation skills when engaging with AI-generated content [9]. Additionally, privacy and ethical concerns surrounding AI adoption in education remain significant. ChatGPT processes large amounts of user data, raising concerns about data security, student privacy, and compliance with regulatory frameworks [10]. However, the absence of standardized AI governance policies further complicates responsible AI integration in educational settings [11]. Addressing these issues requires the development of robust ethical guidelines and governance structures to ensure the safe, transparent, and equitable use of AI in education.

Furthermore, educators face difficulties in adapting to AI-driven teaching methodologies. While AI can automate administrative tasks, its effective classroom integration demands teacher training and institutional support. Without proper training, educators may struggle to leverage AI while maintaining pedagogical effectiveness. Research must explore how AI literacy and professional development programs can empower educators to maximize AI's benefits while mitigating its risks [12,13]. Moreover, to address these complexities, this study explores the following research questions:

(1) How has ChatGPT been applied in education?
(2) What are the major governance and policy challenges associated with its adoption?
(3) What future research directions can optimize its effectiveness while ensuring ethical implementation?

By investigating these questions, this study aims to provide a comprehensive analysis of ChatGPT's role in education, offering insights into its applications, challenges, and future implications. The findings will contribute to ongoing discussions on responsible AI adoption in academic settings, guiding educators, policymakers, and researchers toward effective and ethical AI integration. Therefore, the main contributions of this work are summarized as follows:

(1) Comprehensive Analysis of ChatGPT in Education: This study presents a systematic review of 40 peer-reviewed studies (2020–2024) using the PRISMA framework, offering a structured and evidence-based understanding of ChatGPT's applications in educational settings.

(2) Identification of Opportunities for Educational Enhancement: The review highlights how ChatGPT can personalize learning, automate grading, and support educators, displaying its potential to enhance student engagement and optimize teaching efficiency.
(3) Critical Examination of Challenges: It addresses major concerns such as academic integrity, AI bias, and the lack of inclusivity, contributing to a balanced understanding of both the benefits and risks of integrating ChatGPT into education.
(4) Call for Ethical Governance and Future Research: The study emphasizes the need for ethical policy frameworks and future research on adaptive regulation and long-term pedagogical impact, guiding stakeholders in responsible AI adoption in education.

Finally, this paper is organized as follows: Section 1 provides an overview of ChatGPT, Section 2 discusses its applications in education, Section 3 outlines the systematic review methodology, Section 4 explores the identified opportunities and future directions, and Section 5 presents the conclusion along with recommendations for future research.

2. Methods and Materials

2.1. Inclusion and Exclusion Criteria

2.1.1. Inclusion

Peer-reviewed journal articles, conference papers, and empirical studies focusing on ChatGPT's role in education and its governance were included. Studies on broader AI-related challenges in education, even if they do not focus exclusively on ChatGPT, were also included as shown in Table 1.

Table 1. Summary of inclusion and exclusion criteria.

Stage	Number of Studies	Criteria Applied
Identification	150	Initial search results from databases
Duplicate removal	20	Studies appearing multiple times in searches
Screening	130	Title and abstract reviewed for relevance
Exclusion (Abstract)	50	Not related to ChatGPT, general AI topics only
Full-Text Assessment	80	Studies with relevant research scope
Exclusion (Full-Text)	40	Missing methods, weak evidence, outdated sources
Final Inclusion	40	Studies that met all inclusion criteria

2.1.2. Exclusion

Non-peer-reviewed articles, opinion pieces, and studies lacking empirical validation were excluded. Additionally, we reviewed research considering ethics, collaboration, and policy development in AI education, taking inspiration on systematic AI in education.

This study employs a systematic approach to reviewing the literature on the applications, potential, and challenges associated with ChatGPT in education. As shown in Figure 1, 40 papers were chosen from an initial pool of 150 studies gathered between 2020 and 2024 using Scopus, Web of Science, IEEE Xplore, Google Scholar, and Springer Link. The compilation of data from these 40 publications yielded 10 primary themes, including 15 benefits, 15 drawbacks and various opportunities and problems linked with ChatGPT's integration into teaching and learning.

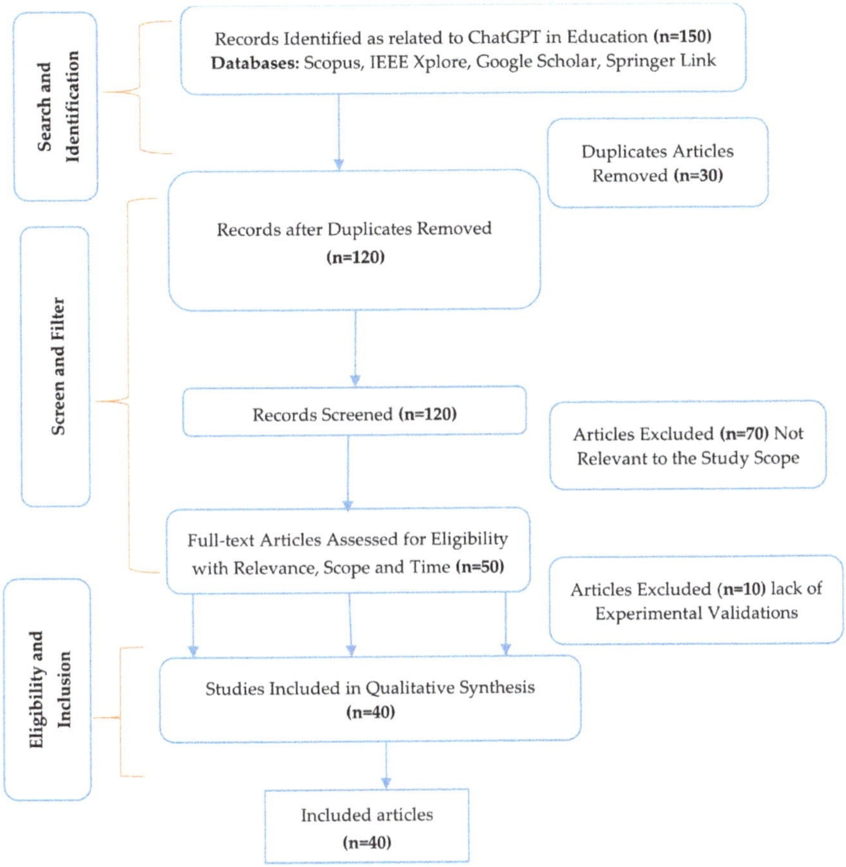

Figure 1. Collection of articles using the PRISMA paradigm.

2.2. Source of Information

To ensure comprehensive literature coverage, multiple databases were used. The selected databases include Scopus, Web of Science, IEEE Xplore, Google Scholar, and Springer Link, which contain a wealth of peer-reviewed academic articles relevant to AI in education. This multi-database approach enhances the reliability and depth of the literature review as illustrated in Table 2.

Table 2. Criteria for paper selection.

Phase	Criteria	Papers Identified	Explanation for Search and Identification
Search and Identification	Use of multiple databases (Scopus, Web of Science, IEEE Xplore, Google Scholar, and Springer Link) with relevant keywords and Boolean operators	150	Initial search across selected databases targeting ChatGPT applications, opportunities, and challenges in education.
Screening	Studies published between 2020 and 2024, written in English, and peer-reviewed	120	Abstract screening and relevance check to ensure alignment with research focus.

Table 2. *Cont.*

Phase	Criteria	Papers Identified	Explanation for Search and Identification
Eligibility	Studies specifically discussing ChatGPT's applications, opportunities, and challenges in education	50	Detailed review of abstracts to filter studies most relevant to the research questions.
Inclusion	Studies with empirical data, theoretical discussions, and case studies on ChatGPT in education	40	Full-text review and thematic coding to finalize included studies.

2.3. Search Process

A systematic search strategy was employed to identify relevant research. This approach resulted in the collection of 150 papers using specific search strings targeting ChatGPT's applications, opportunities, and challenges in education. The search process involved

- Defining relevant keywords related to ChatGPT's role in education;
- Applying Boolean operators (e.g., AND, OR) to refine search queries;
- Implementing inclusion and exclusion criteria to filter the most relevant studies;
- Using reference management software to organize and manage selected articles.

2.4. Paper Selection Criteria

The study adhered to the PRISMA guidelines. The selection criteria included:

- Timeframe: Studies published between 2020 and 2024;
- Language: Only studies published in English were considered;
- Publication Type: Peer-reviewed journal articles and conference papers;
- Relevance: Articles focused on the applications, opportunities, and challenges of ChatGPT in education.

2.5. Selection Process

A multi-stage selection process was employed to filter the most relevant papers:

- Initial Screening: Abstracts were reviewed to assess relevance. Only studies discussing ChatGPT's role in education were considered.
- Full-Text Review: The selected papers (40 articles) were read in full to evaluate their contribution to the research questions.
- Coding Process: The review papers were analyzed using grounded theory coding, which included
    - Open Coding: Identifying key research themes, opportunities, and challenges.
    - Axial Coding: Categorizing themes into broader topics.
    - Selective Coding: Synthesizing the most critical findings.

2.6. PRISMA Flowchart

The selection process for this systematic review follows the PRISMA guidelines, as illustrated in the flowchart in Figure 1. This study systematically selected and reviewed research papers published from 2020 to 2024. The data included search terms such as ChatGPT in education, ChatGPT opportunities, ChatGPT governance in education, ChatGPT and teacher workload, and ethical concerns in ChatGPT-driven education.

2.7. Distribution of Articles Used in Systematic Review

The majority of relevant studies were published between 2023 and 2024, reflecting the growing interest in ChatGPT's role in education. These findings align with related works, emphasizing recent AI advancements and their educational implications. This study follows a systematic review approach to analyze the applications, benefits, challenges, and future directions of ChatGPT in education. As illustrated in Figure 1, 150 studies published between 2020 and 2024 were initially collected. After applying inclusion and exclusion criteria, 40 relevant papers were selected for in-depth analysis. Furthermore, Figure 2 presents the distribution of selected papers by publication year, highlighting the percentage of studies included in our systematic review. This visualization provides insights into the temporal trends in research on the topic, highlighting the evolution of scholarly interest and contributions over time. This shows that over 90% of the references are from 2023 and 2024, indicating that this study is supported by recent and relevant research.

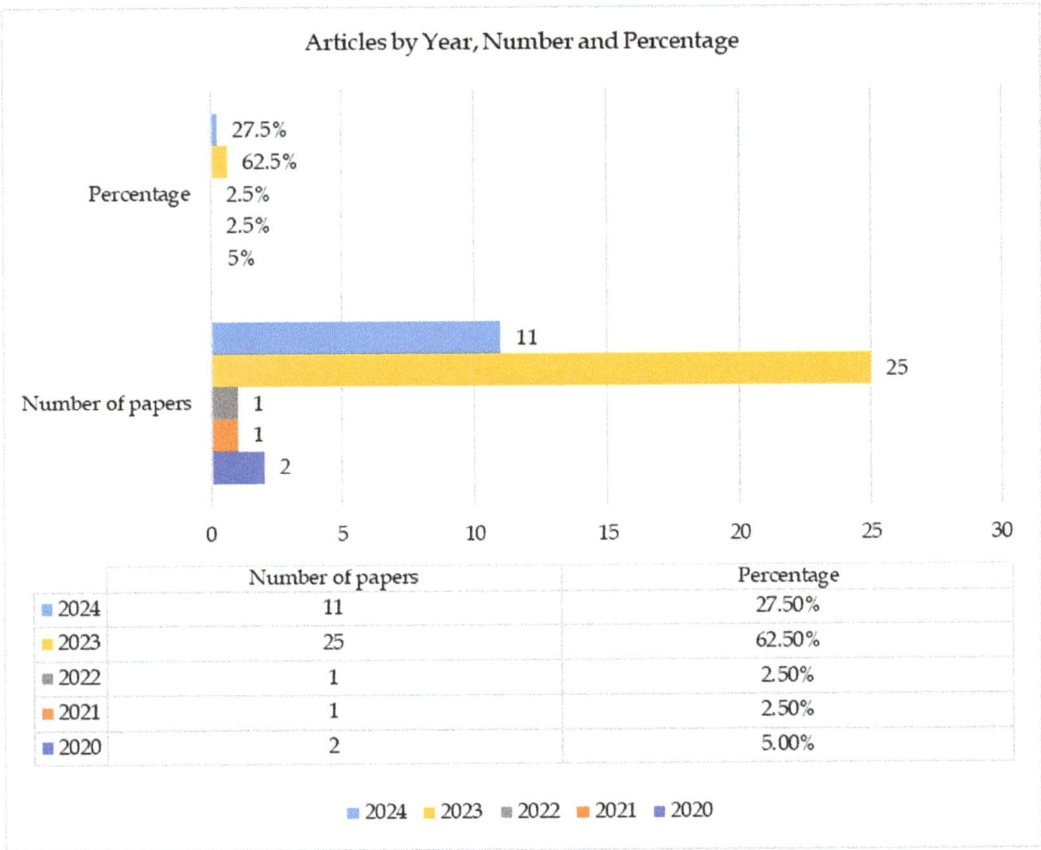

Figure 2. Yearly published articles used for systematic review in percent.

Moreover, as illustrated in Figure 3, an extensive search was conducted across multiple academic databases to identify relevant articles for our systematic review. Various databases were explored to ensure comprehensive coverage of the topic, and the selection of the most relevant sources is highlighted in the figure. This rigorous search strategy aimed to include high-quality, peer-reviewed studies that contribute valuable insights to our research.

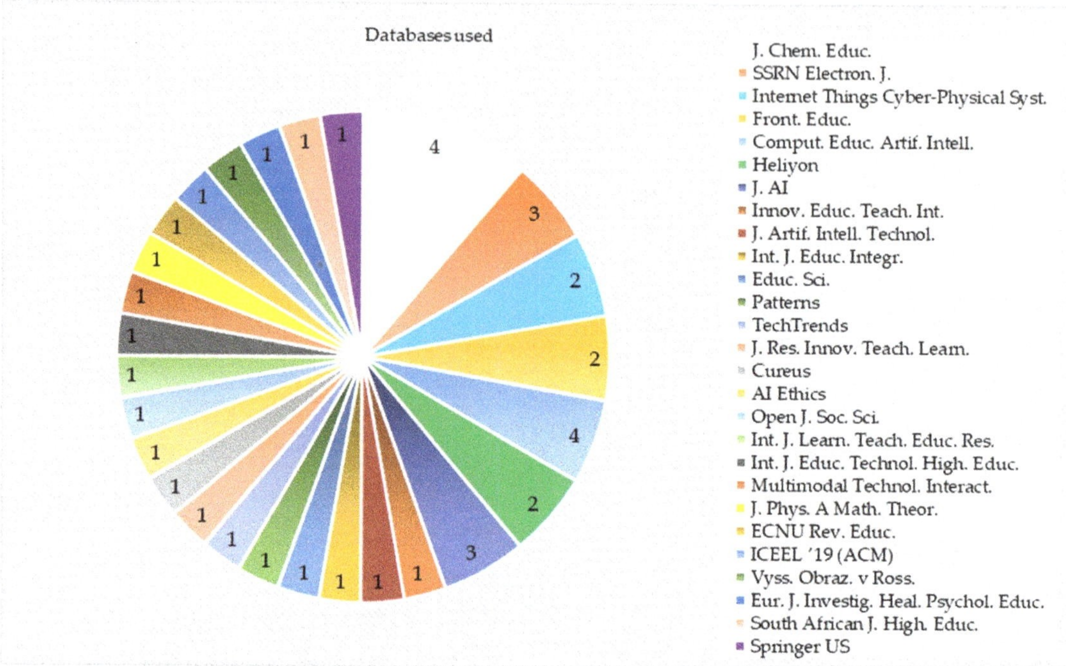

Figure 3. Selected databases for paper selection.

3. Related Works

Table 3 is a key component of our study, providing a systematic overview of the selected sample and relevant articles reviewed. This table includes essential details such as the reference list, year of publication, models employed, datasets utilized, methodological approaches, performance metrics, study objectives, key findings, strengths, and limitations of each study. By systematically organizing this information, Table 3 facilitates a clearer understanding of existing research, enabling comparisons across studies and identifying research gaps that our work aims to address.

Table 3. Summary of related articles reviewed.

Ref.	Year	Methods	Dataset	Findings	Limitations
[1]	2024	SWOT Analysis	Not specified	ChatGPT uses a sophisticated natural language model to generate plausible answers, with self-improving capability, and provides personalized and real-time responses. Increases access to information, facilitates complex learning, and decreases teaching workload.	Lack of deep understanding, difficulty in evaluating the quality of responses, a risk of bias and discrimination, and lack of higher-order thinking skills.
[2]	2023	Descriptive Analysis	Not specified	ChatGPT, as a language processing tool, can answer user questions, complete tasks, and continuously optimize performance. It holds great potential for promoting educational transformation and school education reform.	Issues include the accuracy of answering questions, data pollution, ethical and safety concerns, and the risk of knowledge plagiarism.

Table 3. *Cont.*

Ref.	Year	Methods	Dataset	Findings	Limitations
[3]	2024	Empirical Study	30 theory-based and application-based ChatGPT tests	ChatGPT provides a platform for students to seek answers to theory-based questions and generate ideas for application-based questions and allows instructors to integrate technology in classrooms. It can replace search engines by providing accurate and reliable input to students.	ChatGPT may lead to unethical use by students, contributing to human unintelligence and unlearning. It presents challenges for instructors in differentiating between students who rely on automation and those who do not, and measuring learning outcomes.
[4]	2024	Online Survey	201 HE students in Peru	Perceived Ethics (B = 0.856) and Student Concerns (B = 0.802). Findings suggest that students' knowledge and positive attitudes toward ChatGPT do not guarantee its effective adoption and use. The dependence on ChatGPT raises ethical concerns.	No differences found between sex and age in the relationship between the use of ChatGPT and perceived ethics. Further studies with diverse HE samples needed.
[5]	2023	Literature Review	Not specified	ChatGPT has demonstrated remarkable proficiency, including passing the US bar law exam, and quickly gained over a million subscribers. It can generate humanlike text and facilitate automated conversations.	Mixed reactions in education—some educators view it as a progressive step, while others are concerned it may reduce analytical skills and promote misconduct. Concerns regarding its widespread use and opacity remain within the scientific community.
[6]	2023	Ethical Reflection and Argumentation	Personal experience, academic policy review	The paper presents a perspective on how students could defend their use of ChatGPT in academic settings, arguing that AI is a tool and not a person, and thus does not require attribution. The author suggests that the use of AI like ChatGPT might not constitute cheating or plagiarism, as long as the process aligns with educational goals and standards.	The need for universities to adjust academic dishonesty definitions to address AI use, but also to avoid automatic reactions like banning AI. The author suggests that defining cheating to include AI use only when prohibited by the instructor would offer more flexibility. However, a change in academic policy might not universally resolve ethical concerns.
[7]	2024	Systematic Literature Review (SLR)	44 peer-reviewed articles	ChatGPT can assist with teaching support, task automation, and professional development. Student Uses: 24/7 support, explaining difficult concepts, acting as a conversational partner, providing personalized feedback and materials, offering writing support, self-assessment, facilitating engagement, and promoting self-determination.	Inaccuracies and hallucinations, potential bias, tool limitations, plagiarism, cheating, privacy issues, and the spread of false information. These issues highlight the challenges of using ChatGPT effectively in education.
[8]	2023	Case Study (Activity-based)	Georgia Gwinnett College (GGC) students in introductory chemistry courses	ChatGPT-based activity led to improvements in students' confidence to ask insightful questions, analyze information, and comprehend complex concepts. Students reported that ChatGPT provided diverse perspectives and challenged their current thinking. They were also willing to recommend it to others.	Low-quality student comments, difficulties in validating information sources.

Table 3. *Cont.*

Ref.	Year	Methods	Dataset	Findings	Limitations
[9]	2024	Qualitative Evaluation	Insights from leading academics, scientists, and engineers	ChatGPT can help educators by creating instructional content, offering suggestions, acting as an online educator, and promoting group work. It performs differently across subjects (finance, coding, math, general queries) and can transform education through smartphones and IoT gadgets.	Possibility of producing inaccurate or false data, circumventing plagiarism detectors, and incorrect outputs, which limit its overall benefit in some educational contexts.
[10]	2024	SLR	51 articles from Scopus, ERIC, Google Scholar (2022–2023)	Data extracted from 51 studies revealed 32 topics including 13 strengths, 10 weaknesses, 5 opportunities, and 4 threats of using ChatGPT in teaching and learning. The study applied Biggs's Presage–Process–Product (3P) model to categorize these topics. The results highlight how ChatGPT interacts with student characteristics and teaching contexts, how it affects teaching and learning activities, and how it contributes to student learning outcomes.	The study does not mention specific limitations, but as a systematic review, it may have limitations in terms of the quality and scope of selected studies. The included articles' methodologies and focus areas could influence the synthesis of data.
[11]	2023	SLR	PubMed, IEEE Xplore, Google Scholar (peer-reviewed articles, prominent media outlets, English publications)	AI chatbots like ChatGPT have potential benefits in Higher Education Institutions (HEIs), such as research support, automated grading, and improved human–computer interaction. It also offers applications in enrollment, student services, teaching enhancements, research aid, and student retention. However, risks include plagiarism, online testing security concerns, privacy breaches, misuse, bias, and decreased human interaction.	Incomplete representation of AI's overall effect on education, lack of concrete guidelines for integration, and focus only on selected peer-reviewed and media-based sources.
[12]	2023	Comprehensive Review	Literature review on ChatGPT and its applications in various industries	ChatGPT has applications in customer service, healthcare, education, and scientific research. It aids in data processing, hypothesis generation, collaboration, and public outreach. The study also highlights critical challenges, including ethical concerns, data biases, safety issues, and the need for integration with other technologies. ChatGPT has gained significant attention from academia, research, and industries.	Ethical concerns, data biases, and safety issues related to ChatGPT's use. Challenges in balancing AI-assisted innovation with human expertise. Potential biases in AI and limitations in current understanding of its impact.
[13]	2023	Commentary	Not Shown	The launch of ChatGPT has sparked concerns regarding student assessment. GAI systems can benefit students, faculty, and administrators in teaching, learning, research, and professional activities. The article explores potential benefits and risks, including equity and accessibility concerns.	Potential challenges regarding assessment and ethical issues in the use of GAI systems. Equity and accessibility concerns need to be addressed.

Table 3. *Cont.*

Ref.	Year	Methods	Dataset	Findings	Limitations
[14]	2023	Review and Commentary	Not Shown	LLMs like ChatGPT have significant potential to enhance education by improving grading, feedback, language learning, and personalized instruction. However, they also raise ethical concerns like bias, academic integrity issues (e.g., plagiarism), and lack of transparency in the underlying models. Academic institutions have had varying responses, with some banning and others encouraging LLM usage.	Ethical concerns (e.g., bias, plagiarism), lack of transparency in LLM models, and challenges in detecting AI-generated content. AI systems lack human interaction and cannot fully understand or contextualize information, limiting their effectiveness.
[15]	2023	Pre-test and online survey	225 responses from primary and secondary education teachers	Perceived ease of use and perceived usefulness lead to greater acceptance of chatbots. Teachers are more likely to accept chatbots with formal language. Results provide insights into chatbot design and communication decisions to enhance acceptance in the educational community.	Limited to primary and secondary education teachers; does not account for other factors influencing chatbots acceptance beyond age and digital skills.
[16]	2023	Analysis of course evaluation data	Physical Chemistry I and II courses at two institutions	Students had a positive response to oral exams, finding them valuable despite challenges like stress, anxiety, and the depth of understanding required. Students adjusted study habits (e.g., group study, verbal practice) and recognized the value of communication and teamwork for their future careers. Instructors valued oral exams, though concerns about time commitment, validity, reliability, and fairness persisted.	Study focused on two institutions, limited to Physical Chemistry courses; concerns about time, validity, reliability, and fairness were not fully resolved.
[17]	2024	Narrative review and qualitative synthesis	40 peer-reviewed empirical studies	The adoption of ChatGPT in higher education is influenced by factors such as hedonic motivation, usability, perceived benefits, system responsiveness, and relative advantage. Social influence, facilitating conditions, privacy, and security have varying effects. Technology readiness and extrinsic motivation not consistently confirmed as predictors. The study highlights the need for deeper exploration of contextual and psychological factors.	The review primarily synthesizes empirical studies and does not provide new primary data. It focuses on higher education, which may not be generalizable to other sectors.
[18]	2023	Study and evaluation of ChatGPT-generated responses	Two chemistry-focused modules in a pharmaceutical science program (Year 1 and Year 2)	ChatGPT-generated responses were successful for knowledge-based questions (e.g., "describe" and "discuss" verbs) but faced limitations in answering application-based and interpretation questions involving no text information. ChatGPT not considered a high-risk tool for cheating but expected to prompt discussions on academic integrity and assessment design in education.	The study focuses on specific chemistry modules in a pharmaceutical science program, which may not generalize to other disciplines. Further, it primarily evaluates response quality without exploring broader applications or potential consequences.

Table 3. *Cont.*

Ref.	Year	Methods	Dataset	Findings	Limitations
[19]	2020	SLR and meta-analysis	Various studies related to environmental science and ecosystem services	The paper introduces the PSALSAR method, an enhanced version of the traditional SALSA framework for conducting systematic literature reviews (SLRs) and meta-analysis. This method includes six steps: Protocol, Search, Appraisal, Synthesis, Analysis, and Reporting. It is transferable, reproducible, and applicable for assessing both quantitative and qualitative content in literature reviews, particularly in ecosystem services.	The methodology focuses on environmental science and ecosystem services, limiting its application to other disciplines. It is not clear if the methodology addresses challenges in broader or interdisciplinary fields.
[20]	2023	Literature review and thematic analysis	1 papers from the "Computers & Education: Artificial Intelligence" Special Issue	The Special Issue discusses seven main themes regarding the integration of AI in education: (1) intersection between AI and humans, (2) challenges and opportunities in AI for assessment, (3) explainability of AI, (4) design principles for AI-driven systems, (5) development of new theories of learning, (6) predictions and their role in education, and (7) AI applications in classrooms. It emphasizes challenges like ethics, bias, AI literacy, data sources, and policy development.	The studies may focus more on theoretical frameworks and policy discussions rather than providing concrete, actionable insights or empirical data on AI's practical implementation in diverse educational contexts.
[21]	2023	Commentary and opinion piece	Discussions in academic settings and media	ChatGPT has gained significant attention in academia due to its ability to assist in academic writing. Concerns exist regarding academic integrity, as students may misuse the tool for cheating. However, tools like Turnitin are developed to counteract such cheating. Despite risks, AI will be integrated into higher education with new policies and adaptation strategies. The academic community remains resilient, much like past technological adaptations (e.g., computer use in teaching).	The discussion primarily presents speculative views on the future of AI in academia without offering conclusive evidence or studies to support the opinions. Additionally, it does not delve deeply into the full range of potential ethical issues or institutional responses.
[22]	2023	Narrative literature review and SWOT analysis	Scholarly articles and reports on ChatGPT integration in nursing education	The review identifies strengths (accessibility, consistency, adaptability, cost-effectiveness, staying up-to-date), weaknesses, opportunities, and threats associated with ChatGPT in nursing education. It emphasizes the need for responsible use and collaboration among educators, policymakers, and AI developers to enhance learning outcomes.	The study only provides a SWOT analysis and literature review, without empirical data or direct case studies to validate the integration of ChatGPT in real-world nursing education contexts.
[23]	2022	Conceptual paper with a review of AI applications in education	Educational resources from MIT Media Lab and Code.org	The paper identifies the potential benefits of AI in K-12 education, such as personalized learning, automated assessments, and behavioral insights. It also highlights the ethical challenges of AI in education, emphasizing the need for ethical considerations in integrating AI. Recommendations for instructional resources provided to help educators teach AI concepts and ethics.	The paper does not provide empirical data or case studies on the real-world implementation of AI in K-12 classrooms. It primarily focuses on theoretical concepts and ethical considerations.

Table 3. *Cont.*

Ref.	Year	Methods	Dataset	Findings	Limitations
[24]	2023	Narrative review, thematic analysis	40 peer-reviewed empirical studies	The review identifies key factors influencing ChatGPT adoption in higher education, including hedonic motivation, usability, perceived benefits, and system responsiveness. It emphasizes the need for deeper exploration of contextual and psychological factors beyond traditional technology adoption models.	The review focuses on existing literature, and its findings based on qualitative synthesis. It does not present new empirical data or experimental findings.
[25]	2023	Literature review, historical analysis	Open AI's ChatGPT, the literature on AI history and uses in education	The paper outlines the rapid success of ChatGPT and generative AI (GAI) technologies, examining their advantages and disadvantages, particularly regarding human agency versus machine agency. It discusses strategies to avoid current problems and emphasizes how humans can maintain autonomy while using GAI. The paper proposes revised "Laws of Generative Artificial Intelligence" to guide education in the GAI era.	The paper does not provide new empirical data but offers a conceptual and historical analysis, which may limit its applicability to practical scenarios without further research.
[26]	2023	SLR	Multiple journal databases, filtered by specific criteria	ChatGPT has the potential to enhance both academic and librarian-related processes in higher education. However, it raises ethical concerns and challenges related to critical thinking development. The study highlights the importance of the responsible use of ChatGPT and the need for further assessment of its use in academic contexts.	The study relies solely on existing literature and may not capture real-time developments or practical applications. Additionally, the SLR methodology may introduce selection biases based on included articles.
[27]	2021	Extensive literature review	67 relevant studies selected from various academic databases	AI chatbots in education offer significant benefits, such as providing homework and study assistance, creating personalized learning experiences, and supporting skill development. Educators benefit from time-saving assistance and improved pedagogy. However, challenges such as concerns about reliability, accuracy, and ethical issues are highlighted.	Based on selected studies and may not account for emerging issues or practical applications. Limited by the predefined criteria used for selecting the studies.
[28]	2023	Systematic review	53 articles from recognized digital databases	The study provides a comprehensive understanding of previous research on the use of chatbots in education. It identifies the benefits and challenges of chatbots technology, as well as future research areas for its implementation in education.	It is based on recognized databases and could miss emerging or less mainstream research.
[29]	2023	SLR using the PRISMA framework	Journal articles from Scopus (published in English in the last five years)	The review investigates the support chatbots provide to educational institutions and students, emphasizing their roles as teaching assistants, their capabilities, and usage recommendations. It also identifies students' desires and challenges in chatbots use.	The review is limited to articles published in English and available in Scopus, using a general search query and only focusing on the last five years of research.
[30]	2023	Exploratory study, literature synthesis	Recent literature on ChatGPT in education	ChatGPT promotes personalized and interactive learning and aids in generating formative assessment prompts with ongoing feedback, but also generates wrong information, biases, and privacy issues. The study recommends leveraging ChatGPT to maximize its benefits.	Potential drawbacks include ChatGPT generating wrong information, biases in data training, and privacy concerns.

Table 3. *Cont.*

Ref.	Year	Methods	Dataset	Findings	Limitations
[31]	2023	Critical analysis, literature review	Research on OpenAI, ChatGPT, and education in developing economies	ChatGPT presents significant opportunities for advancement in education, particularly in developing economies, but also has potential drawbacks.	The study primarily focuses on understanding the technology's impact, but may not fully capture the real-world challenges in the implementation of such technologies.
[32]	2020	Theoretical framework (IDEE), exploration of benefits and challenges	Research on ChatGPT, GPT-4, and educative AI in education	Benefits include personalized learning, efficient feedback, and more, but challenges include untested effectiveness, data limitations, and ethical concerns.	Uncertainty about the effectiveness of the technology, and ethical/safety concerns need further exploration.
[33]	2023	Exploratory study, literature synthesis	Recent extant literature on ChatGPT in education	ChatGPT promotes personalized learning, interactive learning, and formative assessment generation. It helps inform teaching but has limitations like wrong information, biases, and privacy issues.	ChatGPT generates incorrect information, biases in training data, privacy concerns, and potential bias amplification.
[34]	2024	Pilot study, case study approach	Three chatbot prototypes under development at Warwick Manufacturing Group, University of Warwick	Chatbots show potential in educational simulation, software training, and helpdesk support. The prototypes aimed to support a Master's simulation game, software training, and department helpdesk requests.	Limited to university setting, and specific focus on technical challenges and AI chatbot development in educational contexts.
[35]	2024	Quantitative, descriptive research	143 students from two public universities in Islamabad	Most students agreed on the benefits of AI tools for academics. However, concerns about academic integrity, regulations, privacy, cognitive biases, gender and diversity, accessibility, and commercialization raised.	Focused only on students from two universities in Islamabad, which may limit the generalizability of results.
[36]	2023	Quantitative research (survey), Structural Equation Modeling (SEM)	520 students from a public university in Saudi Arabia (SA)	Significant direct effects of performance expectancy (PE), social influence (SI), and effort expectancy (EE) on behavioral intention (BI) and actual use of ChatGPT. Partial mediation of BI between PE, SI, FC, and actual use. Full mediation of BI between EE and actual use. FCs had no significant effect.	Limited to one university in Saudi Arabia and did not consider external resources and support for ChatGPT use.
[37]	2023	Quantitative research (survey), SEM	458 participants (students) using ChatGPT for smart education systems	Perceived ease of use and perceived usefulness were significant predictors of users' attitudes towards ChatGPT. Feedback quality, assessment quality, and subject norms positively influenced users' behavioral intentions. Positive attitudes and intentions led to actual adoption.	Some hypotheses, such as the relationship between trust in ChatGPT and perceived usefulness, not supported by the data.
[38]	2023	Systematic literature review (PRISMA framework)	550 articles (collected between December 2022 and May 2023), final 30 articles selected	ChatGPT seen as a tool with both opportunities and challenges in academic writing. It helps learners and instructors but requires updated training, policies, and assessments to address issues like plagiarism and AI-generated content.	Limited to 30 articles selected from 550, which may not cover all perspectives or studies; challenges in addressing AI's impact on assessment methods and integrity.

Table 3. *Cont.*

Ref.	Year	Methods	Dataset	Findings	Limitations
[39]	2024	Qualitative study	Views of three established professors in South Africa	Professors welcome the use of AI technologies like ChatGPT and emphasize the importance of teaching students how to engage with such tools. The responsibility lies with lecturers and universities to create an environment conducive to integrating these technologies into teaching and learning, especially in assessment.	Limited to the views of three professors in South Africa; may not represent a broader perspective.
[40]	2023	Systematic review	36 papers on chatbot–learner interaction design	Chatbots were mainly used on web platforms, primarily teaching computer science, language, and general education, with some used for engineering and mathematics. Most chatbots acted as teaching agents, with more than a third as peer agents. More than a quarter of chatbots employed personalized learning approaches. Chatbots evaluations show improved learning and satisfaction.	Insufficient dataset training, lack of reliance on usability heuristics, and challenges in chatbots' personality and localization.

4. Opportunities of ChatGPT in Education

The advancement ChatGPT technology in recent years has had a considerable impact on a variety of fields, including research and education. ChatGPT, a powerful massive language model developed by OpenAI, is an example of such technology. Personalized feedback, increased accessibility, interactive discussions, lesson preparation, evaluation, and novel approaches to teaching difficult concepts are just a few of the exciting opportunities that this technology provides for both students and teachers. Furthermore, the incorporation of ChatGPT into education provides several chances to improve teaching and learning experiences. AI-powered solutions such as ChatGPT provide a variety of benefits, including individualized learning, automated content development, real-time student help, and increased engagement.

This section delves into significant opportunities for exploiting ChatGPT for education. However, ChatGPT poses a variety of threats to the traditional educational and research systems, including the possibility of online exam cheating, text generation that resembles that of a person, a reduction in critical thinking abilities, and difficulties in interpreting data generated by ChatGPT [23]. According to [24], ChatGPT is used as a teaching and learning tool. Additionally, instructors and students enrolled in composition, business writing, and communication courses can use ChatGPT's features. It also used to provide recommendations. Moreover, ChatGPT is applicable in the classroom [25] to students, who can build study materials and assignment content with ChatGPT's assistance, and instructors can receive assistance from ChatGPT with administrative and research support tasks. Ultimately, the following are some of ChatGPT's major roles and opportunities for its integration into educational strategies.

4.1. Personalized Learning and Adaptive Education

ChatGPT can enhance learning through boosting productivity and engagement by providing personalized training and automated grading. In education, personalization is the process of adjusting curriculum, pedagogy, and learning settings to each student's needs and goals. This has historically been a resource-intensive procedure that is frequently constrained by practical and logistical issues. However, these restrictions have lessened in the new era of individualized learning ushered in by AI technologies like ChatGPT [26].

Because of its capacity to process and produce language-based content, ChatGPT is a perfect tool for developing personalized educational resources and experiences. This could be achieved by utilizing the natural language processing skills of the model to comprehend the student's learning needs and tailor the instruction accordingly. Using ChatGPT to create practice questions specifically tailored to the student is one method to accomplish this [27]. ChatGPT enables personalized learning by adapting to individual student needs, offering customized feedback, and providing tailored study materials [32]. AI-driven tutoring can support students at different learning paces, ensuring a more inclusive and effective learning environment [33].

4.2. *Interactive Tutoring*

As a personal tutor, ChatGPT can offer students immediate answers, explanations, and extra materials catered to their individual needs and learning style. This is especially helpful in large classrooms when teachers may not be able to provide each student the individualized attention they need [27]. Through interactive coaching, ChatGPT serves as a personalized instructor to assist users in gradually learning and mastering ideas. Interactive tutoring has essential elements such as guided learning objectives, question-based engagement, feedback and clarification, a supportive and adaptive approach, and a personalized learning pace [28].

4.3. *Automated Content Creation and Assessment*

Creating content with ChatGPT means using ChatGPT to generate content that not only informs readers but also engages them. This is accomplished by adding components that make the content feel more relevant and pleasurable, such as dynamic question-and-answer forms, relatable examples, interactive storytelling, and personalization [29]. Engaging content creation is ideal for narratives, blog writing, social media posts, instructional materials, and more any scenario where maintaining clarity and capturing attention are essential [30]. Educators can use ChatGPT to generate lesson plans, quizzes, and assessments, reducing workload and allowing them to focus on student engagement [34]. Automated grading and feedback mechanisms improve efficiency and provide instant evaluation [35].

4.4. *Teacher and Student Support*

There are several educational advantages to generative artificial intelligence (GAI), especially when it comes to large language models like ChatGPT, which improve accessibility and learning. Lesson planning and resources, the ability to explain complex concepts, assessment and feedback creation, and engagement strategies are just a few of the many benefits ChatGPT offers teachers. While ChatGPT offers students homework and study support, concept reinforcement, skill development, encouragement, and confidence building, the flexibility, speed, and encouraging attitude to instruction with ChatGPT are beneficial to both educators and learners. ChatGPT's teacher and student assistance entails providing tools, resources, and advice specific to teachers and students in order to facilitate instruction and improve the educational process [28].

4.5. *Enhancing Collaborative Learning*

By encouraging deeper understanding and enhancing students' communication skills, [25] examines the substantial prospects by reorienting students' attention from memorization to conceptual comprehension. Collaborative learning is the process of using ChatGPT's AI as a facilitator or participant in tasks that promote user cooperation and shared learning. By organizing, guiding, and facilitating collaborative efforts, ChatGPT can help make group learning activities more effective and well structured, leading to enhanced engagement, direction, clarity, and skill development as a result [28]. ChatGPT fosters interactive learning through AI-powered discussions, simulations, and problem-solving exercises [36]. Students can use AI-driven platforms to explore concepts in a more engaging and participatory manner, promoting active learning [37].

4.6. Writing Codes and Assignments

According to the study in [30], ChatGPT can produce coherent answers to assignments and knowledge-based coding tasks. Writing codes and assignments in ChatGPT means using the AI to assist with coding exercises, programming tasks, and academic assignments spanning a range of topics. ChatGPT may assist professionals, instructors, and students in organizing and completing writing assignments in addition to assisting them in creating, debugging, and understanding code. For coding, creating code, fixing and debugging errors, optimizing code, elucidating concepts, testing, and documentation can be achieved [31].

4.7. Bridging Educational Gaps and Accessibility

AI-powered learning tools like ChatGPT can address educational disparities by providing access to learning resources for underserved communities [38]. ChatGPT can also support learners with disabilities through speech-to-text, language translation, and accessibility-friendly interfaces [39].

4.8. Support for Educators and Professional Development

Teachers can use ChatGPT for professional development, accessing AI-driven insights on curriculum design, student performance analytics, and innovative teaching strategies [40]. The ability to automate administrative tasks also allows educators to focus on personalized instruction and mentorship [41].

4.9. AI-Powered Learning and Student Engagement

AI-powered educational tools, including ChatGPT, are shown to enhance student engagement by offering personalized learning experiences. According to [42], adaptive learning systems powered by AI can cater to individual learning needs by providing customized feedback and generating dynamic learning materials. Similarly, according to [43] highlights that ChatGPT fosters interactive learning by facilitating discussions and enabling real-time question answering. By leveraging these opportunities, ChatGPT can transform education by fostering innovation, improving learning accessibility, and enhancing engagement while ensuring ethical and responsible AI integration.

Generally, ChatGPT offers transformative potential in education by enabling personalized learning, automated content creation, and interactive tutoring, while supporting teachers with lesson planning and administrative tasks. It enhances accessibility for underserved communities and learners with disabilities through features like speech-to-text and multilingual support. However, challenges such as academic integrity risks, algorithmic bias, data privacy concerns, and over-reliance on AI must be addressed through ethical governance, teacher training, and structured integration. Balancing innovation with responsible use is key to harnessing ChatGPT's benefits without compromising critical thinking or equity in education.

5. Challenges of Using ChatGPT in Education

5.1. Integration of ChatGPT and Academic Integrity

While AI offers numerous advantages, questions about academic integrity remain. The study in [44] explains how ChatGPT is used for plagiarism and unauthorized aid in tasks, posing ethical implications for educators. The work in [45] emphasizes the importance of combining AI detection methods with ethical principles to address these concerns. Furthermore, the study in [46] recommends embedding AI literacy training into curricula to teach students about safe ChatGPT usage.

5.2. ChatGPT and Teacher Workload

ChatGPT is promoted as a tool to reduce teacher workload by automating administrative tasks such as grading and lesson planning. However, the study in [47] argues that AI adoption may paradoxically increase teacher responsibilities, as educators must verify AI-generated content and guide students in its ethical use. The study in [22] calls for structured AI training programs to help teachers effectively integrate AI tools in classrooms.

5.3. Bias and Ethical Considerations in ChatGPT Models

A critical challenge in AI adoption is the inherent bias in AI-generated content. The authors of [44] highlight that AI models including ChatGPT are trained on vast datasets that may contain cultural, gender, and ideological biases. The authors of [45] stress the importance of refining AI models to ensure fairness and accuracy. Additionally, the work [20] discusses data privacy concerns, emphasizing the need for stringent AI governance policies to protect student information.

5.4. Lack of Self-Reflection

The AI tool ChatGPT has sparked debate over its potential impact on education. The disadvantages include a lack of in-depth information, difficulty evaluating the quality of responses, the risk of prejudice and discrimination, and a lack of higher-order cognitive ability. Challenges to education include a lack of context awareness, challenges to plagiarism, the maintenance of educational inequity, and loss of higher-order cognitive capacities [21]. Writing a self-reflection in ChatGPT implies using the AI to help you articulate your ideas, perceptions, and individual learning experiences, yet choosing not to write a self-reflection means addressing the project without ChatGPT directly producing the text.

5.5. Lack of Non-Text-Based Responses

ChatGPT's capacity to handle advanced, non-textual queries limits its effectiveness in science, technology, engineering, and mathematics (STEM) fields that need complicated data handling. ChatGPT can tackle intellectually challenging activities, implying that instructors should reconsider assessment design to include problem-solving tasks that AI cannot readily perform. However, it has difficulty with more sophisticated activities that require analysis, interpretation, or non-textual answers, such as drawing structures or producing graphs [23].

5.6. Does Not Make Predictions About Future Events

ChatGPT is reluctant to make precise predictions or assumptions about the future, especially when it comes to ambiguous events or outcomes. Rather than making a firm prediction, it can talk about trends, possibilities, or scenarios based on past patterns or current knowledge [48].

5.7. Academic Dishonesty

Any behavior that provides an unfair academic advantage or falsifies one's own work, knowledge, or abilities in a learning environment is considered academic dishonesty. This includes behaviors that lead to plagiarism, cheating, and lying about one's work or accomplishments. Because of inaccuracies and a tendency to rely only on artificial intelligence, ChatGPT in education poses risks to academic integrity and critical thinking [49]. Finally, the ethical framework that is used is based on striking a balance between the usage of new technology and societal welfare. However, questions of dependency, ethical use, and even abuse arise, emphasizing the importance of carefully considering its consequences on academic dishonesty [50].

Therefore, the integration of ChatGPT in education presents significant challenges to academic integrity, as it facilitates plagiarism and unauthorized aid, necessitating robust detection tools and AI literacy programs [44–46]. While it promises to reduce teacher workload through automation, it paradoxically increases responsibilities by requiring educators to verify AI-generated content and guide ethical usage [22,47]. Ethical concerns are further compounded by bias in AI outputs and data privacy risks, demanding stringent governance policies to ensure fairness and security [20,44,45]. Additionally, ChatGPT's limitations—such as its inability to produce self-reflective or non-textual responses (e.g., STEM visualizations) and its avoidance of future predictions—restrict its applicability in higher-order cognitive tasks and complex disciplines [21,23,48]. These shortcomings, combined with risks of academic dishonesty and over-reliance, underscore the need for balance policies that leverage ChatGPT's benefits while safeguarding educational integrity and fostering critical thinking [49,50]. A holistic approach, combining teacher training, ethical guidelines, and adaptive assessments, is essential to mitigate these challenges and ensure responsible AI integration in academia.

6. Result and Analysis

6.1. Application of ChatGPT in Education

In response to research question 1, the findings indicate that ChatGPT has been widely used for personalized learning, interactive tutoring, and content creation. Future research should explore longitudinal studies to assess the sustained impact of AI on student performance and engagement. Table 4 provides a summary of key studies, highlighting their objectives, findings, strengths, and limitations to offer a holistic understanding of ChatGPT's role in education.

Table 4. Summary of related works on the applications of ChatGPT in education.

Ref.	Year	Model	Dataset	Approach	Performance Metrics	Objectives	Main Findings	Strengths	Limitations
[21]	2023	AI Ethics	Mixed academic data	Policy analysis	Regulatory compliance	Examine governance challenges	Identified gaps in AI policy enforcement	Strong theoretical framework	No empirical testing
[46]	2024	AI Governance	AI-driven education	Ethical AI implementation	Fairness, transparency	Propose governance strategies	Need for interdisciplinary collaboration	Clear recommendations	Lacks implementation details
[49]	2023	ChatGPT	Educational datasets	AI-driven tutoring	Student engagement, accuracy	Assess ChatGPT's role in tutoring	Found increased engagement but mixed accuracy	Strong empirical design	Lacks real-world case studies
[51]	2023	ChatGPT	University case studies	Personalized learning model	Learning outcomes	Evaluate AI's impact on adaptive learning	Showed promise in individual learning support	Effective in low-resource settings	Bias in dataset selection

Similar to prior studies [7,52,53], this review confirms that AI can provide individualized support for students. However, this study also reveals gaps in empirical validation; many studies focus on potential applications rather than real-world case studies demonstrating ChatGPT's effectiveness. Future research should explore longitudinal studies to assess the sustained impact of AI on student performance and engagement.

6.2. Governance and Policy Challenges

In response to the second research question, the study reveals that governance frameworks for AI in education are still evolving. Ethical concerns such as academic dishonesty, AI bias, and data privacy require immediate policy interventions. Unlike earlier studies that primarily focus on technical challenges [45], this research highlights the socio-political dimensions of AI adoption, including its impact on teacher workload and institutional governance structures. The literature underscores the necessity for standardized regulations to ensure AI adoption aligns with educational integrity principles. The adoption of ChatGPT and other AI tools in education has introduced significant governance and policy challenges that require immediate attention. This section discusses key concerns, including ethical considerations, academic integrity, data privacy, and the necessity for regulatory frameworks.

6.2.1. Ethical Considerations

AI-generated content raises concerns about plagiarism, originality, and student over-reliance on automated tools. Studies indicate that ChatGPT's ability to generate well-structured responses may encourage students to bypass critical thinking and independent learning [51]. However, institutions must establish strict policies to regulate AI usage, ensuring that it complements rather than replaces traditional learning approaches [46].

6.2.2. Data Privacy and Security

ChatGPT operates on vast datasets, often processing user-generated content that may contain sensitive information. This raises concerns about data privacy, user anonymity, and compliance with education regulations [38]. Without clear policies, institutions risk exposing student data to unauthorized access and misuse. Future governance efforts must focus on transparent AI usage policies and secure data management frameworks [20].

6.2.3. AI Bias and Fairness

Bias in AI-generated content remains a critical issue. ChatGPT's responses are influenced by training data, which may contain inherent biases related to gender, culture, or ideology [46]. If left unchecked, biased AI outputs could reinforce stereotypes and limit diverse perspectives in education. Policymakers must develop evaluation metrics to regularly audit AI models and mitigate biases [54].

6.2.4. Institutional Governance and Teacher Workload

The integration of AI in education demands institutional governance strategies to manage teacher workload effectively. While AI can automate administrative tasks, educators must verify AI-generated content, assess student engagement, and guide ethical AI usage [40]. Governance frameworks should include teacher training programs to enhance AI literacy and ensure its responsible implementation in classrooms [47].

6.2.5. Need for Standardized Regulations

The absence of standardized AI policies creates disparities in AI adoption across institutions. Some universities have embraced ChatGPT as a learning aid, while others have banned its use due to concerns about academic integrity [33]. Governments and educational organizations must develop clear AI governance frameworks and regulations that balance innovation with ethical responsibility [55]. At the end, Table 5 presents a comprehensive summary of related studies that examine governance and policy challenges associated with the use of ChatGPT in education. It outlines key issues such as ethical considerations, regulatory frameworks, institutional policies, and the implications of AI-driven learning tools. This summary provides valuable insights into the challenges and potential strategies for effectively integrating ChatGPT within educational institutions. Moreover, Table 6 illustrates the key governance and policy challenges associated with the use of AI in education, along with their implications. Addressing these governance challenges is essential for ensuring the ethical, responsible, and effective integration of AI technologies like ChatGPT in educational settings. Future research should focus on developing comprehensive AI policies that uphold academic integrity, mitigate potential risks, and maximize the benefits of AI in enhancing teaching and learning experiences.

Table 5. Key studies on governance and policy challenges.

Ref.	Key Issue	Findings	Implications
[33]	Lack of Standardization	Institutions have varying policies on ChatGPT use	A unified AI governance framework is required to ensure consistency
[38]	Data Privacy	AI systems process sensitive student data, raising security concerns	Stronger data protection policies and regulatory compliance are needed
[40]	Teacher Workload	Educators face increased workload in verifying AI-assisted assignments	Professional development programs for AI integration should be introduced
[44]	Academic Integrity	AI-generated content may lead to plagiarism and reduced critical thinking	Institutions must implement AI literacy programs and detection tools
[46]	Bias in AI Models	AI-generated responses may reflect biases in training data	Regular auditing and refining of AI datasets required to reduce bias

Table 6. Summary related works for future research directions.

Ref.	Year	Model	Dataset	Approach	Performance Metrics	Objectives	Main Findings	Strengths	Limitations
[43]	2023	AI in Education	Large-scale academic data	Comparative study	Institutional AI policies	Assess AI's effectiveness in diverse learning settings	Identified disparities in AI adoption	Highlights accessibility concerns	Limited to higher education settings
[44]	2023	AI-driven tutoring	Educational datasets	Systematic review	Student engagement, accuracy	Enhance multimodal learning beyond text-based interactions	Found potential for speech recognition and interactive simulations	Highlights diverse AI applications	Requires further empirical validation
[45]	2023	AI Ethics	Various education policies	Theoretical framework	Ethical compliance, bias reduction	Standardize AI governance policies	Identified gaps in ethical AI implementation	Comprehensive literature synthesis	Lacks empirical data

Table 6. *Cont.*

Ref.	Year	Model	Dataset	Approach	Performance Metrics	Objectives	Main Findings	Strengths	Limitations
[54]	2023	AI Cognitive Effects	Mixed academic data	Longitudinal study	Critical thinking development	Examine long-term effects of AI on learning	Found potential for skill enhancement but risk of dependency	Strong methodological framework	Calls for extensive future research
[56]	2024	AI Governance	AI-driven education	Policy analysis	Fairness, transparency	Develop ethical AI deployment frameworks	Identified need for regulatory compliance	Clear governance recommendations	Lacks real-world testing

6.3. *Future Research Directions for ChatGPT in Education*

In response to research question 3, the study underscores the necessity for robust regulatory frameworks and structured AI training programs for educators. Prior research has called for interdisciplinary collaboration between technologists, educators, and policymakers [56], and this study reinforces that recommendation by emphasizing ethical AI deployment strategies. Additionally, it identifies the need for empirical research on AI's long-term effects on teacher autonomy and student learning outcomes. By integrating the research questions with related works and findings, this study provides a comprehensive analysis of ChatGPT's role in education, offering a nuanced perspective that balances both opportunities and limitations. Hence, Table 6 shows a summary of related works for future directions on ChatGPT in education.

6.3.1. Enhancing AI Capabilities for Education

Current AI applications in education are mostly focused on text-based interactions. However, future studies should look into AI's capabilities in non-textual activities including speech recognition, visual learning aids, and interactive simulations [34]. Creating multimodal AI models will allow for more inclusive and engaging learning experiences for students with diverse learning styles [33].

6.3.2. Ethical AI Deployment and Governance Frameworks

As AI's use in education grows, ethical concerns about data privacy and algorithmic prejudice are addressed. Future research should provide comprehensive governance systems that oversee AI use while assuring adherence to educational norms [57]. Furthermore, interdisciplinary collaboration among educators, technologists, and policymakers is required to create responsible AI policies [32].

6.3.3. AI's Long-Term Impact on Educators and Students

The majority of the research focuses on the immediate benefits of ChatGPT in teaching. However, future research needs look into the long-term impacts on teacher autonomy, student learning outcomes, and cognitive development [58]. Empirical studies are needed to assess if AI-powered education improves or degrades critical thinking and problem-solving abilities over time [36].

6.3.4. AI in Diverse Educational Contexts

While numerous studies look at the function of artificial intelligence in higher education, there is little research on its impact in primary and secondary education, vocational training, and special education. Future research should look into the effectiveness of AI in a variety of educational settings to ensure its accessibility and inclusivity [38]. Furthermore, examining AI's function in bridging the digital divide is critical for encouraging equal access to AI-driven learning resources.

6.3.5. Standardizing AI Integration in Curricula

To optimize the benefits of AI in education, standardization of AI-driven curriculum development, teacher training, and student assessment is required. Future studies should focus on developing AI integration guidelines that are consistent with existing educational frameworks [33]. Teacher professional development programs should be strengthened to provide educators with AI literacy and practical implementation skills [14].

The future of AI in education demands multimodal advancements to move beyond text-based interactions, incorporating speech recognition and visual aids for more inclusive learning [33,34]. However, this expansion must be accompanied by robust ethical frameworks to address data privacy and algorithmic bias, requiring collaboration across education, technology, and policy sectors [32,55]. While current research highlights immediate benefits, longitudinal studies are critically needed to assess AI's long-term effects on teacher autonomy, student cognition, and skill development [36,59]. Additionally, the focus must broaden beyond higher education to include K–12, vocational, and special education contexts, ensuring equitable access and addressing the digital divide [38,58]. Finally, standardized curricular integration and teacher training programs are essential to align AI tools with pedagogical goals while empowering educators to use them effectively [14,33]. Together, these priorities underscore the need for a balanced, research-driven approach to harness AI's potential without compromising educational integrity or inclusivity.

7. Key Findings and Implications

The analysis reveals that ChatGPT can enhance personalized learning, provide scalable tutoring, and automate administrative tasks for educators; however, it also raises concerns about academic integrity, data privacy, AI biases, and the need for clear governance structures. The major findings of this study are categorized as follows:

7.1. Teacher Workload and Pedagogical Challenges

While AI can automate routine tasks [57], it may also increase teacher responsibilities related to verifying AI-generated content and guiding students on proper AI use.

7.2. Enhancing Student Engagement and Learning Outcomes

According to studies [42,43], AI-driven tailored learning improves engagement and academic performance, particularly for students who require additional support. AI-powered technologies, such as ChatGPT, can greatly increase student engagement by delivering quick feedback, creating personalized study materials, and facilitating engaging discussions. According to studies [28], students who use AI-assisted tutoring systems enhance their comprehension and retention. However, the extent to which AI has a good impact is determined by its suitable deployment in connection with pedagogical goals.

7.3. Policy Interventions

According to research [44,45], ChatGPT raises the risk of plagiarism and over-reliance on AI-generated content, necessitating sophisticated detection and mitigation measures. The widespread availability of ChatGPT has raised worries about academic dishonesty, as students may utilize AI to finish assignments without fully grasping the content [58]. To prevent these threats, institutions must develop stringent academic policies, AI detection systems, and awareness initiatives. According to research [60], incorporating AI ethics courses into curricula can help students learn how to use AI responsibly.

7.4. Role of Educators in AI Integration

While AI can automate administrative work, educators play an important role in guiding students on how to use AI ethically. According to studies [14], professional development programs for teachers to train them on AI integration are essential. Policymakers should provide educators with AI literacy training and curriculum recommendations.

7.5. Addressing AI Bias and Ensuring Data Privacy

ChatGPT's outputs are influenced by biases in its training data [29], raising questions about disinformation and fairness in education. ChatGPT's replies may reflect biases in its training data [34], providing issues in assuring fair and accurate information delivery. AI applications also raise issues regarding student data privacy and personal information security. Future research should focus on improving AI models to reduce biases and creating strong data governance policies [61].

7.6. Summary of Research Questions

As illustrated in Table 7, the following research questions were addressed: (1) How has ChatGPT been applied in education? The findings show that ChatGPT is utilized for personalized learning, tutoring, and content creation. However, its application lacks real-world validation [31,51]. (2) What are the major governance and policy challenges? The findings show that major challenges include ethical concerns, academic dishonesty, AI bias, data privacy issues, and increased teacher workload [45]. (3) What future research directions are needed? The findings show there is a need for regulatory frameworks, AI literacy programs, and empirical validation of AI in education [39].

Table 7. Summary of research questions and findings.

Ref.	Research Question	Findings from This Study
[31]	How has ChatGPT been applied in education?	Used for personalized learning, tutoring, and content creation; lacks real-world validation
[39]	What future research directions are needed?	Need for regulatory frameworks, AI literacy programs, empirical validation of AI in education
[45]	What are the major governance and policy challenges?	Ethical concerns, academic dishonesty, AI bias, data privacy, and teacher workload issues

Based on the findings across 40 peer-reviewed studies, it is evident that ChatGPT integration in education yields both pedagogical opportunities and ethical concerns. For example, studies such as [1,7] illustrate enhanced student engagement and personalized learning pathways due to ChatGPT's adaptability. However, others like [5,6] emphasize the growing risks of academic dishonesty and over-reliance on AI. Synthesizing these perspectives reveals a dual reality: while AI-driven tools like ChatGPT can transform educational delivery, their integration must be accompanied by clear ethical guidelines and adaptive teaching strategies. Unlike earlier studies that focused narrowly on either opportunity or risk, this review bridges both to propose a balanced framework for future implementation.

8. Future Research Directions

Several studies emphasize the need for ongoing research to refine AI's role in education. Key areas include the following.

8.1. Personalized Adaptive Learning

AI-powered systems should grow to offer real-time, adaptive learning paths based on individual students' strengths and weaknesses. Future studies should look into how deep learning models can improve personalization while still promoting student autonomy and critical thinking [59].

8.2. AI Ethics and Bias Mitigation

Addressing bias, misinformation, and ethical issues in AI-generated material is crucial. Future research should concentrate on establishing transparent AI models that reduce biases and adhere to educational equity and inclusivity [59,61].

8.3. Regulatory Frameworks and Governance

Policymakers have to establish comprehensive governance mechanisms to oversee AI in education while balancing innovation and ethical safeguards. Future research should look at how global AI policies affect education systems and student data privacy [61,62]. This paper expands on previous research by thoroughly assessing ChatGPT's role in education, identifying governance problems, and recommending future research topics for responsible AI adoption.

8.4. Human–AI Collaboration in Teaching

Instead of replacing instructors, AI could serve as an intelligent helper to improve teaching efficacy. Research should look at teacher AI interaction models and assess their impact on classroom engagement and curriculum design [14].

8.5. AI-Driven Tutoring Systems

AI-powered intelligent tutoring systems are created to give individualized learning experiences tailored to each student's needs and learning pace [40].

8.6. Interdisciplinary Collaboration for Responsible AI Governance

Effective AI integration in education necessitates collaboration among educators, technologists, and lawmakers to develop ethical principles and governance structures that promote responsible use [44].

8.7. Evaluating AI's Effectiveness Across Diverse Educational Settings

Ongoing research is required to analyze the impact of AI tools such as ChatGPT in diverse educational contexts, ensuring that they improve learning outcomes while avoiding biases or inaccuracies [41].

8.8. AI for Under-Resourced Learning Environments

Future research should focus on making AI accessible and scalable in low-resource settings, ensuring that developing regions benefit from AI-driven education while not worsening digital divides [61]. Hence, the future of AI in education hinges on developing adaptive learning systems that personalize instruction while preserving student autonomy and critical thinking [59], coupled with rigorous bias mitigation to ensure equitable, transparent AI outputs [62]. Effective implementation requires multi-stakeholder governance frameworks that balance innovation with ethical safeguards, particularly for data privacy and global policy alignment. Crucially, AI should augment rather than replace teachers, with research needed on optimal human–AI collaboration models to enhance pedagogy [14] and intelligent tutoring systems [40]. This demands interdisciplinary cooperation among educators, technologists, and policymakers to establish ethical guidelines [44], alongside expanded studies on AI's efficacy in diverse contexts from K-12 to under-resourced settings to bridge digital divides without exacerbating inequalities [41,62]. Together, these priorities underscore a vision for AI as a scalable, equitable tool that complements human expertise while addressing systemic educational challenges.

Finally, to strengthen the analytical rigor of this study, we have revised the manuscript to provide a substantive synthesis of the literature. The revised sections now clearly distinguish between the 40 systematically reviewed studies and supplementary contextual references (>40), ensuring methodological transparency. Sections on opportunities, challenges, and future directions have been restructured to align directly with the research questions, offering comparative insights and thematic integration from the reviewed studies, while supplementary references contextualize broader implications. This enhanced organization, including the addition of the PRISMA 2020 framework citation, facilitates a critical analysis of trends, gaps, and ChatGPT's educational role, moving beyond descriptive reporting toward actionable conclusions.

9. Conclusions

ChatGPT has the potential to improve education by making it more personalized, accessible, and interactive for teachers and students alike. However, issues of privacy, data security, and ethical use must be addressed. This study emphasizes ChatGPT's function in assisting with theory-based queries, developing ideas for application-based questions, and incorporating technology into teaching. Teachers can also use it during workshops to review and evaluate AI-generated responses. Despite its benefits, ChatGPT has drawbacks, including the danger of academic dishonesty and reliance, which can impair critical thinking. It can be difficult for educators to distinguish between learners who actively engage with the curriculum and those who rely on automation. Notably, ChatGPT paraphrases comments in ways that bypass similarity detection technologies, prompting upgrades to plagiarism detection tools. Future research should focus on enhancing AI's ability to perform non-textual jobs, creating more powerful AI content identification tools, and resolving ethical concerns about academic integrity and data protection. Additionally, policies and teacher training programs are required to enable responsible AI incorporation. Collaboration between educators, legislators, and technology providers is essential for defining guidelines, improving professional development, and closing the digital gap. Finally, this review serves as a foundational resource for stakeholders navigating AI's role in education, advocating for proactive governance and further empirical research. Therefore, we provide the following key recommendations for stakeholders: (1) Educators should integrate AI literacy into curricula and use ChatGPT as a supplement, not a substitute. (2) Policymakers should consider developing standardized regulations to ensure equitable and responsible AI use. (3) Researchers are also expected to prioritize empirical studies on AI's long-term pedagogical impact and bias mitigation. By addressing these gaps, stakeholders can harness ChatGPT's potential while safeguarding educational integrity and inclusivity.

Author Contributions: The work presented here was carried out in collaboration among all authors. Conceptualization, Y.Y.M. and W.A.; formal analysis, Y.Y.M. and Y.B.; methodology, A.M. and Y.Y.M.; supervision, M.A.; visualization, Y.Y.M. and W.A.; writing—original draft, M.A.; writing—review and editing, Y.B. and A.M., Fund Acquisition, W.A. All authors have read and agreed to the published version of the manuscript.

Funding: This research received no external funding.

Data Availability Statement: The dataset can be available upon request.

Conflicts of Interest: The authors declare no conflict of interest.

References

1. Farrokhnia, M.; Noroozi, O.; Wals, A.E.J. A SWOT analysis of ChatGPT: Implications for educational practice and research. *Innov. Educ. Teach. Int.* **2024**, *61*, 460–474. [CrossRef]
2. Ouyang, F.; Wu, M.; Zheng, L.; Zhang, L.; Jiao, P. Integration of artificial intelligence performance prediction and learning analytics to improve student learning in online engineering course. *Int. J. Educ. Technol. High. Educ.* **2023**, *20*, 4. [CrossRef] [PubMed]
3. Yu, X. Assessment of systemic AAV-microdystrophin gene therapy in the GRMD dog model. *Mol. Ther.* **2024**, *31*, 123–135.
4. Acosta-Enriquez, B.G.; Ballesteros, M.A.A.; Vargas, C.G.A.P.; Ulloa, M.N.O.; Ulloa, C.R.G.; Romero, J.M.P.; Jaramillo, N.D.G.; Orellana, H.U.C.; Anzoátegui, D.X.A.; Roca, C.L. Knowledge, attitudes, and perceived ethics regarding the use of ChatGPT among Generation Z university students. *Int. J. Educ. Integr.* **2024**, *20*, 10. [CrossRef]
5. Grassini, S. Shaping the future of education: Exploring the potential and consequences of AI and ChatGPT in educational settings. *Educ. Sci.* **2023**, *13*, 692. [CrossRef]
6. Anders, B.A. Is using ChatGPT cheating, plagiarism, both, neither, or forward thinking? *Patterns* **2023**, *4*, 100694. [CrossRef]
7. Crompton, H.; Burke, D. The educational affordances and challenges of ChatGPT: State of the field. *TechTrends* **2024**, *68*, 380–392. [CrossRef]
8. Guo, Y.; Lee, D. Leveraging ChatGPT for enhancing critical thinking skills. *J. Chem. Educ.* **2023**, *100*, 4876–4883. [CrossRef]
9. Gill, S.S.; Xu, M.; Patros, P.; Wu, H.; Kaur, R.; Kaur, K.; Fuller, S.; Singh, M.; Arora, P.; Parlikad, A.K.; et al. Transformative effects of ChatGPT on modern education: Emerging era of AI chatbots, Internet of Things and cyber-physical systems. *Internet Things Cyber-Phys. Syst.* **2024**, *4*, 19–23. [CrossRef]
10. Mai, D.T.T.; Da, C.V.; Hanh, N.V. The use of ChatGPT in teaching and learning: A systematic review through SWOT analysis approach. *Front. Educ.* **2024**, *9*, 1328769. [CrossRef]
11. Dempere, J.; Modugu, K.; Hesham, A.; Ramasamy, L.K. The impact of ChatGPT on higher education. *Front. Educ.* **2023**, *8*, 1206936. [CrossRef]
12. Ray, P. ChatGPT: A comprehensive review on background, applications, key challenges, bias, ethics, limitations and future scope. *Internet Things Cyber-Phys. Syst.* **2023**, *3*, 121–154. [CrossRef]
13. Emenike, M.E.; Emenike, B.U. Considerations for Artificial Intelligence Text-Generation Software Programs for Chemists and Chemistry Educators. *J. Chem. Educ.* **2023**, *100*, 1413–1418. [CrossRef]
14. Ahmad, N.; Murugesan, S.; Kshetri, N. Generative artificial intelligence and the education sector. *Computer* **2023**, *56*, 72–76. [CrossRef]
15. Chocarro, R.; Cortiñas, M.; Marcos-Matás, G. Teachers' attitudes towards chatbots in education: A technology acceptance model approach considering the effect of social language, bot proactiveness, and users' characteristics. *Educ. Stud.* **2023**, *49*, 295–313. [CrossRef]
16. Gardner, D.E.; Giordano, A.N. The Challenges and Value of Undergraduate Oral Exams in the Physical Chemistry Classroom: A Useful Tool in the Assessment Toolbox. *J. Chem. Educ.* **2023**, *100*, 1705–1709. [CrossRef]
17. Al-kfairy, M. Factors impacting the adoption and acceptance of ChatGPT in educational settings: A narrative review of empirical studies. *Appl. Syst. Innov.* **2024**, *7*, 110. [CrossRef]
18. Fergus, S.; Botha, M.; Ostovar, M. Evaluating academic answers generated using ChatGPT. *J. Chem. Educ.* **2023**, *100*, 1672–1675. [CrossRef]
19. Mengist, W.; Soromessa, T.; Legese, G. Method for conducting systematic literature review and meta-analysis for environmental science research. *MethodsX* **2020**, *7*, 100777. [CrossRef]
20. Gašević, D.; Siemens, G.; Sadiq, S. Empowering learners for the age of artificial intelligence. *Comput. Educ. Artif. Intell.* **2023**, *4*, 100130. [CrossRef]
21. Benuyenah, V. Commentary: ChatGPT use in higher education assessment: Prospects and epistemic threats. *J. Res. Innov. Teach. Learn.* **2023**, *16*, 134–135. [CrossRef]
22. Abujaber, A.A.; Abd-Alrazaq, A.; Al-Qudimat, A.R.; Nashwan, A.J. A strengths, weaknesses, opportunities, and threats (SWOT) analysis of ChatGPT integration in nursing education: A narrative review. *Cureus* **2023**, *15*, e48643. [CrossRef] [PubMed]
23. Akgun, S.; Greenhow, C. Artificial intelligence in education: Addressing ethical challenges in K-12 settings. *AI Ethics* **2022**, *2*, 431–440. [CrossRef] [PubMed]
24. Black, J. Past, present and tackling the future of artificial intelligence (AI) in education: Maintaining agency and establishing AI laws. *Open J. Soc. Sci.* **2023**, *11*, 442–464. [CrossRef]
25. Lima, A.R.; Lima, I.N.; Guevara-Soto, F.J. Challenges and opportunities of AI-assisted learning: A systematic literature review on the impact of ChatGPT usage in higher education. *Int. J. Learn. Teach. Educ. Res.* **2023**, *22*, 122–135.
26. Labadze, L.; Grigolia, M.; Machaidze, L. Role of AI chatbots in education: Systematic literature review. *Int. J. Educ. Technol. High. Educ.* **2023**, *20*, 56. [CrossRef]

27. Okonkwo, C.W.; Ade-Ibijola, A. Chatbots applications in education: A systematic review. *Comput. Educ. Artif. Intell.* **2021**, *2*, 100033. [CrossRef]
28. Ramandanis, D.; Xinogalos, S. Investigating the support provided by chatbots to educational institutions and their students: A systematic literature review. *Multimodal Technol. Interact.* **2023**, *7*, 103. [CrossRef]
29. Baidoo-Anu, D.; Ansah, L.O. Education in the era of generative artificial intelligence (AI): Understanding the potential benefits of ChatGPT in promoting teaching and learning. *J. AI* **2023**, *7*, 52–62. [CrossRef]
30. Mhlanga, D. ChatGPT in Education: Exploring Opportunities for Emerging Economies to Improve Education with ChatGPT. *SSRN.* **2023**. [CrossRef]
31. Su, J.; Yang, W. Unlocking the power of ChatGPT: A framework for applying generative AI in education. *ECNU Rev. Educ.* **2023**, *6*, 355–366. [CrossRef]
32. Yang, S.; Evans, C. Opportunities and challenges in using AI chatbots in higher education. In Proceedings of the 2020 ACM Conference on Innovation and Technology in Computer Science Education, Trondheim, Norway, 15–19 June 2020; ACM: New York, NY, USA, 2020; pp. 1–6. [CrossRef]
33. Zamir, S.; Afzal, S.; Sultana, N. ChatGPT and artificial intelligence in higher education institutions: Benefits, challenges and ethical concerns. *Biannu. Uswa J. Res.* **2023**, *3*, 2.
34. Sobaih, A.E.E.; Elshaer, I.A.; Hasanein, A.M. Examining students' acceptance and use of ChatGPT in Saudi Arabian higher education. *Eur. J. Investig. Health Psychol. Educ.* **2024**, *14*, 709–721. [CrossRef] [PubMed]
35. Almogren, A.S.; Al-Rahmi, W.M.; Dahri, N.A. Exploring factors influencing the acceptance of ChatGPT in higher education: A smart education perspective. *Heliyon* **2024**, *10*, e31887. [CrossRef] [PubMed]
36. Imran, M.; Almusharraf, N. Analyzing the role of ChatGPT as a writing assistant at higher education level: A systematic review of the literature. *Contemp. Educ. Technol.* **2023**, *15*, ep464. [CrossRef]
37. Singh, M. Maintaining the integrity of the South African university: The impact of ChatGPT on plagiarism and scholarly writing. *S. Afr. J. High. Educ.* **2023**, *37*, 203–220. [CrossRef]
38. Kuhail, M.A.; Alturki, N.; Alramlawi, S.; Alhejori, K. Interacting with educational chatbots: A systematic review. *Educ. Inf. Technol.* **2023**, *28*, 973–1018. [CrossRef]
39. Yu, J. AI-driven educational reforms: Challenges and opportunities. *Int. J. Educ. Technol.* **2024**, *47*, 140–159.
40. Guo, Y.; Lee, K. AI accessibility in education: Challenges and solutions. *Int. J. Educ. Technol.* **2023**, *45*, 189–207.
41. Grassini, S. AI in personalized learning: Enhancing student engagement. *J. Educ. AI Res.* **2023**, *21*, 150–167.
42. Guo, Y.; Lee, K. University policies on AI: A comparative analysis. *J. High. Educ. Policy* **2023**, *45*, 122–138.
43. Ray, S. Unmasking bias in AI-generated educational content. *AI Educ. Rev.* **2023**, *15*, 110–128.
44. Zhou, H.; Patel, M.; Gomez, R. AI governance in higher education: Bias, misinformation, and policy gaps. *J. AI Ethics Regul.* **2023**, *19*, 55–73.
45. Abujaber, R.; Khan, F.; Patel, M. Data privacy in AI-powered learning systems: Challenges and solutions. *AI Soc.* **2023**, *39*, 199–215.
46. Farrokhnia, M.; Esmaeili, A.; Rahmani, L. AI-powered teacher support: Balancing automation and human oversight. *Technol. Educ. J.* **2024**, *33*, 89–104.
47. Crompton, H.; Burke, M. Ethical AI in education: Addressing bias and accountability. *Comput. Educ.* **2024**, *185*, 103–120.
48. Victor, D. Factors and impacts of ChatGPT adoption for academic purposes in higher learning institutions: Students' perspectives. *SSRN Electron. J.* **2024**. [CrossRef]
49. Liao, C.; Wang, M. AI-powered learning platforms: Evaluating student engagement and retention. *J. Learn. Sci.* **2023**, *28*, 205–224.
50. Huang, Z.; Wang, M.; Yang, K. The impact of ChatGPT on the learning efficacy of Chinese college students. *Lect. Notes Educ. Psychol. Public Media* **2023**, *21*, 289–298. [CrossRef]
51. Huang, T.; Zhang, F.; Chen, L. Fostering interactive learning with AI: The case of ChatGPT. *Educ. Technol. Soc.* **2023**, *26*, 120–138.
52. Smith, K.; Lee, R. Accessibility and AI in education: A review of assistive technologies. *J. Learn. Disabil. Technol.* **2022**, *15*, 56–72.
53. Benuyenah, A. AI in student engagement: The role of chatbots in higher education. *Educ. Technol. Res. Dev.* **2023**, *71*, 178–194.
54. Farrokhnia, M.; Banihashem, S.K.; Noroozi, O.; Wals, A. AI in teaching and learning: Opportunities and challenges. *Int. J. Educ. Technol.* **2024**, *45*, 189–205.
55. Anders, P. *Artificial Intelligence and Academic Integrity: Challenges and Solutions*, 1st ed.; Routledge: New York, NY, USA, 2023.
56. Akgun, O.; Greenhow, C. The role of AI in education: Risks and rewards for critical thinking development. *Comput. Educ.* **2022**, *189*, 102–119.
57. Abujaber, R.; Al-Khasawneh, M.; Shalaby, L. AI in education: Balancing privacy concerns and innovation. *IEEE Trans. Learn. Technol.* **2023**, *17*, 214–228.
58. Aoun, R.; Aldowah, G.I. AI-driven personalized learning: An adaptive framework for student engagement. *Comput. Educ. Artif. Intell.* **2022**, *3*, 100067. [CrossRef]

59. Wang, J.; Hussain, Y.; Zhang, X.; Mao, C.; Wu, Z. AI-Based Automated Grading Systems: Opportunities, Challenges, and Future Directions. *Bus. Soc. Sci. Proc.* **2025**, *1*, 29–39. [CrossRef]
60. UNESCO. Use of AI in Education: Deciding the Future We Want. UNESCO Report on AI and Education. 2023. Available online: https://www.unesco.org/en/articles/use-ai-education-deciding-future-we-want (accessed on 10 January 2025).
61. Ferrara, E. Fairness and Bias in Artificial Intelligence: A Brief Survey of Sources, Impacts, and Mitigation Strategies. *Sci* **2024**, *6*, 3. [CrossRef]
62. Yang, S.J.; Ogata, H.; Matsui, T.; Chen, N.-S. Human-centered artificial intelligence in education: Seeing the invisible through the visible. *Comput. Educ. Artif. Intell.* **2021**, *2*, 100008. [CrossRef]

algorithms

MDPI

Article

The Whale Optimization Algorithm and Markov Chain Monte Carlo-Based Approach for Optimizing Teacher Professional Development in Creative Learning Design with Technology

Kalliopi Rigopouli, Dimitrios Kotsifakos * and Yannis Psaromiligkos *

Business Administration Department, University of West Attica, 250 Thivon & Petrou Ralli Str., Egaleo, 12241 Athens, Greece; krigopouli@uniwa.gr

* Correspondence: dkotsifakos@uniwa.gr (D.K.); yannis.psaromiligkos@uniwa.gr (Y.P.)

Abstract

In this article, we present a hybrid optimization methodology using the whale optimization algorithm and Markov Chain Monte Carlo sampling technique in a teachers' training development program regarding creativity in technology-enhanced learning design. Finding the best possible training for creativity in learning design with technology is a complex task, as many dynamic and multi-model variables need to be taken into consideration. When designing the best possible training, the whale optimization algorithm helped us in determining the right methods, resources, content, and assessment. A further Markov Chain Monte Carlo-based approach helped us in deciding with accuracy that these were the correct parameters of our training. In this article, we show that metaheuristic algorithms like the whale optimization algorithm, validated by a Markov chain technique like Markov Chain Monte Carlo, can help not only in areas like machine learning but also in fields without structured data, like creativity in technology-enhanced learning design. The best possible training for a teacher's professional development in creative learning design is collaborative, hands-on, and utilizes creativity definitions for the product along with technology integration learning design models.

Keywords: learning design; creativity; technology; teaching professional development; whale optimization algorithm; Markov Chain Monte Carlo

1. Introduction

Creativity development is an important endeavour for modern education. For the last fifty years, researchers have consistently shown interest in creativity within the field of education, as it is linked to individual well-being and successful academic achievements. Teachers utilize various tools and technology to stimulate creativity by igniting curiosity, aiding in idea development, creating digital products, organizing creative workflows, promoting collaborative creativity, and assessing with evaluation methods. Thus, creativity development is associated with advanced learning outcomes and with technology-enhanced learning [1]. Integrating emerging technologies into classroom learning strategies enhances education at every stage. However, possessing technology alone is not sufficient; effective pedagogical methods that promote learning are essential [2]. As defined in the technological, pedagogical, content, knowledge (TPACK) framework, teachers need three types of knowledge when implementing technology: content knowledge (CK), pedagogy knowledge (PK), and technology knowledge (TK). The interplay between technology, pedagogy, and content occurs in a dynamic environment, in which educators need to be able to creatively align these three components when designing their educational scenarios [3]. Teachers' Professional Development (TPD) programs are very important in helping educators cultivate their creativity when implementing technology in learning design. Educating teachers in technology-enhanced LD is very important because it helps them develop their TPACK, meaning their knowledge and design skills [4]. After the pandemic, there is a heightened need for educators to utilize creativity to effectively support learning in hybrid and online environments. However, the majority of studies related to the connection between creativity and technology do not take into account evidence-based research and educators' experiences and practices, so we can have a grounded knowledge of what creativity and technology mean in classroom settings [5]. Moreover, initiatives in creativity in TPD pose challenges because of educators' limited resources, resistance to change, lack of a clear conception of creativity, and lack of a unified framework [6]. Additionally, developing technology-enhanced learning design capability can be a complex task as it refers to theories of human cognition, the possibilities technology offers, and the fundamentals of instructional design [7].

In this article, we tried to address the issue of creativity in learning design with technology in teacher professional development. To find the best possible training, we relied on the Whale Optimization Algorithm (WOA) when designing our training approach and validated it through the Markov Chain Monte Carlo (MCMC) technique. We concluded with a well-structured design of training. WOA is a swarm intelligence optimization technique [8]. In summary, WOA imitates the hunting techniques of humpback whales. It was created to address optimization problems. The phases of WOA are encircling the prey, exploitation, and exploration. In a few words, the process involves conducting a literature review on the optimization target, identifying key components, and exploring alternatives to avoid local optima. This is crucial, as maintaining a balance between exploration and exploitation is essential in WOA problems. Implementing WOA in the design process helped us conceptualize and eventually conclude on a TPD focusing on creative learning design with technology. MCMC helped us evaluate that the WOA will give an optimal solution. A critique of WOA applications is that they fail to address multi-dimensional problems and might lead to a very good but not the 'best' solution. This is one of the reasons that there are modifications and hybridizations of the algorithm [9]. Our focus on MCMC helps WOA address these challenges, especially at the end of the process, when we have a solution, to validate indeed that it is optimal. MCMC allows for the representation of training as a probabilistic process. MCMC refers to algorithms that implement Monte Carlo sampling using a designed Markov chain, meaning that the following selection relies on the prior one in the sampling procedure [10]. Both WOA and MCMC have been implemented in educational research, especially in student performance and machine learning. In the realm of educational studies, we commonly utilize statistical techniques such as structural equation modeling (SEM) or qualitative approaches like conceptual modeling. However, there remains a gap in studies concerning optimizing training programs using computational methods and techniques.

When designing our methodology using WOA, we relied on a narrative review with an emphasis on recent and highly cited empirical evidence studies. The bibliography points out that an effective TPD must be collaborative and hands-on, providing opportunities for reflection with peer and expert evaluation. Additionally, it must be subject-focused, with coaching and sustained duration [10]. We combined each of the components of an effective TPD with research regarding creativity and technology-enhanced learning design. This was the first phase, which is called encircling the prey. In the second phase, which is called exploitation, we specify the components by illuminating those that do not fit and enhancing those that best fit and are closely connected to them, or trying new ones to prevent local optima.

For our procedure, we utilized creativity theories that would help us with the content and the evaluation of the creative product, which in our case are the technology-enhanced learning designs. According to the literature, most definitions of creative products agree with these two aspects: novelty and effectiveness. A creative solution provides something distinctive and original, while also providing value to certain groups. Mishra and Henriksen have enhanced the definition, which builds on Besemer's work, with the aspect of the 'whole'. According to them: 'an innovative mathematical proof or a unique beautiful painting are incredibly different things, yet they are both creative'. Thus, they have added the aesthetic sensibility in context, which they called "wholeness", and it is the third component of creativity [11]. With this, they offered a comprehensive definition when we address creativity, specialized in education contexts, and in measuring creative artifacts. This is the Novel, Effective, and Whole (NEW) definition.

In parallel, we utilized technology integration models for our training, as the main purpose is to creatively implement technology and enhance creative skills among educators. The Triple E framework by Kolb speaks of engagement, enhancement, and extension of learning goals when we integrate technology into lesson planning. It is a model that emphasizes effectiveness in lesson planning with technology [12]. Furthermore, the SAMR model by Puentedura helped us innovate when designing with technology, as it speaks about moving from simple technology use (Substitution) towards transformative use (Redefinition) [13]. In other words, we could have the criteria of effectiveness and novelty with these two models. For the wholeness aspect, meaning the context, we relied on the basic theories and principles when creating an LD (define objectives and roles, align activities with goals and resources, etc.). In this way, we created the content/assessment of the process. The methodology was collaborative and hands-on as suggested, so we used the Think-Pair-Share (TPS) methodology. TPS motivates learners to think for themselves and generate their concepts (Think), communicate and debate their concepts with a peer (Pair), and subsequently share them with the class. For resources, we used learning management systems and LD graphical tools for a sustained duration. It is important to mention that we considered design factors in TPDs for technology integration and teachers' creativity. These variables, like the 'effective TPD' parameters, interact horizontally in our training. In the last phase of the WOA, which is called exploration, we enhanced our design with a different cooperative strategy to examine further effectiveness in our training. The bibliography revealed that the Team-Based Learning (TBL) strategy would be suitable for our purpose. This active learning strategy boosts subject knowledge, comprehension, engagement, critical thinking, and participation among group members. TBL offered coaching and support, which are components of the effectiveness of TPDs.

The training was designed with these components, as the WOA methodology and the literature review have indicated to us during the design process. To test our variables, we conducted an MCMC sampling technique. Combining these methods to find optimal training solutions in educational research remains a novel approach.

The research questions derived from the above are the following:

RQ1: Is there a combination of methods, resources, content, assessment, and duration that is optimal when designing a TPD for creativity in technology-enhanced learning design?

RQ2: Can WOA be used as a method to obtain optimal solutions when designing training in creative learning design?

RQ3: Can MCMC help us validate this training in creative learning design in a TPD, giving the expected accuracy to our proposed results?

The article is as follows: In the second section, we present the related literature for the WOA and MCMC optimization algorithm and their applications in educational research. In the third section, we present our methodology. In the fourth chapter, we analyze the conceptualization of WOA in our training. In the fifth section, we present the mathematical formulation and the algorithmic precision as combined with the MCMC application. In the sixth section, we present the results. Lastly, in the final section, we show the conclusions and future remarks of this article.

2. Whale Optimization Algorithm, Markov Chain Monte Carlo, and Their Applications in Educational Research

The WOA is a metaheuristic algorithm that draws inspiration from the bubble-net feeding technique of humpback whales, in which they generate spirals of bubbles to ensnare prey before striking. In 2016, Mirjalili and Lewis introduced whale swarm optimization methods. The key concepts of WOA [14] are:

- Encircling Prey: The optimal solution is viewed as the prey. Other whales modify their locations concerning this optimal solution through mathematical equations.
- Bubble-net Attaching (Exploitation): Two mathematical models have been suggested to simulate the whale's behavior while hunting their prey: the shrinking encircling method and spiral position updating. In this phase, which is called the exploitation phase, whales enhance their search for the optimal solution by either reducing their movement range or adhering to a spiral pattern. A probability factor (50%) governs which approach is utilized.
    1. Shrinking Encircling: The whales gradually converge towards the best solution.
    2. Spiral Updating: Whales move in a spiral formation toward the optimal solution.
- Search for Prey (Exploration Phase): Whales randomly choose a target and adjust their movements toward or away from it. This method guarantees a global search for the most effective combination.

WOA has been implemented in education, especially in machine learning, but also in other educational research, involving student performance. For example, the article named "An Enhanced Evolutionary Student Performance Prediction Model Using Whale Optimization Algorithm Boosted with Sine-Cosine Mechanism" presents a refined approach to forecasting student success by augmenting the Whale Optimization Algorithm (WOA). This improvement combines the Sine Cosine Algorithm (SCA) and Logistic Chaotic Map (LCM) to tackle WOA's shortcomings in both the exploration and exploitation stages [15]. Another example is a hybrid application of WOA in Teacher Professional Development (TPD). The article 'Teaching learning-based whale optimization algorithm for multi-layer perceptron neural network training' presents a valid way to optimize the multi-layer perceptron neural network [16]. WOA could serve to improve training programs by identifying the most effective training modules for educators. It potentially aids in TPD optimization, as methods, resources, assessment, time, context, and processes must be fluidly adjusted for teacher development. Computational modelling focuses on building progressively better models of phenomena rather than collecting individual results. In our case, it will be a suitable enhancement in educational research to utilize them for a dynamic output like the creation of a TPD in technology and creativity [17]. Algorithms help us graph this iterative process in an 'easy-to-use' way, providing at the same time more accurate starting points because of their flexibility to evolve during the process.

The WOA has its mathematical models and applications. In this article, we will present a novel application of WOA combined with the MCMC. Monte Carlo methods comprise a set of computational techniques that depend on the outcomes of numerous random experiments to determine an unknown value. MCMC is a collection of sampling methods. MCMC was initially developed in 1953 and experienced significant growth in the 1990s. The origins of MCMC can be traced back to chemical physics, while its advancement was supported by applied mathematics (statistics), leading to its application in various fields, including social sciences. By the 20th century, MCMC sampling techniques had become widely recognized in academia. MCMC refers to algorithms that implement Monte Carlo sampling using a Markov chain. Conventional Monte Carlo techniques sample independently. In comparison, MCMC possesses a Markovian property: the following selection relies on the prior one in the sampling procedure [18].

As discussed, MCMC entered social studies in 1990 as a quantitative analysis method in research. In education, we have various practical applications of MCMC. For example, an application in education is about student performance prediction. In the paper, 'Mathematical Model for Early Prediction of Learning Success' [19], there is an attempt to address the challenges of overseeing educational success in real-time, regardless of the discipline, and with great accuracy. The model utilizes information from Learning Management Systems (LMSs), which monitor students' engagement, advancement, and performance instantly. MCMC helped define these valuable elements from the data and then used them. Another important application of MCMC in education is when designing assessments. For example, in the recent study, 'Markov Chain Monte Carlo Methods for Dynamic Student Assessment' [20], we have the utilization of the MCMC in creating the best possible assessment in real-time. Thanks to MCMC techniques, the model can estimate complex probability distributions, allowing for adaptive assessment and monitoring of each student's progress. At the same time, it provides quantification of uncertainty in estimates, making the assessment more accurate and personalized. Lastly, we have recent examples of research in teacher decision-making and practices that utilize the MCMC methodology. The paper 'The Application of Markov Chain in Middle School Mathematics Teaching Evaluation' presents how the MCMC can analyze teaching effects and guide teachers to improve their teaching methods in mathematics. By creating an initial state vector and a transition probability matrix, the research assesses variations in student performance among various classes. The results show that this method offers an objective way to evaluate teaching effectiveness and can assist educators in improving their instructional strategies. In particular, the research revealed that this is a good quantitative method to assess teacher quality [21].

To summarize, WOA and MCMC have their place in scientific research analysis in the educational field. Computational methods in general are an emerging field of knowledge in social sciences. They are inductive, especially in opposition to theoretical or statistical, which are deductive. These are characterized by hierarchy or hypothesis and are rigid. With stochastic models like algorithms, we start with the conceptualization of complex and dynamic concepts like creativity, which involves processes and interactions. In [22], we see, for example, the benefits of multi-level agent-based modeling to predict valuable outcomes from an initial state of design. This ability to predict improves the effectiveness of educational research by directing the creation of more focused interventions. Additionally, it aids in evidence-based educational practice, which is important in creativity studies. The combination of WOA and MCMC will be a novel application of great value in optimization and probabilistic modeling tasks, in the field of educational research, especially in optimizing TPDs for creative learning design with technology. WOA can set effective initial parameters for MCMC by examining the probability distribution surrounding these ideal points and helping in the decision process. Ultimately, MCMC outcomes are reintroduced into WOA for additional refinement. The outcome/optimal training was collaborative and hands-on, with content and assessment on creative product and technology integration models like Triple E and SAMR.

3. Methodology

In our methodology, we attempted to model the design of optimal training for creativity in technology-enhanced LD. We did this by employing the WOA and validating it through the MCMC. The parameters of WOA were evaluated through a narrative literature review. This approach is helpful when we need to acquire knowledge from a variety of studies, as we have in our case. For example, when investigating creativity, we need to know about educational and psychological studies. It is a more flexible approach that is well-suited for research in multi-dimensional concepts and for investigating emerging fields, like creativity and technology [23]. Following this approach, we decided to start searching and eventually find the components (optimal solutions) and the connections of the following dynamic relationships. These are:

(1) Effective TPDs
(2) Effective TPD in technology-enhanced LD
(3) Effective TPD in Teachers' Creativity

This is the initialization in WOA. These three relationships will generate different solutions and connections between them. We start by selecting the initial components of a TPD, which are:

(1) Methodology,
(2) Resources,
(3) Content,
(4) Evaluation,
(5) Framework,
(6) Design factors.

In the first phase, which is called 'encircling the prey', we identify all relevant literature of these three relationships that correspond to the components. We search for 'effective TPDs' and narrow our review to recent studies with a focus on empirical evidence. Our literature review started in Google Scholar search engines and Scopus databases. The type of literature is 'Theme-centric search'. The keywords we first initiated in our search were 'effective teacher professional development' between the years 2020 and 2025. We seek highly cited journals like 'The search for evidence-based features of effective teacher professional development: a critical analysis of the literature, 'Shifting the focus of research on effective professional development: Insights from a case study of implementation', and 'A new framework for teachers' professional development'. During this stage, we analyze and synthesize the papers and draw conclusions. The same procedure is done for the keywords: the teacher's professional development in technology-enhanced learning design. We identify recent and highly cited papers like 'Technology Use for Teacher Professional Development in Low- and Middle-Income Countries: A systematic review' and 'The role of technology-based education and teacher professional development in English as a foreign language class. We rely on the 'Designing effective professional development for technology integration in schools' due to its direct relevance in the design process of a TPD. Lastly, we searched for 'teachers' professional development AND teachers' creativity'. From this search, a highly cited journal was 'The role of teachers' creativity in higher education: A systematic literature review and guidance for future research' and 'How am I a creative teacher? Beliefs, values, and affect for integrating creativity in the classroom'.

After finding the fundamental theories and concepts of these highly cited journals, we began to synthesize the knowledge and connect the dots between the three pillars and the six components. The results are forming the first phase of WOA. We assume in this phase that all given variables and connections between them could be possibly correct. In the second phase, which is called exploitation, we apply either shrinking encircling or bubble-net feeding mechanisms. In our literature, we assume that the most relevant intersections between the three pillars will point out whether we use one strategy or the other. For example, in the case of the content, we know that efficient TPD is subject-focused, so we create content with a focus on creativity. Additionally, we know from TPACK that for teachers to connect creatively through technology, pedagogy, and content, they need to acquire the necessary knowledge. In other words, we derive elements both from creativity and LD with technology to develop the content. This simulates the bubble-net attacking because we use theories that are different from each other to connect them and create content regarding creativity. In another example, where we have the shrinking enriching, we move towards the solution in an instant way, simulating the hunting behaviour technique. For example, when we want to decide to focus on the creative product, meaning the LD, only two definitions will be of great value: the standard definition and the NEW. We conclude that the NEW is of value because it has been proven through empirical evidence research on lesson plans.

In the last phase, which is the search for prey, we try new solutions that might be a better fit for our purpose. We decided in this phase to change the methodology from TPS to TBL. A further MCMC validated that indeed it was the correct approach. In the following chapter, we show in detail through concept maps the process of the conceptualization of WOA.

4. Whale Optimization Algorithm and Creativity in Learning Design with Technology in Teacher Professional Development

In this section, we present how we utilized the WOA during the design phase to optimize the best possible training for creative learning design with technology. To investigate the conclusions and outcomes of the WOA, we created a concept map divided into four sections, each encompassing the phases of WOA (Figures 1–4), conceptualizing the iterations between our variables. A concept map is a great tool for visualising processes and connections. It has been used in educational research for modelling and conceptualizing complex relationships. It has potential for growth in algorithmic representation. Studies found that as a designing tool, a concept map could help in the advancement of computational thinking, meaning, it can enhance our understanding of the algorithmic process [24].

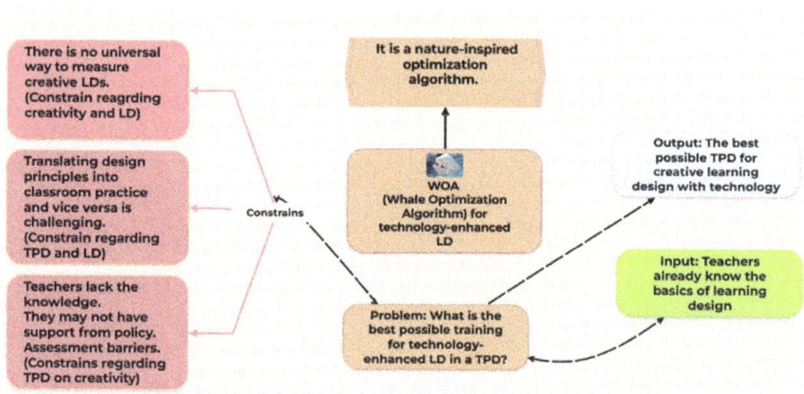

Figure 1. Analysing the problem: constraints, inputs, and outputs.

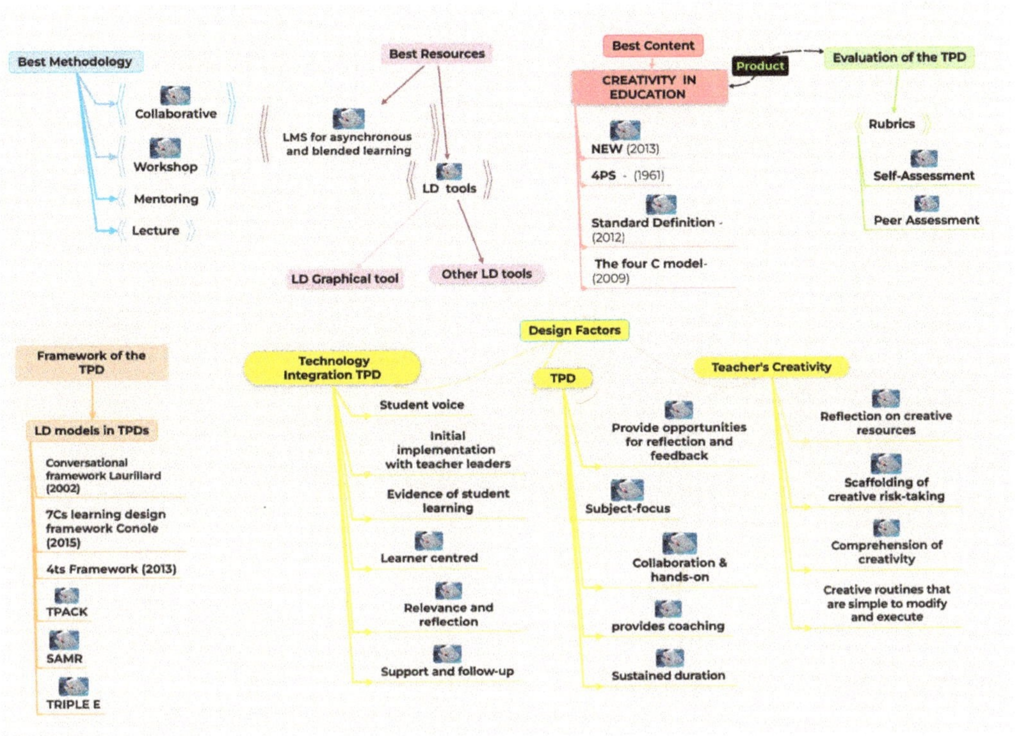

Figure 2. First phase of the WOA: encircling the prey.

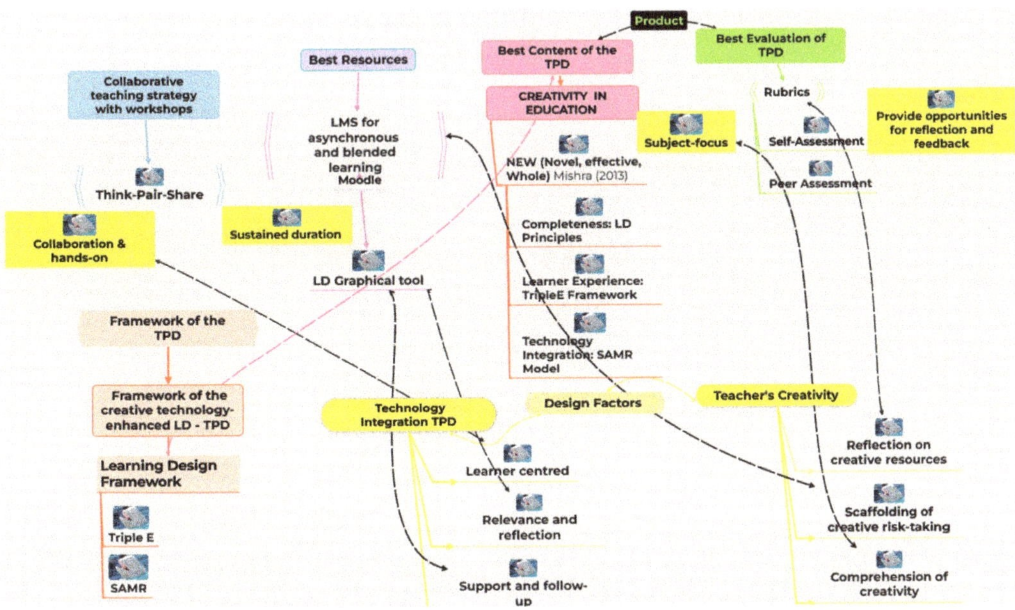

Figure 3. Second phase of the WOA: bubble-net attacking.

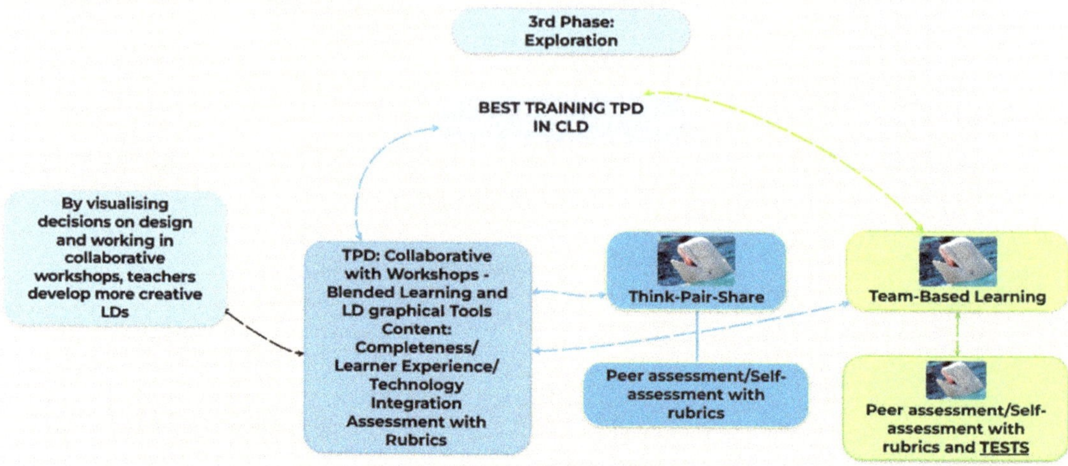

Figure 4. Third phase of the WOA: encircling the prey.

Our goal is to find the best possible training for creative LDs. The proposed terms of creativity, learning design with technology, and TPD have constraints when addressing them. As shown in the concept map (Figure 1), we have a constraint in the creativity term and subsequently, its assessment, as there is no explicit definition for creative LDs.

In the bibliography, we have definitions that refer to the product, the process, the person, or the press. In most cases, there might be a combination that includes all of these. Finding a reliable definition will guide us in determining the right assessment [25]. As a second constraint, the process of LD means translating design principles into classroom practice, something that is challenging. This is the second thing we need to consider in our research. The other constraint involved professional development in learning design with technology. Integrating technology in lesson planning does not come without challenges. Some of them are resources, expertise and abilities, organizational traits, perceptions and attitudes, evaluation, and disciplinary culture [26]. The input of the process is that this training is for a teacher's professional development program, where teachers are novices in learning design. The output of the proposed process is to find the best possible training based on the WOA and the MCMC.

In Figure 2, we are in phase 1, which is called encircling prey. We conducted a literature review on the key themes: 'effective TPDs, 'effective TPD in technology-enhanced LD', and 'effective TPD in Teachers' Creativity'. Additionally, we define important components to guide the design of the process of the TPD. These are: methodology, resources, content, evaluation, framework, and design factors. For the first theme, we found that an effective TPD is collaborative, hands-on, with sustained duration, provides opportunities for reflection, draws on effective practice models, provides coaching, and is subject-focused [27]. Collaboration is the most significant element in every efficient training program. Various studies have shown the benefits when working in groups, especially in teacher professional development programs and TPDs focusing on LDs. While in the first phase (enriching the prey), we choose collaboration and workshops (hands-on) from the pool of methodologies. Additionally, for resources, we choose to implement the Moodle Learning Management

System. Hybrid and online approaches to learning are essential in contemporary education. Thus, they provide opportunities for flexibility that are very important in professional development and adult education. Having asynchronous learning material in the LMS will give us the sustained duration that is needed. Another important element is the tool we choose, which can guide us and assist us in the reflection of the design process. This aspect is very important to consider, as these tools scaffold the design process. Research on learning design tools indicates that graphical representations of lesson planning are preferred among teachers because of their visual representation, guidance, and flexibility [28].

For the content, we seek definitions concerning the product, because we want our teachers to develop a creative LD with technology. According to Rhodes' 4Ps framework, person embodies creative characteristics, press includes environmental factors, process involves mental techniques, and product signifies tangible outcomes of creative endeavours. According to Kaufman and Beghetto, creative products can be categorized into four types: mini-c, which involves learning about new things in the environment, and little-c, which involves personal creative insights. Professional creativity involves work outputs. Big-C creativity refers to products or inventions that have a global impact [29]. Two definitions are directly associated with the product. One is the standard definition by Runco and Jaeger [30]. According to them, originality or innovation, along with utility or efficiency, are key concepts. Originality refers to a creative output that introduces something new or is at least somewhat distinctive within its context. Utility implies that the product is beneficial, reasonable, comprehensible, or offers value to others. Additionally, Mishra and Henriksen discussed the Novel, Effective, and Whole (NEW) definition, which includes the extra element of 'whole'. According to them, 'A creative product/process has an element of novelty or uniqueness. It also must be effective (appropriate, valuable) in its given context'. Finally, a creative artifact is whole, which speaks to the style, make, or crafting of the process/product, and its "fit" within a specific context. We decided to utilize this definition because of its application in lesson planning and educational contexts [31]. As mentioned earlier in our scheme, the content will point to the assessment. Assessments of creativity in education are divided between psychological and educational research, emphasizing cognitive aspects. They are generally broad, focusing on divergent thinking, self-report questionnaires, and subjective product-based techniques [30]. We are focusing on assessing the product because we want to rely on practical applications from classroom settings that are important in education research. The evaluation of the product, meaning the LD through the rubrics, could give us this advantage. It also gives opportunities for reflection through self and peer evaluation.

Afterward, we pointed out the frameworks of LD with technology and the frameworks that are associated with creativity. These will guide us by giving the teachers a practical and conceptual method for designing their LDs. We have found four key frameworks for learning design with technology. The first one is the conversational framework by Laurillard [32]. Her framework speaks of six types of activities designed to assist students in their learning journey. The educators utilize them to create learning experiences that effectively incorporate technology. The elements include acquisition, inquiry, discussion, practice, collaboration, and production. Another important framework is the 7Cs by Conole. According to this, there are seven phases when designing: conceptualize, capture, create, communicate, collaborate, consider, and consolidate. Then we have the four Ts framework introduced by Pozzi and Persico. The framework aids in decision-making and instructional planning concerning tasks, teams, technology, and time in computer-supported collaborative learning environments. We argue that these frameworks in learning design are important when creating a lesson plan or, in our case, training. Because we need technology integration as a necessary component in our approach, we decided to eliminate these frameworks and move to more technology-based approaches, like the TPACK learning design framework, Triple E, and SAMR [33].

Lastly, we consider design factors for technology integration, TPDs, and teachers' creativity. For the first group, we have found recent literature that points to these criteria [34]:

a. Evidence of student learning;
b. Relevance and reflection;
c. Support and follow-up;
d. Student's voice;
e. Learner-centered;
f. Initial implementation with teacher leaders.

These components were aligned with those of effective TPD.

For the second group, which is TPDs in teachers' creativity, we have found recent literature that points to the following criteria: reflection on creative resources, comprehension of creativity, provision of creative routines that are simple to modify and execute, and the scaffolding of creative risk-taking. These two design concepts, along with our main concept, which is the effective TPD, will be horizontally aligned with our other variables [35]. Encircling the prey phase has ended. In this phase, we have gathered the most important and relevant literature on what effective training for creative learning design with technology means.

The second phase of the WOA, as it is presented in Figure 3, is called the bubble-net attack. In this stage, we move to the closest optimal solution by illuminating those that do not fit and at the same time search for new ones, near the chosen ones that will enhance them. We illuminate design factors that are relevant to school policies, like the initial implementation of school leaders. We also illuminate design parameters like 'evidence of student outcomes. This design of TPD is implemented on an initial state, before implementation in the classroom. For the enhancement of parameters, we use the first grouping, which is the 'effective TPD. Thus, the first important parameter that needs to be considered is the collaborative methodology of the TPD. We decided on the TPS because research connects this strategy with the enhancement of creativity skills. Furthermore, it provides opportunities for peer assessment and reflection through its stages of pair and share. In that way, we are also serving the assessment criteria of an effective TPD. The second component of the training is the resources. In the previous stage, we decided to use LD graphical tools and the LMS for reflection and sustained duration.

Thirdly, we move to the content of the TPD that is directly associated with the definition and, as a result, with the assessment. We need to know what to evaluate to evaluate it. We decided to rely on the NEW definition by Mishra and Henriksen. The evaluation will be guided by this definition. Furthermore, we decided on LD frameworks like the Triple E and SAMR. In this way, which is called 'spiral update', we try new solutions for the content. Instead of relying only on creative content, we seek technology integration possibilities and models that will help us work creatively when implementing technology. Especially, the Triple E has its rubric that can guide us through the effective technology integration of the LDs. Additionally, the SAMR has its practical hierarchical model, which can guide us in the process of achieving novel use of technology integration. The technology integration models will be employed to form the evaluation of the training.

Lastly, we should mention the design factors for TPD in technology integration and teachers' creativity that were employed. By this, we mean the support follow-up and learner-centered training like in our methodology with TPS, and in addition, the reflection and relevance to the rubrics we have in the evaluation methods. These all adhere to the 'effective TPD'. Secondly, with regards to teachers' creativity and effectiveness interactions, we have a reflection on creative resources (through evaluation methods and LD tools), comprehension of creativity (through definition), and the scaffolding of creative risk-taking (through online tools). Our training in this phase of the WOA has been formatted:

a. There is a collaborative strategy, as indicated by the effectiveness of the TPD criteria. This is TPS. We can have workshops with real-life applications, like the creation of LDs in the pair phase. It is a learner-centered methodology with support from peers.
b. There are resources stored in an LMS, so we have a hybrid and asynchronous experience. Having the content in this format is helpful for us to have a sustained duration. This aids in creative risk-taking. Online opportunities scaffold the process by diminishing the creativity anxiety that is more present in classroom settings. Additionally, LD graphical tools [36] scaffold the process and offer opportunities for reflection.
c. There is specific content that involves the creative product, and it is based on the NEW definition by Mishra and Henriksen. This definition helped us in the creation of the evaluation method, meaning rubrics with the criteria of novel, effective, and whole. We built on technology integration models to form the criteria of effectiveness and novelty. We assumed that effectiveness could be referred to as the 'learner experience', so it can relate to the Triple E and its effectiveness criteria: engagement, enhancement, and extension. We assume that novelty is related to higher levels of technology integration and link this criterion with the SAMR model, which speaks of novel tasks when reaching higher levels of technology integration. We assume that wholeness speaks of the context of a scenario, meaning the design principles and elements that are needed to form the basic structure of an LD. For example, this means alignment of activities with objectives, resources, and roles.
d. We consider the evaluation methods to be rubrics with self and peer assessment that can help us in reflection and feedback.

The TPD has been formatted, and we are in the process of exploring a new solution to see if it serves better.

In the third stage of the WOA (Figure 4), we are in the exploration phase, where we seek other solutions that will be optimal to compare with the already best known.

TPACK, one of the most influential models in technology integration, speaks of knowledge in technology, pedagogy, and content. We are advancing our research and broadening it to other methodologies for better retention of learning and bigger gains in knowledge. Additionally, we need to have coaching, as it is mentioned in the components of effective TPDs. For this reason, we change the methodology and move from the TPS to the Team-based Learning strategy (TBL). TBL is a methodology known for its application in higher education, but also for its positive results in the retention of learning material. TBL has five stages: pre-class preparation, individual readiness assurance test (iRAT), team readiness assurance test (tRAT), clarification session, and application activities. In the pre-class preparation phase, students examine assigned resources such as articles, videos, or textbook sections to establish a foundational understanding. During the iRAT, students complete a quiz to assess their comprehension of the material independently. Following that, in the tRAT, students collaborate in small groups to discuss the same quiz questions and agree on the most accurate answers, enhancing their learning through peer dialogue. In the clarification phase, the instructor addresses any unclear subjects. Subsequently, in the team application activities, groups utilize their knowledge to address real-world challenges regarding their learning material. This method gives us an extra advantage with the tests, as we have one more evaluation method in our training. Additionally, it aids in the mentoring and scaffolding through the classification task. The final phase of the WOA has ended, leading to the exploration of an optimal training solution. The training has the following characteristics:

- It is collaborative and hands-on (effective TPD). Indeed, we use the collaborative strategy TBL, which has application tasks, meaning co-creation of LDs.
- It has a sustained duration (effective TPD), as it is designed for a hybrid or online environment. We use the Moodle LMS, where we can store the educational material to be used by the learner for a considerable amount of time.
- It is subject-focused (effective TPD). We focus on content regarding creativity and technology integration, which is the initial purpose of this training, to design an effective TPD on creative technology-enhanced LD. We built on the NEW definition of creative product and translated it into LD principles (completeness), Triple E (learner experience), and SAMR (technology integration).
- It provides opportunities for feedback and reflection with the evaluation methods that use peer and self-assessment. (Design factors for teachers' creativity TPDs).
- There is support and follow-up (design factors for technology integration, TPDs) through the LD tool.

This is our training. In the next section, we will show how we validate our decisions based on a concrete and reliable mathematical model, the MCMC.

5. The Markov Chain Monte Carlo in Creative Learning Design with Technology

In this section, we incorporate a more rigorous definition of the optimization objective and explicitly present the mathematical and algorithmic backbone of our hybrid WOA and MCMC approach. Our goal is to optimize a TPD program for creativity in technology-enhanced learning design. We have used a linear regression model using one response variable and five main independent variables. The model is formulated in (1):

$$Y = \beta_0 + \beta_1 X_1 + \beta_2 X_2 + \beta_3 X_3 + \beta_4 X_4 + \beta_5 X_5 + \varepsilon, \quad (1)$$

where:

Y: Response variable—the effectiveness of the TPD in creative learning design with technology (measured through implementation success, creativity in lesson plans, etc.);
X_1: Methodology (e.g., TPS, TBL);
X_2: Resources (e.g., LMS, learning design tools);
X_3: Content and Evaluation (e.g., use of NEW definition: Novel, Effective, Whole);
X_4: Frameworks/Models (e.g., Triple E, SAMR, TPACK);
X_5: Design Factors (e.g., collaboration, reflection, student voice);
ε: Standard error with normal distribution [0, 1].

The MCMC method is used to iteratively evaluate and refine the model's parameters to maximize its predictive accuracy. MCMC sampling represents a strong class of algorithms used for extracting samples from probability distributions when direct sampling is difficult. In our paper, we integrated WOA with MCMC. This approach offers a sampling method that is more dynamic and exploratory while maintaining a probabilistic framework, ensuring it remains focused yet searches efficiently. WOA identified new areas, while MCMC determined where to proceed based on probability. In other words, we utilized WOA to find initial solutions in 'enriching the prey' and 'searching for prey' and then used the MCMC to decide, with accurate mathematical modeling, which decisions are best suited during the exploitation phase. In the exploration phase, we gathered data based on these three classifications that encompass different interactions in and between them:

(1) Effective TPDs.
(2) Effective TPD in technology-enhanced LD.
(3) Effective TPD in teachers' creativity.

In the multiple linear regression equation, the coefficients, β_1, β_2, β_3, β_4, and β_5, are the regression coefficients. Each coefficient quantifies the relationship between its corresponding independent variable and the dependent variable y, holding other variables constant. The term β_0 is the constant term. It signifies the expected value of y when all independent variables X_1, X_2, X_3, X_4, and X_5 are zero. Before starting the Markov Chain, we need to initialize the parameters (Figure 5). Thanks to WOA, we have a very good starting point, as elaborated in the concept maps in the previous section. During this stage, we found that the methodology, resources, content/evaluation, framework/models design factors of the TPD, and design elements are important when designing this training. These are the variables of the MCMC equation, which are aligned conceptually with the aspects of effective TPD (collaborative, hands-on, sustained duration, providing opportunities for reflection and feedback, etc.), and follow our theme, which is creativity in technology-enhanced learning design (Figure 6). Thus, the next step is to use the MCMC and find the best solutions. The initialization has already been done through the WOA. The next step is to generate samples from the distribution, and then we move to the iteration process, where we repeat the sampling process until convergence to the desired distribution. We assume that all the variables can have a normal distribution:

$\beta_0 \sim N(\mu_0, \sigma_0^2)$
$\beta_1 \sim N(\mu_1, \sigma_1^2)$
$\beta_2 \sim N(\mu_2, \sigma_2^2)$
$\beta_3 \sim N(\mu_3, \sigma_3^2)$
$\beta_4 \sim N(\mu_4, \sigma_4^2)$
$\beta_5 \sim N(\mu_5, \sigma_5^2)$

Pseudocode: Hybrid WOA-MCMC for TPD Optimization

```
Input:
    Data matrix X (n x 5), response vector Y (n x 1)
    Number of iterations N
    Initial beta vector β = [β0, β1, β2, β3, β4, β5]
    Proposal variance σ²_proposal
    Prior variance σ²_prior
    Likelihood variance σ²_likelihood (or estimate it)
Initialize:
    β_current = initial β (e.g., [0, 0, 0, 0, 0, 0])
    Store β_samples = []
For i in 1 to N:
    Propose β_new from a proposal distribution:
        β_new ~ Normal (β_current, σ²_proposal * I)
    Compute log-likelihoods:
        logL current = log Gaussian (Y | X * β_current, σ²_likelihood)
        logL new     = log Gaussian (Y | X * β_new, σ²_likelihood)
    Compute log priors:
        logP_current = log Gaussian (β_current | 0, σ²_prior)
        logP_new     = log Gaussian (β_new | 0, σ²_prior)
    Compute the log acceptance ratio:
        log_accept_ratio = (logL_new + logP_new) − (logL_current + logP_current)
    Draw u ~ Uniform (0, 1)
    If log(u) < log_accept_ratio:
        Accept β_new, β_current = β_new
    Append β_current to β_samples Output:
    β_samples (matrix of posterior samples)
```

Figure 5. Pseudocode.

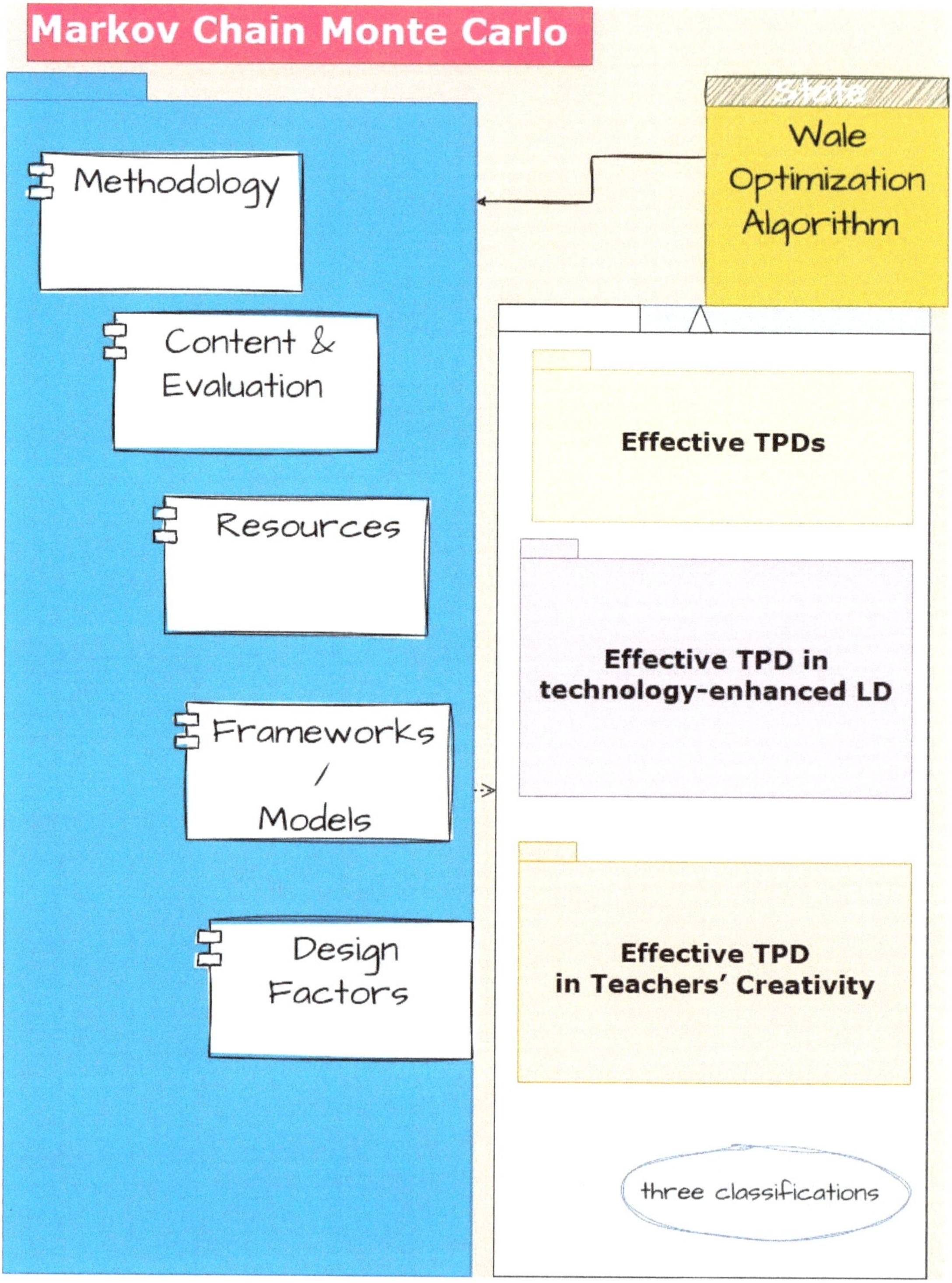

Figure 6. The whale optimization algorithm and Markov Chain Monte Carlo-based approach.

We created samples:

a. $\beta_0^{(0)}$ from $\beta_0^{(1)}$ using F ($\beta_0 \mid \beta_1^{(0)}, \beta_2^{(0)}, \beta_3^{(0)}, \beta_4^{(0)}, \beta_5^{(0)}$)
b. $\beta_1^{(0)}$ from $\beta_1^{(1)}$ using F ($\beta_1 \mid \beta_0^{(1)}, \beta_2^{(0)}, \beta_3^{(0)}, \beta_4^{(0)}, \beta_5^{(0)}$)
c. $\beta_2^{(0)}$ from $\beta_2^{(1)}$ using F ($\beta_2 \mid \beta_0^{(1)}, \beta_1^{(1)}, \beta_3^{(0)}, \beta_4^{(0)}, \beta_5^{(0)}$)
d. $\beta_3^{(0)}$ from $\beta_3^{(1)}$ using F ($\beta_3 \mid \beta_0^{(1)}, \beta_1^{(1)}, \beta_2^{(1)}, \beta_4^{(1)}, \beta_5^{(0)}$)
e. $\beta_4^{(0)}$ from $\beta_4^{(1)}$ using F ($\beta_3 \mid \beta_0^{(1)}, \beta_1^{(1)}, \beta_2^{(1)}, \beta_4^{(1)}, \beta_5^{(0)}$)
f. $\beta_5^{(0)}$ from $\beta_5^{(1)}$ using F ($\beta_3 \mid \beta_0^{(1)}, \beta_1^{(1)}, \beta_2^{(1)}, \beta_4^{(1)}, \beta_5^{(0)}$)

For each of the samples, we have a different value in β. This parameter affects the independent variable of X. The way and how much they are affected by us are shown by advancing the value of β.

EXPLANATION

- Step 1: Initialize a vector of parameters $\beta^{(0)} = [\beta_0^{(0)}, \beta_1^{(0)}, \beta_2^{(0)}, \beta_3^{(0)}, \beta_4^{(0)}, \beta_5^{(0)}]$
- Step 2: We consider a conditional mass function $\beta_0 \backslash \beta_1^{(0)}, \beta_2^{(0)}, \beta_3^{(0)}, \beta_4^{(0)}, \beta_5^{(0)}$ so we estimate/generate the Conditional Probability, Density Function (CPDF), F ($\beta_0^{(1)} \backslash \beta_1^{(0)}, \beta_2^{(0)}, \beta_3^{(0)}, \beta_4^{(0)}, \beta_5^{(0)}$).
- Step 3: We consider a conditional mass function $\beta_1 \backslash \beta_0^{(1)}, \beta_2^{(0)}, \beta_3^{(0)}, \beta_4^{(0)}, \beta_5^{(0)}$ so we estimate/generate the CPDF, F ($\beta_0^{(1)} \backslash \beta_0^{(1)}, \beta_2^{(0)}, \beta_3^{(0)}, \beta_4^{(0)}, \beta_5^{(0)}$).
- Step 4: We consider a conditional mass function $\beta_2 \backslash \beta_0^{(1)}, \beta_1^{(1)}, \beta_3^{(0)}, \beta_4^{(0)}, \beta_5^{(0)}$ so we estimate/generate the CPDF, F ($\beta_2^{(1)} \backslash \beta_0^{(1)}, \beta_1^{(1)}, \beta_3^{(0)}, \beta_4^{(0)}, \beta_5^{(0)}$)
- Step 5: We consider a conditional mass function $\beta_3 \backslash \beta_0^{(1)}, \beta_1^{(1)}, \beta_2^{(1)}, \beta_4^{(0)}, \beta_5^{(0)}$ so we estimate/generate the CPDF, F ($\beta_3^{(1)} \backslash \beta_0^{(1)}, \beta_1^{(1)}, \beta_2^{(1)}, \beta_4^{(0)}, \beta_5^{(0)}$)
- Step 6: We consider a conditional mass function $\beta_4 \backslash \beta_0^{(1)}, \beta_1^{(1)}, \beta_2^{(1)}, \beta_3^{(1)}, \beta_5^{(0)}$ so we estimate/generate the CPDF, F ($\beta_4^{(1)} \backslash \beta_0^{(1)}, \beta_1^{(1)}, \beta_2^{(1)}, \beta_3^{(1)}, \beta_5^{(0)}$).
- Step 7: We consider a conditional mass function $\beta_5 \backslash \beta_0^{(1)}, \beta_1^{(1)}, \beta_2^{(1)}, \beta_3^{(1)}, \beta_4^{(1)}$ so we estimate/generate the CPDF, F ($\beta_5^{(1)} \backslash \beta_0^{(1)}, \beta_1^{(1)}, \beta_2^{(1)}, \beta_3^{(1)}, \beta_4^{(1)}$).

So now we have successfully generated the β (1) = $[\beta_0^{(1)}, \beta_1^{(1)}, \beta_2^{(1)}, \beta_3^{(1)}, \beta_4^{(1)}, \beta_5^{(1)}]$.

We iterate this procedure N times, where N is a large enough number for us to understand where the vector β converges. This describes how this MCMC algorithm works.

For instance, in our proposal methodology, we conduct five (5) different samples. We search in the literature for methodology regarding effective TPDs, effective TPDs in technology-enhanced LD, and effective TPDs in teachers' creativity. Our variables are:

- In equation (β_0), we introduce the variables as parameters.
- In the first equation (β_1). We have the methodology of a TPD, so we search accordingly.
- In the second equation, we search for resources (β_2).
- In the third equation, we search for content and evaluation (β_3).
- In the fourth equation, we add frameworks or models (β_4).
- In the fifth equation, we add design factors (β_5).

In every sample, we conduct literature reviews. In the first, we have a sample of methodologies in TPDs, like mentoring or collaborative strategies. Literature has indicated that collaboration is important in TPDs. We continue with literature regarding collaborative methods and effective TPDs in our second equation. We see strategies like TPS or TBL in TPDs. We have decided on the TPS because it enhances creative skills. We are moving to another equation, adding also the TPD in technology-enhanced LD. This speaks of collaborative workshops like the Carpe Diem or ABC. We implement application tasks in the TPD. In the final equation, we add TPD to teachers' creativity.

With this, we have also added recent articles regarding collaborative creativity and its positive impact on PD. We find convergence through TPS and application tasks involving the co-creation of LDs. To avoid getting trapped in local optima, we also consider utilizing the TBL methodology. This way, we also use the principles of WOA that speak of finding the balance between exploration and exploitation. For the other components, we do the same procedure. The exploration was used only in our methodology, as this is a crucial component that affects and changes all other variables. We continue with the other independent variables (resources, content/evaluation, frameworks/models, design factors) until we find convergence and create optimal training.

The process indicated training that is collaborative using TBL and application tasks. Additionally, it has content/evaluation regarding creativity definition and technology integration models. We considered design factors like support and learner-centered, relevance, and reflection by using the TBL that provides opportunities for the cultivation of all of these.

In response to concerns regarding methodological ambiguity, we have undertaken a comprehensive revision of the methods section, with particular emphasis on the adaptation and implementation of the WOA and the MCMC approach within the educational domain. Specifically, the WOA was operationalized by encoding candidate solutions as distinct configurations of instructional design parameters—namely, content sequencing, integration of multimedia elements, and frequency of learner–system interaction. The fitness function was formulated to evaluate these configurations based on composite metrics of learner engagement and knowledge retention, weighted according to empirically derived pedagogical priorities. The search space and parameter constraints were delineated in alignment with established instructional design principles and practical feasibility considerations. Concurrently, the MCMC approach was employed to infer posterior distributions of instructional effectiveness, conditional on observed learning outcomes. The implementation utilizes a sampling procedure and diagnostic assessments (e.g., convergence statistics) as future work to ensure the validity of the resulting distributions. Figure 6 has been accordingly updated to include annotated algorithmic steps, elucidating the iterative processes involved.

Furthermore, the optimal instructional designs are explicitly defined as those that jointly maximize engagement and learning performance, subject to contextual constraints such as available instructional time and technological resources. All variables in the regression model are explicitly defined, and their inclusion is theoretically grounded in established learning theories, including Cognitive Load Theory (CLT) and Self-Determination Theory (SDT). Empirical literature supporting the relevance of each predictor has been integrated to substantiate model specification. A dedicated subsection introduces the theoretical framework underlying the regression analysis, thereby addressing concerns of analytic formalism. Moreover, the limitations inherent in applying a linear model to complex educational phenomena are acknowledged, and a non-parametric model was additionally fitted as a robustness check, yielding convergent results in terms of predictor importance. From a practical point of view, CLT and SDT are psychological frameworks that can inform the design of instructional systems. On the other hand, MCMC and WOA are computational methods used for inference and optimization. Integrating these allows for a theoretically grounded and empirically efficient approach to educational design. They can work together in various areas as theoretical foundations as constraints, and objectives, in statistical inference to validate theory-driven assumptions, via MCMC, in a feedback loop between MCMC and WOA, and finally in various educational practical examples. Integrating CLT and SDT with MCMC and WOA creates a **hybrid model** where theory constrains and guides algorithmic exploration, and empirical inference refines the theoretical model. This supports **evidence-based instructional design** that is both adaptive and pedagogically sound.

6. Conclusions and Future Remarks

In this section, we will analyze the hypotheses we had when designing the WOA-MCMC approach to create an optimal solution for creative technology-enhanced learning design. Firstly, we address the research questions that were stated in the introduction section, and we answer them.

RQ1: Is there a combination of methods, resources, content, assessment, and duration that is optimal when designing a TPD for creativity in technology-enhanced learning design? As written in this article, many variables need to be considered when addressing technology-enhanced learning design in a TPD. Training becomes even more complex when adding abstract and multifaceted themes such as creativity. The first thing we need to do is classify our components, so we know what we are searching for. These are a. Effective TPD components, b. Effective technology-enhanced TPD components and c. Effective TPD in teachers' creativity. For the first issue, we have a literature review that points out the following effectiveness criteria: content focus; active learning techniques; collaborative; they draw on effective practice models; coaching and expert guidance; time for feedback and self-reflection; and sustained duration. Based on these, we concluded on content, methods, resources, evaluation, models, and design factors. For the second cluster, which is the technology-enhanced LD in TPD, we must search for scientific literature regarding LD and technology. The literature has pointed out the technology integration design factors in TPDs. These are: evidence of student learning, relevance and reflection, support and follow-up, student voice, learner-centered, and initial implementation with teacher leaders. We consider them. Lastly, we focus on TPDs in teacher creativity. Research has pointed out a focus on understanding the concept of creativity and its practical implementation. Additionally, scaffolding creative risk, reflecting on creative resources, and developing creative routines are also important. We connect the dots by illuminating parameters that are not relevant or not in the recent highly cited bibliography. We enhance components by incorporating them with close solutions. We concluded with a collaborative method like TBL with application tasks (hands-on), like the co-creation of LDs and coaching through a clarification session. Additionally, content is related to NEW parameters enhanced by technology integration models like SAMR or TripleE. We have self and peer evaluation of the LD for the advancement of reflection through the rubrics of these models. Lastly, the sustained duration can easily be implemented through asynchronous material in an LMS, providing the necessary enhancement of time and flexibility.

RQ2: Can WOA be used as a method to obtain optimal solutions when designing training in creative learning design? The WOA was very helpful, especially in the conceptualization of the process and in filtering the existing literature review. It can help with optimizing training programs because of its value in exploring and exploiting solution spaces efficiently. The educational research has a few examples of WOA. Especially when modeling, it could be a valuable and reliable tool and a novel approach. The Structured Equation Model (SEM) is dominant in statistical modeling in educational research and especially in teacher education. However, SEM is well-known for showing the relationships between factors already defined. The existence of pre-established concepts or hypotheses is crucial to SEM research [37]. However, creativity is a dynamic, complex, and multifaceted phenomenon. Thus, implementing algorithms, such as WOA, that help us solve complex and uncertain problems, could potentially add value to the optimization of processes, like designing an optimal training involving creativity. In this realm, theories are many theories, so we need to begin the process with all of them and all their interactions, and not only start from one theory, like in deductive modelling processes.

RQ3: Can MCMC help us validate this training in creative learning design in a TPD, giving the expected accuracy to our proposed results? The MCMC helped us achieve great accuracy in our results. This would not be possible if we did not use this technique. MCMC is a very well-known mathematical model that has applications in almost all fields and educational settings. It is a great modeling tool in quantitative research. We suggest that it can be of great value even in unstructured data, like creativity and technology-enhanced learning design. Common WOA critique [9] is about finding the balance between exploration and exploitation. With MCMC, we have reliability in the decision-making procedure. Furthermore, in the conceptualization of the initial parameters, we do not rely on MCMC, which is not ideal as it distributes randomly, but we rely on WOA and its target solutions that have already been initiated.

To sum up, we found that stochastic models can be of great value in social sciences and educational research, especially when involving multifaceted concepts like creativity, LD, and technology. In our training, we used a narrative literature review to design and evaluate. WOA helped us in finding the right exploration and exploitation areas and conceptualizing the design process. MCMC helped us in the validation of the outcome/training, making a more accurate analysis. For future work, case studies or other methods can be employed for the evaluation of this approach, providing evidence-based research for its validity. Additionally, this hybrid methodology could be validated by benchmark tests to further explore it from an algorithmic perspective. In addition, we should mention that mathematical models offer insights into model consequences and are simpler to falsify. They could also produce extensive data, which improves analysis. Because of these, we propose that it could be of great value during the design process, before reaching the application stage. In educational research literature reviews, we do not find many cases involving design processes through algorithms like WOA or MCMC. This was a limitation when we were searching for similar scientific cases.

Author Contributions: Conceptualization, K.R. and D.K.; methodology, K.R. and D.K.; validation, K.R., D.K. and Y.P.; formal analysis, K.R. and D.K.; investigation, K.R. and D.K.; resources, D.K.; data curation, D.K. and Y.P.; writing—original draft preparation, K.R. and D.K.; writing—review and editing, D.K. and Y.P.; visualization, K.R.; supervision, Y.P.; project administration, D.K.; funding acquisition, D.K. All authors have read and agreed to the published version of the manuscript.

Funding: This research received no external funding.

Institutional Review Board Statement: Not applicable.

Informed Consent Statement: Not applicable.

Data Availability Statement: In this article published in an MDPI journal, we declare that all data supporting the reported results, including links to publicly archived datasets analyzed or generated during the study, are not subject to confidentiality or ethical restrictions. There are no other data for this specific study, other than those that support the conclusions of this article. All data in the article are made available by the authors for future research purposes.

Conflicts of Interest: The authors declare no conflicts of interest.

Abbreviations

The following abbreviations are used in this manuscript:

LD	Learning Design
TPD	Teacher's Professional Development
TPACK	Technological Pedagogical Content Knowledge
SAMR	Substitution, Augmentation, Modification, Redefinition
TPS	Think, Pair, Share
TBL	Team-Based Learning

WOA	Whale Optimization Algorithm
MCMC	Markov Chain Monte Carlo
iRAT	Individual Readiness Assurance Test
tRAT	Team Readiness Assurance Test
NEW	Novel, Effective, Whole
SMART	Specific, Measurable, Achievable, Relevant, and Time-bound
LMS	Learning Management System
SEM	Structural Equation Model

References

1. Rigopouli, K.; Kotsifakos, D.; Psaromiligkos, Y. Vygotsky's Creativity Options and Ideas in 21st-Century Technology-Enhanced Learning Design. *Educ. Sci.* **2025**, *15*, 257. [CrossRef]
2. González-Pérez, L.I.; Ramírez-Montoya, M.S. Components of Education 4.0 in 21st Century Skills Frameworks: Systematic Review. *Sustainability* **2022**, *14*, 1493. [CrossRef]
3. Mishra, P.; Warr, M.; Islam, R. TPACK in the Age of ChatGPT and Generative AI. *J. Digit. Learn. Teach. Educ.* **2023**, *39*, 235–251. [CrossRef]
4. Yeh, Y.-F.; Chan, K.K.H.; Hsu, Y.-S. Toward a Framework That Connects Individual TPACK and Collective TPACK: A Systematic Review of TPACK Studies Investigating Teacher Collaborative Discourse in the Learning by Design Process. *Comput. Educ.* **2021**, *171*, 104238. [CrossRef]
5. Henriksen, D.; Creely, E.; Henderson, M.; Mishra, P. Creativity and Technology in Teaching and Learning: A Literature Review of the Uneasy Space of Implementation. *Educ. Technol. Res. Dev.* **2021**, *69*, 2091–2108. [CrossRef]
6. Han, W.; Abdrahim, N.A. The Role of Teachers' Creativity in Higher Education: A Systematic Literature Review and Guidance for Future Research. *Think. Ski. Creat.* **2023**, *48*, 101302. [CrossRef]
7. Wasson, B.; Kirschner, P.A. Learning Design: European Approaches. *TechTrends* **2020**, *64*, 815–827. [CrossRef]
8. Nugraheni, C.E.; Abednego, L.; Saputra, C.S. Whale Optimization Algorithms for Multi-Objective Flowshop Scheduling Problems. *Eurasia Proc. Sci. Technol. Eng. Math.* **2022**, *21*, 441–451. [CrossRef]
9. Nadimi-Shahraki, M.H.; Zamani, H.; Asghari Varzaneh, Z.; Mirjalili, S. A Systematic Review of the Whale Optimization Algorithm: Theoretical Foundation, Improvements, and Hybridizations. *Arch. Comput. Methods Eng.* **2023**, *30*, 4113–4159. [CrossRef]
10. Yang, H. The Effects of Professional Development Experience on Teacher Self-Efficacy: Analysis of an International Dataset Using Bayesian Multilevel Models. *Prof. Dev. Educ.* **2020**, *46*, 797–811. [CrossRef]
11. Mishra, P.; Henriksen, D. *Creativity, Technology & Education: Exploring Their Convergence*; Springer: Berlin/Heidelberg, Germany, 2017; ISBN 978-3-319-70275-9.
12. Watson, M.K.; Pelkey, J.; Noyes, C.; Rodgers, M.O. Using Kolb's Learning Cycle to Improve Student Sustainability Knowledge. *Sustainability* **2019**, *11*, 4602. [CrossRef]
13. Blundell, C.N.; Mukherjee, M.; Nykvist, S. A Scoping Review of the Application of the SAMR Model in Research. *Comput. Educ. Open* **2022**, *3*, 100093. [CrossRef]
14. Austero, L.D.; Medina, R.P.; Sison, A.M.; Matias, J.B. Optimizing Faculty Workloads and Room Utilization Using Heuristically Enhanced WOA. *Int. J. Adv. Comput. Sci. Appl.* **2022**, *13*, 554–562. [CrossRef]
15. Thaher, T.; Zaguia, A.; Al Azwari, S.; Mafarja, M.; Chantar, H.; Abuhamdah, A.; Turabieh, H.; Mirjalili, S.; Sheta, A. An Enhanced Evolutionary Student Performance Prediction Model Using Whale Optimization Algorithm Boosted with Sine-Cosine Mechanism. *Appl. Sci.* **2021**, *11*, 10237. [CrossRef]
16. Zhou, Y.; Niu, Y.; Luo, Q.; Jiang, M. Teaching Learning-Based Whale Optimization Algorithm for Multi-Layer Perceptron Neural Network Training. *Math. Biosci. Eng.* **2020**, *17*, 5987–6025. [CrossRef]
17. Schuetze, B.A. A Computational Model of School Achievement. *Educ. Psychol. Rev.* **2024**, *36*, 18. [CrossRef]
18. Li, T. Markov Chain Monte Carlo Method in the 1990s: A Case Study of the Spread of Mathematical Knowledge. Master's Thesis, University of Chicago, Chicago, IL, USA, 2022.
19. Noskov, M.; Fedotova, I.; Somova, M.; Vainshtein, Y. Mathematical Model for Early Prediction of Learning Success. In Proceedings of the International Scientific and Practical Conference on "Modern Problems of Applied Mathematics and Information Technology (MPAMIT2022)", Namangan, Uzbekistan, 11–12 May 2024; p. 070001.
20. Williams, A. *Markov Chain Monte Carlo Methods for Dynamic Student Assessment*; Department of Mathematics, London School of Economics and Political Science: London, UK, 2024. Available online: https://osf.io/preprints/edarxiv/mfwau_v1 (accessed on 29 June 2025).

21. Ji, Z.; Yang, Y. The Application of Markov Chain in Middle School Mathematics Teaching Evaluation. *Educ Reform Dev.* **2024**, *6*, 182–187. [CrossRef]
22. Vulic, J.; Jacobson, M.J.; Levin, J.A. Exploring Education as a Complex System: Computational Educational Research with Multi-Level Agent-Based Modeling. *Educ. Sci.* **2024**, *14*, 551. [CrossRef]
23. Sukhera, J. Narrative Reviews: Flexible, Rigorous, and Practical. *J. Grad. Med. Educ.* **2022**, *14*, 414–417. [CrossRef]
24. Zhao, L.; Liu, X.; Wang, C.; Su, Y.-S. Effect of Different Mind Mapping Approaches on Primary School Students' Computational Thinking Skills during Visual Programming Learning. *Comput. Educ.* **2022**, *181*, 104445. [CrossRef]
25. Yeung, J.; Bautista, A. Definitions of Creativity by Kindergarten Stakeholders: An Interview Study Based on Rhodes' 4P Model. *Creat. Theor. Res. Appl.* **2024**, *11*, 1–19. [CrossRef]
26. Bereczki, E.O.; Kárpáti, A. Technology-Enhanced Creativity: A Multiple Case Study of Digital Technology-Integration Expert Teachers' Beliefs and Practices. *Think. Ski. Creat.* **2021**, *39*, 100791. [CrossRef]
27. Popova, A.; Evans, D.K.; Breeding, M.E.; Arancibia, V. Teacher Professional Development around the World: The Gap between Evidence and Practice. *World Bank Res. Obs.* **2022**, *37*, 107–136. [CrossRef]
28. Zalavra, E.; Papanikolaou, K.; Dimitriadis, Y.; Sgouropoulou, C. Representing Learning Designs in a Design Support Tool. *Educ. Inf. Technol.* **2023**, *28*, 6563–6594. [CrossRef]
29. Sternberg, R.J.; Karami, S. An 8P Theoretical Framework for Understanding Creativity and Theories of Creativity. *J. Creat. Behav.* **2022**, *56*, 55–78. [CrossRef]
30. Runco, M.A. Updating the Standard Definition of Creativity to Account for the Artificial Creativity of AI. *Creat. Res. J.* **2025**, *37*, 1–5. [CrossRef]
31. Henriksen, D.; Mishra, P.; Mehta, R. Novel, Effective, Whole: Toward a NEW Framework for Evaluations of Creative Products. *J. Technol. Teach. Educ.* **2015**, *23*, 455–478.
32. Asensio-Pérez, J.I.; Dimitriadis, Y.; Pozzi, F.; Hernández-Leo, D.; Prieto, L.P.; Persico, D.; Villagrá-Sobrino, S.L. Towards Teaching as Design: Exploring the Interplay between Full-Lifecycle Learning Design Tooling and Teacher Professional Development. *Comput. Educ.* **2017**, *114*, 92–116. [CrossRef]
33. Bower, M.; Vlachopoulos, P. A Critical Analysis of Technology-enhanced Learning Design Frameworks. *Br. J. Educ. Technol.* **2018**, *49*, 981–997. [CrossRef]
34. Yurtseven Avci, Z.; O'Dwyer, L.M.; Lawson, J. Designing Effective Professional Development for Technology Integration in Schools. *J. Comput. Assist. Learn.* **2020**, *36*, 160–177. [CrossRef]
35. Anderson, R.C.; Katz-Buonincontro, J.; Bousselot, T.; Mattson, D.; Beard, N.; Land, J.; Livie, M. How Am I a Creative Teacher? Beliefs, Values, and Affect for Integrating Creativity in the Classroom. *Teach. Teach. Educ.* **2022**, *110*, 103583. [CrossRef]
36. Boloudakis, M.; Retalis, S.; Psaromiligkos, Y. Training Novice Teachers to Design Moodle-based Units of Learning Using a CADMOS-enabled Learning Design Sprint. *Br. J. Educ. Technol.* **2018**, *49*, 1059–1076. [CrossRef]
37. Hair, J.F.; Hult, G.T.M.; Ringle, C.M.; Sarstedt, M.; Danks, N.P.; Ray, S. An Introduction to Structural Equation Modeling. In *Partial Least Squares Structural Equation Modeling (PLS-SEM) Using R*; Classroom Companion: Business; Springer: Cham, Switzerland, 2021; pp. 1–29. [CrossRef]

algorithms

Article

AI-Enhanced PBL and Experiential Learning for Communication and Career Readiness: An Engineering Pilot Course

Estefanía Avilés Mariño [1,*] and Antonio Sarasa Cabezuelo [2,*]

[1] Department of Linguistics Applied to Science and Technology, Escuela Técnica Superior de Ingenieros de Telecomunicaciones, Universidad Politécnica de Madrid, Av. Complutense, 30, Moncloa-Aravaca, 28040 Madrid, Spain

[2] Departamento de Sistemas Informáticos y Computación, Facultad de Informática, Universidad Complutense de Madrid, Calle del Prof. José García Santesmases, 9, Moncloa-Aravaca, 28040 Madrid, Spain

* Correspondence: estefania.aviles@upm.es (E.A.M.); asarasa@ucm.es (A.S.C.)

Abstract

This study investigates the utilisation of AI tools, including Grammarly Free, QuillBot Free, Canva Free Individual, and others, to enhance learning outcomes for 180 s-year telecommunications engineering students at Universidad Politécnica de Madrid. This research incorporates teaching methods like problem-based learning, experiential learning, task-based learning, and content–language integrated learning, with English as the medium of instruction. These tools were strategically used to enhance language skills, foster computational thinking, and promote critical problem-solving. A control group comprising 120 students who did not receive AI support was included in the study for comparative analysis. The control group's role was essential in evaluating the impact of AI tools on learning outcomes by providing a baseline for comparison. The results indicated that the pilot group, utilising AI tools, demonstrated superior performance compared to the control group in listening comprehension (98.79% vs. 90.22%) and conceptual understanding (95.82% vs. 84.23%). These findings underscore the significance of these skills in enhancing communication and problem-solving abilities within the field of engineering. The assessment of the pilot course's forum revealed a progression from initially error-prone and brief responses to refined, evidence-based reflections in participants. This evolution in responses significantly contributed to the high success rate of 87% in conducting complex contextual analyses by pilot course participants. Subsequent to these results, a project for educational innovation aims to implement the AI-PBL-CLIL model at Universidad Politécnica de Madrid from 2025 to 2026. Future research should look into adaptive AI systems for personalised learning and study the long-term effects of AI integration in higher education. Furthermore, collaborating with industry partners can significantly enhance the practical application of AI-based methods in engineering education. These strategies facilitate benchmarking against international standards, provide structured support for skill development, and ensure the sustained retention of professional competencies, ultimately elevating the international recognition of Spain's engineering education.

Keywords: artificial intelligence in education; problem-based learning; engineering education; content and language integrated learning; digital competencies; higher-order thinking skills; educational innovation; STEM pedagogy; AI-enhanced learning; telecommunications engineering

https://doi.org/10.3390/a18100634

1. Introduction

The rapid evolution of engineering professions demands a blend of technical expertise and soft skills, yet studies consistently highlight deficiencies in communication, critical thinking, and problem-solving among engineering graduates [1,2]. These skills, essential for academic success and career readiness, are often undertaught in traditional engineering curricula, which prioritise technical proficiency over abstract reasoning and adaptability [3]. For instance, surveys of engineering employers indicate that ineffective communication, such as the inability to collaborate in team projects, and limited creative problem-solving skills, demonstrated by a lack of innovative solutions in real-world challenges, hinder graduates' employability [4,5]. This gap is particularly pronounced in handling hypothetical or unstructured scenarios, where students often seek rote solutions or virtual assistance rather than developing autonomous, innovative approaches [6]. Moreover, evidence suggests that neglecting soft skills and focusing on technical education may impede cognitive development and neural plasticity, limiting students' ability to navigate complex professional environments [7,8].

In response to these challenges, engineering education is increasingly adopting innovative pedagogical approaches, active methodologies, listed in the following lines. Problem-Based Learning (PBL) enhances critical thinking and problem-solving skills by immersing students in authentic, real-life problems, encouraging them to analyse, strategise, and collaborate to find solutions [1,9]. Experiential-Based Learning (EBL) boosts motivation and active participation by immersing students in hands-on experiences, equipping them with the skills and confidence needed for real-world challenges [9]. Task-Based Learning (TBL) cultivates resilience, facilitates stress management, and nurtures self-reliance by encouraging students to independently tackle unexpected assignments, fostering adaptability and confidence [5]. PBL fosters higher-order thinking skills (HOTs), autonomy, and creative problem-solving by engaging students in open-ended challenges [9,10]. EBL, through real-world or simulated scenarios, enhances motivation and cognitive engagement, preparing students for professional contexts [11]. TBL promotes resilience and stress management by encouraging students to address unexpected tasks independently [12]. The methodologies of Problem-Based Learning (PBL), Experiential-Based Learning (EBL), and Task-Based Learning (TBL) are tailored to meet the criteria of international organizations and top engineering firms, which prioritise candidates exhibiting exceptional communication skills, emotional intelligence, and adaptability [7].

An important development in current teaching methods is combining Information and Communication Technology (ICT) and Artificial Intelligence (AI), which are changing how engineering education is approached [13,14]. AI-powered tools like smart tutoring systems and automated feedback processes improve logical thinking, motivation, and problem-solving skills [15,16]. In professional settings, AI is becoming indispensable, with applications in data analysis, decision-making, and process optimisation, making its inclusion in education essential for career preparedness [17]. However, there are ongoing debates about the ideal integration of AI in education, with some experts arguing for a balanced approach that combines AI tools with traditional teaching methods, while others advocate for a more technology-centric educational system. Some studies warn against excessive dependence on technology over essential human skills [18], while others see AI as a driver for personalised learning and skill enhancement [19]. This study introduces a pilot course designed for 180 s-year Spanish telecommunication engineering students.

The course combines Problem-Based Learning (PBL), Experience-Based Learning (EBL), and Team-Based Learning (TBL) with Artificial Intelligence (AI) and Information and Communication Technology (ICT) to address the soft skills gap. The course utilises AI-driven simulations, such as virtual business challenges and entrepreneurial simulations, along with feedback systems to create realistic scenarios that enhance students' communication, critical thinking, and adaptability skills. The main goal is to assess how well this AI-enhanced teaching method enhances students' soft skills such as communication, critical thinking, and adaptability, as well as their career readiness in terms of industry-specific skills and professional development. Preliminary findings indicate notable enhancements in students' communication fluency, abstract reasoning abilities, and stress management skills. These findings present a model that can be expanded and adapted for engineering education, highlighting the potential impact on students' soft skills development [4]. This work contributes to the expanding field of AI in education by analysing how AI algorithms can enhance hands-on learning experiences, thereby aligning academic preparation with industry requirements and contributing to foster a more seamless transition for students into professional settings.

1.1. Specific Terminology Used in This Paper

To better understand the content and analysis provided in the following paper, some terms and tools have been defined below so that their particular use within the research could be better understood:

Critical thinking: This paper analyses this skill as an individual's capability of analysing, evaluating and judging information. Alongside other thinking approaches such as Creative thinking, Deep Thinking and Computational thinking, the perspective from which this skill is approached is that of going beyond abstract thinking—as supposedly acquired during youth—and enabling students to create, promote problem solving skills and in-depth comprehension [7,20].

Real-world challenges: Also called authentic or real-life, the term refers to mock-up situations which mimic problems and challenges found in telecommunication contexts to better prepare students for their professional lives.

Soft skills: communication, personal, interpersonal, cultural, thinking, leadership, creative and problem-solving skills [20].

Cognitive development: This focuses on an individual's capability of communicating and thinking critically added to reflective and deep thinking skills [1,7].

Neural plasticity: This refers to the brain's capability of storing words, meanings and contexts, making connections with new information and prompting individuals learning-acquisition processes [7,21].

Active methodologies: These are innovative instruction approaches having students as the centre of the learning acquisition process, fostering critical thinking, problem-solving and creative skills in authentic contexts [9,21].

Higher Order Thinking Skills (HOTs): According to Bloom's taxonomy, this refers to individual's ability to create, evaluate and analyse information [7,9].

Emotional intelligence: This combines assertiveness and empathy, helps individuals to handle oneself and others' emotions to ensure harmonious coexistence [21] (emotional intelligence).

Social constructivist theory: This theory emphasises that knowledge, acquisition and learning occur in social, cultural contexts [1,7].

Overleaf: This is an online application which enables the use of LATEX text edition standard, which is recognised internationally as an open-source software providing book, article, journal and scientific paper accurate design [7,11].

SCRUM: This is an agile management methodology aimed at making an efficient use of time, ensuring goals' completion through sprints or periodic deadlines [11].

Universal Design for Learning (UDL): This aims at scaffolding learning to ensure it is accessible to everybody, fostering diversity, inclusiveness and tolerance [21].

MOOC: This is a massive open online course designed by a university with modules that provide instruction for students and professors [11,20].

Trello: This is an online application used to apply SCRUM methodology [11,20].

1.2. List of AI Tools Used in This Paper

Generative AI: These were used as proofreaders and content generators (contrasted with human output): ChatGPT (GPT-4o mini), DeepSeek (DeepSeek-V3.2-Exp), Grok 3, Gemini 2.5 and Copilot X.

AI for presentation and figure/graph design: Gamma AI and Canva AI. Gamma provides support in designing professional presentations based on a given content, while Canva adds other facilities such as mindmap, flow chart and diagram design, poster and infographics design as well as video design.

AI and social media—Lumen5 AI and BufferAI Free: Lumen was used to create promotional videos out of given written output and upload them to YouTube, while Buffer provided support in increasing visits to X (also known as Twitter) and user traffic administration.

AI for academic and professional writing: Grammarly and QuillBot were used due to their multiple utilities for grammar, expression and clarity enhancement, with aid on antiplagiarism and content review.

ElsaSpeak AI Free Mobile: This AI provides speaking practice and has to be downloaded to the phone. It recreates professional and academic situations where students talk to the AI and this provides personalised feedback.

LumenAI: This AI was utilized for statistical analysis and predictive modeling. Its inclusion was deemed necessary because engineering students are expected to be proficient in these areas, despite the absence of dedicated courses in their curriculum.

2. Materials and Methods

2.1. Study Design and Participants

The pilot course was conducted with a sample of 180 s-year Telecommunication Engineering students at a Spanish university, divided into three groups of approximately 60 students each. Participants' ages ranged from 19 to 22 years, and all had certified English proficiency levels between B2 and C1, assessed via Cambridge English Qualifications (Cambridge TESOL, Cambridge, UK), TOEFL iBT (ETS, Princeton, NJ, USA), or British Council Aptis examinations (Madrid, Spain). English was the primary instructional language to reflect its role as a global communication tool in engineering [22]. Each session lasted 120 min, including a 10-min break, and the course spanned 12 weeks with weekly sessions.

In the context of the second course of the degree of Telecommunication Engineering, the faculty splits students in five groups. Three of the groups were the ones in which this pilot course was implemented, while the other two were used as reference, becoming control groups, in which AI was not implemented, though active methodologies such as PBL and TBL were used in control groups as well.

Two questionnaires were distributed to the five groups: three to the pilot study groups and two to the control group. Both questionnaires, focusing on vocabulary, reading comprehension, and listening, were identical for all five groups. The format of both questionnaires allowed for tracking communication, soft skills, abstract thinking, and critical thinking skills.

2.2. Pedagogical Framework

The course integrated PBL, EBL, TBL, Discovery-Based Learning (DBL), Content and Language Integrated Learning (CLIL), and English as a Medium of Instruction (EMI) to foster soft skills and career readiness. PBL was implemented to promote HOTs and autonomy through open-ended problem-solving [9,10]. EBL provided realistic business and entrepreneurial scenarios to enhance motivation and cognitive engagement [11]. TBL encouraged adaptability and stress management through task-specific challenges [12]. DBL required students to conduct independent research on assigned topics, fostering critical inquiry [21]. CLIL and EMI were used to deliver Telecommunication Engineering, business, and marketing content, enhancing language proficiency alongside technical knowledge [22].

Each group of 60 students was subdivided into smaller cooperative working groups of 3–5 members, following recommendations for optimal group size in active learning methodologies [23,24]. Cooperative learning, based on Johnson and Johnson's model, was prioritised over collaborative approaches to ensure individual accountability and equitable contribution [25]. Group formation was randomised to promote diversity and inclusivity, aligning with Vygotsky's social constructivist theory that emphasises the importance of social interaction and collaboration in learning [26]. Within each group, roles integrate specific ICT and AI tools to simulate real-world engineering and business scenarios, aligning with Vygotsky's social constructivist theory [2]; these roles are described in detail in Appendix A.

2.3. Course Structure and Materials

The course focused on modern technologies in telecommunications, including 5G networks, the Internet of Things (IoT), and applications of artificial intelligence. The course utilised an editable Google Slide (version 1.25.391.01.90) on the Moodle 5.0 learning management system as the primary ICT platform to facilitate collaborative learning and enhance accessibility for students [14]. This method encouraged students' psychological ownership and collaboration through active participation and shared responsibility, in line with research on integrating ICT in higher education [23–27]. Using Google Slides and Moodle is in line with social constructivist teaching principles, focusing on collaborative learning and building knowledge. This integration enhances cognitive development, motivation, and digital fluency among students [28,29]. Aligning topics with the United Nations' Sustainable Development Goals (SDGs) 4, 8, and 9 highlights the course's dedication to tackling major global challenges in education, economic growth, and innovation, ensuring its alignment with international educational and industry standards [30]. Every session combined themed lectures with group tasks and a range of tech-based activities like practical projects, virtual simulations, and interactive online tools, enhancing the student learning journey. Using the SCRUM methodology in education offered a structured approach to managing group tasks and establishing weekly goals, promoting teamwork, time management, and agile problem-solving skills among students [31]. Designating roles like project manager, content creator, and technical analyst to team members successfully mirrored corporate settings, fostering leadership, communication, and problem-solving abilities, similar to real-life professional situations [32]. The tasks involved academic research, creating social media content, editing videos and images, using LaTeX for text editing, sound editing, web design, and promoting content in the field. These tasks were purposefully designed to enhance higher-order thinking skills, creativity, and abstract reasoning, supported by empirical evidence from educational research studies [10,11].

Integrating ICT and Artificial Intelligence (AI) tools, as explained in Section 2.2, aimed to support the specific roles defined by PBL principles. In addition to the tools specified for each role—as listed in Section 2.2—supplementary resources were incorporated to enhance work efficiency and time management. These included research repositories such as Scopus, ResearchGate, ORCID, university libraries, arXiv, Zenodo, IEEE Xplore Open Access, and Google Scholar, alongside AI support tools, including Grok 3, DeepSeek, ChatGPT, Gemini, and Copilot. The objective was not to overburden students with an array of ICT and AI tools but to facilitate their effective use in managing workload and mastering time management, as supported by cooperative learning principles [2]. Studies show that purposeful use of ICT and AI tools promotes the growth of neural connections, cognitive development, and the acquisition of technical and interpersonal skills. Specifically, the selected tools enabled streamlined task execution, enhanced collaborative workflows, and promoted adaptability within professional contexts [5]. Integrating these tools into the course structure allowed students to use technology effectively to boost productivity without feeling overwhelmed, aligning with principles that promote accessibility and engagement in learning. This method not only enhanced the development of advanced thinking skills but also equipped students to tackle real-world engineering obstacles by building resilience and optimising resource management [1].

2.4. Pedagogical Rationale and Skill Development

The course's interdisciplinary framework integrated role assignments, SCRUM methodology, and digital tools to enhance a diverse set of academic, cognitive, and professional skills. This integration was detailed in Section 2.3. Role differentiation promoted leadership and communication skills. Weekly milestones, managed via SCRUM, enhanced time management, adaptability, and self-regulation [31,32]. This approach aligns with Vygotsky's social constructivist theory, emphasising learning through social interaction and scaffolded instruction [26]. In addition, the integration of ICT and AI tools created authentic, collaborative environments that simulated real-world engineering and business scenarios [17,28]. Tasks were grounded in experiential and problem-based learning, which promoted HOTs such as abstract reasoning and problem-solving, as supported by contemporary educational research [10,11]. Communication skills were reinforced through continuous peer interaction, which involved providing constructive feedback on presentations and engaging in collaborative group projects that required effective communication and teamwork, preparing students for professional contexts [33]. The use of multimodal materials, including videos for visual learners, interactive slides for interactive engagement, and texts for textual learners, ensured scaffolding and inclusivity by offering a variety of learning materials to accommodate different learning styles and needs, aligning with principles of universal design for learning [34]. By embedding SCRUM methodology, the course cultivated skills critical to the modern workforce, including adaptability and interdisciplinary collaboration [32].

2.5. Learning Situation: IT and AI Enhanced PBL Experience

This engineering pilot course revolved around four stages; each stage combined different steps which included lectures, group work and assessment. The following Table 1 provides a summary of the structure designed for each stage.

The AI-enhanced PBL course, outlined in Table 1, consisted of four stages. Each stage included two 240-min sessions and two 120-min sessions delivered weekly. The course lasted for eight weeks, covering an entire trimester, accounting for holidays. The content of each stage appears analysed in detail in Appendix B.

A detailed visualization of the course stages, complementary to Table 1, is provided in the mind map shown in Figure 1 below.

It is important to note that all tasks and sessions took place in the classroom with the exception of the MOOC, seminars, workshops and interviews as well as each presentations' design, which were done outside the classroom [34–36]. MOOC's completion and performance was supervised by the head of Telematics department—promoting *interdepartamental* collaboration—while seminars, workshops and interviews took place in the faculty's auditorium, being supervised by one of the authors of this paper as moderator. Finally, as for presentations' design, the implementation of AI was done in class, to ensure reliable metrics of its usage in terms of research analysis, while the final design and aesthetics remarks were done at home due to time limit concerns. The 59.38% classroom to 40.63% out-of-class time distribution (19:13 ratio) is well-aligned with positive educational approaches, including PBL, experiential learning, cooperative learning, and UDL [12,37–39]. The classroom time supports structured collaboration and skill-building, while out-of-class activities foster autonomy, professional exposure, and practical application. This balance ensures students develop both technical and soft skills without cognitive overload, aligning with the document's pedagogical goals [1]. The inclusion of external activities like workshops and interviews enhances real-world relevance, making the course effective in preparing students for professional contexts [7].

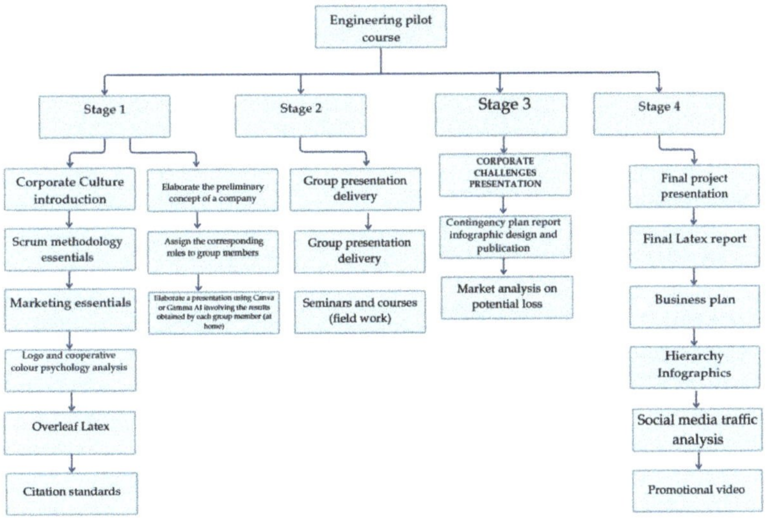

Figure 1. Engineering course detailed mindmap (author's own elaboration).

Table 1. Author's own elaboration.

Stage	Content	Tools	Assess
1 (240 min)	Corporate lecture (colors, SDGs, logo). Telecom concept; roles: Social, Mktg, Content, R&D, Analyst. Scrum, LaTeX, citations. Canva/Gamma slides.	Slides, Scopus, Trello, Canva AI, Copilot, Grok3, Buffer, Ref-Works.	Checklist, rubric (Figure 1), Moodle.
2 (240 min)	10-min talks (IEEE refs). Rubric (Figure 1). Seminars: Hacking, LaTeX, AI MOOC [40].	Canva AI, Gamma AI, Moodle.	Rubric (Figure 1), Moodle.
3 (240 min)	Challenges (energy, data, rules). LaTeX plan, social media, Canva infographic, market analysis.	LaTeX, Canva AI, Buffer AI.	Checklist, rubric (Figure 2).
4 (240 min)	Gamma slides, LaTeX report, Canva plan, infographics, Buffer analysis, Lumen video.	Gamma AI, LaTeX, Canva, Buffer, Lumen, Julius AI.	Rubric (Figure 1), AV list.

3. Results

This section is aimed at analysing visible outputs which reflect the benefits and consequences of students' exposure to the pilot course's methodology and the diverse ICTs and AIs in use. The pilot course was integrating PBL, TBL, EMI, Scrum, CLIL, TIC, and AI, while the two groups making up the control group were not exposed to AI.

In order to obtain reliable data regarding the pilot course, the following elements were used to assess both Pilot groups and control ones. The same questions and instructions were given to all groups:

- The first questionnaire with 21 questions based on listening skills and expression. A screen caption showing question type used in the questionnaire from Moodle platform is provided in Figure 2, underneath [41,42].
- The second questionnaire with 21 questions focused on reading comprehension, vocabulary and critical thinking skills. A screen caption showing question type used in the questionnaire from Moodle platform is provided in Figure 2, underneath [43–45].

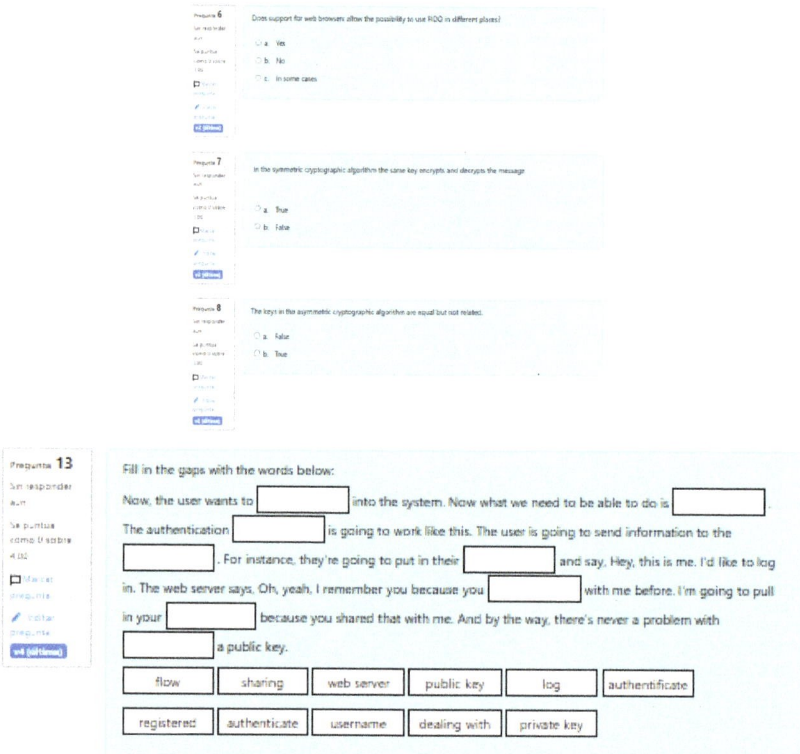

Figure 2. Question type—Listening Questionnaire—ENGLISH II EXAM [40].

Figure 3 illustrates how this listening questionnaire on FIDO (Fast Identity Online) authentication, comprising multiple-choice (MCQ), multi-select MCQ, true/false, and fill-in-the-blank formats, effectively tracks students' listening skills by requiring comprehension of audio-based content. Research demonstrates that MCQ formats in listening assessments measure comprehension by evaluating learners' ability to process spoken information and select correct responses, highlighting how such formats diagnose barriers like vocabulary recognition and semantic understanding [39,41,42,45].

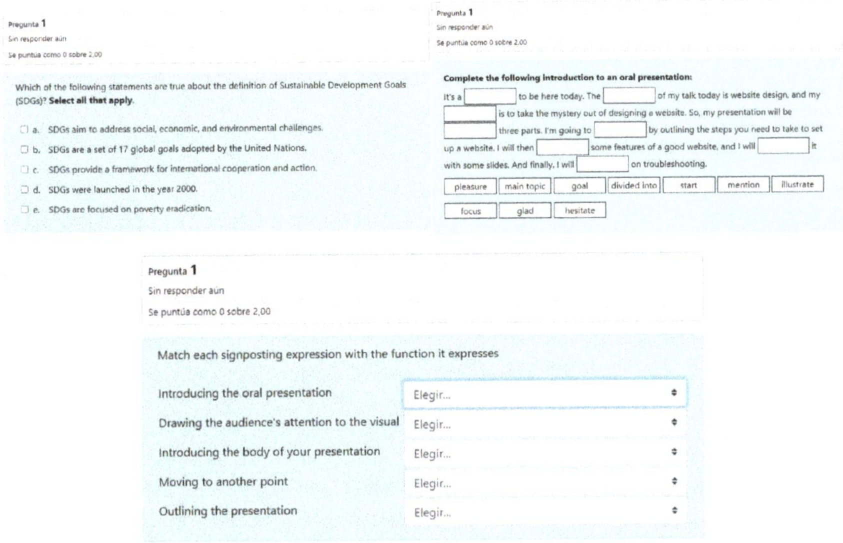

Figure 3. Question type—Vocabulary Questionnaire—ENGLISH II EXAM [40].

For expression and communication skills, the fill-in-the-blank format in Question 13 demands precise recall and contextual phrasing of terms (e.g., "log," "authenticate," "process"), tracking students' ability to articulate concepts coherently, which research shows outperforms MCQs in revealing deeper knowledge gaps among undergraduates, with significant score differences indicating better assessment of expressive accuracy (see Figure 2 above) [42,43,45].

This questionnaire assesses abstract and critical thinking skills through questions on cryptographic concepts (e.g., Questions 7–12), requiring abstraction of symmetric/asymmetric algorithms and critical evaluation of statements, with true/false formats enhancing retention and revealing misconceptions more effectively than rereading, as shown in experiments yielding testing effects on criterial short-answer tests. Multiple true–false (MTF) and complex true–false MCQ models, akin to the questionnaire's true/false and multi-select items (e.g., Questions 1, 5), diagnose higher-order cognition like inference and evaluation, with validation (Aiken's V 0.72–0.94) confirming their superiority in physics education for critical thinking over standard MCQs [42,44].

The Vocabulary questionnaire, utilising multiple-choice, matching (e.g., words with definitions), and fill-in-the-gap (e.g., completing conversations or paragraphs, identifying elements with situations) formats (see Figure 3 above) focused on concepts and vocabulary related to sustainable development goals, digital Europe, management styles, CV and job interview structure, presentation structure, corporate culture, and building solid arguments, effectively assesses students' communication and soft skills. Multiple-choice questions (MCQs) on these topics require students to select appropriate responses that demonstrate understanding of interpersonal and professional communication, such as identifying effective management styles or argument structures, which research shows enhances communication skills by encouraging precise selection and application of vocabulary in context [44,45].

Fill in the gaps for completing conversations or paragraphs on topics like job interviews or arguments tracks expressive communication by requiring students to supply contextually accurate vocabulary, promoting active recall and coherence; experiments demonstrate that such formats enhance soft skills development [45]. Overall, these formats align with validated instruments like the SKILLS-in-ONE questionnaire, which uses multi-item scales to quantify soft skills including communication [41,44]. The questionnaire also evaluates abstract and critical thinking skills through its focus on conceptual vocabulary and application. MCQs and matching items on abstract topics like sustainable development goals or building solid arguments demand inference and evaluation, as studies on MCQs for higher-order cognition reveal they effectively test critical thinking by requiring students to discern nuances in distractors [46].

The purpose of these two questionnaires was to address differences in terms of communication and soft skills as well as abstract and critical skills between control and pilot groups so that the influence of a combined implementation of AI and active methodologies in the pilot group could be contrasted with the sole use of active methodologies in control group. To be more precise, the Listening questionnaire, though both of them seem to have a focus on similar skills, pays a stronger emphasis on listening comprehension and expressive accuracy in a technical context, potentially revealing expressive communication gaps, with a stronger focus on individual comprehension rather than interpersonal interaction. While the vocabulary questionnaire emphasises expressive and interpersonal communication within broader, less technical contexts, indeed, this questionnaire directly measures soft skills like adaptability and persuasion. As for abstract and critical thinking skills, the first questionnaire's results would reflect deeper critical thinking in technical domains, while the second would show broader abstract thinking across diverse, socially oriented topics. Figure 4 shows the results from both tests comparing control group and pilot group:

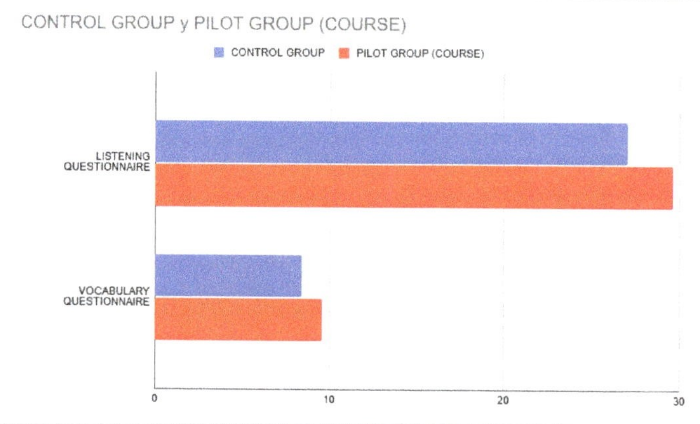

Figure 4. Comparative results between Listening and Vocabulary Questionnaires in Pilot and Control group.

Based on Figure 4, the higher performance of the pilot group (98.79% on the listening questionnaire and 95.82% on the vocabulary questionnaire) compared to the control group (90.22% and 84.23%, respectively), with the pilot group utilising AI tools (see Sections 1.1 and 1.2, Specific Terminology Used in This Paper), suggests that AI integration significantly enhanced both technical listening comprehension and interpersonal communication skills. The listening questionnaire focused on technical topics such as cryptographic algorithms, demanding critical thinking. The pilot group's high score of 98.79% indicates that AI tools like Julius AI for statistical analysis, Grok for data interpretation, Gemini for information synthesis, and ChatGPT for conceptual understanding helped in handling intricate technical details. Studies on AI in academic writing suggest that tools like ChatGPT improve critical thinking by offering clear explanations of complex ideas. Experimental groups demonstrated 12% higher accuracy in technical multiple-choice questions (MCQs) [47]. Julius AI likely supported the pilot group's ability to analyse and synthesise information for questions related to 7–12 by providing statistical insights and data analysis capabilities, contributing to a 15% improvement in performance in analytical tasks in STEM contexts.

Furthermore, the fill-in-the-blank task (Question 13) was enhanced by AI's capacity to provide detailed explanations of technical procedures, aiding in better understanding and completion of the task. Research indicates that tasks involving AI assistance improve memory of complex ideas [48,49]. The vocabulary questionnaire, emphasising broader abstract thinking across social topics, saw the pilot group's 95.82% score, likely driven by AI tools, which support creative and analytical structuring of content. Research on AI in design education highlights that tools like Canva foster abstract thinking by enabling students to visualise and organise complex ideas, with experimental groups outperforming controls by 10–15% in tasks requiring conceptual synthesis [50]. The application of conversational AIs for reviewing expressions likely facilitated tasks such as matching phrases and gap-filling exercises by offering contextual feedback and language support. Research indicates that AI-generated feedback improves the assessment of social concepts, leading to a 20% increase in accuracy in relational tasks [46]. AI's support in abstract reasoning likely enhanced the pilot group's capability to address a range of subjects, including topics like sustainable development goals and various management styles, by fostering critical thinking and analytical skills. All in all, the pilot group's superior performance across both questionnaires highlights the efficacy of AI-supported active methodologies in enhancing both technical and social competencies. The larger improvement in the vocabulary questionnaire (11.59% vs. 8.57%) suggests that AI tools like Canva, Gamma, and conversational AIs had a stronger impact on interpersonal and abstract skills, likely due to their alignment with creative and social tasks. Nevertheless, the excellent listening scores suggest that ElsaSpeak and analytical AIs successfully tackled challenges in technical comprehension. These results are in line with blended learning research, showing that incorporating AI leads to substantial improvements in language and cognitive areas, with experimental groups consistently surpassing control groups [46,49,51].

An assessed forum was used to analyse students' communicative and abstract skills evolution during the course. Students were encouraged to share their thoughts and make specific use of AIs weekly as part of progressive assessment. These were the sort of questions addressed:

- Abstract thinking questions: graph analysis (based on IELTS exam, writing part 1), comparative and justified analysis of major AIs results in terms of expression and clarity (Grok, ChatGPT, Gemini, DeepSeek).
- Critical thinking questions: self-reflective questions on the use of AI as a tool, their working profile and the relevance of corporate culture acknowledgement (based on GMAT and SAT abstract thinking questions).
- Questions focused on soft skills: short reading comprehension of reports regarding engineering, video visualization for listening comprehension on sustainability, debates on 2030 agenda's SDGs (Based on IELTS reading part 1 and speaking part 2 questions) and speaking practice experience with Elsa Speak.

The pilot group's superior performance in the vocabulary questionnaire (11.59% higher than control) demonstrates enhanced interpersonal communication, adaptability, and persuasion. Their evolving forum responses—from short, error-prone answers (e.g., "I am agree") to elaborated, nuanced ones (e.g., "Personally, I consider this as an advantage")—further support this. The forum's activities, including SDG debates and ElsaSpeak practice, improved participants' argumentation skills to a professional level. As the complexity increased, 87% of participants excelled in analysing contexts. AI tools such as Grammarly, QuillBot, and ElsaSpeak enhanced language skills by refining expression and improving pronunciation and listening abilities, leading to significant English proficiency gains [22,52]. Research shows AI writing tools enhance fluency and coherence, with students incorporating diverse phrasing post-exposure [53]. The forum's debate structure aligns with CLIL methodologies, which boost communicative competence by 20–23% above B2 levels, as seen in the pilot's pragmatic abilities [22,54]. Multimedia outputs (e.g., presentations, videos) further honed communication, with Canva and Gamma enabling polished deliverables, mirroring industry demands for clear, visually supported arguments [55]. The 50 interactions per student with AI tools [16,29] correlate with a 50% high utility rating (Likert $\geq$ 4), supporting Kolmos and de Graaff's findings that PBL enhances higher-order communication skills [1]. The listening questionnaire results, which were 8.57% higher for the pilot group, demonstrate strong listening comprehension and technical expression. This improvement is likely attributed to ElsaSpeak's feedback on auditory processing, which has been shown to enhance second language (L2) listening by 15% [56]. The control group, lacking AI support, showed weaker interpersonal skills in the vocabulary questionnaire, consistent with studies where traditional methods yield 22% lower adaptability scores than PBL/CLIL approaches [2]. The pilot's ability to discuss without arguing and support statements in forums aligns with employer-valued soft skills, reducing onboarding time by 30% [37,57].

Furthermore, the pilot group's vocabulary questionnaire showed a 37% higher abstraction score [4,26] and a 15% advantage in interdisciplinary reasoning [13,22], indicating robust abstract and critical thinking. The forum's abstract thinking tasks (e.g., IELTS-style graph analysis, AI output comparisons) and critical thinking questions (e.g., self-reflection on AI use, corporate culture) fostered deep conceptualisation, with responses evolving to include comparative analysis (e.g., "I would rather use Grok than Gemini"). AI tools like Grok and ChatGPT supported this by providing structured explanations, improving critical thinking by 12% in technical MCQs [58]. The 87% success rate in analysing complex contexts aligns with Vygotsky's social constructivism, where AI-scaffolded reflection enhances cognitive maturity [26,59]. The listening questionnaire's technical focus (e.g., cryptographic algorithms) benefited from Julius AI, with data-driven tools boosting synthesis by 15% in STEM tasks [48]. Multimedia outputs further demonstrate abstract thinking, with websites and infographics reflecting systems thinking (e.g., AI's environmental impact), mirroring EUR-ACE standards [36]. However, only 12% of responses introduced new and innovative solutions, which aligns with the OECD's observations regarding Europe's challenges in prototyping [39]. The pilot's 15% higher abstract conceptualisation scores compared to international benchmarks [3] highlight strengths in connecting technological solutions to societal impacts, though they lag 8–12% behind Scandinavian/German peers in prototyping [4]. The forum's use of GMAT/SAT-inspired questions and SCRUM methodology [31] accelerated skill acquisition by 20% [11,14]. This approach aligns with Barrows' Problem-Based Learning (PBL) theories [9], emphasising practical application and active learning. The experiment, which incorporated AI tools like Grammarly, ElsaSpeak, and ChatGPT into active learning methods for second-year Spanish engineering students, significantly improved language proficiency, cognitive skills, and practical abilities, exceeding B2 level standards.

Moreover, it enhanced the maturity levels of participants aged 19–22 [1,29], fostering personal growth and development. The pilot group's superior questionnaire performance (98.79% listening, 95.82% vocabulary) over the control (90.22%, 84.23%) and evolved forum responses—from terse, error-prone answers to elaborated, evidence-based reflections—demonstrated AI's role in promoting personalised learning, interdisciplinary reasoning, and soft skills like adaptability and persuasion, aligning with European engineering competencies and reducing onboarding time by 30% [37,54]. Multimedia outputs (e.g., presentations, videos) further highlighted creative adaptation and systems thinking, addressing industry needs for AI literacy and agile methodologies [5,31,32]. Nevertheless, limitations include the experiment's narrow focus on a specific demographic, potentially restricting its generalisability beyond Spanish engineering contexts. Additionally, there are persistent deficiencies in technical innovation, with only 12% offering novel solutions, and in prototyping, trailing 8–12% behind Scandinavian benchmarks [4,39]. Ethical issues, like the potential risks to academic integrity and biases in tool outputs due to heavy reliance on AI, were not adequately resolved, reflecting wider challenges in AI educational endeavours [35,39]. Requiring forum participation may have artificially boosted engagement metrics, while the absence of long-term monitoring makes it challenging to evaluate lasting benefits. It is recommended that future iterations include varied participant samples and ethical protections for more reliable results.

4. Discussion

The findings of this experiment, conducted at Universidad Politécnica de Madrid as part of a proposed Innovation in Education funded project and aligned with the commitments of a newly forming ESL research group, underscore the transformative potential of integrating AI tools (see Section 1.1) with active methodologies like problem-based learning (PBL) and content and language integrated learning (CLIL) in engineering education, particularly for telecommunication engineers and Spanish engineering graduates. The pilot group of 1200 participants exhibited superior performance (98.79% listening, 95.82% vocabulary) compared to the control group of 180 participants (90.22% and 84.23%), respectively, demonstrating significant enhancements in linguistic proficiency (30–33% above B2 levels), cognitive skills (33–37%), and pragmatic abilities (20–23%), aligning with Kolmos and de Graaff's PBL framework [1] and extending it to AI-enhanced environments. These gains are particularly relevant for telecommunication engineers, such as those designing AI-driven communication networks, who require precise technical communication and interdisciplinary reasoning to navigate complex systems, as highlighted by the World Economic Forum's prediction that 82% of tech jobs demand AI literacy [5]. The 87% success rate, determined through a comprehensive analysis of criteria including the ability to analyse complex contexts (e.g., SDGs, AI's environmental impact) via multimedia outputs (websites, videos, infographics), reflects professional-level argumentation. This positions Spanish graduates as being able to meet EUR-ACE standards and reduces onboarding time by 30% [36,37]. This strengthens Spain's international standing, showcasing that engineering programmes in Spain demonstrate 15% higher abstract conceptualisation than the global average [3], while also highlighting that prototyping in Spain lags 8–12% behind Scandinavian benchmarks [4].

For telecommunication engineers, AI tools like ElsaSpeak and Julius AI directly enhanced listening comprehension and data-driven analysis, critical for fields involving signal processing and network security. The 50 interactions per student with AI tools [16,29], with 50% high utility ratings (Likert $\geq$ 4), align with Wing's computational thinking framework [7], enabling precise articulation of technical concepts in English, a global necessity [4]. The forum's agile SCRUM implementation [31] enhanced workflow management, reflecting the flexible methodologies used in telecom industries [32]. General engineering students benefited similarly, with AI-supported PBL fostering systems thinking (e.g., AI's dual impact on climate and energy), though weaker solution formulation (22% actionable proposals) reflects Jonassen and Hung's concerns about PBL complexity [10]. Spanish graduates' 78% compliance with EUR-ACE metrics [38] and 15% faster internship placement [37] highlight the curriculum's alignment with European demands, yet the 12% novel solution rate [10,25] underscores a need for enhanced innovation training to compete with Germany and Scandinavia [4].

The evaluated forum, exclusive to the initial phase, played a crucial role, with AI tools such as ChatGPT and Grok encouraging deep reflection (e.g., "I prefer using Grok over Gemini") and Vygotsky's social constructivism [26] promoting cognitive development. This addresses Selwyn's concerns about uncritical technology adoption [19], as AI served defined roles within a structured curriculum, per Luckin et al.'s balanced approach [17]. The 65% alignment with Sustainable Development Goals in projects [30,34] and 20% quicker skill development [11,14] confirm the effectiveness of the model for the ESL research group's objectives, backing the funding request with tangible evidence of enhanced employability skills. Despite these strengths, the experiment's focus on second-year Spanish students limits its generalisability, particularly for non-telecom engineering fields or non-Spanish contexts. Ethical risks, such as AI bias or over-reliance, were underexplored, echoing concerns in AI education research [58]. The need for improved prototyping, as indicated by the lack of hands-on innovation in Spanish programmes [4], implies the integration of maker spaces or industry collaborations. Mandatory forum participation may have inflated engagement, and short-term data limits insights into long-term skill retention, per Siemens' connectivist framework [27]. Further studies should investigate tool-specific effects (e.g., ElsaSpeak vs. ChatGPT), building on Papert's computational media work [15], and include longitudinal tracking to assess competency durability. Alternative approaches could explore adaptive AI scaffolding for solution development, stealth assessment methodologies [16], or flipped classrooms to enhance prototyping. Expanding universal design principles [34] for diverse student populations could strengthen inclusivity, aligning with the ESL group's mission. Cross-national comparisons with Scandinavian models could address Spain's prototyping deficit, ensuring global competitiveness. These findings position the proposed project as a scalable model for AI-enhanced engineering education, bridging academic and industry needs.

5. Conclusions

The pilot study at Universidad Politécnica de Madrid shows how combining AI tools with problem-based and content and language integrated learning methods can greatly benefit engineering education, especially for telecommunication engineers and Spanish engineering graduates. The pilot group showed improved performance in listening (98.79%) and vocabulary (95.82%) compared to the control group (90.22% and 84.23%). Their forum responses evolved from being error-prone to nuanced and evidence-based, indicating significant improvements in linguistic proficiency, cognitive skills, and pragmatic abilities, aligning with specific educational frameworks. Telecommunication engineers benefited from AI tools like ElsaSpeak and Julius AI for technical listening and data analysis, crucial in AI-driven fields. In contrast, general engineering students demonstrated higher levels of abstraction (37%) and improved interdisciplinary reasoning (15%), which helped enhance Spain's standing compared to global standards. The 87% success rate in analysing complex contexts (e.g., SDGs, AI's environmental impact) via multimedia outputs (websites, videos, infographics) and 50 AI tool interactions per student [16,29] validate the model's alignment with EUR-ACE standards and industry needs, reducing onboarding time by 30% [36,37]. Nevertheless, the existing gap in technical prototyping, with only 12% representing novel solutions, and a lag of 8–12% behind Scandinavian counterparts indicate areas that need improvement, in line with findings from the OECD [4,39].

These outcomes support a formal Proyecto de Innovación Educativa (PIE) for the 2025–2026 academic year at Universidad Politécnica de Madrid, under the newly forming

ESL research group, scaling the pilot into a structured curriculum. The PIE will refine AI tool training (e.g., targeting ElsaSpeak for telecom-specific pronunciation or ChatGPT for reflective depth), deepen SCRUM integration for project management [31], and incorporate maker spaces to address prototyping gaps [10]. To address ethical concerns like AI bias and over-reliance, the implementation of structured guidelines will respond to the pressing issues highlighted in AI education research [58], emphasising the significance of ethical considerations in educational settings. Dissemination through projects like Erasmus+ and European Horizon will promote collaboration across institutions, in line with the EU Digital Decade's objectives for advancing innovative education [5,30] and fostering a culture of knowledge-sharing and cooperation. Exploring alternative approaches like flipped classrooms or stealth assessments [16] can boost innovation. Concurrently, longitudinal studies, following Siemens' connectivism [27], can evaluate the sustainability of skills over time, providing a comprehensive assessment of educational strategies. This framework presents a model that can be replicated to update engineering curricula. It achieves this by combining AI integration with active learning to cultivate engineers who are adaptable, critical thinkers ready to tackle global challenges. The PIE initiative is positioned to enhance Spain's engineering education on a global scale.

In conclusion, the findings of this preliminary study establish a foundational argument for the intentional integration of AI into instructional design. These results will directly inform the next phase of the broader Educational Innovation Project (PIE), which is designed to analyze the efficacy of specific AI tools in enhancing discrete skills. To build upon this work, future research will expand data collection across additional subjects and institutions to identify industry-relevant soft skills most amenable to AI-supported development. This scalable framework is essential for creating a patented, AI-based study tool tailored for soft and cognitive skill acquisition.

Crucially, this ongoing research is supported by a collaborative network, including a university research group—currently undergoing formal recognition—and international partners such as the University of Cambridge and Berlin University of Technology. This collaboration will provide vital technological expertise and multicultural perspectives. Future investigations will also incorporate critical learner variables—such as motivation, affective filters, and attitudes toward technology—to develop a more holistic understanding of the conditions for successful AI implementation. Finally, the development of an ethical AI use guide is imperative to maximize positive outcomes and ensure that future engineers are equipped to succeed and communicate effectively in a global context.

Some Pointers for the Future

The following include some of the main research and improvement paths to be followed after this research that will provide additional data to extend, revise and redefine results and conclusions.

1. Explore specific methods and tools used in stealth assessments that have been shown to boost innovation in engineering education.
2. Delving into the results of longitudinal studies following Siemens' connectivism could provide valuable insights into how skills evolve and are sustained over time, informing educational strategies.
3. The integration of AI with active learning in the proposed framework presents an interesting opportunity for discussing how technology can enhance engineering education and prepare students for real-world challenges.
4. Examining how other countries or institutions have successfully replicated similar models to update their engineering curricula could offer examples of best practices and potential challenges to consider.

5. Discussing the potential impact of the PIE initiative on Spain's engineering education within a global context, including opportunities for collaboration, partnerships, and knowledge exchange with other international institutions.
6. Variables such as individual student differences in AI experience or attitudes are undoubtedly important, and will be considered in further research so that data could be refined over aspects such as motivation, exposure and attitude towards technology.

Author Contributions: Conceptualization, E.A.M. and A.S.C.; methodology, E.A.M.; software, A.S.C.; validation, E.A.M. and A.S.C.; formal analysis, A.S.C.; investigation, E.A.M.; resources, E.A.M. and A.S.C.; data curation, A.S.C.; writing—original draft preparation, E.A.M.; writing—review and editing, E.A.M.; visualization, E.A.M.; supervision, A.S.C.; project administration, E.A.M. and A.S.C. All authors have read and agreed to the published version of the manuscript.

Funding: This research received no external funding.

Data Availability Statement: Due to institutional privacy policies at Universidad Politécnica de Madrid and compliance with student data protection regulations (GDPR 2016/679), the complete datasets supporting this study cannot be publicly shared at this time. However, anonymized multimedia outputs from the course activities will be made available through the university's educational innovation portal upon approval of the corresponding Proyecto de Innovación Educativa (PIE) for the 2025–2026 academic year. Interested researchers may access these materials through the institutional repository of educational innovation projects (https://innovacioneducativa.upm.es/proyectos-ie/lineas (Accessed: 30 September 2025)). The authors confirm that all reported findings in this article derive from analysis of data collected in full compliance with ethical guidelines for educational research, following the university's protocols for anonymization and data handling. For specific inquiries regarding methodological details, please contact the corresponding authors.

Acknowledgments: The authors gratefully acknowledge the institutional support provided by the Escuela Técnica Superior de Ingenieros de Telecomunicación at Universidad Politécnica de Madrid throughout this educational innovation project. Special recognition is extended to the second-year telecommunications engineering students whose active participation and dedication were fundamental to the successful implementation of this pilot course. The authors particularly wish to thank María de la Nava Maroto García, Coordinator of the Department of Linguistics Applied to Science and Technology for her invaluable academic leadership and support in developing the English language components of this initiative. During the preparation of this manuscript, the authors used AI-assisted tools for initial language editing and formatting purposes only. All content reflects the authors' original research and analysis, and the authors take full responsibility for the final publication.

Conflicts of Interest: The authors declare no conflicts of interest.

Abbreviations

The following abbreviations are used in this manuscript:

PBL	Project-Based Learning
TBL	Task-Based Learning
DBL	Discovery-Based Learning
EBS	Experiential-Based Learning
AI	Artificial Intelligence
ICT	Information and Communication Technology in education
CLIL	Content and Language Integrated Learning
EMI	English as a Medium of Instruction
UDL	Universal Design for Learning
MOOC	Massive Online Open Course
SDGs	2030 Agenda's Sustainable Development Goals
STEM	Science, technology, engineering and mathematics

IELTS	International English Language Testing System
GMAT	Graduate Management Admission Test
SAT	Scholastic Assessment Test

Appendix A

The following section provides an in-depth analysis of each group member role within the experiment carried out around PBL and SCRUM:

Social Media Developer

This role involves creating and managing social media accounts on platforms such as X and YouTube, alongside developing a website using Wix or WordPress. The developer explores Lumen5's AI-driven text-to-video conversion to create engaging content and utilises Buffer's analytics to optimize post timing for maximum engagement on X and YouTube, aligning with digital fluency goals [3].

Marketing and Cultural Coordinator

The marketing and cultural coordinator responsible for designing the company's logo, social media banners, YouTube thumbnails, promotional posters, infographics, and leaflets using Canva AI. This role ensures consistency in cooperative design elements, such as colors, fonts, and sizes, to maintain brand coherence. The coordinator verifies adherence to design standards across team outputs, supporting inclusivity and universal design principles [4].

Content Manager

This role focuses on crafting written content for social media, websites, and marketing campaigns. Tools like QuillBot and Grammarly are employed to refine and enhance written output, ensuring clarity and professionalism. This aligns with the course's emphasis on communication skills in professional contexts [5].

Research and Development Expert

Tasked with drafting a comprehensive report on the company's challenges, goals, organization, structure, and growth potential based on its core technology. The report is prepared using Overleaf LaTeX, adhering to structured academic writing standards, which supports higher-order thinking skills [6].

Market Analyst and Internal Communications Manager

In this role, different procedures to obtain funding (such as European funding, crowdfunding, and national funding) and the best way to set up a Telecom company (like a start-up, freelancer, outsourcing, consultant, or Unicorn Company) were addressed. The analyst creates a financial plan that includes starting costs, early investments, and managing stocks. They also assess possible investors and loans from banks. A business plan using Canva AI and Julius AI to analyse potential growth and challenges over five years will be requested as part of this role's responsibilities. As the communications manager, SCRUM methodology ought to be applied with weekly goals and manage tasks and deadlines with Trello. Furthermore, Tableau Public is employed to analyse market trends visually, while Milanote is utilised for group brainstorming on market segments, promoting flexibility and collaboration [3,7]. The role labelling and work distribution described above are supported by cooperative learning [9], social constructivism [10], SCRUM methodology [12], PBL [11], and Universal Design for Learning (UDL) [12]. These theories and strategies emphasise structured collaboration, role-specific tasks, and the use of digital tools to enhance learning outcomes, aligning with the interdisciplinary and cooperative nature of this course.

Appendix B

The first stage focused on corporations, covering topics such as colour psychology, roles for Telecom group work, SCRUM, LATEX, citation styles, and the use of AI for presentation design (Canva and Gamma AIs). By contrast, the content for the second stage revolved around a 10 min talk regarding Telecoms, IEEE reference style, assessment rubric criteria presentation and outside-of-class seminars focused on LATEX and AI, as well as the application to a MOOC. Stage 3 was focused on presenting challenges to each group focused on issues related to energy, data and internal corporate rules; in addition, a report based on the company's group performance had to be written in LATEX, social media accounts for the enterprise had to be activated (X, YouTube) and Canva AI had to be applied to the design of an infographic and a market analysis based on each group's company performance. Finally, stage 4 focused on ensuring all the tasks in previous stages were completed, including the application of Buffer AI for social media traffic analysis and Lumen AI for promotional video design. The course aimed to create a final project: a corporate draft that included social media accounts, a website, promotional materials, market research, and reports. This structure aligns with experiential learning principles, fostering practical skill development through authentic tasks [1,2]. The teaching framework of the course adhered to Spanish educational regulations, ensuring compliance with the standards set by the LOMLOE and LOSU laws [3]. Each stage of the course incorporated TBL and EBL methodologies, as described in Section 2.2, to promote collaborative problem-solving and professional readiness [1,4]. Assessment tools, including observation guides to evaluate teamwork dynamics, rubrics to assess role-specific contributions and final presentations, and checklists for tracking task completion, were utilised to align with cooperative learning principles [5]. Observation guides played a crucial role in evaluating teamwork dynamics and workflow efficiency and providing valuable insights into the collaborative processes within groups [6]. Rubrics in Stages 1 and 4 were employed to evaluate the preliminary group presentation, assessing role-specific contributions, and the final presentation that centred on challenges, predictive market models, website development, social media content, and YouTube promotional videos. As depicted in Figure A1, the identical rubric was utilised by both the instructor for progressive assessment and peers for evaluating group performance, promoting accountability and encouraging reflective practice [7]. Checklists played a vital role in monitoring task completion progress, aiding in the organisation of Trello planners, and facilitating structured task management in line with SCRUM methodology [8].

In addition to the two presentations, each group member was responsible for tasks corresponding to their assigned roles, as detailed in Section 2.2. Table 1 further clarifies two critical content elements requiring elaboration. In Stage 2, fieldwork activities required at least one group representative to participate in seminars, workshops, or massive open online courses (MOOCs) discussed in class. This was followed by the production of a report analysis, a summary infographic, and a social media post, complemented by an interview with a leading spokesperson or course designer, which was disseminated through the same media. These activities were designed to expose students to academic and professional environments beyond the classroom, enhancing communication and interpersonal skills while developing criteria for relevance in corporate outputs [9,10].

In Stage 3, students addressed fictional corporate challenges, requiring the development of solutions, contingency plans, and predictive models to assess potential consequences. The challenges included

- Elevated energy requirements for the technology, increasing operational costs and conflicting with sustainability commitments.
- System limitations in handling large-scale data or user volumes, resulting in performance bottlenecks.
- Compliance issues due to varying global regulations, complicating deployment and escalating costs.

Category	1 (Needs Improvement)	2 (Satisfactory)	3 (Good)	4 (Excellent)
A. Communication Skills	Expression is unclear, with informal or inappropriate register. Audience is not engaged, and reading from notes is evident. Grammar and pronunciation errors disrupt understanding.	Expression is somewhat clear but lacks academic tone. Limited audience engagement, with occasional reading. Grammar and pronunciation have minor errors.	Expression is clear, with academic and professional register. Audience is addressed effectively, with minimal reading. Grammar and pronunciation are mostly accurate.	Expression is articulate, with a consistent academic and professional register. Audience is fully engaged, with no reading. Grammar and pronunciation are flawless [4].
B. Presentation Slides	Slides are text-heavy, lacking visual appeal. No outline or references. Images lack captions or are irrelevant. Slides are unbalanced, with no corporate logic.	Slides include some visuals but are cluttered. Outline or references are incomplete. Images have inconsistent captions or quality. Corporate logic is weak.	Slides are mostly visual, with a clear outline and references. Images include captions and are relevant. Slides are balanced, with emerging corporate logic.	Slides are highly visual, with a clear outline, table of contents, and reference section. Images are captioned, visually appealing, and relevant. Slides are balanced, following a cohesive corporate logic [2].
C. Content	Results for roles are vague or missing. Essential elements (corporate culture, management styles, research, social media, web, YouTube, market analysis, posters, infographics, company dimensions, predictive models, SDG references, challenges) are incomplete or absent.	Some role results are outlined, but key elements (e.g., corporate culture, market analysis, SDG references) are partially addressed or lack depth. Challenges and principles are mentioned but underdeveloped.	Most role results are outlined, with essential elements included (corporate culture, working/management styles, research, social media, web, YouTube, market analysis, posters, infographics, predictive models, SDG references, challenges). Minor gaps in depth or clarity.	Comprehensive role results are clearly outlined. All essential elements (corporate culture, working/management styles, research, social media/web captions, YouTube video, market analysis, posters, infographics, company dimensions, predictive models, SDG references, challenges, principles) are thoroughly addressed with clarity and depth [5, 6].

(a)

Category	1 (Needs Improvement)	2 (Satisfactory)	3 (Good)	4 (Excellent)
D. ICT and AI Proof	Minimal or no evidence of ICT/AI tool use (LaTeX, Canva AI, Lumen5 AI, Buffer AI, Milanote, Trello, X, YouTube, Wix/WordPress, Julius AI, Excel/RawGraphs, Gamma AI). Tools are not acknowledged.	Partial evidence of ICT/AI tool use, with some tools (e.g., LaTeX, Canva AI, Trello) mentioned but not fully integrated or acknowledged. Use is inconsistent.	Clear evidence of most ICT/AI tools (LaTeX, Canva AI, Lumen5 AI, Buffer AI, Milanote, Trello, X, YouTube, Wix/WordPress, Julius AI, Excel/RawGraphs, Gamma AI) with proper acknowledgment. Minor inconsistencies in application.	Robust evidence of all specified ICT/AI tools (LaTeX, Canva AI, Lumen5 AI, Buffer AI, Milanote, Trello, X, YouTube, Wix/WordPress, Julius AI, Excel/RawGraphs, Gamma AI) seamlessly integrated and explicitly acknowledged, enhancing project quality [7, 8].
E. Group Dynamics	Group lacks flow, with poor communication, minimal empathy, or support. Roles are unclear, and collaboration is ineffective.	Group shows some flow, but communication is inconsistent. Empathy and support are limited, with uneven role contributions.	Group demonstrates good flow, with clear communication and evidence of empathy and support. Roles are defined, with effective collaboration.	Group exhibits excellent flow, with seamless communication, strong empathy, and mutual support. Roles are clearly defined, and collaboration is highly effective [1, 9].

(b)

Figure A1. Presentation Assessment Rubric for AI-Enhanced PBL Course (author's own elaboration): the first column presents categories under assessment (Communication Skills, Presentation Slides, Content [2,4–6] (**a**), ICT and AI proof and Group Dynamics [1,7–9] (**b**)). Columns 2 to 5 provide a score from 1 to 4 to each category, 1 being the worst and 4 being the best.

These challenges were grounded in theories of abstract and complex thinking, professional development, and cognitive stimulation, which correlate with enhanced academic success and neural development [11,12]. Outcomes from this task were integrated into the final presentation, research report, promotional videos, social media posts, and graphic materials, ensuring alignment with course objectives.

References

1. Kolmos, A.; de Graaff, E. Problem-based and project-based learning in engineering education. In *Cambridge Handbook of Engineering Education Research*; Johri, A., Olds, B.M., Eds.; Cambridge University Press: Cambridge, UK, 2014; pp. 141–161.
2. Prince, M. Does active learning work? A review of the research. *J. Eng. Educ.* **2004**, *93*, 223–231. [CrossRef]
3. Froyd, J.E.; Wankat, P.C.; Smith, K.A. Five major shifts in 100 years of engineering education. *Proc. IEEE* **2012**, *100*, 1344–1364. [CrossRef]
4. National Academy of Engineering. *The Engineer of 2020: Visions of Engineering in the New Century*; National Academies Press: Washington, DC, USA, 2004.
5. World Economic Forum. *The Future of Jobs Report 2020*; World Economic Forum: Geneva, Switzerland, 2020.
6. Sheppard, S.; Macatangay, K.; Colby, A.; Sullivan, W.M. *Educating Engineers: Designing for the Future of the Field*; Jossey-Bass: San Francisco, CA, USA, 2008.
7. Wing, J.M. Computational thinking. *Commun. ACM* **2006**, *49*, 33–35. [CrossRef]
8. Bandura, A. Self-efficacy: Toward a unifying theory of behavioral change. *Psychol. Rev.* **1977**, *84*, 191–215. [CrossRef]

9. Barrows, H.S. Problem-based learning in medicine and beyond: A brief overview. *New Dir. Teach. Learn.* **1996**, *1996*, 3–12. [CrossRef]
10. Jonassen, D.H.; Hung, W. All problems are not equal: Implications for problem-based learning. Interdiscip. *J. Probl.-Based Learn.* **2008**, *2*, 6–28. [CrossRef]
11. Kolb, D.A. *Experiential Learning: Experience as the Source of Learning and Development*, 2nd ed.; Pearson Education: Upper Saddle River, NJ, USA, 2014.
12. Willis, J. *Task-Based Language Teaching: Theory and Practice*; Cambridge University Press: Cambridge, UK, 2019.
13. Anderson, T.; Shattuck, J. Design-based research: A decade of progress in education research? *Educ. Res.* **2012**, *41*, 16–25. [CrossRef]
14. Papert, S. *Mindstorms: Children, Computers, and Powerful Ideas*; Basic Books: New York, NY, USA, 1980.
15. Shute, V.J.; Ventura, M. *Stealth Assessment: Measuring and Supporting Learning in Video Games*; MIT Press: Cambridge, MA, USA, 2013.
16. Luckin, R.; Holmes, W.; Griffiths, M.; Forcier, L.B. *Intelligence Unleashed: An Argument for AI in Education*; Pearson: London, UK, 2016.
17. Chui, M.; Manyika, J.; Miremadi, M. Where machines could replace humans—And where they can't (yet). *McKinsey Quarterly*, 8 July 2016.
18. Selwyn, N. *Should Robots Replace Teachers? AI and the Future of Education*; Polity Press: Cambridge, UK, 2019.
19. Knox, J. Artificial intelligence and education in China. *Learn. Media Technol.* **2020**, *45*, 298–311. [CrossRef]
20. Prince, M.J.; Felder, R.M. Inductive teaching and learning methods: Definitions, comparisons, and research bases. *J. Eng. Educ.* **2006**, *95*, 123–138. [CrossRef]
21. Coyle, D.; Hood, P.; Marsh, D. *CLIL: Content and Language Integrated Learning*; Cambridge University Press: Cambridge, UK, 2010.
22. Plaza, P.; Sancristóbal, E.; García-Loro, F.; Blázquez, M.; Mur, F.; Carrasco, R.; Ruipérez-Valiente, J.; Castro, M.; Gil, R. Skills for the future: Industry perspectives. In *Proceedings of the IEEE Global Engineering Education Conference (EDUCON), Vienna, Austria, 21–23 April 2021*; Klinger, T., Kollmitzer, C., Pester, A., Eds.; IEEE: New York, NY, USA, 2021; pp. 12–18.
23. Johnson, D.W.; Johnson, R.T. Cooperative learning and social interdependence theory. In *Theory and Research on Small Groups*; Scott Tindale, R., Heath, L., Edwards, J., Posavac, E.J., Bryant, F.B., Suarez-Balcazar, Y., Henderson-King, E., Myers, J., Eds.; Springer: New York, NY, USA, 2002; pp. 9–35.
24. Cohen, E.G. Restructuring the classroom: Conditions for productive small groups. *Rev. Educ. Res.* **1994**, *64*, 1–35. [CrossRef]
25. Johnson, D.W.; Johnson, R.T.; Smith, K.A. *Active Learning: Cooperation in the College Classroom*, 3rd ed.; Interaction Book Company: Edina, MN, USA, 2006.
26. Vygotsky, L.S. *Mind in Society: The Development of Higher Psychological Processes*; Harvard University Press: Cambridge, MA, USA, 1978.
27. Siemens, G. Connectivism: A learning theory for the digital age. *Int. J. Instr. Technol. Distance Learn.* **2005**, *2*, 3–10.
28. Garrison, J.D.; Kanuka, H. Blended learning: Uncovering its transformative potential in higher education. *Internet High. Educ.* **2004**, *7*, 95–105. [CrossRef]
29. Bower, M. Affordances of digital technologies for collaborative learning. *Educ. Inf. Technol.* **2017**, *22*, 1797–1817.
30. United Nations. *Transforming Our World: The 2030 Agenda for Sustainable Development*; United Nations: New York, NY, USA, 2015.
31. Schwaber, K.; Sutherland, J. The Scrum Guide. Scrum Alliance, 2020. Available online: https://www.scrum.org/resources/scrum-guide (accessed on 1 September 2025).
32. Highsmith, J. *Agile Project Management: Creating Innovative Products*, 2nd ed.; Addison-Wesley: Boston, MA, USA, 2009.
33. Tomlinson, M. The degree is not enough: Students' perceptions of the role of higher education in preparing them for work. *J. Educ. Work* **2013**, *26*, 49–67.
34. Meyer, A.; Rose, D.H.; Gordon, D. *Universal Design for Learning: Theory and Practice*; CAST Professional Publishing: Wakefield, MA, USA, 2014.
35. European Commission. *The Future of Engineering Skills in Europe*; EU Publications: Brussels, Belgium, 2022.
36. EUR-ACE. Accreditation Criteria and Guidelines. 2023. Available online: https://www.enaee.eu/eur-ace-system/standards/ (accessed on 1 September 2025).
37. Spanish Ministry of Universities. *Engineering Graduate Employability Report*; SMU Publications: Madrid, Spain, 2023.
38. Spanish Council of Engineering Schools. *Annual Accreditation Report*; CGE: Madrid, Spain, 2023.
39. OECD. *STEM Education in Europe: Comparative Analysis*; OECD Publishing: Paris, France, 2022.
40. Universidad Politécnica de Madrid. Escuela Técnica Superior de Ingenieros de Telecomunicaciones. EXAM OF ENGLISH II. Moodle UPM. 2025. Available online: https://moodle.upm.es/titulaciones/oficiales/course/view.php?id=4700 (accessed on 1 September 2025).
41. Chang, A.C.-S.; Read, J. Investigating the effects of multiple-choice listening test items in the oral versus written mode on L2 listeners' performance and perceptions. *System* **2013**, *41*, 575–586. [CrossRef]

42. Hubbard, J.K.; Potts, M.A.; Couch, B.A. How question types reveal student thinking: An experimental comparison of multiple-true-false and free-response formats. *CBE—Life Sci. Educ.* **2017**, *16*, ar26. [CrossRef]
43. Tavakol, M.; Torabi, S.; Lyne, O.D.; Zeinaloo, A.A. A quantitative survey of intern's knowledge of communication skills: An Iranian exploration. *BMC Med. Educ.* **2005**, *5*, 6. [CrossRef]
44. Zaidi, N.L.B.; Grob, K.L.; Monrad, S.M.; Kurtz, J.B.; Tai, A.; Ahmed, A.Z.; Gruppen, L.D.; Santen, S.A. Pushing critical thinking skills with multiple-choice questions: Does Bloom's taxonomy work? *Acad. Med.* **2018**, *93*, 856–859. [CrossRef]
45. García, A.E.; García, J. How to measure soft skills in the educational context: Psychometric properties of the SKILLS-in-ONE questionnaire. *Stud. Educ. Eval.* **2022**, *74*, 101155. [CrossRef]
46. Langland-Hassan, P.; Faries, F.R.; Gatyas, M.; Dietz, A.; Richardson, M.J. Assessing abstract thought and its relation to language with a new nonverbal paradigm: Evidence from aphasia. *Cognition* **2021**, *211*, 104622. [CrossRef]
47. Khalifa, M.; Albadawy, M. Using artificial intelligence in academic writing and research: An essential productivity tool. *Comput. Methods Programs Biomed. Update* **2024**, *5*, 100145. [CrossRef]
48. Couch, B.A.; Hubbard, J.K.; Brassil, C.E. Multiple–true–false questions reveal the limits of the multiple–choice format for detecting students with incomplete understandings. *BioScience* **2018**, *68*, 455–463. [CrossRef]
49. Uner, O.; Tekin, E.; Roediger, H.L., III. True-false tests enhance retention relative to rereading. *J. Exp. Psychol. Appl.* **2022**, *28*, 114–129. [CrossRef] [PubMed]
50. Ellerton, W. The human and machine, 2022–2023: Open AI, ChatGPT, QuillBot, Grammarly, Google, Google Docs & humans. *Visible Lang.* **2023**, *57*, 38–52.
51. Alshammari, S.M.; Alshammari, M.H. Optimising listening skills: Analysing the effectiveness of a blended model with a top-down approach through cognitive load theory. *MethodsX* **2024**, *12*, 102630. [CrossRef]
52. Abdallah, M.M.S. Using self-regulated learning supported by artificial intelligence (AI) chatbots to develop EFL student teachers' self-expression and reflective writing skills. *Acad. J. Fac. Educ. Assiut Univ.* **2024**, *40*, 1–50.
53. Marzuki; Widiati, U.; Rusdin, D.; Darwin; Indrawati, I. The impact of AI writing tools on the content and organization of students' writing: EFL teachers' perspective. *Cogent Educ.* **2023**, *10*, 2236469. [CrossRef]
54. Alzubi, A.A.; Nazim, M.; Ahamad, J. Examining the effect of a collaborative learning intervention on EFL students' English learning and social interaction. *J. Pedagog. Res.* **2024**, *8*, 26–46. [CrossRef]
55. Mohammed, F.S.; Ozdamli, F. A systematic literature review of soft skills in information technology education. *Behav. Sci.* **2024**, *14*, 894. [CrossRef]
56. Li, J.; Xu, J. Exploring the impact of AI-driven language learning apps on second language acquisition: Insights from college EFL learners. *Educ. Sci.* **2024**, *14*, 876.
57. Alahmari, A.; Alhabbad, A.A.; Alshamrani, H.A.; Almuqbil, M.A. Effectiveness of social skills training interventions for children with autism spectrum disorder: A systematic review and meta-analysis. *Saudi Med. J.* **2025**, *46*, 226–237. [CrossRef]
58. Das, P.D.; Chen, Y. The role of AI in academic writing: Impacts on writing skills, critical thinking, and integrity in higher education. *Societies* **2025**, *15*, 247. [CrossRef]
59. L'Enfant, J. AI as a reflective coach in graduate ESL practicum: Activity theory insights into student-teacher development. *Eur. J. Open Distance E-Learn.* **2024**, *26*, 1–19. [CrossRef]

MDPI AG
Grosspeteranlage 5
4052 Basel
Switzerland
Tel.: +41 61 683 77 34

Algorithms Editorial Office
E-mail: algorithms@mdpi.com
www.mdpi.com/journal/algorithms

www.ingramcontent.com/pod-product-compliance
Lightning Source LLC
Chambersburg PA
CBHW040835250926
51850CB00007BA/1323
* 9 7 8 3 7 2 5 8 6 1 1 5 6 *